Rudi Matthee is John and Dorothy Munroe Professor of Middle East History at the University of Delaware. He is the author of *Persia in Crisis: Safavid Decline and the Fall of Isfahan* (I.B.Tauris, 2012); *The Pursuit of Pleasure: Drugs and Stimulants in Iranian History, 1500–1900* (Princeton University Press, 2005); and *The Politics of Trade in Safavid Iran: Silk for Silver, 1600–1730* (Cambridge University Press, 1999).

Willem Floor is an independent scholar specializing in the socio-economic history of Iran. His publications include *A Social History of Sexual Relations in Iran*; *Iran and the World in the Safavid Age* (with Edmund Herzig, eds, I.B.Tauris); *Labor and Industry in Iran, 1850–1941* and *The Persian Gulf: A Political and Economic History of Five Port Cities 1500–1730.*

Patrick Clawson is Deputy Director of Research at the Washington Institute for Near East Policy and Senior Editor of *Middle East Quarterly.*

The Monetary History of Iran

From the Safavids to the Qajars

Rudi Matthee
Willem Floor
Patrick Clawson

I.B. TAURIS
LONDON · NEW YORK

Published by I.B.Tauris & Co. Ltd
In association with the Iran Heritage Foundation

Published in 2013 by I.B.Tauris & Co Ltd
6 Salem Road, London W2 4BU
175 Fifth Avenue, New York NY 10010
www.ibtauris.com

Distributed in the United States and Canada Exclusively by Palgrave Macmillan
175 Fifth Avenue, New York NY 10010

Iran and the Persianate World Series

ISBN: 978 1 78076 079 7
eISBN: 978 0 85773 353 5
ePDF: 978 0 85772 172 3

A full CIP record for this book is available from the British Library
A full CIP record is available from the Library of Congress

Library of Congress Catalog Card Number: available

Contents

PART 3: THE QAJAR PERIOD 1779–1925

Tables

Maps, Illustrations and Coin Images

Maps (p. xxiii)

PLATE SECTION

Illustrations

Coin Images

Gold

5. Safavid: Isma'il I, 1501–24, ashrafi, Ardabil, AH 927 (courtesy of Steve Album, Auction 13, Lot 852)
6. Safavid: Soltan Hoseyn, 1694–1722, reduced ashrafi, Isfahan, AH 1129 (courtesy of Steve Album, List 243, Item No. 815089)
7. Afsharid: Nader Shah, 1735–47, mohur, Isfahan (Dar al-Saltaneh), AH 1153 (courtesy of Steve Album, List 243, Item No. 79314)
8. Zand: Karim Khan, 1753–79, ¼ mohur, Kashan, AH 1192 (courtesy of Steve Album, List 260, Item No. 826737)
9. Qajar: Fath `Ali Shah, 1797–1834, tuman, Yazd, AH 1220 (courtesy of Steve Album, List 266, Item No. 108797)
10. Qajar: Naser al-Din Shah, 1848–96, 2 tumans, Mashhad, AH 1281 (courtesy of Steve Album, List 243, Item No. 72370)

Silver

11. Safavid: Isma`il I, 1501–24, ½ shahi, Astarabad, AH 929 (courtesy of Steve Album, List 265, Item No. 113337)
12. Safavid: Isma`il I, 1501–24, shahi, Sari, AH 929 (courtesy of Steve Album, List 240, Item No. 49045)
13. Safavid: Isma`il I, 1501–24, larin, Lar, ND
14. Safavid: Tahmasp I, 1524–76, ½ mesqal, Soltaniyeh, ND (courtesy of Steve Album, Lists 218, Item No. 47278)
15. Safavid: Tahmasb I, 1524–76 shahi, Bistam, ND (courtesy of Steve Album, List 227, Item No. 58750)
16. Safavid: Isma`il II, 1576–78, 2 shahi, Shamakhi, AH 984 (courtesy of Steve Album, List 225, Item No. 58751)
17. Safavid: Mohammad Khodabandeh, 1578–88, 2 shahi, Ordubad, ND (courtesy of Steve Album, List 240, Item No. 38321)
18. Safavid: Mohammad Khodabandeh, 1578–88, shahi, Ordu, AH 988 (courtesy of Steve Album, Auction 12, Lot 659)
19. Safavid: `Abbas I, 1578–1629, bisti, Mazandaran, ND (courtesy of Steve Album, List 228, Item No. 59344)
20. Safavid: `Abbas I, 1588–1629, `abbasi, Nimruz, ND (courtesy of Steve Album, Auction 11, Lot 740)
21. Safavid: Safi II, 1666–68, `abbasi, Iravan (Yerevan), AH 1079 (courtesy of Steve Album, List 260, Item No. 100242)

Civic copper

41. fals (7.30 g), Yazd, AH 1186 (courtesy of Steve Album, Auction 13, Lot 954)
42. fals (16.25 g), Khuy, AH 1190 (courtesy of Steve Album, List 222, Item No. 45935)
43. fals (4.61 g), Dezful, ND, late eighteenth century (courtesy of Steve Album, Auction 12, Lot 744)
44. fals (17.72 g), Rasht, ND (courtesy of Steve Album, Auction 7, Lot 483)
45. fals (8.03 g), Rasht, ND, ca. 1820 (courtesy of Steve Album, Auction 12, Lot 756).
46. fals (11.44 g), Lahijan, ND, early nineteenth century (courtesy of Steve Album, List 225, Item No. 54940)

Banknotes

47. Naser al-Din Shah, 1848–96, 3 tumans
48. Ahmad Shah, 1909–25, 5 tumans

Note on Transliteration

The Persian transliteration used in this book follows the system used by *Iranian Studies*, without the diacritic marks. Dates in the text are given according to the Common Era calendar, except when there is a compelling reason to give the Islamic lunar or the Iranian solar *hejri* date as well. The Russian transliteration used in this book follows the Library of Congress system.

Abbreviations

AAE	Archives des Affaires Etrangères, Paris
AP	*Accounts and Papers*
BBME	British Bank of the Middle East
DCR	*Diplomatic and Consular Reports*
EI	*Encyclopedia of Islam*
EIC	East India Company
EIr.	*Encyclopaedia Iranica*
IJMES	*International Journal of Middle East Studies*
IOR	India Office Records, British Library London
IS	*Iranian Studies*
JESHO	*Journal of the Social and Economic History of the Orient*
JRGS	*Journal of the Royal Asiatic Society*
NA	*Nationaal Archief (Dutch National Archives), The Hague*
RGS	*Royal Geographical Society*
St.Ir.	*Studia iranica*
US	United States
VOC	Verenigde Oostindische Compagnie
ZDMG	*Zeitschrift der Deutschen Morgenländischen Gesellschaft*

Acknowledgements

We would like to thank Stephen Album and Angie Hoseth for their indispensable assistance with the mint maps; Stephen Album for granting us permission to publish many coins from his price lists and auction catalogues; and Stefan Heidemann and Massumeh Farhad for helping us to obtain the images of the money-changers. We acknowledge the extraordinary service and dedication of the staff at the various archives where we have worked over the years, most notably the Nationaal Archief in The Hague and the National Archives in Kew Gardens. We are grateful to HSBC for granting us access to the archives of the Imperial Bank of Persia. Paul Tompsett, finally, deserves our praise for guiding us through the editorial phase of the book in such an efficient and courteous manner.

Preface

The history of Iran between 1500 and 1925 is the story of the rise, peak and fall of two major, relatively stable states – the Safavids in the sixteenth and seventeenth centuries and the Qajars in the nineteenth century – interspersed with the lifespan of various more ephemeral dynasties and more protracted periods of decentralized, tribal power frequently shading into chaos. The bookend dates of this long period are in part imposed by the nature of the available source material – for the period after 1500, foreign, mostly Western, documents supplement indigenous, Persian-language records – but arguably arise from an internal logic as well. Whether or not one subscribes to the 'early modern' paradigm, the Safavid dynasty, while inheriting the patterns and practices from previous regimes, forged a new state-society relationship, intertwining territorial and religious identity, that carried over into the Qajar period and that still marks Iran as a unique country in the Islamic Middle East. As for the closing date, a good case can be made for the argument that the overthrow of the Qajars and the rise of Reza Shah mark the beginning of Iran's full modernization and thus of modern Iranian history.

One of the many threads that hold the period considered in this book together, giving it texture and contributing to its continuity, is the monetary system and the role it played in economic exchange – determining the ways in which the state collected revenue and remunerated its administrators and soldiers, subjects paid their taxes, and merchants made deals with their domestic and foreign partners. Despite the many changes that took place in the ways money functioned and was handled in these four centuries, many features of the system remained the same or at least show strong elements of continuity.

The use of coined money grew out of the desire to simplify exchange, by using standardized units instead of units that needed to be weighed and tested for quality on each occasion. This development received further impetus from governments wishing to simplify public finances, in particular the collection of taxes and tribute. Coins differ from earlier forms of media of exchange in that they are (1) standardized monetary units and (2) guaranteed by the state as a valid mode of payment. However, from 1500 – the approximate date for which we have substantially more information than the surviving coins – to 1925 – the onset of the reign of the Pahlavis and with it the introduction of a modern monetary system – Iranian money did not fully have either of these two characteristics; that is, the coins were not standardized units which could be seamlessly interchanged, and the state did not guarantee the value of coins as a medium of payment without discounts. In other words, the Iranian monetary system until 1925 was much more complicated and much less organized than what we are used to in modern times.

The disorganized and chaotic character of Iran's money from 1500 to 1925 was exacerbated by three factors. First, three metals were used for coins. Copper was used for most local trade and silver for most long-distance trade, with gold playing a limited role. To make the system even more confusing, accounts were often kept in imaginary monetary units – that is, in 'ghost monies'. Second, Iran experienced chronic shortages of money due to poor metal supply, large trade imbalances that had to be financed by substantial coin shipments, and stressed government finances. Transactions among people in rural areas were often conducted through barter. Third, Iran did not have much of a national economy. Moving money from one place to another was not cheap or easy. The money system in use often varied considerably from city to city.

Thus far, the obvious importance of this topic has not translated into a comprehensive study on the monetary system of pre-modern and early modern Iran. Adjacent states and empires have fared better in this regard. For the Ottoman Empire and Mughal India, not to mention China, important studies have appeared in the recent past. Until now, no comparable monograph existed for those interested in the monetary history of early modern Iran. H. L. Rabino de Borgomale's *Coins, Medals, and Seals of the Shahs of Iran. 1500–1941* (1945), while informative, is more a catalogue than an analytical study of the subject. Beyond that, only a handful of articles, mostly written by the authors of the present volume, addressed aspects of the subject in the Safavid and Qajar period.

The present work is designed as a first and major attempt to fill this gap. We offer this study with the understanding that, in many ways, the monetary history of pre-modern Iran remains rudimentary in that many of its facets are yet to be studied or have only been partially examined.

This book presents Iran's monetary history predominantly as a story of economic issues and questions in connection with the state and its policies. It does so chronologically. The second part of this preface offers an overview of Iran's pre-modern monetary system, and of its enduring characteristics and peculiarities. The body of the study, comprising chapters 1 to 7, is divided into three parts. Part 1 covers the Safavid period; Part 2 deals with the eighteenth century – the reign of Nader Shah and the Zands; and Part 3 considers the Qajar period, 1779–1925.

As the subsections in the table of contents indicate, each chapter considers the specific monetary conditions in a particular period, involving the use of ready money and its circulation, the quasi-trimetallic system involving gold, silver and copper coins, and the changing conditions of the country's mints. Each chapter also addresses the role played by the state in managing money by way of striking coins and tampering with the coinage, either by lowering weight standards or through debasement – lowering the metal alloy of coins – for profit.

This book is about Iran yet its scope is expansive. Throughout, we look at Iran not as a self-contained unit but as part of a larger, regional, trans-regional and even global economic structure. Monetary sovereignty may have been a desideratum on the part of the central state but, as always, reality fell far short of the ideal. This is especially true in the case of Iran, a country which, devoid of gold and silver mines and chronically short on ready money, until the discovery of oil in the twentieth century, depended on the outside world for the influx of its precious metal. Because of its chronic trade imbalance, the land of the shah also saw much of its bullion disappear to India via the Persian Gulf ports. The seventeenth-century French cleric and long-time resident of Isfahan Raphael du Mans famously summed this up by calling Iran a caravanserai with one gate open to the west and the other the east. Hence the attention this study pays to the interplay between domestic money and international bullion movements between Europe and India. The section on the Safavids thus engages with the vexed (and now somewhat hoary) question of whether the sixteenth-century Islamic world witnessed a 'price revolution'. More importantly, each chapter pays particular attention to government attempts to prevent or at least curb the bullion flow toward India through bans or taxation.

MAPS

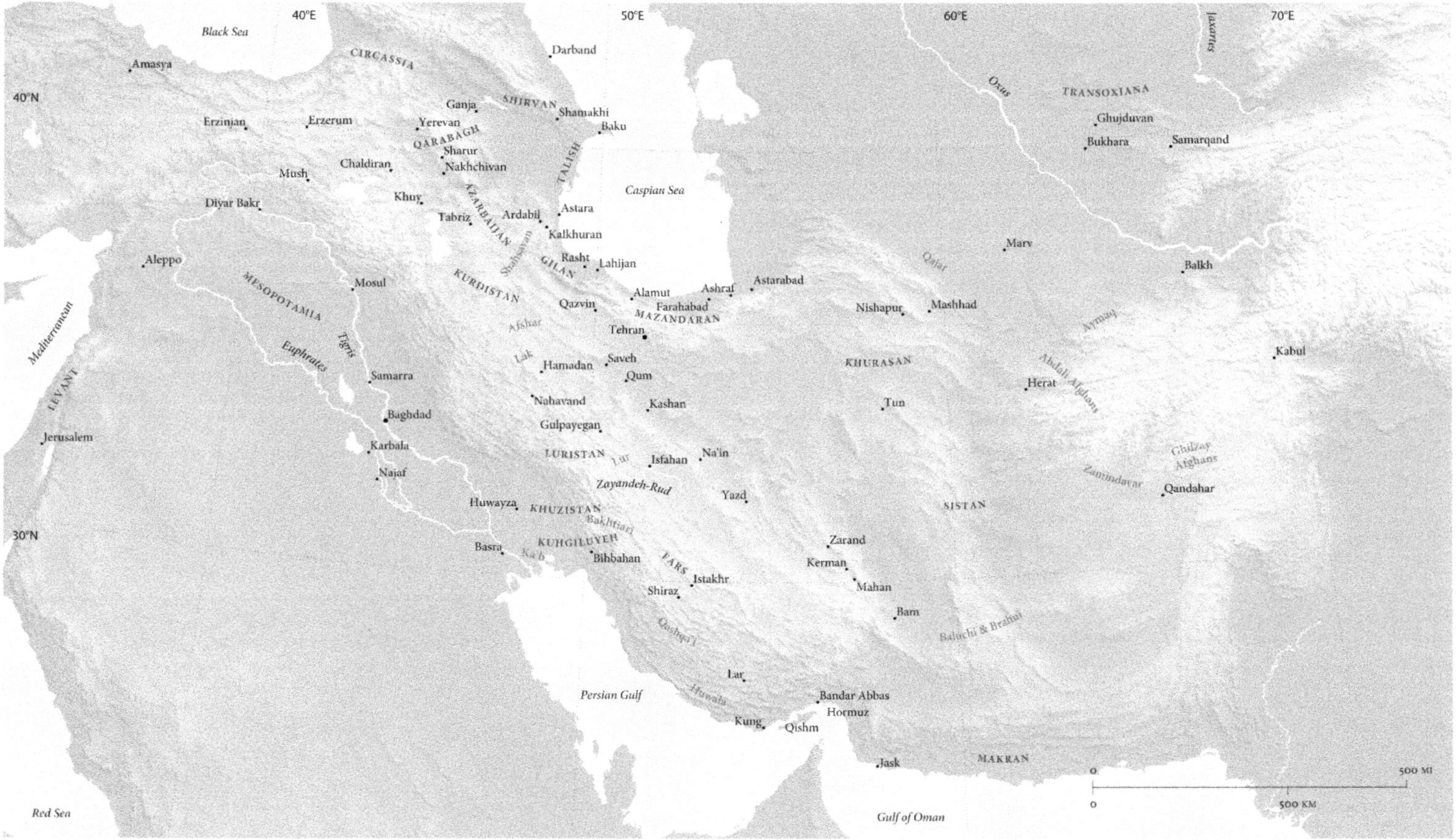

Map 1: Iran and the Surrounding World

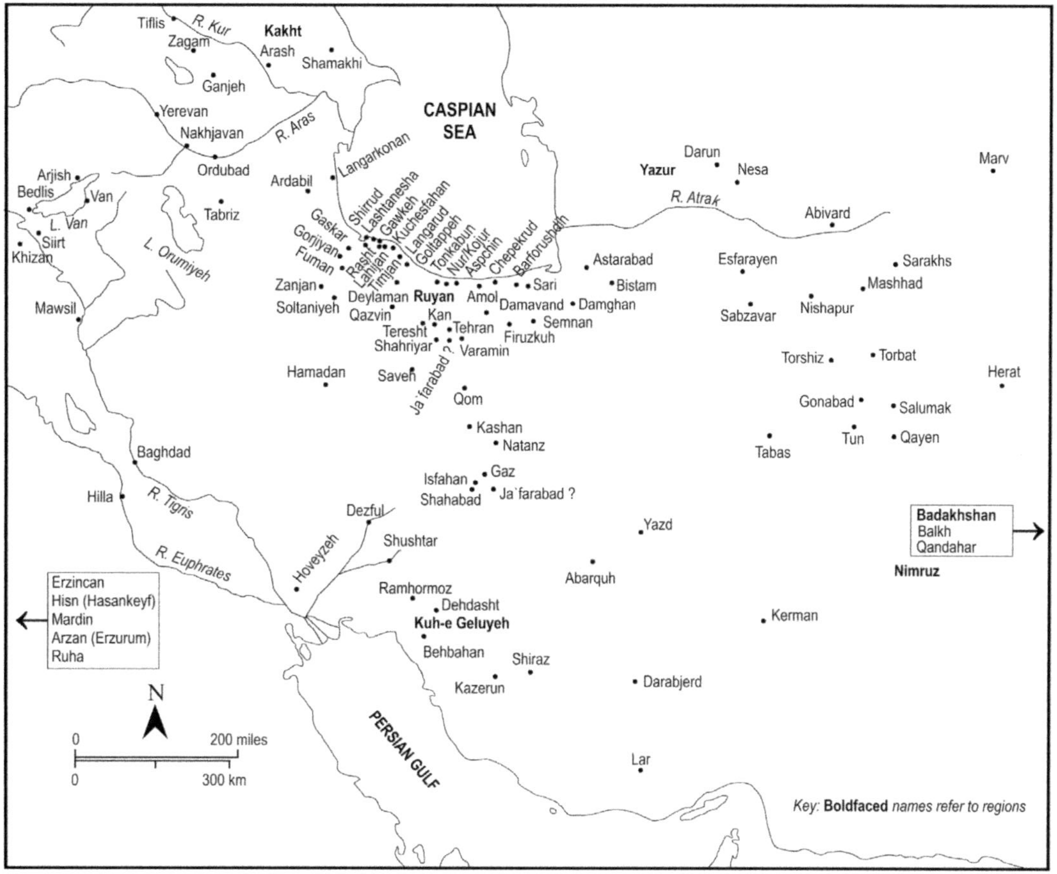

Map 2: Location of Safavid Mints 907–95/1501–87

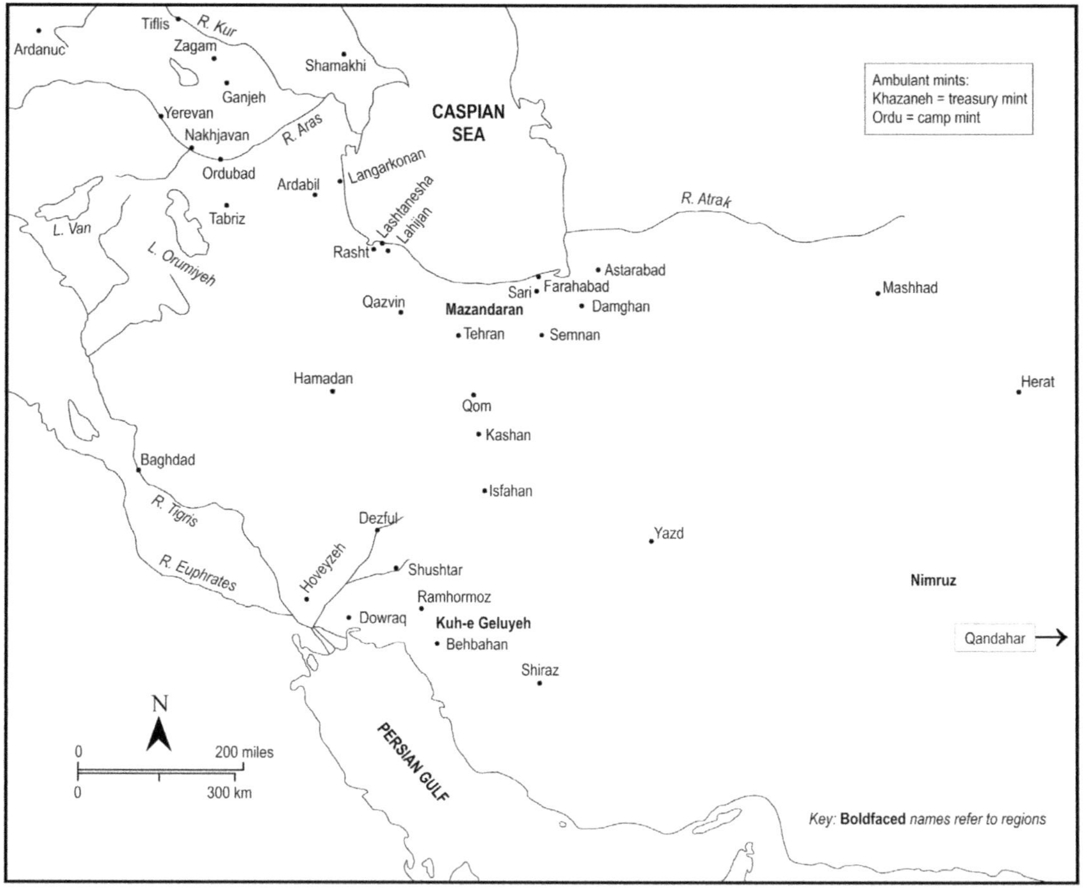

Map 3: Location of Safavid Mints 995–1052/1587–1642

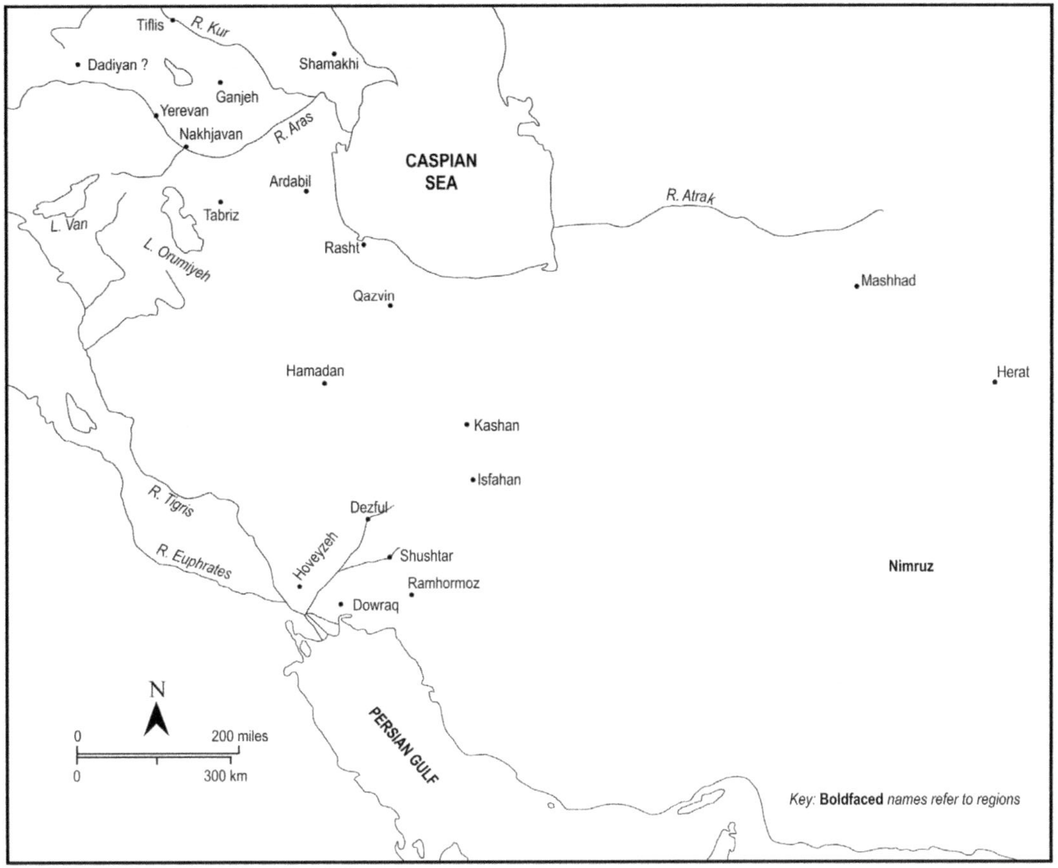

Map 4: Location of Safavid Mints 1052–1105/1642–94

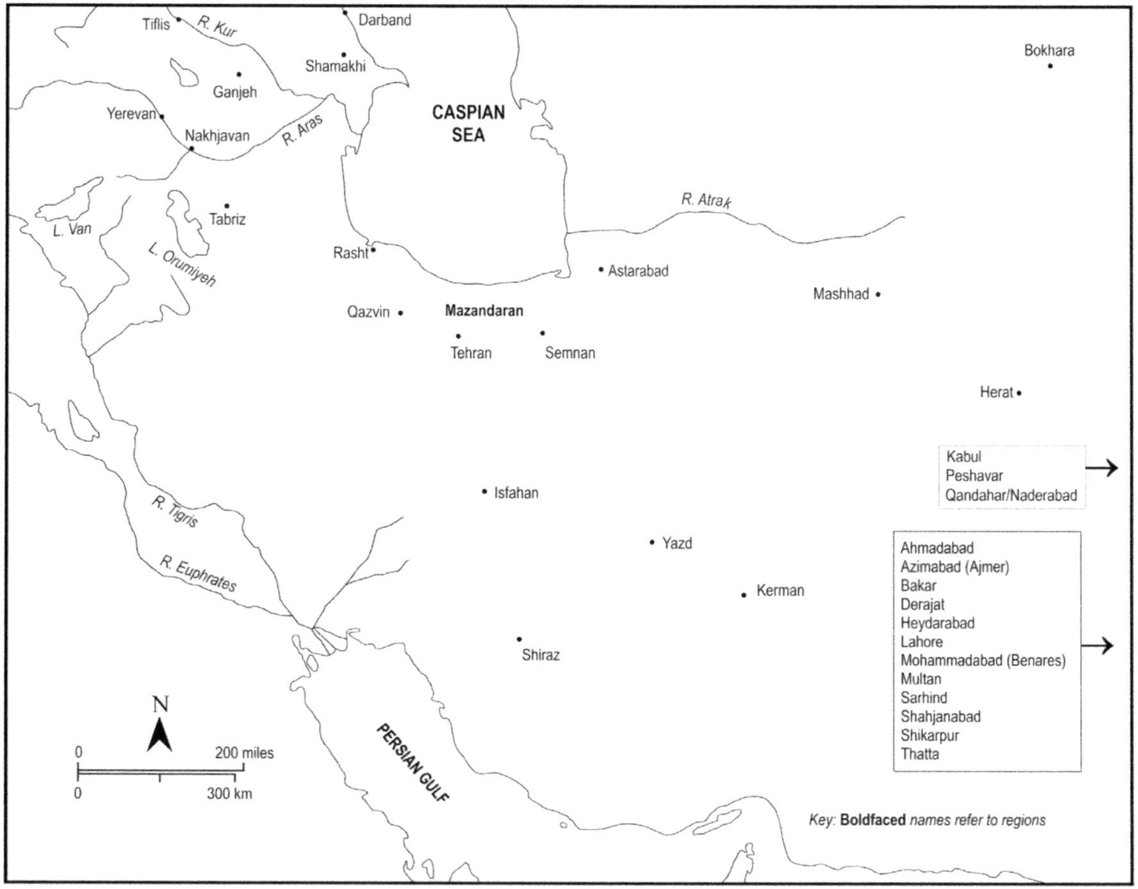

Map 5: Location of Afsharid Mints 1148–60/1735–47

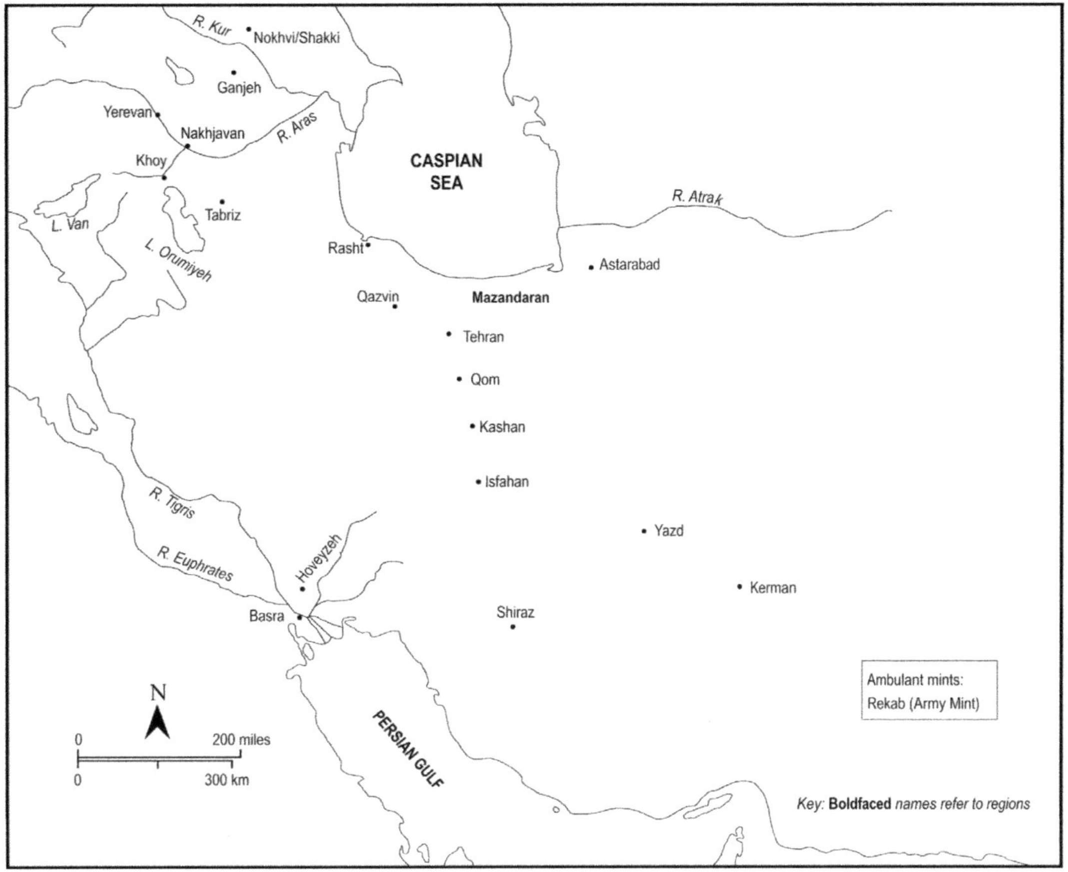

Map 6: Location of Zand Mints 1166–1209/1753–95

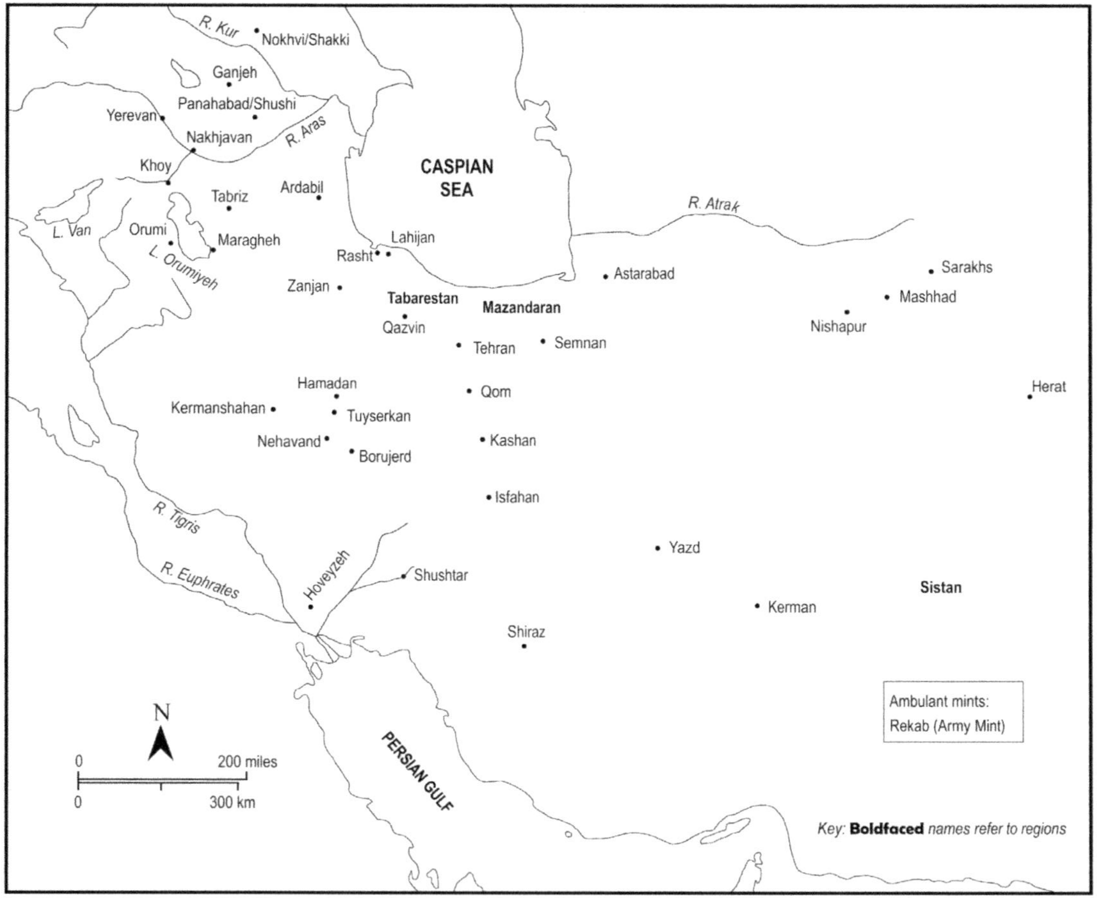

Map 7: Location of Qajar Mints 1193–1344/1779–1925

Introduction

A note about weights: a common Iranian measure of weights which was unchanged for centuries was the *nokhud* (meaning pea), which weighed 192 milligrams. Also unchanging was the *mesqal*, which was 24 nokhud, i.e., 4.61 g. An additional term for weights was the *man*, which was often but not always 640 mesqal, i.e., 2.94 kg. A common way in which the monetary standard was calculated was how many nokhud there were to the (notional) *tuman*, e.g., an 800 nokhud standard, a 1,200 nokhud standard, and so on.

And to remind the reader, 'specie' is 'coined metal', while 'bullion' is usually defined as 'gold or silver considered as so much metal, specifically uncoined bars or ingots', though the term will be used here to also cover uncoined copper. 'Precious metal' or 'monetary metal' is composed of both specie and bullion.

Copper, Silver and Gold

As was the case in Mongol times, Iran from 1500 until 1925 had copper, silver and gold coins.[1] The state typically kept its accounts and levied its taxes in silver, but the actual currency used for most ordinary transactions was copper. The copper coins were often issued by local authorities, especially provincial governors. Furthermore, the value of the copper coins was typically well in excess of the value of copper metal in those coins.

The system of coins in three metals was not fully a 'trimetallic' system in which the value of coins of each metal is fixed relative to coins in the other two metals and the value of each coin is determined by the metal in it. The state typically established an official ratio for exchanging copper coins and gold coins into silver coins, but those ratios were not necessarily enforced rigidly: the typical practice was to require an 'agio', which is a discount

1 Album et al., 'Coins and Coinage'; Smith and Plunkett, 'Gold Money in Mongol Iran'; Martinez, 'Regional Mint Output', 137.

on exchange from one coin to another. In other words, there was a certain looseness in how copper, silver and gold coins were exchanged one for the other, as well as a certain flexibility in how the value of the coin related to the value of the metal in the coin.[2] Nevertheless, the system relied to some extent on official rates of conversion from coins in one metal to coins in the other metals. Therefore, the system came under strain when the market prices of metals varied. In particular, Iran suffered from the problem that over time, the principal metal it was using – silver – declined in value relative to the main metal used for money in Europe and India, which was gold.

Although the shahs coined gold, these gold coins served mainly a special use, such as to affirm the royal right of coinage; to be used as presents, in particular on *Nowruz* occasions; and to show off with heavy so-called presentation coins. Silver, however, was the high-quality currency for tax, administrative and trading purposes. The silver coins had a fine alloy relative to coins of many other realms. When they melted European or Turkish coins, Iranian minters purified them before re-striking the metal as Iranian currency. European travelers were impressed with the fineness and weight of the silver currency of the Safavids. But despite the fact that generally Iranian currency was of good weight and fineness, in trade people never forgot to check this premise. Normally, the weight of coins was correct, so that for large payments, both merchants and government officials made use of bags containing a standard number of coins. Known as *kiseh* and *bolsa* in Safavid times, these bags contained a guaranteed value of 50 tuman. A special inspector, the *sarraf-bashi*, was responsible for the quality of the coinage in the bags, which he sealed personally. This checking of money certainly held true until the end of the nineteenth century.

Another complication in the monetary system was that accounts were often kept using 'ghost monies' – that is, units which did not correspond to any coin. That provided a constant method of recording monetary values even when over time the value of coins changed. From the beginning of the Muslim Empire, the dinar was the monetary unit.[3] In 1260 the Mongols introduced the *tuman*, a word meaning 10,000. It was originally used to refer to 10,000 gold dinars. However, in the Safavid period, after 1500, the tuman was a unit of account, not a gold coin. Furthermore, in actual practice the

2 Hennequin, 'Nouveaux aperçus'; Ibid. 'Problèmes théoriques'; and Ricardo, 'High Price of Bullion'. This also explains why at any given moment a large variety of antique, old, debased, and false coins would circulate in Iran. According to O'Donovan, *Merv Oasis*, 484, visiting Mashhad in 1880, 'The variety of coins current in this place would delight the heart of the numismatist'.

3 Nizam al-Molk, *Book of Government*, 57.

value of the tuman also fluctuated and was not always equal to 10,000 dinars; al-`Omari, for instance, put the tuman at 20,000 dinars.[4] Also, the Tabriz or Iraq tumans were often four times the value of the Khorasan tuman. Only in 1883, under Naser al-Din Shah, was an actual tuman coin minted, in silver.[5]

In general throughout this period, the value of the actual coins was expressed in relation to the dinar/tuman system. There were several intermediate coins whose value changed depending on time and location. Often during the Safavid period, 50 dinars made a *shahi*, 4 shahis made an *`abbasi*, and 50 `abbasis made a tuman; there was often also a *mahmudi*, usually of 2 shahis. Often during the Qajar period, a *riyal* or *qran* was valued at 1,250 dinars or 25 shahis, with a tuman being 8 riyals or qrans, but this was by no means always the case.

Especially for Europeans, a standard of reference was the Venetian gold ducat, whose weight and fineness remained unchanged from 1284 to 1914 at 3.49 g of 98.6 per cent gold.

Shortage of Coins

Expanding the supply of money required (1) production of metal from mines; (2) acquisition of booty through conquest; or (3) a positive trade balance. Neither of the first two factors was particularly important during this time. Iran lacked significant gold and silver mines; a few mines were occasionally brought into operation, but their output invariably was more expensive than what was available in the market. While copper was mined, even that metal had to be imported throughout most of the period. Conquest brought only temporary relief. The fiscal effect was often negative, in that the cost of the conquest and the additional spending in the aftermath tended to exceed the booty seized. It would seem that the monetary effects were also often short-lived; that is, the additional spending led to additional imports such that the money went to finance a balance of trade deficit, and money was in as short a supply as before the conquest.[6]

Throughout this period, Iran, benefiting from its large exports of raw silk, apparently had a positive trade balance with Russia and the Ottoman Empire. Istanbul was evidently running a positive trade balance with the rest of Europe, with a considerable amount of specie flowing into Anatolia,

4 Spuler, *Mongolen*, 255.
5 Rabino, *Coins, Medals, and Seals*, 13.
6 For the Ghaznavids, see Bosworth, *Ghaznavids*, 78.

and much of that in turn going to Iran.[7] On the other hand, Iran had a trade deficit with the Indian Ocean lands, such as Mughal India, and this had to be paid for in precious metal. The two trade deficits – positive with the lands north and west of Iran, negative with the lands south and east of Iran – meant that large amounts of coin and bullion were flowing into and out of Iran. Sustaining this flow was a considerable strain; after all, moving so much metal was expensive and risky in unsettled times. In this system, transport expenses of specie and bullion were a vital factor, as was the profitability of alternative export articles.

Another way to describe the trade pattern of the centuries in question is that the West received large amounts of silver and gold from the Americas, and that precious metal was being used in part to finance the West's persistent balance of trade deficit with South and East Asia. Such a description highlights the intermediary role Iran played in the global flow of money.

Whereas we often think of gold when considering the bullion originating in the Americas, actually silver played a greater role. The exploitation of American deposits changed the centuries-old ratio between silver and gold, with silver becoming cheaper – at first gradually, then more rapidly during the late nineteenth century. Depending on transport costs and risks en route, the changing silver–gold ratio often made arbitrage profitable; that is, shipping silver from the west to the east in return for sending gold the other way. It is not clear how much of a role Iran played in arbitrage; the country does not seem to have shipped much gold to the West.

The need to ship large amounts of metal over long distances gave extra importance to having good-quality coinage. The best coin for trade was a unit of high value, being both of elevated purity and substantial weight, which would retain these qualities and thus its value over time, issued by a ruler overseeing a sound economy, who would not be tempted to devalue the coin for temporary fiscal advantage.[8] Such trade coins, widely recognized for their quality and enjoying prestige everywhere, were in high demand, dominated international trade and, as a rule, circulated at a premium over their metallic value.

The export of monetary metal from Iran followed maritime as well as overland routes through the nineteenth century, with most of the exports generally consisting of specie rather than bullion.[9] Despite the trend for gold to retain its historically higher value relative to silver in India longer than

7 Şahillioğlu, 'Role of International Monetary and Metal Movements', 283.

8 Ederer, *Evolution of Money*, 23–24.

it did in the West, gold was often favored for export to the subcontinent because at least until the 1670s it got a better rate in India, and especially in Coromandel. But silver was almost always preferred over merchandise in the trade with the east, although this naturally depended on prices for silver and for commodities in India.

From time to time Iran's rulers issued edicts against the exportation of coin from the kingdom, but only with temporary results, as merchants could easily evade these regulations indirectly, or even directly, by bribing the authorities. In Safavid times the first documented export ban on specie occurred in 1618, during the reign of Shah `Abbas I. Similar bans were issued frequently thereafter by successive rulers.

In Safavid Iran, many of the coins circulating were foreign, mainly European ones. Lacking any domestic source of precious metal coins, Safavid mints in practice functioned primarily by processing – melting and restriking – imported foreign coins. Consequently, the mint suffered if it established a price for a foreign coin which was lower than the market price. Much of the precious metal arriving from the Ottoman Empire came as bullion in the form of silver bars; some was specie, usually either Spanish *reals of eight* or Dutch *rijksdaalders*, which were approximately equal in value. On arrival in Iran these were often brought to the mints of Yerevan, Tabriz and Tiflis, to be melted and coined into `abbasis and mahmudis. The seignorage (*vajebi*) demanded by the state when metal was brought to the mint for coining was partly a tax and partly a fee for minting. With a good excuse a merchant could get a certificate allowing him to take the bullion to Isfahan. But this was not in the interest of the minter who stood to lose his seignorage share.

While most of the money entered Iran from the northwest, some came via Basra by caravan from Aleppo. The market price of Iranian coins therefore could not be too far out of line with the market price in Basra. The importance of the local mint of Hoveyzeh in Khuzestan and the concentration of mints in the region in the Safavid period is also explained by the proximity of Basra.

The large-scale shipments of specie and bullion to and from Iran made the money supply dependent on factors over which the state had little control. War beyond the borders would keep the caravans from the north and west away and thus raise the price, for example.[10] So would an increase

9 Lorimer (ed.), *Gazetteer*, 63.

10 *NA*, VOC 1304, Gamron to Batavia, 4 Sept. 1674, fol. 519v; VOC 1732, Isfahan to Heren XVII, 30 Sept. 1705, fol. 234.

in banditry in Anatolia.[11] Similar circumstances affected the demand side in India, with war, unsafe roads, robberies or changes in the gold–silver ratio affecting prices.[12] Also, the market was volatile because of rumors, which, simply by relating whether an expected specie caravan was about to arrive or not, might send the price up or down.[13] Furthermore, the market was subject to strong seasonal pressures, ranging from the departure of annual pilgrim caravans to Mecca to seasonal fluctuations in trade.[14]

Besides Iran's trade deficit with India and the needs of commercial life, the demand for money was also a function of the 'hoarding' habits of the rich, above all the shah himself. While the term 'hoarding' implies irrational behavior, in fact holding and hiding coins was one of the few secure ways of having liquid savings in an economy without a banking system. And such liquid savings were useful for large purchases or as a fallback in the event of hard times in the form of unrest, crop failure or epidemics.

Rulers were often tempted to manipulate the coinage as a quick way of raising funds. Iran had a long tradition of maintaining the alloy percentage in its coinage. When the government decided to devalue the coinage, the usual method was either to raise the accountancy value of the existing coins or to reduce the weight of coins, principally by clipping old coins. Such measures typically were accompanied by a ban of the export of good coins and the bullion these were made of. Clipping old coins was facilitated by the fact that Iranian coins were unmilled and hammer-struck, and that they tended to be small and thick. At times when many of the old coins had been clipped, new coins at reduced standards were introduced to reflect the general state of the coins in circulation. The practice of devaluing the coins was limited by the widespread use of foreign coins and the large-scale trade in bullion. Devaluation was also complicated by the use of coins of three different metals, which meant that if the coins of one metal (typically copper) were devalued, the working of Gresham's Law might prompt merchants to switch to the use of coins of that metal at the expense of the use of coins of another metal (typically silver), with unintended consequences.

Barter was common in Iran throughout this entire period. In many parts of the country much of commercial exchange took place outside the cash economy, so that for most of the population money played no or a limited role. In most rural parts, production was anyhow not for the market. Money

11 *NA*, VOC 1291, Gamron to Batavia, 21 Mar. 1673, fol. 558r; VOC 1304, Gamron to Batavia, 24 May 1674, fol. 437r.

12 *NA*, VOC 1226, Gamron to Batavia, 1 Mar. 1658, fol. 800v. See also Van Santen, *Verenigde Oost-Indische Compagnie.*

13 *NA*, VOC 1549, Gamron to Batavia, 24 Oct. 1694, fols. 600v-01r.

14 See, for example, *NA*, VOC 1694, Isfahan to Gamron, 8 June 1703, fol. 71.

was mostly used in payments to the state, and even there, cash payments were often optional; although the tax burden was expressed in monetary units actual payments were settled in-kind. The state also often paid its officials with assignments on the produce of land, not in coin. According to Chardin most of the shah's taxes were in-kind and consequently many of its payment orders were in-kind as well.[15] The *tas'ir*, or system of conversion rates, was used to set a value for commodities when the state was collecting taxes or making payments; the rates fluctuated some with the demand-supply situation of the particular commodity.

Local Economies rather than a National Economy

The collapse of the Il-Khanid state in the 1330s led to a breakdown of political as well as monetary unity in Iran. In the late-fourteenth century Iran became divided into a series of distinct monetary zones, each with its own standards and its own sequence in weight reductions of its silver coinage. Album labeled these, after their principal cities, the Baghdadi, Tabrizi, Nishapuri, the Shirazi and the Lari zones.[16] Some of this regionalism persisted into the Safavid and even the Qajar period.[17]

During much of this period, Iran had a proliferation of mints, in part because the shah would order the establishment of a mint in a newly conquered city to demonstrate his control. Rabino identified 124 mint cities, besides the treasury mint and the mints at army camps, that were operational between 1500 and 1877.[18] At any one point in time, the number of operational mints was substantially smaller.

Although shahs set up mints, they did not have full control over them. The mints were typically farmed out, and the farmers were under varying degrees of control by the ruler. Until the establishment of one national mint in 1877, the weight and fineness of coins were based less on a national norm than on local practice. Throughout much of the period 1500 to 1925, there was a difference between Tabrizi or Iraqi tumans and those of Khorasan.[19]

15 Chardin, *Voyages*, 5:414–15.

16 Album et al., 'Coins and Coinage'; Album, 'Coinage of Nur Award', 222, fn 28.

17 Gemelli-Careri, *Giro del mondo*, 235; Gmelin, *Travels*, 78.

18 For a list see Simmons, 'Evolution of Persia's Monetary System', 81, with explanation on pp. 82–83.

19 Monshi, *History of Shah 'Abbas*, 1:497 (The Khorasani tuman was one-fourth the value of the Iraqi one); Fraser, *Narrative of a Journey into Khorasan*, 455, 468 (One Khorasani tuman was equal to 20 riyals, while an Iraqi tuman was equal to 8 riyals); Forbes, 'Route from Turbat Haideri'. (30 Khorasan = 70 Irak tumans).

For the period before 1877, it makes more sense to study the changes in weight and fineness of each mint rather than combining the results of several mints into a theoretical national average. For Iran such histories exist only for Tiflis, Rayy, Amul, Wasit and Azerbaijan.[20]

Because the coins from one mint were not necessarily equal to the coins from another mint, merchants and money-traders often demanded a discount to convert the coins from another mint into the local coins – the technical term is 'agio'. That discount could be due to many reasons, including differences in the reputation of certain coins (how much their actual metal content varied from the nominal amount), or changes in the demand and supply of currency at that location at that time.

Differences in the relative value of different coins – for instance, in the ratio between copper and silver coins – from one area to another led to the shipment of coins from one town to another in order to capture the difference in their value. The relative value was monitored closely in each city by the *sarrafs* whose business it was to move metal and bullion.[21] This system of regional diversity persisted until 1877, when a uniform national standard was imposed, based on the existence of one national central mint and one standard of currency.

In Iran the state permitted governors the authority to issue token copper coins – that is, coins whose value is materially greater than the value of the metal of which it is composed. The state guaranteed their convertibility with full-bodied coins – coins whose value is equal to that of its component metal – in a limited area and for a limited time. This system stemmed in part from the fact that the cost of production of valuable coins was practically the same as that of petty coins. With the unit cost of petty coins being much higher relative to their value, the production of those petty coins was more attractive if the value of the petty coins exceeded their metallic content. Token coins tempted the counterfeiter, because of the large difference between metal and face value. Counterfeiting was most easy when minting technology was primitive and rough, as it often was at provincial mints.

Governors issuing copper coins used no standard size or shape. The *folus* differed in size, weight and value by area, also because the issuing authority, the local governor, decided on whether to strike copper and what its value

20 For Tiflis, see Pakhomov, *Monety Gruzii*; for Rayy, see Miles, *Numismatic History of Rayy*; for Amul, see Stern, 'Coins of Amul'; for Wasit, see Welin, 'Wasit, the Mint-Town'; and for Azerbaijan, see Pakhomov, *Monety Azerbaidzhana*. All these are now somewhat dated, because new material has become available.

21 *NA*, VOC 1763, Gamron to Batavia, 21 Dec. 1707, fol. 110.

would be. Each governorate had its own particular copper coinage and mark. The marks struck on copper coins by the Safavids, Afsharids, Zands and Qajars were old Iranian images as well as eponymous animals of the Zodiac and Tatar cycle, although this did not mean that the date of issuing these signs coincided with the calendar year indicated by the sign. Kuteliia, basing himself on the available coins studied by him, observed that on the obverse side of the Safavid copper coins some forty different presentations can be found.

Often at the end of the year, the mark on the coin was changed. Old coins were to be turned in at the mint, where they were melted, coined anew and given a new mark by Nowruz. Coins with an old mark were usually valid for only half the amount of coins with the current year's mark. To that end, by the end of the year, around February, the old copper coins were cried down in value, a practice which hurt the poor considerably. However, existing coins are often badly worn, to the point where their marks on one or both sides are often obliterated. This heavy wear implies that these coins were in circulation for long periods. Thus, it would seem that the annual change was not as automatic as some have intimated, but that this varied per mint and per period.

The Transition to a Modern Monetary System

With the establishment of the Imperial Bank of Persia in 1889, Iran began to use paper money on a systematic basis. As the Qajar dynasty drew to an end in the 1920s, Iran was making the transition to a modern monetary system based primarily on paper money issued by a state-controlled bank, with a subordinate role for coins whose value is determined by state decree rather than by metal content. That was a fundamental break from the monetary system which had prevailed for many long centuries – the complicated and chaotic system we describe in this volume.

Part 1

THE SAFAVID PERIOD 1502–1722

1

Money, Metals and Minting

The Safavid state, like its predecessors, claimed the monopoly of the right of coinage and control over its fineness and weight. Its monetary policy had several objectives which were not fully consistent with each other: to use mints as a source of revenue; to maintain a readily verifiable standard for measuring tax obligations and for making payments; and to promote trade, so as to maximize the income and power of the state.

Minting Coins

Supervision of Minting

To achieve these objectives, the state established mints as its main executive agency in the field of monetary policy, laid down rules for their operation, and appointed staff to operate them – or granted to concession-holders the right to operate mints for a fee – and to make sure that the integrity with regard to the fineness and weight of the coins they produced was respected. The minting of coin was free to all who wanted to bring bullion, foreign and outdated official coins to the royal mints. These mints were state-regulated, but the state farmed them out to the highest bidder.

During the Safavid period, the grand vizier appears to have been tasked with the overall supervision of the coinage.[1] In 1685, for instance, it was Sheykh `Ali Khan who, in the face of a monetary crisis caused by silver shortage, commissioned the exploitation of silver mines in the province of Kermanshah.[2] This was but the logical consequence of the grand vizier's total control over the country's revenues and expenditures.[3] At the same time, the *mo`ayyer al-mamalek* or 'controller of the assay' exercised practical control over all aspects of the mint. He appointed and dismissed all personnel, from high to low. Nobody was allowed to engage in the

1 Kaempfer, *Am Hofe*, 81.

2 *NA*, VOC 1398, Van den Heuvel, Gamron to Batavia, 30 Sept. 1685, fol. 640.

3 Minorsky (ed.), *Tadhkirat al-Mulūk*; and Floor, *Safavid Government Institutions*, 27.

production or trade of precious metals without his permission. He was also in charge of the purity of the metals used for minting.[4] Little information is available about the incumbents of this important position, though we know that it was repeatedly held by Armenian *gholams* – imported slave soldiers and bureaucrats – who originally hailed from Tabriz. Thus the mo`ayyer al-mamalek under Shah Safi was Mir Mohammad Sa`id from Tabriz, who had earlier been *zargar-bashi* (head of the jewelers).[5] In the early days of Shah `Abbas II's reign, Mohammad Beg, an Armenian gholam, also from Tabriz, occupied the position.[6] When he was appointed *nazer* (steward of the royal household) in 1651, his brother Oghan Beg succeeded him as controller of the assay.[7] Oghan Beg was probably succeeded by another of Mohammad Beg's brothers, Hoseyn Beg, who assumed the position in 1654. Hoseyn Beg, in turn, made room for one of Mohammad Beg's sons, Amin Beg, who held the post from 1656 to at least 1658.[8] In 1693, Shah Soleyman appointed another Armenian, Hajji Piri, who was a merchant, as controller of the assay of Isfahan.[9] Musa Beg, who served as mo`ayyer al-mamalek in 1713–14, was of Armenian background as well, his grandfather having converted to Islam.[10] The fact that so many Armenians from Tabriz, some of them merchants, served as mo`ayyer al-mamalek, is of course no coincidence. Armenians were the pre-eminent and most active long-distance merchants of the realm, dealing especially with silk, Iran's greatest export revenue earner, and their activities outside Iran gave them unrivalled knowledge of monetary matters, including issues of bullion flows and international prices. In local mints, too, we encounter Armenians. Thus the *zarrab-bashi*, master of the mint, of Nakhjavan was an Armenian in 1691, while the mints of Tiflis and Yerevan, two other key cities located in the forefront of the influx of precious metal, in the 1660s and 1670s were held by a series of local Armenians as well.[11]

The technical manager of the mint was the zarrab-bashi, or master of the mint, who had the daily supervision of the mint and its finances. It was

4 Floor-Faghfoory, *Dastur al-Moluk*, 57, 247–49; Nasiri, *Titles & Emoluments*, 50–52.

5 Torkaman and Mo'arrekh, *Zeyl-e tarikh*, 280.

6 For Mohammad Beg, see Matthee, 'Career of Mohammad Beg.'

7 *NA*, VOC 1195, Gamron to Batavia, 20 Feb. 1652, fol. 798b. Vahid Qazvini, *Tarikh-e jahan-ara-ye `Abbasi*, 149, states that the position went to Mohammad Beg's brother, Hasan Beg.

8 See *NA*, VOC 1203, Gamron to Isfahan, 12 Apr. 1654, fol. 798b; VOC 1210, Willemsz., Gamron to Grand Vizier, 12 June 1656, fol. 890; VOC 1224, Gamron to Batavia, 1 Mar. 1658, fol. 800.

9 *NA*, VOC 1507, Gamron to Heren XVII, 2 Aug. 1693, fol. 469.

10 Khatunabadi, *Vaqaye` al-sennin*, 551; De Bruyn, *Reizen*, 183; *NA*, VOC 1886, Isfahan to Gamron, 23 Oct. 1715, fol. 271.

11 Zak`aria of Agulis, *Journal*, 78, 84, 93; [Villotte], *Voyage*, 191.

the task of the zarrab-bashi to see to it that coins were minted properly, that the fineness of the assay was respected, and that no counterfeit coins were produced.[12] Chardin claimed that, for a first offense, a counterfeiter had his hand chopped off, and that a subsequent violation was punished with disembowelment.[13] In 1683, Shah Soleyman punished the master of the mint who had debased the coinage without his permission.[14] Yet according to Sanson, this was an exception. The zarrab-bashi remains more obscure in the sources than the mo`ayyer al-mamalek. But in this function, too, officials from the ranks of the gholams, Georgians and Armenians, seem to have prevailed. Alexander Gorganizadeh, a scion of a high-ranking Georgian family whose members held high positions at the Safavid court, served as zarrab-bashi in the 1660s.[15] In 1670, Shah Soleyman appointed as zarrab-bashi of Isfahan one Simon, an Armenian from Yerevan, who in the 1660s had been zarrab-bashi of that city.[16] The *moshref*, supervisor, of the mint was in charge of collecting *vajebi* or seignorage (really a tax on metal), which he had to transfer to the zarrab-bashi. The latter had to enforce the royal decree that coins were only produced at the mint. [17] Other taxes were also collected as *tamgha*, which were abolished in 1565, but seem to have been collected later again as *vojuh-e kopek*.[18]

New coins were struck when a new shah acceded to the throne. The same day or night that the old shah died new coins were struck to be ready for distribution among the courtiers after the enthronement. Within a few hours, the coining dies at the mint were changed to reflect the new political reality.[19]

Because much of Iran's gold and silver was imported from the Ottoman Empire, the mints, and especially those located near the northwestern borders, such as Tiflis and Yerevan, played an important role in converting foreign specie into Iranian coins. Silver coins had to be declared on arriving at the borders and handed over at the closest mint.[20] To facilitate merchants and tradesmen in the process of handing in and obtaining coins, city mints

12 Minorsky (ed.), *Tadhkirat al-Mulūk*, 69; Floor-Faghfoory, *Dastur al-Moluk*, 117–18, 248–49; Nasiri, *Titles & Emoluments*, 51.
13 Chardin, *Voyages*, 6:115.
14 Kaempfer, *Am Hofe*, 71–72.
15 Gorgijanize, *Istoriia Gruzii*, 13; Brosset (ed.), *Histoire de la Géorgie*, 2/1:509–14.
16 Zak`aria of Agulis, *Journal*, 100.
17 Minorsky (ed.), *Tadhkirat al-Mulūk*, 69; Floor-Faghfoory, *Dastur al-Moluk*, 249.
18 Mostafavi, 'Yek farman', 134; Honarfar, *Ganjineh-ye asar*, 435.
19 For the striking of new coins at the time of Shah Soleyman's accession, see Kaempfer, *Am Hofe*, 57, 58–59.
20 Chelebi, *Travels in Iran*, 44.

were usually found in or near the bazaar.[21] The Isfahan mint was directly opposite the Qeysariyeh bazaar. The only existing drawing of it appears in Bembo's travelogue.[22] The mint in Kerman had been constructed by Ganj `Ali Khan, the town's governor from 1596 to 1624, and measured 18.5 x 5.7 meters.[23] We have very little additional information about the location and appearance of most other mints in Safavid times. In the bazaar of Qazvin in 1603 the English merchant Cartwright observed that 'In this place do sit daily twelve Sheriffes [sarrafs], that is, men to buy and sell Pearle, Diamonds, and other pretious stones, and to exchange Gold and Silver, to turne Spanish dollars to great advantage into Persian Coyne; and to change the great piece of Persian Coyne, as Abbasses, Larines, and such like into certaine Brasse Monies for the poore. They will also lend upon any pawne, and that with as great interest as our divillesh Brokers and Scriveners take in London.'[24] The same system continued to exist in Iran until 1877.

Large quantities of coin were typically checked by weighing them. For large payments, both merchants and government officials made use of bags containing a standard amount of coins. These bags were referred to as *kiseh* and *bolsa*. According to Chardin, such bags held 50 tumans in silver.[25] For the Nader Shah period, we have a reference to a similar bag holding 500 tumans in gold.[26] A special inspector, the *sarraf-bashi*, was responsible for the quality of the coinage in the bags, which he sealed personally. In return, he received 1 to 1.5 `abbasi per bag. According to Du Mans, it was his responsibility to replace any false coins at his own expense.[27] In 1661, the Dutch paid one per mill of the purchase price of silk as a fee to 'the sarrafs, who checked the coins after payment, because the shah's agent only would accept the money after checking'.[28]

The provincial mints were formally under the direct control of the central government, at least with regard to the striking of gold and silver coins. The example of Shah `Abbas I, who sent for the Mint master of Shiraz for having 'exceeded the said value of 13 shahis cost', and had him

21 Olearius, *Vermehrte newe Beschreibung*, 561.
22 It was a bank branch and tourist office in the 1970s. See Gaube and Wirth, *Der Bazar von Isfahan*, 177, 262.
23 Bastani-Parizi, *Ganj `Ali Khan*, 83.
24 Purchas, *Purchas his Pilgrims*, 8:507.
25 Chardin, *Voyages*, 4:170.
26 Marvi, *Tarikh-e `alamara-ye Naderi*, 2:540.
27 Richard (ed.), *Raphaël du Mans*, 2:267; Minorsky (ed.), *Tadhkirat al-Mulūk*, 69; Kaempfer, *Am Hofe*, 121–22.
28 *NA*, VOC 1234, Gamron to Batavia, 5 May 1662, fol. 210.

beheaded, suggests that this control was more than theoretical, at least under the forceful Shah `Abbas.[29] Yet in most cases the local rulers, under whose auspices the mint operated, and especially the *vali*s, had a great deal of autonomy in their minting practices, and not just for copper (which was by definition local and thus not subject to central government control). Some controversy exists over the exact nature of this autonomy. Some Russian numismatists, using the example of the most extensively studied Safavid mint, that of Georgia, have argued that local rulers were entirely deprived of their right of coinage as a symbol of royal sovereignty.[30] There is no question that the minting of silver was subject to central control and supervision. A local chronicle makes clear that it was the shah who granted – and could revoke – the minting right of the vali of Khuzestan.[31] Similarly, the example of the Indian prince who, returning to his homeland and reaching Mashhad in 1696, was unable to have his silverware minted into silver coin because the proper dies carrying the name of the shah had not been sent from Isfahan, suggests that dies were provided by the central government.[32] It is perhaps best to follow the Georgian numismatist Kuteliia, who makes a useful distinction between political legitimacy and economic reality in this regard. Kuteliia argues that from a juridical perspective the mint of Tiflis in Georgia, a semiautonomous region, *velayat*, was an Iranian or a Safavid one adhering to Safavid types, legends and weight standards. Economically speaking, however, matters were different, for the shah did not or perhaps could not interfere directly in the affairs of local mints.[33] The money issued by the mint of Tiflis, for instance, was used for the local population rather than for the shah's Qezelbash garrison in Tiflis, and profits accruing from the Georgian mints are said to have benefited the local vali.[34] Franz Caspar Schillinger, who visited the Caucasus at the turn of the eighteenth century, noted that Shah Soltan Hoseyn had permitted the local ruler to strike coins as he had done before, on condition that the coins issued would bear the name of the shah on one side.[35] The example of

29 Sainsbury (ed.), *Calendar of State Papers*, Isfahan, 5 July 1620, 379.

30 Pakhomov, *Monety Gruzii*, 217.

31 Kasravi, *Tarikh-e pansad saleh-ye Khuzestan*, 87, citing al-Sayyid `Abd Allah, *Tarikh al-Musha`sha`yin*; and Sistani, *Ehya al-Moluk*, 301. Until 998/1589–90, the ruler of Sistan struck coins in his own name.

32 Nasiri, *Dastur-e shahriyaran*, 118. See also Kasravi, *Tarikh-e pansad saleh-ye Khuzestan*, 87; and Matthee, 'Safavid Mint of Huwayza'.

33 Kuteliia, *Gruziia i sefevidskii Iran*, 26–27.

34 Ibid., 29–30.

35 Schillinger, *Persianische und Ost-Indianische Reise*, 217–18.

Hoveyzeh in the southeastern province of `Arabistan (modern Khuzestan), like Georgia a velayat, also shows that local rulers enjoyed the income of the mint under their jurisdiction and were only held to strike coins that in legend and type conformed to the overall Safavid coinage.[36]

Olearius claims that all mints were farmed out to the highest bidder.[37] This assertion is not confirmed by other sources. The *Tazkerat al-Moluk* notes that in Isfahan the production of silver and copper was farmed out for a sum of between 500 and 700 tumans.[38] In 1667, Agha Vali, the farmer of the mint in Yerevan, received orders from Shah Soleyman to strike `abbasis of 4 shahis, instead of 5 shahis, the ones that until then had been in circulation. However, he remained in charge of the mint only for six months, after which the job reverted to the khan [of Yerevan] who farmed it out to a certain Simon (Shemavon), an Armenian who held the position under four successive governors.[39]

The emoluments of the moshref of the mint in Isfahan were as follows: In wages (*mavajeb*) he received 12 tumans before the Afghan invasion, and 15 tumans under Shah Tahmasb II (1730). In addition, his official daily ration (*jireh*) included one plate [of food], which had a value of 1,000 dinars per day or 36 tumans per year. Concerning his fees (*rosumat*), which did not exist initially, yet had become a custom, he received the following. On account of gold that was turned into gold ashrafis at the mint, he received 10 dinar per mesqal; copper from which coins (*folus*) were struck paid 10 dinars per *man-e shah*; and silver that yielded silver coins half a dinar per misqal. His total annual income with these benefits came to 200 tumans.[40]

The Technical Process

While the Safavids were in power in Iran, Europe began to experiment with various forms of mechanized minting. In several countries hand-operated machinery was introduced in the seventeenth century. French mints began to work with screw presses in 1643, and in England hammer-struck minting was discontinued in 1662. Even the Ottoman Empire saw the beginning of machine-struck coinage in the late seventeenth century.[41] Iranians were not wholly unfamiliar with these new techniques.

36 Kasravi, *Tarikh-e pansad saleh-ye Khuzestan*, 87; and Matthee, 'Safavid Mint of Huwayza'.
37 Olearius, *Vermehrte newe Beschreibung*, 560.
38 Minorsky (ed.), *Tadhkirat al-Mulūk*, 61.
39 Radzhabli, 'Iz istorii monetnogo dela', 59; McCabe, *Shah's Silk*, 157.
40 Nasiri, *Titles & Emoluments*, 51–52.
41 Şahillioğlu, 'Introduction of Machinery'.

Shah `Abbas II (1642–66) was informed about the more efficient, new mechanical European minting technology. Although he is said to have admired its quality of output, he showed no interest in acquiring this technology,[42] and until the nineteenth century no Iranian government made any attempt to introduce mechanized minting.

For the situation after 1650, we have several descriptions, which yield the following picture of the minting process. The coins were hammer struck, though some of the heavier ones may have been cast. The dies, which were of iron, were about 15 cm long, varied in diameter and were irregular in shape. The same dies were used for gold and silver. The size and shape of the coins varied, and no standard appears to have been adopted. Most coins were round, but some were oblong. The same type of coin could be struck both round and oblong, as was for example the case with the copper *paisas* in the early eighteenth century. Despite the skills demonstrated by the mint workers their output was not always quality work. The coins differed in thickness, in shape, and the flan often was smaller than the die. Some have an extra margin, whilst on others there is hardly room for the inscription.[43]

Gemelli-Careri, who was in Iran in the 1690s, gives a short description of the minting process in Safavid Iran:

> They make coins in Persia in the following manner. [The metal] is put in a ditch [fossa], with charcoal and wood on top of it to heat the metal. This is done with the help of two bellows to keep the fire going, which causes the metal to become liquid. In this liquified form they make bars, which they later flatten, and reduce to a laminated form. These they extend, others then cut it up, the next [workers] reduce these to round pieces, which others then weigh, while finally yet other [workers] flatten them. After this, the metal is coined by being hammer-struck.[44]

This description corresponds with what the *Tazkerat al-Moluk* reports about the minting procedure:[45]

1. The foundry (*sabbaki*). The staff of this shop turn impure gold into pure, and base silver into pure by putting them into crucibles.
2. In the shop of the *qors-kubi*, the genuine bullion is beaten in order to produce gold [of the necessary solidity].

42 Tavernier, *Les six voyages*, 1:550–51.
43 Rabino di Borgomale, *Coins, Metals, and Seals*, 8.
44 Gemelli-Carreri, *Giro del mondo*, 2:12.
45 Minorsky (ed.), *Tadhkirat al-Mulūk*, 58–59.

3. Ditto of *ahangari*. After the completion of the previous operations the gold is shaped into forged bars.
4. Ditto of the *charkh-kashi*. After the previous operation gold and silver are drawn through a steel plate with holes.
5. Ditto of *qatta`i*: where gold and silver are cut for the production of coins.
6. Ditto of *kahleh-ku'i*; where the pieces cut from the ingot are given the thickness of an `abbasi or panj-shahi.
7. Ditto of blanching (*safid-gari*) where the surface of money is made refulgent.
8. Ditto of *takhsh-kuni* ('sorting') where the `abbasis which, judging by sight, are underweight are set aside and melted anew.
9. Ditto of *sekkeh-kuni*: where the masters striking coins are every day engaged in this work.

In the best years, 400 workers were daily employed by the nine departments of the mint.[46] In addition to minting, gold-smithing activities were also undertaken by the mint.[47]

While gold was seldom coined in Safavid times, some mints did not even strike silver coins on a regular basis. An example is the mint of Shiraz, which in the late seventeenth century mainly struck copper.[48] Herbert reports about 'the King's Mint, wherein all forreigne Coines are new stampt, with the Persian Characters. One day is for money, a second for Gold, a third for Brasse.'[49]

A Fragmented System

The fall of the Il-Khans not only fragmented Iran's monetary unity but also further tilted the proportion of metals used in Iran's currency toward silver, which now virtually became the sole metal in the monetary system. While copper coinage became relatively scarce, gold was no longer minted in any significant quantity, and most if not all gold coins struck in this period appear to have been for celebratory or donative purposes.[50] The Safavids did not, as is sometimes claimed, introduce a new currency system. Instead, they adopted the Aq-qoyunlu and Timurid prototype. Some of the local

46 Ibid., 60
47 Kaempfer, *Am Hofe*, 157.
48 Gemelli-Carreri, *Giro del mondo*, 2:239
49 Herbert, *Travels in Persia*, 87.
50 Album et al., 'Coins and Coinage'.

variations in currency units persisted into the Safavid period. Besides the standard shahi coinage used in the west, there were two major regional coinages.

The Safavid monetary system is heir to the coinage that was introduced by the Il-Khans, the Mongol dynasty that controlled the eastern Islamic world for much of the thirteenth and fourteenth centuries. Especially the predominance of silver goes back to conditions that came into being under the Il-Khans. The Il-Khanid system was based on the simultaneous circulation of silver and gold (copper circulated as well but was not a regal coinage and was used strictly for local purposes and in low-volume transactions). Silver *derhams* comprised the bulk of the coins struck in this period,[51] and silver was the only real currency in that only silver coins were minted according to a fixed weight standard. The Il-Khans struck gold coins mostly for commemorative and sometimes economic reasons, not to any standard but at random weight, presumably in response to an erratic supply of gold owing to the fact that only one gold mine was found in all of Iran.

The most salient feature inherited from the Mongols is perhaps the money of account used by the Safavids. Dinars figured in the monetary system of the Mongols in the form of the *kepeki* dinar, a unit that goes back to the Chagatay ruler Kebek Khan (r. 716–27/1316–26), who issued this coin, weighing 2 mesqal or 8.53 g as part of a monetary reform.[52] Kepeki dinars continued to be used as silver coins of various weight and value under the Jalayerids, the Timurids and the Qara-qoyunlu, and in the sixteenth century were still in use in Khorasan as well as in Central Asia.[53]

During the first century of the dynasty's reign, the Safavid monetary system was based on one tuman = 200 shahis = 10,000 dinars. This system remained in place for the duration of Safavid rule, even though neither the tuman nor the dinar referred to actual coins. The Englishman Barker in 1626 reported: 'The people do not make their account by naming so many abbassees or shahees, but by tomauns (the greatest denomination and thousands, hundreds, fifties, etc. decimally).'[54] Olearius in 1637 similarly stated: 'The tuman is a unit of account, just as the Russians with their

51 Martinez, 'Regional Mint Output', 137, estimates that about 35 per cent of the total mint output in the Il-Khanid state was in gold.

52 Seifeddin, 'Monetnaia sistema v Azerbaidzhane', 199–200.

53 Monshi, *Tarikh-e `alamara-ye `Abbasi*, 1:497 (50,000 dinar-e kepeki = 50 tuman-e `eraqi); Rumlu, *Ahsan al-Tavarikh*, p. 122; Sam Mirza, *Tazkereh-ye tohfat-e Sami*, 28 (40 tuman-e kepeki = 200 tuman-e Tabrizi). See also Davidovich, 'Monetary Reform'.

54 Simmons, 'Evolution of Persia's Monetary System', 268.

rubles.'[55] Whereas ghost money like the tuman was used for accounting, the actual coins in use were quite different. As of 1600, the following main monetary face values existed: `abbasi (200 dinars); mahmudi (half `abbasi or 100 dinars); shahi (¼ `abbasi or 50 dinars); and bisti (1/10 of an `abbasi or 20 dinars), which were all silver coins. For copper, finally, there was the qazbaki or qazbegi (1/40 of an `abbasi or 5 dinars) with its fractional values.[56] Coin names, generally, were synonymous with their dinar values, e.g., bisti means 'twenty'. In the case of a devaluation by way of weight reduction, the same coin name and dinar value was applied to the lighter coin; otherwise a different dinar value was applied to the coin. This system, with silver `abbasi adjustments under the shahs `Abbas II, Soleyman, and in particular Soltan Hoseyn (1720), remained in place until the Afghan invasion. After Nader Shah's accession to the throne in 1736 a monetary reform was attempted. New silver and gold coins were struck, based on the Indian silver rupee and golden *mohr.*

The monetary unity of Iran under the Il-Khanids, as well as its political unity, broke down with the collapse of their rule following the death of Soltan Abu Sa`id in 1336. A variety of local currencies circulated in the later fourteenth century; Stephen Album hypothesizes that Iran became divided into four distinctive monetary zones.

Such distinct monetary zones also were characteristic for the Safavid period, in particular the sixteenth century. Album concluded, based on numismatic evidence:

> What is clear is that even within a single weight standard, designs were regional rather national. Moreover, during these reigns [of Esma`il I and Tahmasb I] at least three different weight standards were maintained simultaneously for different portions of the kingdom (silver coinage only). Besides the standard shahi coinage used in the west, there were two major regional coinages. The first was a separate shahi sequence for the eastern region, including the provinces of Khurasan, Quhistan, Sistan and Astarbad, maintained until 974. The second was a fixed tanka standard of just over 3.6 g for Mazandaran province, inherited from the Aq Qoyunlu and maintained until sometime during he reign of `Abbas I.[57]

55 Olearius, *Vermehrte newe Beschreibung*, 560.

56 The term qazbegi seems to go back to Ghazi Beg, who ruled Shirvan between 906–07/1501–02. See `Abdi Beg Shirazi, *Takmilat al-akhbar*, 135.

57 Album, *Checklist*, 274.

From the time of the accession of Esma`il II in 984/1576 onward, there is a regular sequence of uniform types used everywhere in the empire. The only prominent exceptions to the uniform coinage are Mazandaran and Khuzestan.[58] In Mazandaran, a *tangeh* or *tankeh* of 3.6 g, derived from an Aq-Qoyunlu prototype, was in circulation from the reign of Shah Esma`il until the early part of the seventeenth century.[59] The tangeh also continued to be in circulation in the Caucasus and Hormuz until the end of the sixteenth century.[60]

The most prominent local currency was the *lari*. The lari takes its name from Lar, the capital of Larestan, which first minted this coin. But under Shah Tahmasb it was struck at numerous mints throughout Iran. It was known among Europeans as *larin*. The larin was a bent silver wire in the form of a hairpin. Stamped on both sides, it was struck to a 5.15 g standard, introduced by the Timurid ruler Shahrukh in 827.[61] After Shah `Abbas I conquered Lar in 1010/1601–02 the production of this coin was discontinued. However, due to its fineness the lari had become a popular currency in international trade, so much so in fact that it was the standard currency in the Indian Ocean trading area as of the mid-sixteenth century. The European companies trading in the Indian Ocean area also, for a time, adopted it as their unit of account for bookkeeping purposes.[62] The lari was minted in a region stretching from Tabriz, Shiraz, Lar, and Basra to southwest India (Dapoli), Ceylon and the Maldive Islands. It continued to play a role as a unit of account, as a measure of value, and as a unit of land measurement in west India into the mid-eighteenth century.[63] Some derivates of lesser alloy, such as the *tawilah*, the long [coin], continued to circulate in the Arab peninsula well into the twentieth century.[64]

While the lari served as a low-value trading coin in the Indian Ocean basin well into the eighteenth century, in the Persian Gulf basin it lost its importance in the 1600s. It is unclear why the lari faded, to be replaced by the mahmudi of Hoveyzeh as the workhorse of the Persian Gulf basin.[65] It

58 Ibid.

59 Ibid., Fumeni, *Tarikh-e Gilan*, 17. (It was known as the *tangeh-ye now.*)

60 The currency in Hormuz 'is called "lari e tanqua", 7 of which equal one ducato d'oro', in a Mingrelian town it was called 'cutatis' [kutaisi], also tangua, with Iberian letters'. Membré, *Mission to the Lord Sophy*, 14, 51, 54; see also Purchas, *Hakluytus Posthumus* 8: 460–61.

61 Album, *Checklist*, 276.

62 See, e.g., Dunlop (ed.), *Bronnen*, index: laryn.

63 Perlin, 'Money-use in Late Pre-colonial India', 335, n. 147.

64 See Wood, '*Gampola Larin Hoard*'; and Van Laere, 'Larin'.

65 Some sources claim that the lari was used in the Maldives into the nineteenth century.

has been suggested that the popularity of either coin is perhaps attributable to the absence of a universally accepted copper coinage in the area.[66]

A Trimetallic System

As said, during the entire Safavid period, Iran had what, for lack of a better term, may be called a trimetallic system. We use this term here with the understanding that the normal connotation – that all three metals exist in a fixed, government-controlled ratio of convertibility to one another – is not applicable to pre-modern Iran. Economists would also assume that a trimetallic system would be severely stressed by debasement of the currency, because the coins of each metal type might be debased at different rates. The trimetallic system would also be undermined during periods of deflation, when coins of all three types were debased so that less metal was necessary to purchase a fixed basket of goods.

However, it appears that the use of three metals in Iran did not experience significant amounts of arbitrage and that the system was rather stable, despite considerable currency debasement and, it would seem, some deflation. Part of the reason is that the coins in each of the three metals were largely separated by their uses: the copper coins were mostly for local trade; the silver for government use and long distance trade; the gold equally for long distance trade as well as for hoarding and luxury items. In Safavid times, as in all pre-modern states, these precious metals merely circulated side by side. The shahs coined gold – albeit infrequently – silver and copper, which in theory could be used for all kind of payments. In fact, as we will see, they were used as such in various periods in Iranian history.

The system of coins in three metals persisted even though the relative values of the three metals changed considerably. During the 250 years under consideration, the relative prices of these metals underwent tremendous changes in the various parts of the world market because of the flood of metals from the New World, from which silver came in greater relative quantities than gold. The ratio of the gold price to the silver price, which had been roughly constant for centuries, in the course of the seventeenth

66 Broome, *Handbook List of Islamic Coins*, 172. That does not seem likely, though, given the fact that these silver coins were mainly used in international trade at a time that copper was not used for that purpose.

century rose from 11:1 to 15:1 in European markets.[67] At the same time, sharply higher production from northern Europe, including the Great Copper Mountain in Falun, Sweden, drove down the value of copper. To be sure, the changes in the relative values in any one market did not necessarily translate into similar changes on other markets; moving metal was expensive and insecure, and governments often created barriers to flows of metal. Nevertheless, slowly and unevenly across the world, the value of gold over the decades rose relative to silver and copper.

Copper Coins

Copper coins were called *folus*, the plural of the Arabic word *fals*. Copper coins were also known as *pul*, *pul-e siyah* or *qara pul* (black, i.e., copper, money).[68] Olearius insisted that all copper coin was called pul, while the French envoy Gardane in 1718 noted that the qaz was called a pul.[69] In 1540 in Tabriz, the copper coin was known as *casipeghi* or *qazbaki*.[70] Originally a weight of about 0.28 g, a qazbak was later used as the name of a coin with the same weight. The names of the copper coins at the beginning of the seventeenth century were double gaz or qazbak, equal to 10 dinars. We also hear of the small qaz or qazbak of 5 dinars and the folus of 0.5 dinars.[71] The qazbaki equaled ¼ bisti. Copper was issued in various other denominations as well, such as 1 bisti (0.58 g), and ½ bisti (0.28 g). It is, however, difficult to identify the presumed weight of the copper coins, for the weight of coins from different cities does not always coincide.[72] There was anyhow no standard for copper coins, since they were not exchanged by weight, but by tale. Consequently, the copper folus differed in size, weight and value by area. Indeed, it was the issuing authority, the local governor, who decided on whether to coin copper and what its value would be. Copper coins typically had eponymous animals of the Zodiac and Tatar cycle printed on them, no doubt to make it easy for a largely illiterate populace to identify and differentiate between them.[73]

67 Braudel, *Mediterranean*, 473, restating and updating the classic statement in Braudel and Spooner, 'Prices in Europe from 1450 to 1750'.
68 Richard (ed.), *Raphaël du Mans*, 2:150.
69 Olearius, *Vermehrte newe Beschreibung*, 560; Rabino, *Coins, Medals, and Seals*, 17, n. 3.
70 Membré, *Mission to the Lord Sophy*, 51.
71 Rabino, *Coins, Medals, and Seals*, 17.
72 Pamokhov, *Monety Gruzii*, 216.
73 Rabino, *Coins, Medals, and Seals*, 20, Simmons, 'Evolution of Persia's Monetary System', 97; Chelebi, *Travels in Iran*, 44.

Because of their low value, copper coins do not readily show up in hoards. Relatively few Safavid copper coins have therefore survived to the present time. Copper coins usually have a date and the mint stamped on them, but typically do not indicate their face value. Only three coins with their face value stamped on them are known for the sixteenth century and none for the seventeenth century. The coins in question were struck in Qonduz, Termiz, and Hesar (957/1550) and state their value as 'two dinars'.[74] They weigh 2.20 g and 2.25 g respectively. Rabino therefore believed that in the sixteenth century the main face value of the Safavid copper coin was the dinar of 1.09 g. In contemporary Central Asia the copper coin also had one dinar as its main face value, which weighed 1.23 g. However, its actual average weight was 0.95 g. The term dinar as the designation for the face value of copper money in Central Asia superseded that of *`adl* as of the second half of the fifteenth century, though the term `adl continued to be used as well. A copper coin minted in Tabriz (954/1547–48) displays the term `adl and weighs 0.77 g.

Kuteliia confirms Rabino's thesis that in the sixteenth century there were three groups of copper coins. These had a ratio of 4:2:1, representing respectively 2, 1 and ½ dinar pieces. Kuteliia arrives at an average weight of 1.85 g, 1.00 g, and 0.35 g for these three different coin values. The one-dinar coin had a weight that is close to Rabino's suggested 1.09 g standard for a copper coin. Under Tahmasb I, the unit for the copper coin was the dinar of 1.11 g. There are also some heavier copper coins from the second half of the sixteenth century minted in Orumiyeh (980/1572–73) weighing 2.78 g and in Zafarabad (978/1570–71) weighing 2.75 g. These probably had a higher face value than the usual two-dinar coins.[75]

In the Indian context, copper has been called a humble kind of coinage used by small people.[76] In Safavid and Afsharid Iran, copper performed the same function. Retail prices and wages were in copper coins, soldiers and the lower-class urban artisans used copper, and nothing but copper probably ever passed through the hands of the poor. Retail prices and wages were in copper coins. Struys in the 1670s noted that 'merchants seldom have gold, but they have a lot of copper coins, which they call pull'. He also observed that in Isfahan, religious figures preaching on the street had 'a pile of pull and other small coins formed in front of them'.[77] Copper coins also had some

74 Rabino, *Coins, Medals, and Seals*, 17 (has Qandahar, which is an erroneous reading of Qonduz); Album, *Checklist*, 303, types 3009 and 3010.

75 Kuteliia, *Catalogue of the Iranian Copper Coins*, 48ff.

76 Perlin, 'Money-use in Late Pre-colonial India', 237.

77 Struys, *Drie aanmerkelijke en seer rampspoedige reysen*, 336.

limited use for dealings with the government. As in Mughal India, taxes were sometimes assessed in copper.[78] For instance, Shah Soltan Hoseyn in or around 1701 introduced a new tax for the Armenians known as *shesh-dinar* (six dinars), which probably was collected in copper, because there were no small silver coins of such a low dinar unit.[79] Generally, however, the state and big traders required payment in full-bodied coins, i.e., silver or gold.

The copper coins were an exception to the general Safavid rule that the value of coins was determined by their precious metal content. The copper coins generally circulated at a value – as measured in silver or gold – that exceeded their metallic worth; that is, they were token money. Copper coinage thus represented a cost-effective means of providing poor people with circulating coin as well as an effective means of additional exploitation. The copper coinage was allowed to circulate in the jurisdiction of the governor who minted the coin. These coins were the monopoly of governors. The local state guaranteed their convertibility with silver and gold coins – referred to as big, full-bodied coins – in a radius limited in time and space. Outside the issuing area their value in terms of silver or gold coins was only 50 per cent of their face value, which was typically less than the value of the copper metal in the coin. Della Valle, talking about the town of Firuz Kuh on the road between Tehran and Mazandaran, offers indisputable evidence for this when he says, 'This town is the last of the province of Iraq, in consequence of which the copper money of Hispahan ceases to pass for more than half its value. It is remarkable circumstance in Persia, that although silver coin be universally current at the same value, copper should pass in a different province too that in which it was issued at only half its price, notwithstanding it be larger and heavier than that in circulation of the stamp of the province in which it is tendered.'[80]

Note that the state's dictation of a fixed, silver value for copper coins – even though the fixed ratio was for a limited time and space – gave the Safavid monetary system some of the character of a classic bimetallic system, rather than a system in which the value of coins fluctuated based on the precious metal content. Furthermore, the usual practice of expressing the value of copper coins both in silver and gold meant that the state was establishing a fixed ratio between silver and gold, though this was generally theoretical, since it was rare indeed that copper was exchanged for gold.

78 For the Indian situation, see Habib, 'System of Trimetallism', 151.

79 Floor, *Fiscal History*, 205.

80 Della Valle, *Viaggi*, 1:586; trans. in Della Valle, 'Extract of the Travels'.

The value of copper coins sometimes lasted for one year only, after which its mark was changed. To that end, by the end of the year, around February, all old copper coins were cried down in value. Those not handed in kept only 50 per cent of their value, which hurt the poor considerably. Once turned in to the mint, the copper coins were melted, stamped anew and given a new mark by Nowruz (21 March).[81] That the practice was officially proscribed or at least controversial is suggested by the inscription on a series of sixteenth-century copper coins: '*Peyvasteh be-la`nat-e elahi taghayyordeh-ye folus-e shahi*,' May God's curse forever on him who changes the royal folus.[82] Although conclusive evidence is still lacking, Kuteliia has argued that it is quite likely that under normal conditions the value of copper coins was cried down periodically, but not necessarily on an annual basis. However, he admits that more complete chronological series of coin issues for a larger sample of towns needs to be established before this issue can be settled.[83]

The mint farmer or government made a considerable profit on this type of operation. As one observer put it: 'The shah used each year to renew the money, by halving its value, and he would not strike new money, forbidding that, and almost all of that was melted in the Mint and doing so, he would be able to get a lot money from this in the other cities, that does not show in his accounts ... On his death, among much gold, silver and jewels, and it hard to believe, but it has been confirmed by more than one reliable person, they found 80 million ducats of which 17 million in gold.'[84] In 1637 the price of one pound of copper was 40 qazbaks (one `abbasi), while at the mint 64 qazbaks were produced from one pound of copper.[85] The difference of 24 qazbaks thus represented a gross profit of 60 per cent for the minter. This shows the special nature of copper coins, which allowed governors to make extra revenue by imposing a rate for copper coins that was higher than the market value of the metal they contained.[86] This profitable activity also explains why the EIC, seeking to export copper to Iran in 1619, found that coined copper was cheaper than the ordinary metal; yet when the EIC agents tried to melt 'ten maunds of pice', they found that there was an

81 Olearius, *Vermehrte newe Beschreibung*, 561–62; for a detailed discussion of this type of monetary policy, see Davidovich, *Istoriia deneshnogo obrasheniia*, ch. 4.

82 Album, *Checklist*, 318.

83 Kuteliia, *Catalogue of the Iranian Copper Coins*, 50–51.

84 Berchet (ed.), *La repubblica di Venezia e la Persia*, 279.

85 Olearius, *Vermehrte newe Beschreibung*, 561–62.

86 Ibid., 561. According to Kuteliia, *Catalogue of the Iranian Copper Coins*, 58, the profit was even higher. A copper coin weighed less than it should have based on its dinar value and therefore 96 instead of 64 copper coins could be minted from one pound of copper.

official prohibition against melting down copper money.[87] This was also true for the other metals, gold and silver. After all, the government did not want to forgo collecting the minting fee, which it was able to obtain only by making it compulsory for all other coin but its own to be reminted or to pay an export fee. Barker, an EIC agent in Isfahan, therefore remarks that 'when making mention of a commodity being sold for such a price, [they?] mean the ordinary and current coins of the country, all foreign being sold as merchandise'.[88]

The poor lost considerably every year because of this annual crying down in value of their money. One Safavid governor who did not avail himself of this mechanism to enrich himself was commemorated for this. The chief mosque in Astarabad features an inscription, dated 1 Jomadi II 937/27 January 1531, which records that Soltan Mohammad Zu'l-Qadr, son of Mir `Ala al-Dowleh, did not change the copper currency.[89] *Taghayyordeh*, 'he who changes', does not mean counterfeiter here, but refers to the governor who changes the face value of the folus at a rate profitable for himself.[90] It therefore seems that, officially, copper coins were to remain unchanged until they were worn down. This is also indicated in the couplet on the late Tahmasb folus, as well as by the fact that not every year the value of the folus was altered by changing the legal marks on them. The surviving folus show heavy wear, often obliterating their marks on one or both sides. This implies heavy wear following heavy use over long periods of time. Thus, it would seem that the annual change was not as automatic as some have suggested, but that this varied per mint and per period. Krusinski, for example, clearly indicates that things were better when governors were not rotated every year:

> None, but the King has a Right to coin Silver Money, the Governors of the Province have a Right to coin Copper: And this Money, which is fixed at a certain value in their Province while they command there, sinks one Half in the Value when they are displaced, and never goes for any more in the other Provinces; so that a Piece of Copper which is worth Ten Pence in the Province where the Governor commands with whose Stamps it was coin'ed, is worth but Five Pence in all the other Provinces of the Kingdom; and suffers the same Abatement in his own too, the Moment

87 Foster (ed.), *English Factories in India 1618–21*, 142, 144.
88 Simmons, 'Evolution of Persia's Monetary System', 268.
89 Rabino, *Mazandaran and Astarabad*, 27, Persian text.
90 Album, *Checklist*, 318, n. 785.

> he gives Place to his successor. By this means, a Man who goes to bed at Night with a Ten penny Piece in his Breeches, finds but Five Pence there in the Morning, if the Governor was chang'd in the Night. And it was hardly possible but these Alterations must often happen under a Prince so weak as Schah-Hussein, led too by People who, at the same Time that they governed him, could not agree with one another.[91]

This changing of the guard was a heavy burden on the populace, all the more so because they also bore the cost of welcoming a new governor. In the late seventeenth century such impositions only grew in frequency. Prior to the reign of Shah Soleyman (r. 1666–94), governors tended to be in charge of a governorate for longer periods. The period of Shah Soleyman also witnessed the introduction of the sale of offices, and this drove up the price of a governorship and thus the need for money.[92]

The limited role that copper coinage played in inter-regional and foreign trade was thrown into relief during periods of tight money, when traders would complain that they were forced to accept copper, despite its heavy weight.

Gold Coins

Good-quality coinage was important for trade, for administrative purposes, and for national tax collection. The greater the distance a coin had to travel, the better and more reliable its quality had to be. Coins, as a rule, circulated at a premium over their intrinsic value, due to their value added and especially local conditions of supply and demand. Such trade coins dominated international trade and enjoyed prestige everywhere, being much more in demand and more easily accepted than other coins. These coins were often imitated in weight, fineness and even design (e.g., the lari, the 'Ottoman' shahi, the `abbasi).

Gold, or at least gold minted within the country, was not particularly important in Iran at this time. Prior to the Safavid period, Iran is said to have had one gold mine, located near Damghan, in Khorasan.[93] There is no evidence that this mine was in operation in Safavid times, and the presumed existence of a gold mine in the vicinity of Tabriz notwithstanding, all indications are that all gold had to be imported.[94] The shahs coined gold,

91 Krusinksi, *History of the Late Revolutions*, 1: 89.

92 See the discussion in Matthee, *Persia in Crisis*, 148ff.

93 Mustawfi, *Nuzhat al-qulub*, 193.

94 Germelli-Careri, *Giro*, 2:46, claims that there was a gold mine three miles from Tabriz.

but the resulting coins served only a special use, viz. to affirm the royal right of coinage, to be used as presents, in particular on the occasion of a royal accession, *jolus*, and the Iranian New Year, Nowruz, and to show off. In sum, they did not circulate among the people.[95] However, gold and silver was siphoned off for other, non-monetary purposes. Aside from hoarding, much gold and silver was transformed into jewelry, gold and silver wire, plates, vases, goblets and the like. In 1576, according to Sharaf Khan Bedlisi, who had been commissioned by Esma`il II (r. 1576–77) to make an inventory of the royal treasury, the latter contained among other things 380,000 tumans in gold and silver coins, 600 gold and silver ingots (each weighing 3,000 mesqals), silk, gold brocade robes and arms. Bedlisi did not list any jewelry or the various eating and drinking vessels.[96] About a century later, Du Mans claimed that the value of the eating and drinking utensils at the Safavid court amounted to some 10 million gold pieces.[97] Another end-use contributing to the withdrawal of gold and silver from the market was the production of gold and silver brocade and other metal textiles and the gilding of various accoutrements such as reins, stirrups and other horse trappings. We do not know what the annual production of such textiles was and how much precious metal these contained or how much of it was used in ornamenting horses and the like. Both in transforming the metals (gold and silver wire drawing) and through their end-use (wear and tear) losses occurred. These could be significantly high, so that, for example, in the Ottoman empire at times the gilding of horse trappings, the gold and silver embroidering of caps and robes as well as the operation of gold and silver wire manufactories were forbidden or subject to strict limitations.[98] Sanson notes that, whereas neighboring countries restricted the use of gold brocade, Iran was a major producer of that product.[99] We only know of one restrictive ordinance in Safavid Iran. In 1716, when Iran was in the midst of a deep economic crisis, the grand vizier forbade the production of gold and silver wire, gold and silver brocades as well as the wearing of these textiles, including their use for horses. However, this interdiction did not last long, for the craftsmen concerned offered a present to the grand vizier who then lifted the ban.[100]

95 Tavernier, *Les six voyages*, 1:551; Gemelli-Careri, *Giro del mondo*, 2:46 and 211; Album, *Checklist*, 274.

96 Bidlisi, *Scheref-nameh*, 1:453; 2:251–52.

97 Richard (ed.), *Raphaël du Mans*, 2:299; Kaempfer, *Am Hofe*, 120; Chardin, *Travels in Persia*, 96.

98 Şahillioğlu, 'Introduction of Machinery', 276, n. 17, 285, n. 43.

99 Sanson, *Estat présent*, 161.

100 *NA*, VOC 1897, 4th fasc., Gamron to Batavia, 30 Nov. 1716, fol. 17.

Du Mans's claim that the shah did not even strike new gold coins, but used Venetian gold ducats, points to the important role non-Iranian gold coins, mostly Venetian but also Ottoman imitations, played in the country's trade circuit.[101] So prevalent was foreign gold that some travelers maintained that there were only foreign gold coins in Iran.[102] Treated as a commodity rather than a currency, these coins passed from Iran to India in great quantity. More about this role will be said in the chapter on bullion flows.

The gold coin struck in Iran had no proper name and were referred to as *tela*. With a few exceptions, Safavid gold coins were based on the standard of the ashrafi of 3.55 or the mesqal of 4.61 g. The name often used for these coins, *ashrafi*, came into use with the introduction of Egyptian gold coins into Iran struck by Ashraf Bars-bey (1421–38). The striking of gold coins under the Safavids may have followed developments in the Ottoman Empire, where in 882/1477–78 a new gold coin, the *soltani*, was introduced. Gold in Ottoman lands remained rare before the reign of Süleyman I (1520–56), but became abundant with the conquest of Egypt in 1517 and the subsequent receipt of tax money from that country in gold.[103] The export of gold through the Red Sea and the Persian Gulf dates from the same period and may have enabled the Safavids to reintroduce a gold coinage as well. Iran indeed acquired an indigenous gold coin under the first Safavid ruler, Shah Esma`il (r. 1501–24), who began to issue gold ashrafis shortly after acceding to power.[104] Gold continued to be struck in only moderate quantities until 1019/1610–11, when emissions ceased for more than a century.[105]

`Abbas I struck gold gold `abbasis of 2.22 g. These coins were still in use in 1745, although their production had been discontinued at the end of the Safavid era.[106] The coinage of gold in Iran all but ceased round about the middle of Shah `Abbas I's reign, and no gold would be struck until the decade preceding the fall of Isfahan and the eclipse of Safavid rule in 1722. It was Shah Soltan Hoseyn (r. 1694–1722), the last effective Safavid monarch, who resumed the striking of gold coins. Desperate to finance a military campaign to meet the challenge against marauding and invading tribesmen, he initiated the coinage of the gold ashrafi in 1129/1717.

101 Richard (ed.), *Raphaël du Mans*, 2:23.
102 Fryer, *New Account*, 3:152.
103 Pamuk, 'Money in the Ottoman Empire', 954–56.
104 Album et al, 'Coins and Coinage', 30.
105 Islamic *hejri* dates will only be given whenever they represent years of minting or occur in Persian sources.
106 Hanway, *Historical Account*, 2:20.

Table 1.1: Gold coinage of the first four Safavid shahs (1501–88)

Shah	Coin	Weight in grams	Coin standard period	Coin standard period dates
Esma`il I	ashrafi	3.45		907–27
	¼ ashrafi	.88		
	1, ¼ and ½ mesqal	ca. 4.7; ca. 3.25; ca. 1.17	mesqal standard introduced in 928	
Tahmasp II	1, ½ and ¼ mesqal	4.67, 2.33, 1.16	1st gold standard	930–40
	ashrafi	ca. 3.90	2nd golden standard	938–40 [western mints]
	½ ashrafi	4.1 – 4.2	3rd gold standard	940–54 [west + east mints]
	1, ½ , ¼ mesqal	4.65; 2.33; 1.16	4th gold standard	954–
Esma`il II				
	½ mesqal; 2, 1 shahi	2.34; 4.61; 2.30		984–85
Khodabandeh				
	2, 1, ½ mesqal	9.22;4.61; 2.30		985–95
Abbas I				
	2, 1, ½ mesqal	9.22; 4.61; 2.30		
	Heavy, ½ idem, light ashrafi	3.9; 1.95; ca. 3.5		
Safi	-	-	-	-
Abbas II	ashrafi	-	-	presentation only
Soleyman	1, ¼ ashrafi	-	-	idem
Soltan Hoseyn	mesqal; ashrafi; ¼ mesqal	4.61; 3.46; 1.15		

Note: ca. = circa

Silver Coins

Gold remained a distant second to silver during the entire Safavid period. In contrast to the limited use of gold, silver was the main currency for tax, administrative and large-scale or long-distance trading purposes.[107] The general name for silver coins under the Safavids was derham. The term derham went out of use in the nineteenth century, although it was used to refer to a weight as late as the 1930s. Other terms used to denote silver coins were *hazar*, i.e., hazar dinar, or 1,000 dinars. Some Europeans therefore mistakenly referred to this coin as *zar*, which means gold.

The silver coins were of fine alloy, and when European coins were melted after crossing the border and being handed over to the nearest mint, they were purified before being rerstruck as Iranian currency.[108]

> The shah used each year to renew the money, by halving its value, and he would not strike new money, forbidding that, and almost all of that was melted in the Mint and doing so, he would be able to get a lot of money from this in the other cities, that does not show in his accounts ... On his death, among much gold, silver and jewels, and it hard to believe, but it has been confirmed by more than one reliable person, they found 80 million ducats of which 17 million in gold.[109]

European travelers were impressed with the fineness and weight of the silver currency of the Safavids. Thévenot, calling `abbasis the pieces that were the most current in Iran, claims that Iranian silver money was the best money in the world:

> They are of the finest silver, and the Officers of the Mint dare not coyn one single piece, until they have first refined the Piasters and other pieces of silver, that are appointed for the making of Abassis: They are stamped (as all the rest of the money) with a hammer, and not milled, and there is so great equality in their weight, that in great payments, they are weighed after this manner. They put five and twenty Abassis, in one scale of the balance, and as many in the other, and is the one weigh more or less than the other, they conclude for a certain that there are some false Abassis amongst them, and fail not to examine then; in which they are never out, for each Scale ought most exactly to weigh alike. They then put the five

107 Tavernier, *Les six voyages*, 1:151.

108 Thévenot, *Relation*, *Suite du voyage*, 128; Tavernier, *Les six voyages*, 1:152.

109 Berchet (ed.), *La repubblica de Venezia e la Persia*, 279.

> and twenty of the one Scale into the other, which by that means contains fifty, and that number makes the Toman: afterward they count no more of the money, but onely filling up the empty Scale of the balance, until it weigh as much as the other wherein the Toman is counted, and when they find that both sides weigh not alike, they examine the pieces.[110]

Despite this alleged fineness, there was ample reason to check the value of coins with great care. Kaempfer reports that when Shah Soleyman had the standard of the coins in his treasury assessed, of the 30,000 tumans valued in there, only 300 tumans were found to be correct.[111] As a result, the shah had all money declared invalid, except that of Hoveyzeh. This measure hurt trade, for not only did it effectively depreciate the currency, but the new coins also had been tampered with. On learning this, Shah Soleyman had the mo`ayyer al-mamalek executed.[112] De Bruyn, writing in 1703, mentions that the Hoveyzeh mahmudis were still appreciated, because of their weight and fineness, and were traded at a premium of 1–2 per cent and up to 6 per cent.[113]

Despite these incidents, it would seem that normally, the weight of coins was correct, so that for large payments, both merchants and government officials, made use of the aforementioned bags containing a standard amount of coins. A special inspector, the sarraf-bashi, was responsible for the quality of the coinage in the bags, which he sealed personally. He received 1.5 `abbasi per bag for this responsibility.[114]

Profiting from Metal Price Differences

Since the ratio at which coins of different metals were exchanged was not rigidly fixed by the state, the Safavid monetary system was able to accommodate changes in the market value of one metal against another. However, the accommodation was imperfect in several ways. For one thing,

110 Thévenot, *Relation, Suite du voyage*, 89; see also *NA*, VOC 1297, Gamron to Heren XVII, 5 Oct. 1674, fol. 32v which confirms that the `abbasi was the most available coin in Safavid Iran. This is also clear from Table 1.1, where most remittances listed are in `abbasis; see also Chelebi, *Travels in Iran*, 44 ('the purity of their coins is unrivalled').

111 Kaempfer, *Am Hofe*, 54–55.

112 Ibid. 55; Chelebi, *Travels in Iran*, 154 ('Whoever meddles with or counterfeits these coins is not tolerated for one moment and is executed.').

113 De Bruyn, *Reizen*, 175–76.

114 Minorsky (ed.), *Tadhkirat al-Mulūk*, 69; Kaempfer, *Am Hofe*, 121–22; Chardin, *Voyages*, 4:170.

the state often tried to keep prices of the three metals at ratios different from those on the world market by imposing rules that prevented the export of specie or that required the use of only local coins. As Chapter 2 will show, all these measures had only a limited impact. Foreign coins were as freely accepted in payment, as if they were legal coin, as were the local or national ones, and the import and export of specie occurred on a large scale.

Another imperfection was that, as discussed earlier, the copper coins had a nominal value in relation to silver and gold coins; that is, those issuing copper coins claimed that they were worth a certain amount of silver or gold. This is a significant difference from the usual Safavid practice in which the value of a coin was determined by market forces based on the precious metal content of the coin. Not surprisingly, the governors or mint farmers who issued copper coins claimed their coins had a value in terms of silver or gold exceeding the value of the copper metal in the coins relative to what they claimed was the silver or gold equivalent. That provided the coin-issuer with an opportunity for profit if the copper coins were accepted at, or close to, the face value relative to silver and gold coins. Part of the way in which the mint farmers drove up the value of copper coins was to require their surrender at the end of each year as described earlier.

This discount between the copper content and the face value of the coins became particularly important when merchants or the state used copper coins as if they had a fixed value in silver – for instance, when a tuman paid in copper was considered to be equal to a tuman paid in silver. Not surprisingly given the lower metal content of copper coins, prices expressed in copper coins were substantially higher than prices in silver. One VOC account relates, 'One counts here never with black [i.e., copper], but always with white [i.e., silver] money at 50 per cent agio for white money, so that 100 mahmudis in reality is 150 mahmudis copper money.'[115] Another VOC report relates the purchase of copper cleaned by smiths with fire to get rid of iron and rust at a price of 1,800 tumans in black or 1,200 tumans in white money.[116]

A further complication was that, as could be expected, the silver–copper ratio in one area – e.g., along the coast, where international prices mattered more – was different from elsewhere – e.g., inland. These local differences prompted movement of specie to capture the difference in their value. For example, Hajji Mohammad Baqer Beg, vizier of Yazd, caused much misrule

115 *NA*, VOC 2448, Bushehr to Gamron, 21 Apr. 1738, fol. 2429.

116 For a detailed discussion of this subject, see ch. 6.

in his jurisdiction, resulting in a loss a value of the `abbasi in Yazd in 1667. Its value fell from 15 to 45 per dinar. This development made gold merchants come to Yazd with `abbasis from elsewhere (which had appreciated in value) to buy cloth. The vizier next abandoned the normal exchange rate, so that all `abbasis had the same value. The result was that many weavers became destitute and some even left Yazd.[117]

Other accounts of problems adjusting to changes in the price of the three metals appear during periods of tight money. When money became scarce, the effects were first felt on gold and silver bullion (which was easier to move and more likely to be traded internationally) and only later on copper. In the 1730s, for instance, when money became tight, gold and silver were first affected. In 1733, the Dutch observed that for export purposes the loss was less on copper money than on silver `abbasis or golden ducats. (The copper coins were equal in quality and assay to Japanese copper.)[118] But copper prices rose, due to the general scarcity of money.

In general, however, the Iranian economy does not seem to have suffered all that much from the considerable fluctuations in the relative value of gold, silver, and copper on the world market between the sixteenth and the eighteenth century. Consider that, throughout the period, there continued to be used two types of accounting money, one notionally representing an amount of silver (the tuman) and one notionally representing an amount of gold (the ashrafi). The metal content of the gold unit appears to have stayed quite constant during the sixteenth century, even though its silver counterpart lost three-fourths of its metal weight. To be sure, at that time, the world market ratio of silver to gold changed by two-to-one, but still the ratio in Iran changed substantially more than the world market price.

Limits on the Use of Money and the Scarcity of Current Coin

Scarcity of Currency

Another important feature of the Safavid monetary system was the scarcity of current coins. This problem, common in the entire early modern world, was endemic in Iran, with its severe constraints in the supply of specie and where the ruling classes, including the shah himself, were wont to hoard huge quantities of money. Periodic fiscal crises only made the problem

117 Mofidi Bafqi, *Jame`-ye Mofidi*, 3:205.
118 *NA*, VOC 2322, Gamron to Batavia, 1733, fols. 78–97.

worse. In 1633, an English East India Company employee reported that the mints in Iran could only be maintained on imported rials.[119] In 1701 the Dutch insisted that 60,000 rials of eight were annually brought to Isfahan for reminting adding that, without this supply, Iran would be without silver within a few years.[120]

Much of governmental monetary policy can only be understood in light of this structural scarcity. The same is true for the temporary reversions to commodity money by the entire economy in times of chaos, when government authority was either absent or impotent. In 1618, the EIC agents Pettus and Barker remarked that money was 'the principall want of this countrey'. They attributed this scarcity to the wars between the Ottomans and the Safavids and their negative effect on trade.[121] In 1626, money was so scarce in Iran that the VOC had to retail many of its products to various cities to get its money.[122] The records of the maritime companies are replete with similar complaints, but the problem long preceded the arrival of the Europeans on Iran's southern shores. As early as the reign of Shah Esma`il (1501–24) we hear of an empty royal treasury.[123] Eskandar Monshi relates how, before putting `Abbas I on the throne, his self-styled protector, Morteza Qoli Khan, in 989/1581–82 'announced that his troops would receive a handout of gold, intending to raise the money from the rich citizens of Mašhad'. Having exhausted this source, he proceeded to 'lay hands on the shrine treasury; he seized possessions of the shrine ornaments, including all the gold and silver chandeliers and candlesticks ... and used the money to provide his men with pay and allowances'.[124] Hamzeh Mirza, Khodabandeh's son, in 995/1586 had to break up 'all the gold and silver vessels belonging to his establishment and distributed them among the Qezelbash'.[125]

Little changed under Shah `Abbas I. When around 1590 `Abbas wanted to take revenge for an Uzbeg invasion he found himself short of funds. The ruler therefore ordered that all his service of plate be melted down. His administrators stalled, telling him that it had cost 90,000 ducats to make, and that all this would be wasted. But the plate was melted anyway and the

119 Rabino, *Coins, Medals, and Seals*, 3.

120 *NA*, VOC 1667, Isfahan to Gamron, 11 Nov. 1701, fol. 412.

121 Ferrier, 'English View', 192–93.

122 Dunlop (ed.), *Bronnen*, 199, Isfahan to Amsterdam, 17 Aug. 1626.

123 Qazvini, *Javaher al-akhbar*, 140, describes the shah as a ruler in whose 'treasury no one ever saw more than 100 tumans in gold'.

124 Monshi, *Tarikh-e `alamara-ye `Abbasi*, 1: 406–07.

125 Ibid, 468.

army of 80,000 marched.[126] Before joining `Abbas's army, Allahverdi Khan, the powerful governor of Fars, sent out messengers to mobilize his troops in Fars; he also had to pay the *gholaman-e khasseh* and his *molazeman*, retainers.[127] While en route he distributed considerable amounts of red and white gold from Qasr-e Zard in Yazd to his troops.[128] Such problems continued to plague the state throughout the shah's reign. During the siege of Baghdad in 1622, `Abbas I had no money to pay his troops. He therefore gave the soldiers round pieces of leather, marked with the name of the shah and the town of Baghdad. He promised to pay them later in coinage, exchanging the leather pieces for copper money on return to Isfahan, which promise he kept.[129] Two years later, `Abbas intended to pay his army with cloth that he had traded with the EIC. Some 3,500 soldiers would get 2 covids, representing 2,000 pieces of cloths yearly, according to the EIC agent.[130]

As such problems were really endemic, the result of Iran's poverty and the lack of a modern financial system, Shah `Abbas's successors fared little better. Shah Safi I, for example, between 1630 and 1640 was forced to rid himself of 20,000 *man* of tin by paying his soldiers at the rate of 40 shahis, which they sold for 30 shahis in the bazaar.[131] The Ottoman-Venetian war that raged during the reign of Shah `Abbas II (1642–66), further aggravated the situation, causing little money to be carried between Aleppo and Baghdad to Isfahan.[132] That money remained scarce in this period is further suggested by a continuing high interest rate of between 12 and 20 per cent in the Persian Gulf ports, in Isfahan, and probably elsewhere as well.[133]

126 Don Juan, *Don Juan of Persia*, 221–22; `Abbas I distributed quantities of gold jewelry, dinars, derhams, and arms among his horse and foot soldiers in 1598 during the Khorasan campaign. Siyaqi, 'Futuhat-i Humayun', 434. That the derham was still used as a unit of account is clear from other contemporary sources. In 1605, *nim derham* = 50 dinar-e `eraqi; 2 derham = 200 dinar-e `eraqi. See Monshi, *`Alamara-ye `Abbasi*, 2: 688; Molla Jalal, *Tarikh-e `Abbasi*, 306.

127 Adle, 'Futuhat-i Humayun', 441.

128 Ibid., 442.

129 Brosset (ed.), *Collection*, 2:26–27.

130 Ferrier, 'Anglo-Persian Relations', 330.

131 Ibid., 342.

132 *NA*, VOC 1162, Gamron to Batavia, 16 Apr. 1647, fol. 317–20.

133 In 1638–39 the interest rate was 20 per cent in Bandar `Abbas. This rate remained virtually unchanged in the next thirty years. The lowest recorded rate in this period was 12 per cent, in 1660. This compares with interest rates at Surat that dropped from 12 to 6 per cent in the same period and a 6 per cent rate in the Netherlands in 1660. See VOC, Generale Missiven, 15 Feb.1638, in Dunlop (ed.), *Bronnen*, 642; 18 Dec.1639, in Coolhaas, ed. *Generale Missiven, 1639–55*, 32; 12 Dec.1641, in ibid., 143; and *NA*, Coll. Geleynssen de Jongh, vol. 141, 1641, unfol.; Tavernier, *Les six* voyages, 1:471, mentions that the Banyan money lenders in Isfahan charged up to 18 per cent. The rates in the Netherlands and Surat are given in Van Santen, *Verenigde Oost-Indische Compagnie*, 118.

As will be shown in the next chapter, money shortages grew even worse under Shah Soleyman.

Fiduciary Money

Because of the scarcity of coins, which at times brought trade to a standstill, the use of quasi monies such as checks and drafts played an important role in commerce. Although barter trade was widespread, merchants and in particular the European companies generally preferred to sell their goods for hard cash or some form of fiduciary money. Trade was thus not conducted solely in cash as Fragner has it.[134] Merchants were not keen to sell their goods on credit, yet credit transactions were a standard feature of commercial life, not just in Iran but all around the Indian Ocean basin. Bills of exchange, known as *softajeh* and *havaleh*, had been widely used since early medieval times. They were also standard in long-distance trade in Safavid Iran. Known as *havaleh*, *barat* and *tamassok*, they served both as bills of exchange and as assignments on revenues.[135]

> It remains for me to speak of bills of exchange, and how they work in Persia. There sometimes arrives at Gomron (Bandar `Abbas) such a quantity of vessels that there is more merchandise than money, and the merchants at once give notice to Lar, to Shiraz, and to Isfahan and other cities of Persia. Those who have ready money and who are in commerce do not fail to dispatch to Gomron. From the day when one takes money one is obliged to repay at the end of three months, and the exchange fee is from 6 to 12 per cent. When the merchandise has arrived in Isfahan or some other place, the merchant cannot touch it until he has repaid the sum borrowed, unless his creditor, trusting in his good faith, permits him to open his bales. If it is a Persian merchant who does not live in Isfahan and who wishes to carry his merchandise further, he again borrows money to pay what he owes, and repays it at the place he is going to. There are some Turkish and Armenian merchants who borrow money in Surat to repay it in Bandar `Abbas, where they borrow more for Isfahan, and they do the same thing in Isfahan for Erzerum or Babylon (Baghdad), paying the old with the new that they borrow in each place. The money one borrows in Erzerum is paid back in Bursa, Constantinople or Smyrna. That which is borrowed in Baghdad is paid

134 Fragner, 'Social and Internal Economic Affairs', 527.

135 For details, see Floor, *Economy of Safavid Persia*, 101 f.

> back in Aleppo; and as there are some Armenians and even a few Turks who, being in Constantinople or Smyrna, wish to go to Leghorn (Livorno) or Venice, they borrow money in these two former cities to repay their previous bills of exchange, and repay them in the two latter when they are in Italy. I have always reckoned in my voyages that to borrow money in Golconda for Livorno or Venice, after all the exchanges the money would cost 95 per cent. at best, but more often 100 per cent.[136]

There were no standard rules and the credit terms depended on one's reputation, market conditions, timing and place, where and when, and in which currency, the money had to be paid. Prominent merchants usually would get a better credit rating, which meant that their bills had a longer maturity than of the other, less important merchants. This distinction was, however, not applied when prices for the goods were low. Endorsing or discounting bills was not unknown, but not widely practised. As for the trade in broadcloth, for example, the local trade practice among the Iranians was that the purchaser was granted a 2 per cent discount at 8–10 months' sight. If the buyer would pay earlier he would receive 1 per cent for each month that he paid earlier.[137]

The charging of interest was prohibited as usury. To avoid the accusation of usury, which was punishable by the hammering of one's teeth into one's head, both Muslim and non-Muslim sarrafs used legal subterfuges, following age-old tradition and practice. Whether for letters of credit or loans, the ban on interest was honored in the breach through the use of *hiyal-e shar`i* or legal subterfuge, a system developed by the ulama to make the practice of commercial life compatible with the precepts of Islam. Moneylending was mostly the business of Hindus and Jews, but Muslims engaged in the practice as well. If one was known and had sufficient collateral a substantial sum could be lent the next day. To circumvent the religious ban the interest payment was included in the principal. The lender paid the money to the borrower in the presence of witnesses, stating the amount and the borrower accepting it, and giving a promissory note or *sanad*. Another legal subterfuge was when the principal was given interest-free, while the borrower bought some worthless object from the lender at a price equal to the interest for the period of the loan. Loans could be for a specific period, or open-ended. A letter of credit could be endorsed and transferred to another party, just like a check today. The interest rate ranged from 0.5 per cent to 2 per cent per

136 Tavernier, *Les six* voyages, 1:767; see also Chardin, *Voyages*, 3:153.

137 *NA*, VOC 1667, Isfahan to Heren XVII, 30 Apr. 1702, fol. 463.

month, but was mostly 0.75 per cent per month among Armenian merchants trading with and in India. The Dutch borrowed money, in amounts of 15,000 to 20,000 tumans, in the Isfahan market during the period between 1636 and 1643, and paid 20 per cent per year or 1.5, 2, and 4 per cent per month.[138]

A local letter of credit, used to borrow and lend money, was called *mowhak,* and the rate of interest charged was a minimum of 0.75 per cent per month or 9 per cent per year. These mowhaks could be transferred to a third party. An international letter of credit, drawn on someone in another country, was called an *avak*. The rate of interest was higher and could reach 27 per cent per annum. The avak could even be more specific, such as in *yak gusheh*, i.e., an avak borrowed in one port to be repaid in another; or *du gusheh*, i.e., an avak borrowed and to be repaid in the same port.[139]

The barat was another financial instrument. It was an avak with collateral that could be seized in case of default. The barat (or for that matter any other financial instrument) could be secured against the borrower's property with a so-called *gerow*, security. This could take the form of a so-called *shartnameh* or *shart* clause in the barat dealing with the eventuality of a borrower's default. In addition, there were simple loans designed to increase capital, obtained from persons outside the family firm. These loans, called *moddati* (time-bound loan) and *amanat* (trust), were not equity capital but only interest-bearing debts. The rate of interest on these varied from 6 to 9 per cent per year. When Visnich, the VOC director in Iran, lent money in 1627 he asked 2 per cent per month with security. Loans made with merchandise as security and with repayment in three months were at 6–12 per cent for three months. The Armenians, keen to maintain a good credit rating, met their debts, even if some member of their community had defaulted, whether there was a receipt or not. The local Armenian merchants would send the case for a decision to Jolfa where a council of merchants would raise the money to pay the debt. The defaulter would of course be blacklisted from having any dealing with fellow Armenian merchants. The stipulated period of time for the payment of money, in case of the sale of goods, was known as *vada*. For example, goods were sold with 'fifteen months vaddaw, to abate 1 per cent per month'. We know of one transaction, with a twelve-month vada, which did not go through, 'for they would give no manner of security for the payment of the money'.[140]

138 Herzig, 'Armenian Merchants', 241–42, 251; Floor, *Economy of Safavid Persia*, 103.

139 Herzig, 'Armenian Merchants'.

140 Baladouini and Makepeace (eds), *Armenian Merchants*, 257–58, 245; Herzig, 'Armenian Merchants', 257–58; Floor, *Economy of Safavid Persia*, 104.

The office of the Banyan money lenders in Isfahan was located in the `Ali Qoli Khan caravanserai. These were believed often to double their money in 20 months, which seems quite a reasonable rate compared with contemporary financial rates of return. The moneylenders, really bankers, borrowed money from men of substance at 8 to 10 per cent and on-lend it at 30 per cent a year. Naturally, these rates were even higher when money was tight.[141] The repayment of loans ordinarily took place in monthly installments. The rate of interest varied from 18 to 20 per cent per annum. Of course, in the trade with India in particular, and with the East in general, Indian sarrafs had a comparative advantage. The fees demanded for a money transfer depended on distance and risk, and varied from 1 to 8 per cent. The rates on the bills varied depending on market conditions and the direction of the bill. In 1629, the EIC agent in Isfahan drew 150 tumans on Bandar `Abbas with a 5 per cent rate. In 1645, the rate was 3 per cent for payment in 2.5 months in Isfahan; in 1649 we hear of a rate of 1.25 per cent; two years later a shortage of money had made the rate go up to 5 per cent.[142] In 1665, according to Chardin, the rate of interest was 7.5 per cent and in 1699 the Indians lent to the Carmelites at 24 per cent. In 1721, the Indian sarrafs of the VOC, out of kindness, offered Mgr. Pidou credit at only 1 shahi per month per tuman, whereas usually they charged 1 `abbasi (or 4 shahi) or 24 per cent per year. Bishop Elias had forwarded 1,000 *ungari* to the brother of a rich Catholic merchant of Astrakhan to be paid to him at Shamakhi, where he found him to be bankrupt. Defaulters sometimes put pressure on their creditors to avoid paying or get an extension. Tavernier described a case of a draper who in 1662 had borrowed 7 tumans at 2.5 per cent per month from a Banyan and was unable to pay the first installment. He then joined other bad debtors in organizing a conspiracy against the Banyans.[143]

In sum, the economy of Iran had a wide array of effective and flexible financial instruments at its disposal. In addition to loans, promissory notes, bills of exchange and bills of credit, there were also sale and purchase on credit. The system of forward buying, *pish-forush* or *pish-kharid*, was widely practised in the area of major cash crops such as silk and goat hair as well as in the production of carpets. In short, credit, loans and other forms

141 Chardin, *Voyages*, 7:364; Thévenot, *Travels*, 2:111; Tavernier, *Les six voyages*, 1:471.

142 Ferrier, 'British-Persian Relations', 257. In general, the interest rate for normal customers varied between 12–20 per cent per year during most of the seventeenth century. See Dunlop (ed.), *Bronnen*, 642; Coolhaas, *Generale Missieven*, 2:32, 143; van Santen, *Verenigde Oost-indische Compagnie*, 118.

143 Chick (ed.), *Chronicle of the Carmelites*, 1:403, 532, 491 (Elias), 552 (Pidou); Tavernier, *Les six voyages*, 1:587–88.

of fiduciary money were the lubricants that fueled the Iranian engine of trade, including the part European played in it.[144]

Barter

As a final note, it is important to emphasize that money in the form of gold and silver coins played a limited role in the Iranian economy in Safavid times. In many parts of Iran and for most of the population, money occupied a place of minor importance. The economy of much of rural Iran, for instance, operated on the basis of barter. All of our direct evidence for this comes from the north, but there is little question that the situation was no different in other parts of the country. Membré in 1540 noted that, in western Georgia, people would come to the market 'with silks, which they exchange for, cloth for cloth, without other money being used'.[145] Evliya Chelebi's observation that in Daghestan trade took place 'not for money, but by exchange',[146] is echoed by others. A report from Georgia from 1687 affirms that cash played no role or only a limited role in the region's economy.[147] Concurring with this, Pitton de Tournefort, who wrote in 1701, claimed that in large parts of Georgia people preferred to be paid in bracelets, rings, glass necklaces and other items.[148]

Cash money was mostly used in payments to the state and in trade. Even then, cash payments were often optional, for although the tax burden was expressed in monetary units, actual payments were settled in-kind. For instance, Gilan province paid its taxes in silk, although the shah converted this in ready cash by selling it to the silk merchants. According to Chardin, most of the shah's taxes were in-kind and consequently many of its payment orders were in-kind.[149] The state also often paid its officials with assignments on the produce of land, not in coin.[150] The existence of the *tas`ir* or system of conversion rates, which fluctuated with the demand-supply situation of the particular commodity that served as a means of exchange, facilitated such payments in-kind. Thus, the means of exchange were not necessarily always coins, but could be other commodities. Coins, however, served as a standard of value for all payments. In trade, in particular foreign trade, the rule was that coins were both the means of exchange and the unit of value.

144 Floor, *Commercial Conflict*; and Matthee, *Politics of Trade*, 43–44.
145 Membré, *Mission to the Lord Sophy*, 14.
146 Evliya Effendi, *Narative of Travels*, 2:169.
147 Propaganda Fide, Rome, SC, Georgia I, Notizie di Mengrelia, 17 Feb. 1687, fol. 368–81.
148 Tournefort, *Relation d'un voyage*, 2:301.
149 Chardin, *Voyages*, 5:414–15.
150 See Floor, *Fiscal History*.

2

The Trading in Bullion

Iran's Bullion Situation

European records about trade with Safavid Persia present a paradox: they show that Iran, a country that did not produce either gold or silver, exported both metals to pay for the merchandise that the European traders imported into the country. Furthermore, Iran also needed a continuing supply of bullion to provide coins for domestic trade. Are the European accounts of bullion exports plausible, and if so, where did Iran get the bullion that it was exporting? The present chapter discusses the single most important external determinant of Iran's financial condition, the movement of bullion in and out of the country. It will consider the nature and volume of specie imported from the Ottoman Empire and Russia and carried to India via the overland trade and the Persian Gulf ports. The volume of commodities Iran exported continually exceeded imports. Bullion exports closed this trade gap.

Local Production

Safavid Iran was a metal-poor country with no gold or silver mines and a limited production of copper.[1] This does not mean that there were no ores; on the contrary, the Iranian soil abounds with them. These metal resources were difficult to mine, however, because they were located in remote areas where there was generally a lack of other necessary inputs (such as charcoal for smelting; water for processing), while the available technology for extraction was rather primitive. The expenditure of extracting precious metal ore simply made it impossible to make a profit on it, as is suggested by a saying quoted by Tavernier: *noqreh-ye Kervan dah kharjeh noh hasel* – the

1 Texeira states that in Azerbaijan some silver was mined, but no other source does so. Teixeira, *Travels of Pedro Texeira*, 245. On mining and mineral resources in Safavid Iran, see Floor, *Economy of Safavid Persia*, 303–08.

silver of Kervan: ten in expense for nine in yield.[2] The ready availability of precious metal from abroad did not serve as an incentive to indigenous mining either. Gold is a case in point. Shah `Abbas I apparently intended to extract gold from a mine near Hamadan, and had wood and charcoal brought to the site from afar. He abandoned the venture, however, when he discovered that the output equaled the expense.[3] Even copper, despite the very rich deposits in Iran, was mostly imported from Asia and even Europe. Copper, to be sure, had long been mined in Iran; Pliny shows that in Antiquity, copper from Kerman had been shipped to the Persian Gulf and the Red Sea ports.[4] In Safavid times, too, copper was mined in Khorasan, but it had to be mixed in with European copper before it could be turned into a final marketable product.[5] A passage in the *Tarikh-e `Abbasi* pertaining to the period of Shah `Abbas refers to the mining of copper. At the command of the shah a village was created where a well had been dug and water enough for two pair of oxen was flowing. To cultivate it, fifty male and fifty female Indian slaves were bought in, made to marry and settled there. They stayed in the village fortress until housing and cultivation were ready. Meanwhile, they were to dig for copper on a rent basis and they did not have to pay taxes.[6] In the 1640s the Dutch refer to the mining of copper in Khorasan, adding that it had led to a decrease in the price of the metal.[7] Copper was mined in Azerbaijan as well.[8] Kerman province, too, abounded in copper (and silver) deposits, something that Strabo already alluded to.[9] During the reign of Shah Soleyman, when Iran suffered a grave economic crisis, efforts were made to exploit the silver of the Kerman region. According to one chronicle, in 1083/1673 this yielded 60,000 mesqal of silver for the central treasury.[10]

2 Tavernier, *Les six voyages*, 1:373.
3 Leandro di S. Cecilia, *Persia*, 24–25.
4 Warminton, *Commerce between the Roman Empire and India*, 268.
5 According to one foreing observer, there were 'no mines of gold and silver or of copper, but only of iron'. See Grey (ed.), *Narrative of Italian Travels*, 2:225. Yet in 985/1577–78, there was a copper mine in Sabzavar which was leased for 5,000 tumans. Rumlu, *Ahsan al-tavarikh*, 647; Richard (ed.), *Raphaël du Mans*, 2:7, 335. See Floor, 'Copper'; and Idem, 'Coal'.
6 Molla Jalal, *Tarikh-e `Abbasi*, 327–28.
7 *NA*, VOC 1146, Gamron to Batavia, 12 Feb. 1646, fol. 905.
8 Gemelli-Careri, *Giro del mondo*, 2:46.
9 Strabo, *Geography*, 7:153.
10 Mashizi (Bardsiri), *Tazkereh-ye Safaviyeh-ye Kerman*, 283ff., 292–94, 377, 381, 392–93 and 408ff.

Bullion Imports: Causes and Implications

It was seen in Chapter 1 how much of economic life in Safavid Iran was conducted through barter. However, barter existed alongside the monetized economy: good-quality coinage was important for trade, for administrative purposes, and for national tax-collection. The greater the distance a coin had to travel, the better and more reliable its quality had to be. Coins, as a rule, circulated at a premium over their intrinsic value, due to their value added and especially local supply and demand conditions. Such trade coins dominated international trade and enjoyed prestige everywhere, being much more in demand and more easily accepted than other coins. These coins were often imitated in weight, fineness and even design. Good examples are the Spanish real and the Dutch *leeuwendaalder* (lion-dollar), which circulated in abundance in the Safavid realm and were employed in the country's long-distance trade alongside the silver ʽabbasi and mahmudi (two-shahi), the two principal Safavid silver coins, throughout the seventeenth century.

Copper Imports

Although Iran had its own copper mines it still needed to import copper, because foreign copper was often cost competitive, and until the 1670s it was necessary to mix Iranian copper with foreign, Swedish and Japanese copper before it was fit to be used.[11]

We know little about Iranian copper imports before the advent of the maritime companies in the early seventeenth century. Just as the Safavid copper currency fell somewhat outside of the economic circuit of supply and demand, so the copper imports were not part of the west–east movement of precious metals through which most gold and silver entered the country. Copper neither came from the countries with which Iran had a trade surplus, nor did it flow to areas with which the country had a deficit. Copper, in other words, was a true commodity like all other commodities: imported to be turned into coins but also to be used for the manufacturing of cooking vessels.

The Dutch were actively involved in the importation of copper into Iran. As soon as the VOC started trading in Iran copper was among its import goods. On 10 November 1623 the Company imported 100 pieces of Japanese copper weighing 5,765 catty (about 3,459 kg) at 35 Dfl. per picol (about 62 kg) or a total of Dfl. 2,017. It was sold at 35$^{7}/_{10}$ shahis for a total amount of

11 Kaempfer, *Am Hofe*, 94.

Dfl. 4,027, thus realizing a profit of almost 50 per cent.[12] Visnich, the first VOC director in Iran, noted that clean copper could be sold at 50 shahis per man in large quantities. He, therefore, in his contract with the royal factor, Molayem Beg, agreed to sell 7,206 lbs. of copper at Dfl. 6,000.[13] However, not any copper would do. Visnich commented that 'the copper imported by the Company was considered to be coarse and not suitable for processing before it had been refined again. For the sample that we marketed we may only make 30 shahis or 2.5 reals of eight per man of about 12 lb; if copper was of a good quality we could sell it at 50–60 shahis.'[14] This message had to be repeated, because in 1628 once again coarse copper was sent.[15] The Governor-General in Batavia was positive about the trade results of copper in Iran, as were the Heren XVII (the VOC directors in Holland), who instructed Batavia to send as much copper as possible to Iran.[16]

Therefore copper remained on the list of VOC exports to Iran, although a preference was expressed for copper rods over copper vessels.[17]

VOC headquarters in Batavia remained up-beat about copper. In 1634 they boasted that 'the Dutch are the only ones who can bring that commodity, and if we saturate the market it will scare others away, so that the trade is ours, in which case we can do with the price whatever we want.'[18] In fact, Batavia wanted Iran to take 6,000 picols (about 75,000 kg) of copper annually, for copper was the VOC's most profitable export commodity from Japan.[19] In 1635, Gamron ordered 300,000 lbs. of Japanese copper (in rods), even though at that point the market was rather saturated because of the war with the Ottomans.[20] Sales indeed dropped, but profits continued to be satisfactory, though now it appeared that the market preferred copper in plates rather than in rods.[21] The order for 1636, therefore, was reduced to 160,000 lbs., which sold even more profitably.[22] The VOC in this period also experimented with Hungarian and Swedish copper. This only yielded a profit of 30 per cent, however.[23]

12 Dunlop (ed.), *Bronnen*, 28, see also 79, 84–85, 117, 467.
13 Ibid., 41–42; Gamron to Batavia, 18 Jan. 1624.
14 Ibid., 59, Gamron to Batavia, 24 July 1624.
15 Ibid., 232, Journael Dirck van der Lee, June 1628.
16 Ibid., 185, 123, 125, 130, 185.
17 Ibid., 259, 264, 278, 317, 362, 459.
18 Ibid., 499, Batavia to Gamron, 15 Aug. 1634.
19 Ibid., 501.
20 Ibid., 542, Sept. 1635, 549, Isfahan to Amsterdam, 15 Dec. 1635.
21 Ibid., 555, Gamron to Surat, 10 Jan. 1636, 565–66, Gamron to Batavia, 25 Mar. 1636.
22 Ibid., 589, 608, Gamron to Amsterdam, 25 Jan. 1637.
23 *NA*, VOC 1139, Gamron to Batavia, 7 Mar. 1642, fol. 541.

In 1648, the Dutch found that Japanese copper was difficult to sell at the required profit rate owing to the discovery of some new copper mines in Iran. Also, that year's lot consisted of thick cast plates, which were of lower quality than copper in rods, which could 'be used without double raffinage for tableware, for which it is mostly used here'.[24] Although still profitable, the VOC sold less of it. In the 1650s the Dutch typically imported about 200,000 lbs. per year, but in the 1660s this quantity was halved, which the VOC agent considered to be more than enough. He also noted that copper from 'Vingurla and Ragiapur is being sold in small lots, and is now shipped to Masqat'.[25] In 1664, some 80,202 catty (48,000 kg) of Malacca copper was imported into Iran.[26] The Dutch usually sold their wares to some 50 merchants who annually descended upon Bandar `Abbas. But 'copper was also bought by the governor of Lar, who always has it in stock to keep his copperworks busy. He only supplies it to the coppersmiths' bosses.'[27] The trade in copper was still profitable enough to attract competitors. For, during the second half of the seventeenth century, Iranian merchants were also attracted to the profits of that trade. They had agents in Sweden to buy copper there.[28]

The 1648 discovery of domestic mines had no immediate effect on the importation of copper. Matters were different in the 1670s, when the mines came into production, probably following the economic crisis of the moment. The copper mines of Kerman produced so much copper that imports were discontinued. Iran in this period even exported massive amounts to India, with up to 400,000 lbs of copper being taken to Surat in 1680.[29] Much copper was also produced in Sabzavar and Mashhad. At 8.5 to 10 mahmudis per Kerman man or 5 Dutch lbs., it was somewhat more expensive than Japanese copper, yet it was of similar quality. [30] The Dutch, to see whether they still could sell copper in Iran, took samples of these various ores to have them tested in the Netherlands.[31] This abundant domestic production was not to last, however. It is unclear why the amount of available copper leveled off,

24 *NA*, VOC 1174, Gamron to Batavia, 28 Aug. 1648, fol. 749.
25 *NA*, VOC 1243, Gamron to Batavia, 5 May 1663, fol. 1002.
26 *NA*, VOC 1242, Gamron to Heren XVII, 9 Apr. 1664, fol. 1054.
27 *NA*, VOC 1252, Gamron to Batavia, 19 Jan. 1665, fol. 704.
28 Ferier, 'British-Persian Relations', 380; Dunlop (ed.), *Bronnen*, 556; Rabino, *Coins, Medals, and Seals*, 27.
29 *NA*, VOC 1352, Generale missiven, 1680, fol. 95v. Coolhaas, *Generale Missiven*, 4:414, has 'Chirwanse' (from Shirvan) but this is a misreading of 'Chirmanse' (from Kerman).
30 *NA*, VOC 1642, Gamron to Batavia, 22 Nov. 1701, fol. 1548; VOC 1669, Isfahan to Gamron, 11 Jan. 1701, fol. 219; Ibid., 30 Apr. 1702, fol. 453.
31 *NA*, VOC 1667, Gamron to Batavia, 27 Jan. 1702, fol. 33.

though one possible reason is the loss of direction in government policy after Sheykh `Ali Khan lost his firm control over state affairs in the course of the 1670s. A decade later, Japanese copper was imported again for a number of years at a level of about 20,000 lbs. per year, but its profit rate was low.[32] After 1719 there is no more mention of VOC copper imports.

Silver and Gold Imports

Raphael du Mans, a long-time resident of Isfahan and a keen observer of Iran, in 1665 rather pessimistically wrote, 'The wealth of Persia is therefore is like the humidity of water that attaches itself to canals, for it only passes through to unload itself in its basin ... thus, very little remains in the country itself.'[33] Iran derived considerable advantage from the passage of specie through its territory and Du Mans's famous observation that Iran was like a caravanserai, with only two gates, one on the side of Turkey through which money enters from the West ... the other gate Bandar `Abbas or Gombroon on the Persian Gulf, the exit toward the Indies, can therefore not be taken at face value. To be sure, much of the money that entered the country in one form or another left it again. Speculation and the prospect of profit underlay much of the eastward bullion flow. In the second half of the sixteenth century the Italian traveler Vincentio d'Alessandri, commenting on the movement of bullion into Iran, had noted:

> In this country of Persia there are no mines of gold and silver or of copper, but only of iron; so that those who introduce silver from Turkey gain twenty per cent, gold fourteen and fifteen per cent, and copper sometimes eighteen and sometimes twenty percent; it is true that there are great expenses, as the exportation of metals is forbidden.[34]

Bullion and specie, in other words, gained in value from the moment it entered the country in the west. For a good understanding of the mechanism of the export of precious metals it is important to understand that bullion and specie, except for the current coin used in small-scale transactions, was considered a commodity like all other commodities and operated as such. This circumstance was not peculiar to Iran; it

32 *NA*, VOC 1848, 13 Apr. 1715, fol. 3375; VOC 1913, Gamron to Batavia, 31 Dec. 1717, fol. 41; Ibid, Gamron to Batavia, 30 May 1718, fol. 256; VOC 968, 19 July 1718, fol. 608.

33 Richard, ed, *Raphaël du Mans*, 2 :150.

34 Grey (ed.), *Narrative of Italian Travels in Persia*, 2:225–26.

was the hallmark of all non-modern monetary systems. The seignorage imposed on coin at the mint and the charges on it whenever it crossed borders must be understood in this light: these were taxes like the duties on any commodity.[35] Gold especially tended to perform as a commodity. There is no better illustration of this than the appreciation of the ducat on its journey from the borders with the Ottoman Empire to Bandar `Abbas. Thus Venetian ducats ordinarily sold for one-half mahmudi more in Isfahan than in the western border towns, and each ducat gained another half mahmudi before it reached Bandar `Abbas.[36] A good example is on record for the year 1701, when the ducat was worth 12 mahmudis in Tiflis, but could only be bought at slightly less than 15 mahmudis in Bandar `Abbas. In Isfahan, meanwhile, the ducat was half a mahmudi cheaper than on the southern coast.[37]

A good understanding of the traffic in gold and silver in and out of Iran thus requires insight into the country's trade conditions and in particular its relative strength in imports and export flows and balances. In the following section the movement of bullion will therefore be discussed as part of an overview of commercial relations between Iran and its neighbors.

Sources of Imports

From the fifteenth century onward, the Ottoman state was the most important immediate source of Iran's bullion influx. Long predating the entry of the Western maritime companies into the Levantine trade, this situation was intensified by the influx of New World treasure in the early 1500s. As a result of these developments, the entire Mediterranean basin was flooded with the precious metal that came in shipments from the New World. Of the gold and especially the silver that entered Italy, a large proportion found its way to the Levant, where it was used to pay for Italian trade imbalances. All this is reflected by the energy with which in the 1570s Iranian and other merchants siphoned off silver from the Eastern Mediterranean ports to Iran.[38] The surge in trade once the French, the Dutch, and the English joined the Venetians and the Ottomans in the Levant trade can only have increased the influx of precious metal. Fernand Braudel described the movement as follows: 'In the Mediterranean there

35 Simmons, 'Evolution of Persia's Monetary System', 92.

36 The mohammadi or, as the Europeans pronounced it, mahmudi, was introduced by Shah Khodabandeh as a 100-dinar piece.

37 Tournefort, *Relation du voyage*, 2:311; *NA*, VOC 1307, Gamron to Batavia, 21 Dec. 1675, fol. 638r.

38 Tournefort, *Relation du voyage*, 283.

was a demand for pepper, spices, and silk; a feverishly eager demand. But if there had not been a passionate thirst for silver metal in India and China, that demand might well have gone unsatisfied.'[39] Much of this precious metal found its way to Iran as it was transported from Turkey by merchants who in October and November of each year returned to Iran via Tabriz or Baghdad, having sold their wares, mostly silk, in Aleppo and Smyrna. Already before the entry of the Western maritime companies into the Levantine trade, private Iranian merchants were active satisfying the enormous demand for silver in Iran.[40] The expansion of West European trade activity beginning in the seventeenth century and, in particular, the rise to dominance of the Armenians in the silk trade between Iran and the Ottoman Empire, no doubt caused a great increase in the movement of treasure. Armenians became the largest importers of specie from the Ottoman Empire in the seventeenth century. It is said that each caravan of Julfan merchants returning from Europe carried 200,000 silver *scudi*, the equivalent of more than 13,000 tumans.[41]

Whether the surplus money was brought to Isfahan predominantly in gold or silver depended on the relative price of both – in Iran, but even more in India.[42] Gold, either in the form of ducats or in unminted bars, was usually favored because it could get better rate at Coromandel in southern India, at least until the mid 1670s. Until that time silver was the second favorite. Still, silver was always preferred over merchandise. The decision by merchants of what kind of coins to change for export purposes in turn depended on availability, price, and the nature of the demand from India.

In the seventeenth century much of the bullion entering Iran continued to be transported from Ottoman territory. The main carriers in late Safavid times were the merchants, most of them Armenians, who in October and November of each year returned to Iran via Tabriz or Baghdad, having sold their wares, mostly silk, in the Levantine cities of Aleppo and Smyrna (Izmir). The Ottomans also imported various kinds of Persian silken fabrics (*parcheh*), mainly varieties of cotton garments and brocade, *zarbaft*, and, in the eighteenth century, in diminishing quantities, Persian *karbas* (*bez*) and *alacheh*.[43] Available evidence suggests, moreover, that large quantities

39 Braudel, *Mediterranean*, 1:185.

40 Şahillioğlu, 'The Role of International Monetary and Metal Movements', 283.

41 A. Alpoiadzhian, *Istoriia armianskoi emigratsii*, quoted in Baiburtian, *Armiankaia koloniia*, 60. The scudo was an Italian coin which was introduced as a counterpart to the thaler. The first scudi were struck in Mantua in 1536. In 1561 Venice introduced its scudo.

42 *NA*, VOC 1224, Gamron to Batavia, 3 Sept. 1657, fol. 318v.

43 Zarinebaf-Shahr, 'Tabriz under Ottoman Rule', 172–79.

of the Indian indigo and textiles only crossed Iran in transit and were in fact destined for the Ottoman markets.[44] One Dutch report strongly suggests that the east-west textile trade was essentially a transit trade, with the Iranian market being no more than a side-effect.[45] In addition to the proceeds of the sale of these goods, it also appears that merchants were engaged in exporting specie to Iran with the purpose of reselling it at higher price to India.[46] These bullion imports indicate that Iran enjoyed a trade surplus with the Ottoman Empire and the Mediterranean basin. This surplus was to persist over time, for the capital influx from the Ottoman Empire continued well after the Safavid era.

The bullion that arrived from the Ottoman Empire was mostly in the form of silver bars and Spanish reals of eight or rijksdaalders (rix dollars). All these were accepted and reminted into `abbasis and mahmudis.[47] This reminting took place in the provincial mints, which were heavily concentrated in the border area with the Ottoman Empire, in cities such as Tabriz, Yerevan and Tiflis.[48] Tavernier noted that everyone entering Iran from the Ottoman Empire was obligated to submit his silver for recoinage to the mints in these border cities. Poullet describes how, upon entering Iranian soil, caravans coming from the Ottoman Empire were contained in a specific place and no one was allowed to leave until it was clear how much money the caravan was carrying.[49] With a good excuse a merchant could get a certificate that allowed him to take his money to Isfahan. But since the minter stood to lose his share of the seignoriage (*vajebi*), he would not let many merchants pass through without submitting their treasure.[50] The newly minted coins gave a 2 per cent profit in Gilan buying silk. The reason, Tavernier explained, was that the coins one received in return were a little altered, which means that they were slightly lower in silver content, but were nevertheless accepted in the silk-producing areas.[51]

44 Zarinebaf-Shahr, 'Tabriz under Ottoman Rule', 177–78, 189–90; Van Santen, *Verenigde Oost-Indische Compagnie*, 64–65.

45 Dunlop (ed.), *Bronnen*, 670, report by merchant Nicolaes Jacobsz. Overschie with regards to the trade in Persia, 15 Dec. 1638; Ibid., 566; see also VOC 1178, Gamron to Batavia, 29 Mar. 1650.

46 Şahillioğlu, 'Role of International Monetary and Metal Movements', 279 [n. 22], 283ff.

47 Olearius, *Vermehrte newe Beschreibung*, 560.

48 *NA*, VOC 1297, Gamron to Heren XVII, 5 Oct. 1674, fol. 32v; VOC 1304, Gamron to Batavia, 4 Sept. 1674, fol. 519v; VOC 1343, Resolution on trade conditions in Persia, 13 Feb. 1680, fol. 600r; also in VOC 1360, fol. 1891r-v; Tavernier, *Les six voyages*, 1:134.

49 Poullet, *Nouvelles relations*, 2:297–98.

50 Tavernier, *Les six voyages*, 1:361.

51 Ibid., 1:134.

Silver also came from Ottoman lands in the form of shahis minted at Ottoman mints, coins that until 962/1555 carried the inscription 'shah' for the Ottoman sultan and that continued to be called by that name even after the Ottoman rulers renamed them 'padishahis'.[52] These shahis were 'exclusively minted for export, but were extensively used within the Ottoman economy'. Ottoman mints also struck laris and mahmudis for export purposes, mostly for trade in the Persian Gulf and Indian Ocean. This was permitted with a view to collecting the minting fees on silver that would be smuggled to Iran and the Gulf anyway. However, at times the minting of the two latter coins was ceased, because it was believed that this would facilitate the outflow of silver from Ottoman territories.[53]

Reals of eight and rijksdaalders usually were available in some quantity at Basra as well. Located outside Safavid jurisdiction but within Iran's economic orbit, the port of Basra received the overflow of the bullion destined for Iran, serving as a convenient point for money transports to India. Its strategic position on the Persian Gulf made Basra into the gauge of Iran's monetary soundness. The greater the discrepancy between the price paid by the royal mint in Isfahan and the market value, the greater the amount of coins that converged on Basra. The mint of Hoveyzeh in adjacent `Arabistan (Khuzestan), in turn, derived its importance from its proximity to Basra.[54] Much of the money found in Basra was brought in by caravans from Aleppo. The huge quantities involved are suggested in the observation by a missionary in 1653 that 'there have been to this port [Basra] more than 3 million Spanish reals in gold, and more than 6 million gold reals have gone off to Gambrun ...'.[55] In Basra, these coins, together with the Venetian *zecchino* (ducat), were coveted by those who exported bullion to India. For this reason much better prices were paid for these coins in Basra than in Europe. Thus, while in 1661 the gold ducat sold for 6 *livres* 3 *sols* in Lyon, in Aleppo and Basra 7 livres to 7 livres 10 sols was given.[56] In the same year the profit to be made on a real was 8 per cent in Aleppo and Baghdad, but 10 to 12 per cent in Basra.[57] The Venetian ducat sold for 15 mahmudis in 1665, but at that time this coin seems to have been rarer than before in Basra, judging by the information of Thévenot who noted that ducats were purchased at that price by those who wanted to send specie to India.[58]

52 Pamuk, *Monetary History*, 102.
53 Şahillioğlu, 'Role of International Monetary and Metal Movements', 278.
54 For this, see Matthee, 'Mint Consolidation'.
55 Chick (ed.), *Chronicle of the Carmelites*, 2:1140.
56 De Bourge, *Relation du voyage*, 62.
57 Ibid., 42.
58 Thévenot, *Livre troisième de la suite du voyage*, 565.

Throughout the seventeenth century, silver remained the most common and the most profitable precious metal in the border areas of the Ottoman Empire and Iran. Jean de Thévenot claimed that the most current coins in Basra were the Persian five-shahi pieces minted by the basha of the city, and Persian `abbasis.[59] The French missionary Bénigne Vachet in 1690 observed that it was much better to have piasters than ducats when traveling to Iran. The former, he claimed, could be changed into mahmudis at a 30 to 40 per cent profit.[60] Of the silver coins, the Persian `abbasi over time continued to be the coin most available in Basra and elsewhere.[61]

In addition to the two routes from the Ottoman Empire via Baghdad and Tabriz, Russia served as a source of some of the precious metal that entered Iran. Similar to its position vis-à-vis Turkey, Iran had long had a positive trade balance with the expanding Muscovite state.[62] Already in the sixteenth century Dutch money had entered Iran from Russia in some quantity.[63] From the sporadic information available it is evident that then, as later, Muscovite tsars and private merchants purchased goods from the Ottoman state and Iran and paid for these in part with export merchandise such as furs and iron wares, in part with ingots.[64] A contemporary source claims that the Russians had to pay half to one third of the price of the goods they received from Iran in the form of silver and gold coins.[65] According to another source, in 1663 silver accounted for 9 per cent, copper for 5 per cent, and gold for 4 per cent of Russian imports into Azerbaijan and Iran.[66] These percentages accord well with the 17,000 rubles worth of copper, silver and gold coins out of a total value of 76,749 rubles in goods and cash carried by a caravan that arrived from Moscow in the same year.[67]

Bullion Exports

Much of the evidence used about Safavid Iranian trade has been about trade with the West conducted by European maritime companies. However, India,

59 Ibid. The shahi was a 50-dinar silver coin. Four shahis made one `abbasi. Some contemporary sources assert that the shahi was a real coin; others claim that it was only a money of account.
60 [Bénigne Vachet], 'Journal du voyage', fols. 295–96.
61 *NA*, VOC 1297, Gamron to Heren XVII, 5 Oct. 1674, fol. 32v.
62 Attman, *Bullion Flow*, 123.
63 Morgan and Coote (eds), *Early Voyages and Travels*, 2:436.
64 Olearius, *Vermehrte newe Beschreibung*, 249.
65 Attman, *Russian and Polish Markets*; Idem, *Bullion Flow*, 110.
66 Geidarov, *Remeslennoe proizvodstvo*, 77.
67 Ibid., 190–91; Attman, *Bullion Flow*, 110.

not Europe was Iran's dominant trading partner at the time. During the early modern period, India was a great commercial power, and the trade in the Persian Gulf, from Bandar `Abbas to Masqat and Basra, was dominated by Indian goods. For instance, more Indian textiles were exported to Europe than vice-versa. Iran, by contrast, a country with far fewer resources and a fraction of the Indian population, was a minor economic player during the Safavid period.[68] In the words of an East India Company agent, Iran was 'a most miserable poore countrey of money [with] little Commerce and trade within itselfe'.[69] Chardin described Iran as 'dry, barren, mountainous, and but thinly inhabited', while India – which he visited at least twice during his stay in Iran from 1666 to 1677 – was 'a Country very Rich, Fruitful and populous'.[70] The best estimate is that Iran's population in the seventeenth century was no more than one-tenth of that of India – approximately 5 to 8 million compared to 60 to 100 million – with the qualification that Iran's population is known with less confidence than that of India, for which Abu'l-Fazl `Allami's gazeteer *A'in-e Akbari* provides good information.[71]

Trade routes between Iran and India were well maintained and protected during most of the Safavid period. Highway police (*rahdars*) patrolled roads effectively enough for merchants, even in small caravans, to travel without need for armed guards, at least until the late Safavid period when security conditions deteriorated.[72] Shah `Abbas I built numerous caravansarais and rebuilt or improved roads. Examples are the metalling of a highway across a swampy stretch north of Isfahan and the building of a famous causeway running along the Caspian littoral. After reviewing the conditions along the trade routes among Iran, India and the Uzbek state of Central Asia, Stephen Dale concludes, 'The simultaneous pacification of trade routes and construction of roads and caravansarais throughout northern India, Iran, and Turan in the late sixteenth and seventeenth century established exceptionally favorable conditions for trade throughout the entire region.'[73]

Safavid Iran imported textiles, sugar, indigo (a widely used dye), rice, cinnamon, pepper, camphor, cardamon, ginger, radix china, tropical woods, steel, salarmoniac, lac and a variety of odd things from Mughal India. Its exports primarily consisted of specie, dates, auripigmentum, madder

68 For this, see Matthee, 'Safavid Economy'.
69 Ferrier, 'English View of Persian Trade', 192–93.
70 Chardin, *Travels in Persia*, 130.
71 The sources are summarized in Dale, *Indian Merchants*, 15–19.
72 Emerson and Floor, 'Rahdars and their Tolls'.
73 Dale, *Indian Merchants*, 41.

and rose water, in addition to luxuries, especially silk and specialty foods (such as melons and dried apricots). Also, large quantities of almonds were exported to Gujarat, where they were used as currency. One of the financially important export products was horses from Iran, which were a vital military commodity for India.[74] As Dale writes, 'Silk, like fruit and nuts, was a luxury import [for India] whose end products were destined for a small stratum of the Indian population, and while the value of imported silk thread and cloth has to remain a matter of conjecture it could not have balanced India's staple exports of cotton cloth, indigo and sugar.'[75]

The main reason why gold and silver were taken out to India in such large quantities was Iran's much noted trade deficit with the subcontinent, which stood in contrast to the country's position vis-à-vis the Ottoman Empire and Russia. Safavid Iran simply did not produce enough exportable wares to compensate for the huge quantities of spices and manufactured goods, mainly cloth in myriad varieties, brought in from India. The Mughal Empire's insatiable appetite for cash money is epitomized by the incessant flow of gold toward the coast of Coromandel, but was visible in the north and the south alike. This is illustrated in the figures for Bengal given by Om Prakash, who estimates that of the total English and Dutch East India Company (EIC and VOC, respectively) imports into Bengal between 1660 and 1720, only 20.6 and 12.5 per cent respectively was in the form of goods.[76] The rest consisted of bullion, much of which came from Iran.[77] Iran's position in this entire scheme was exactly the opposite of most of the rest of Asia, where the inability of the Europeans to produce enough goods that were of local interest necessitated the import of gold from Europe.[78]

This situation long predates the Safavid period. A pattern of precious metal moving from Europe to Asia in return for luxury goods, reflecting an imbalance of payments between West and East, can be traced as far back as the early medieval period and well before the advent of Islam. From those early days until relatively modern times, Asia – and especially

74 Foor, *Economy of Safavid Persia*, ch. 5.

75 Ibid., 25. The analysis of the commodity composition of Iranian-Indian trade is from ibid., 21–25 and Van Santen, *Verenigde Oost-Indische Compagnie*, 63–68.

76 Prakash, 'Foreign Merchants and Indian Mints', 172.

77 Around the turn of the nineteenth century it was still estimated that nine-tenth of the goods imported into Iran from India were paid for in specie. See Lorimer (ed.), *Gazetteer*, 1/i, 163.

78 Prakash, *Dutch East India Company*, 11–13. Iran's position was rather similar to Japan's after 1696 when, despite that county's devaluation of gold, this metal continued to be shipped out by the Dutch, not because they chose to do so, but because first, gold was still in high demand in Coromandel and, second, because little else could be profitably exported from Japan.

China and India – tended to offer commodities that were in demand in the West, while Europe produced little of interest for Asian consumers.[79] The Portuguese, discussing the role of Hormuz during the first decade of the sixteenth century, observed that money, both silver and gold, was plentiful there, while the money earned by merchants was used in India.[80]

The export of bullion to the subcontinent took place via maritime as well as overland channels. In 1639, it was estimated, for example, that each year some 20,000 to 25,000 camels laden with Indian textiles arrived in Isfahan.[81] Of course these camels had to return, and much of their return cargo seems to have consisted of coin. Chardin called the Qandahar caravan trade a multi-million-tuman affair. Although Tavernier claimed that the Qandahar trade had fallen off by the 1650s compared with previous times, the volume of bullion carried to India via the land route continued to be very large.[82] Several sources insist that during the robbery of an Isfahan to Qandahar caravan in 1667, 40,000 tumans worth of gold were stolen.[83] Six years later, in 1673, the large regular August India-bound caravan was robbed of its coin on its way to India and lost the reported (and surely exaggerated) sum of between 150,000 and 300,000 tumans.[84]

The Participants in the Bullion Trade

All merchants engaged in commercial relations between Iran and India participated in the capital flight to the subcontinent. Numerous references in the literature point to the Banyans, Hindu merchants, as domestic merchants who were active in the movement of gold and silver to India. The Armenians, too, were engaged in large-scale shipments of the same kind. Unfortunately, almost all references to these and other indigenous and regional merchants are found in the European maritime sources and the accounts of Western travelers. No clear picture emerges from these sources with regard to the volume of bullion and specie that Armenian, Arab and

79 Lombard, 'Les bases monétaires'; Spufford, *Money and its Use*, 50–55, 60–61.

80 Barbosa, *Book of Duarte Barbosa*, 1:100–01. For a detailed discussion of this trade, see Subrahmanyam, 'Precious Metal Flow and Prices'; and Haider, 'Precious Metal Flows'.

81 Van Santen, *Verenigde Oost-Indische Compagnie*, 65.

82 Chardin, *Voyages*, 2:47–49; 347–49; Tavernier, *Les Six voyages*, 1:771. For a general analysis of the overland itinerary via Qandahar, see Steensgaard, 'Route through Qandahar'.

83 *NA*, VOC 1265, Gamron to Batavia, 8 July 1667, fol. 955v; VOC 1255, Gamron to Heren XVII, 6 Aug. 1667, fols. 904–05; Chardin, *Voyages*, 10:68.

84 *NA*, VOC 1291, Gamron to Heren XVII, 21 Mar. 1674, fol. 558; VOC 1304, Gamron to Batavia, 24 May 1674, fol. 437; Chardin, *Voyages*, 2:349.

Indian merchants exported from Iran, but the existing information suggests that considerable sums were involved. A most telling example of the extent of their activity is the story from 1690 about Armenian merchants who brought a considerable sum in silver and gold money to Basra, to load it there into a Dutch vessel, with the intention of shipping the specie directly to India. The Iranian authorities apprehended the ship and brought it to Bandar `Abbas, where the money belonging to the Armenians was unloaded. The amount of 434,809½ rix-dollars seized from the Armenians apparently was only part of the total sum on board, for it was said that, aside from the Armenians, Turks, Arabs, 'Moors', and Banyans had brought specie on board in both Basra and Kong.[85]

The above story exemplifies a pattern of Western companies transporting money belonging to indigenous merchants. Another good example of such cooperation is the caravan in 1666 that carried gold from Isfahan to Bandar `Abbas for Armenian merchants. Their attempt to clandestinely ship this gold was foiled when, after finding out, the Iranians intercepted the caravan in the vicinity of Lar.[86] Indigenous merchants found it advantageous to transport their gold and silver from Isfahan to Bandar `Abbas with European caravans since foreigners were less vulnerable to government control. If caught, they would always invoke the agreements with the Safavid crown that promised them freedom of trade. On the other hand, the indigenous merchants were usually the ones who suffered first and most from the frequent export prohibitions issued by Isfahan. If the chances of being caught became too great, the European maritime companies naturally first tried to avoid being implicated in transporting money for others.

The involvement of the maritime companies in the transportation of bullion for local merchants did not stop at the port of Bandar `Abbas. Both the Dutch and the English carried large amounts of precious metal belonging to private Asian merchants as 'freight' in their own ships. Thus in 1699 we hear of Armenian merchants exporting 100,000 gold ducats on the Hampshire, belonging to the EIC.[87] The price of this service was 1 per cent of the value of the bullion carried. On 'Moorish' ships, the freight price was only ½ per cent ad valorem.[88] However, many local merchants were quite willing to pay this freight charge because company ships provided relative

85 *NA*, VOC 1476, Gamron to Isfahan, 20 Sept. 1690, fols. 479–483; ibid., Gamron to Heren XVII, 29 Nov. 1690, fols. 508r-09v. The story is also told by Sanson, *Estat présent*, 12–14.

86 IOR, G/40/2, Surat to Company, 4 Apr. 1666, fol. 7; the same letter is found in E/3/29/3157.

87 Ferrier, 'British-Persian Relations', 317.

88 *NA*, VOC 1635, Aanwijzingen vracht (freight instructions), 1700, fols. 811–12.

security against pirates, who were a growing problem in the Persian Gulf in the later seventeenth century.

Most available information on the movement of bullion and specie concerns operations that the maritime companies undertook for their own accounts. These companies entered Iran in the early seventeenth century with the intent of establishing a trade of Asian commodities for Iranian goods, primarily silk. Since the Safavids needed and desired cash above all else, they forced the VOC and the EIC to pay for at least part of the merchandise they bought in Iran with current coin. What resulted was a tug of war between the Safavid crown and the Europeans over the terms of payment. When the Dutch first started trading with Iran in 1623, they supplied some bullion. Between 1623 and 1629, the VOC was obliged by treaty to import specie to pay for one-third of its sales in coin or an amount of 10,000 tumans.[89] While Shah `Abbas I was desperate for cash, the VOC did not as yet have sufficient capital, in either goods or cash, to finance the silk trade with Iran. In fact the VOC was unable to comply with the term of the contract, certainly as far as the cash component was concerned, just as Molayem Beg, the shah's factor, failed to deliver the silk mandated by the contract. For example, in 1628, the VOC only supplied 3,000 tumans in cash to Molayem Beg, or 17 per cent instead of 33 per cent, because the total of the transaction amounted to 17,153 tumans.[90] Under Shah Safi (1629–42) this type of contract continued for some years. The last time was in 1634, when Overschie concluded an agreement with Khvajeh Qasem, the royal factor, for the supply of 357 bales of silk in exchange for goods and cash to an amount of 6,856 tumans, of which 5,500 tumans, or 83 per cent, was to be in cash.[91] Occasionally the VOC made a profit on such cash imports, but it sometimes lost money as well. For example, in 1635 the VOC imported Dfl. 135,000 in specie. The Mint paid 5 mahmudis for each *daalder* which resulted in a loss of Dfl. 1,430 on the 45,000 pieces, but on the 24,000 *rijksdaalders* (rix-dollars) the Company made a profit of 1 qazbegi or 6.5 pennies.[92]

The Dutch generally preferred to export gold rather than silver, and European or Indian coins rather than Safavid (and Ottoman) ones, but often had no choice but to export whatever was available. The Company insisted that its staff in Iran try and export as many reals of eight and

89 Dunlop (ed.), *Bronnen*, 186, 23 Apr. 1626.

90 Ibid., 259. For this question in general see Steensgaard, *Asian Trade Revolution*, 380ff.; and Matthee, *Politics of Trade*, 115–16.

91 Dunlop (ed.), *Bronnen*, 469, Gamron to Batavia, 28 Mar. 1634.

92 Ibid., 504, Isfahan to Amsterdam, 27 Oct. 1634.

rijksdaalders as possible. When metals became scarce, however, any metal was moved, depending on its relative market price. Thus in 1649 Batavia instructed Gamron to obtain Hasani rupias and send these to Surat, because they yielded a loss of only 1.25 per cent.[93] In addition to Hasani rupias, the Company exported Sasiam rupias, Tolpura `abbasis, Safavid silver `abbasis, as well as gold and silver in bullion.[94] Occasionally, golden Visiapur pagodas were also exported.[95] The Dutch naturally tried to keep their losses on the export of specie to a minimum. They were generally successful in this effort, for, reinvested in India, the money bought goods that yielded a considerable profit for the Company. Also, in the absence of specie imports from Iran, the VOC agent in a place like Surat would have had to borrow money locally, or alternatively, money would have to be sent from the Netherlands, both of which were expensive options.[96] The Dutch did not base their decision to trade with a country or in a particular commodity, in this case specie on which it seemingly lost money, on the availability of one single commodity. Rather, they calculated how such trade would fit into their existing trading pattern, and assessed the opportunity cost of that particular trade, the activities of their competitors and, naturally, the state of the market. From the very beginning, the VOC, much more so than its main rival the EIC, turned the intra-Asian trade into a mainstay of its operations. In fact, this trade became a major factor in the VOC's prosperity in the seventeenth century. The energetic Jan Pietersz. Coen, who served as Governor-General from 1619 to 1623 and again between 1627 and 1629, sought to create a so-called *Indies Fund*, which would be formed by the revenue yielded by the VOC's participation in the Asian trade. He hoped that enough profits would be made for Batavia to be able to reduce, if not eliminate, the export of specie from the Netherlands altogether. Although Coen's dream was never fully realized it is clear that during the seventeenth century the success of the intra-Asian trade increased the VOC's capital in Asia to the point where the Dutch managed to reduce the export of bullion from the Netherlands. Within this trade Iran would play an important role. Not only did the VOC operation in Iran yield substantial profits, but it also gave the Company the opportunity to acquire gold and silver to finance its trading activities elsewhere in Asia. In fact, the VOC factory in Gamron was the Company's

93 *NA*, VOC 873, Gamron to Batavia, 23 Oct. 1649, fol. 159 vs.

94 For example, *NA*, VOC 1177, Gamron to B atavia, 29 Aug. 1650, fol. 618 v; VOC 1178 bis, Gamron to Batavia, 2 Feb. 1650, fol. 652; VOC 1177, Gamron to Heren XVII, 5 Apr. 1651, 574–89v.; ibid., Gamron to Heren XVII, 25 Mar. 1651, 591–94.

95 *NA*, VOC 1242, Gamron to Heren XVII, fol. 1089; VOC 1245, Gamron to Heren XVII, 9 Jan. 1665, fol. 364.

96 *NA*, VOC 868, 9 Aug. 1644, fol. 522.

most important exporter of specie in West Asia, and 'around 1700 Persia was the greatest source of treasure for the VOC in Asia'.[97]

Given the disappointing trade results with silk, the Dutch early on tried to reduce the amount they had to buy from the shah. The 'silk for cash and goods' contract with the shah was not renewed in 1635. Since Iran had little to offer besides silk and sundry goods, the Europeans soon began to export specie.

The first export of gold and silver by the VOC took place in 1643 with a sum of Dfl. 235,000.[98] Before long, these transports, to Surat, Coromandel, Pulicat, Ceylon and Batavia, became a routine matter, continuing until 1765, the last year that the VOC was commercially active in Iran. The amounts quickly increased, reaching more than Dfl. 1 million in 1650. Verburgh, the new VOC Director in Iran, in 1648 wrote to Batavia, almost apologetically:

> During the past few years we have been able to assist Surat with 3 tons of gold (Dfl. 300,000), while we can assist Coromandel with not more than 4 tons of gold (Dfl. 400,000), of which half has been send already with de Overschie to Paliacatta [Pulicat]. The merchants [here] are strapped for cash at the moment now toward the end of the monsoon.[99]

During the early reign of Shah Soleyman (1666–94) Iran's economic problems caused specie exports to drop off, but after 1674 the amounts remitted usually were above the Dfl. 200,000 level per year.

Although the export of gold and silver was important for the Company, it too was not necessarily the most profitable line of business. In 1653, for example, VOC Director Sarcerius reported that he lost 12.5 per cent in Surat and 20 per cent in Coromandel on the export of specie.[100] Such losses continued until the very end of the Dutch trading activities in the Persian Gulf.[101] Batavia (now Jakarta), the Company's Asian headquarters, therefore kept a sharp eye on the movement of specie. In 1656, the Governor-General instructed Willems, at that point VOC director in Iran, to send all 'Moorish' (Ottoman) ducats to Coromandel, because the loss there was only 4 per cent as against 10 per cent in Surat.[102] Consequently, a lively and continuous

97 Gaastra, 'Exports of Precious Metals', 465 [447–76].
98 Coolhaas (ed.), *Generale Missiven*, 2:205.
99 *NA*, VOC 1277 bis, Gamron to Batavia, 28 Mar. 1648, fols. 762–64.
100 *NA*, VOC 1201, Gamron to Batavia, 16 Aug. 1653, fol 821.
101 Floor, 'Decline of the Dutch East Indies Company'; and Idem, 'Dutch on Khark Island'. See also Idem, *Persian Gulf: Rise of the Gulf Arabs*, chs. 3 and 5.
102 VOC 783, fol. 443.

Table 2.1: VOC exports of gold and silver from Iran, 1643–74 (in Dfl.)

Year	Amount	Year	Amount
1643	235,000	1661	
1644	250,000	1662	250,000
1645	400,000	1663	348,081
1646	383,000	1664	
1647	531,000	1665	
1648	715,605	1666	545,000
1649	660,000	1667	100,000
1650	1,094,451	-	
1651		1669	259,862
1652		-	
1653		-	
1654	549,195	1674	500,000
1655	583,000	1675	120,000
1656	589,174	1676	
1657		1677	
1658	1,500,000	-	
1659		-	
1660	772,560	1683	158,865

Source: Coolhaas, *Generale Missieven*, 2:205, 247, 274, 294, 317, 377, 418, 550–51, 735; 3: 39, 173, 228, 334,437, 502, 545, 561, 569, 703; 4: 17, 68, 124, 144 198, 204, 637. This table is slightly different from the one published by Gaastra. Both tables have the problem that they are incomplete and probably understate the annual amount of cash exports, for they do not include, for example, the not negligible revenues of the freight trade with Surat.[103] For a more accurate picture, more research needs to be done in the records of the trading stations that received specie from Iran.

103 Van Santen, *Verenigde Oost-indische Compagnie*, 55, Table 4.

correspondence was conducted between various VOC factories and the Asian headquarters in Batavia, concerning prices, profit rates, production data, and other relevant commercial news.

The English, too, were actively involved in the bullion trade, and not just for third parties. Their contractual arrangement with the shah was similar to what the Dutch obtained, in that it stipulated that part of the payment for the royal silk they procured was to be made in cash. Initially the English were made to pay two-thirds in current coin for their silk. Under Shah Safi this ratio was lowered to one-fourth.[104] And, just like the Dutch, who faced an Iranian market of limited export potential, they soon tried to take specie rather than merchandise out of the country. As early as 1639 they sent all their specie to Surat where, as they said, riyals sold 'at a much better price than at either Persia or Masulipatam'.[105] The English were as creative as the Dutch in concealing their money from the Safavid customs inspectors. In 1685 the EIC superiors in India instructed their agents in Iran to transport silver to Bandar `Abbas at night, with the advice to 'pack it up in wine chests matted over, that you may stuffe up with strawe, soe that the parcells of money doe not shake ... '.[106] The Company practised other means of hiding money as well. In 1695 agent Bruce transported 23,000 ducats packed in galbanum (a gum resin), while in 1697 17,000 ducats were brought down in ammoniacum (another gum resin).[107] In the latter year 83,000 ducats, called *chequins* (zecchini) in the English sources, were exported to Bombay by the EIC.[108] In 1699, cash-strapped shah issued another ban on the export of ducats. In 1707, 120,806 sequins were sent to Bombay.[109] Little other information is available on the quantities exported by the EIC, not to mention the numerous English private traders.

The flow of gold in the intercontinental bullion transfers was minimized by the introduction and the rapid spread across Asia of the Spanish *real of eight*. In addition, Ottoman currency adjustments, amounting to a devaluation of the indigenous *akçe* without an attendant price reduction at the mints, led to a growing outflow of silver to Iran.[110]

104 Matthee, *Politics of Trade*, 134.
105 Ferrier, 'British-Persian Relations', 256.
106 IOR, G/36/92, Swally to Gombroon, 23 Feb. 1685, fol. 43.
107 In Ferrier, 'British-Persian Relations', based on IOR, G/36/112, Gombroon to Surat, 7 Mar. 1695, fol. 165; EIC, G/40/5, Isfahan to Surat, 30 Apr. 1697, fol. 33.
108 IOR, G/40/5, Isfahan to Surat, 10 Sept. 1697, fol. 35.
109 Ferrier, 'British-Persian Relations', 316.
110 Şahillioğlu, 'Role of International Monetary and Metal Movements', 285–86.

Short-term Fluctuations in the Bullion Trade

As the pre-eminent market in the country and the most centrally located city of the realm, Isfahan was of crucial importance to those engaged in the bullion trade. The pivotal crucial issue, the rate of exchange, was elusive, however, and to follow it required a close following of the daily fluctuations of the market.[111] To do so, all merchants with a stake in the currency market, no doubt did as the Dutch, who to that effect kept in daily touch with the sarrafs (money-changers) they dealt with. To avoid being dependent solely on this source of information, however, the VOC resident in Isfahan also maintained close contact with some prominent Armenian merchants, whose involvement in the Ottoman trade made them the ones most intimately familiar with the prices of bullion that came from the Ottoman Empire.

The daily fluctuation of the money market in Isfahan was a function of a multitude of factors. These can be identified and classified under various rubrics, beginning with those of supply and demand. Within those categories factors related to domestic economic and political conditions and those of an external nature need to be distinguished. A further distinction is that between cyclical and contingent factors. Finally, there is the role of market forces and that of government intervention and regulation.

The impact of domestic factors on bullion, its price and its currency in the market, was mainly demand-related and mostly short-term in nature. Some were seasonal and could therefore be anticipated (though never counted on), while others were unpredictable in their effects, either because they involved market fluctuations or because their occurrence could not be anticipated. The most conspicuous seasonal factor that affected above all the price of gold involved the New Year's gift-giving ceremony. The magnitude of the collective demand for precious metal was such that the approach of each spring season invariably sent the price of gold up.[112] A second factor was the perennial tendency among the rich and powerful to hoard gold and silver. The effect of this practice on prices and circulation can only be surmised, since the sources only occasionally yield a reference to the phenomenon without giving clues to its impact on market prices. In

111 *NA*, VOC 1763, Gamron to Batavia, 21 Dec. 1707, fol. 110.

112 In seventeenth-century Russia a similar phenomenon could be observed. There, too, the price of gold would rise before holidays. See Kil'burger, in Kurts, *Sochinenie Kil'burgera*, 159. According to Stephen Album the Iranian *Nowruz* currently has the same effect on the price of gold in Los Angeles. For more on this, see Matthee, 'From Venice to Surat'.

times of scarcity, finally, competition among those in search of scarce gold tended to make already expensive ducats even more expensive.[113]

A most interesting demand factor, finally, was formed by the annual hajj to Mecca and, to a lesser extent, the visitation (*ziyarat*) of the holy Shi`i places (*`atabat*), Najaf and Kerbala in Mesopotamia. At the beginning of the pilgrimage season those who were about to embark on their year-long journey to the Arabian peninsula would buy up large amounts of gold, this being the only specie that lent itself to being carried over great distances, as a result of which prices would go up. This practice is briefly referred to in Tavernier's comment that the ducats would be bought up during the pilgrimage season and rise in price to 27 and 28 shahis (13.5 and 14 mahmudis), or even higher.[114] The pilgrims to Mecca and Medina, the same source noted, carried nothing but gold ducats, which were indispensable for the payment of Turkish and Arab tolls as well as for the expenses of alms and presents at the shrines.[115] The pilgrims passed through either Basra or Baghdad, where they would buy camels – to be resold at greatly reduced prices upon return – and pay for safe conduct. The Frenchman Jean de Thévenot noted that each pilgrim paid 35 ducats.[116] It is unclear whether the gold carried by pilgrims consisted of Venetian or Ottoman ducats, or both.

Precisely the wish to forestall the deleterious effect of the currency flight which accompanied the yearly pilgrimage was one of the reasons that prompted Shah `Abbas I to encourage the veneration of Imam Reza and the visitation of his tomb in Mashhad.[117] These attempts, it appears from the sources, may have worked in the short run, but did not meet with lasting success. Under `Abbas's successors the pilgrimage to Mecca by large numbers of people resumed. Chardin noted that up to 10,000 people would

113 See IOR, E/3/52/6283, Isfahan to Company, 1 Oct. 1696, which complains that Dutch competition had driven up the price of ducats to the unprecedented price of '29 shahis, 5 cazbegis'.

114 Tavernier, *Les six voyages*, 1:136.

115 The amir of Mecca in the later seventeenth century is said to have taken eleven gold dinars from pilgrims and to have charged them six dinars upon entry into the city; entering Madina cost five dinars. See Ja`fariyan, *`Elal-e bar oftadan-e Safaviyan*, 362, citing Abu Salim `Ayyashi, *al-Madinah al-munawwarah fi rihlat al-`Ayyashi* (Kuwait, 1408), 190.

116 Thévenot, *Suite du voyage de Levant*, 321–22. That the hajj business must have been immensely lucrative for the officials in Basra is indicated by the competition between Basra and Baghdad over which city was to serve as the starting point for the Iranian pilgrims, as well as by the Arab envoys periodically sent to Isfahan with rich gifts to petition for the annulment of bans on the pilgrimage. See Chardin, *Voyages*, 3:134–36; and 7:183–85.

117 Tavernier, *Les six voyages*, 1:588–89. Shah `Abbas's project was not the first of its kind, for already in the fifteenth century we hear of an attempt to substitute the veneration of a shrine of an Iranian sheykh for the costly hajj to Mecca. See Aubin, 'Deux sayyids de Bam', 301.

set out for Arabia each year.[118] Permission to go was withheld a number of times under the Shahs `Abbas II and Soleyman, but this was done more on account of the frequent abuse of pilgrims in Ottoman territory than because of concern over money.[119]

The supply and value of bullion in Safavid Iran was affected above all by external factors. By definition extraneous, the supply was, however, not entirely unpredictable. Short-term tergiversations were in part cyclical, related as they were to the seasonal character of long-distance commerce, land-based and maritime alike. The rumored approach of a richly laden caravan from Ottoman territory, which usually arrived in the fall or the early winter, tended to cause an immediate decline in the price of specie in Isfahan.[120] On the other hand, the uncertainty surrounding the long-distance caravan trade routinely turned perceptions and rumors into price-determining factors. Hazardous terrain, harsh climatic conditions and poor communications all played an important role in this regard. In a society where most reliable news was ordinarily preceded by a flurry of rumors, the mere rumor of the pending arrival of a large caravan from Tabriz, with only the likelihood, never the certainty, of a supply of specie, would send the price of ducats in Isfahan down. Conversely, any delay of anticipated caravans from Tabriz would cause prices to rise. War or the threat of war had the same effect. Thus in 1674 rumors about an impending war between the Ottomans and Safavids kept many Turkish merchants from coming to Iran with cash.[121]

Since most precious metal used in Iran was transmitted through the Ottoman Empire, the price and availability of gold and silver naturally depended in large measure on the rhythm of supply from across the northern and northwestern borders. Supply, in turn, was related to political and economic conditions in an area that stretched far beyond Iran or even West Asia. Indeed, circumstances in places as far away as Europe had a demonstrable effect on the price and availability of specie in Iran. The high price of gold in the early 1670s, for instance, may in large part be attributed to the ban on minting and exporting of ducats that Venice issued in 1670 with the aim of encouraging the export of goods

118 Chardin, *Voyages*, 3:135.

119 Chardin, *Voyages*, 7:185, claimed that in the twelve years he was in Iran he saw four ambassadors from Arabia pleading the Safavid court to revoke its ban on the hajj. Two recent studies of the history of the hajj in the early modern period are Faroqhi, *Pilgrims and Sultans*; and Pearson, *Pilgrimage to Mecca*. Both discuss the economic dimension of the pilgrimage, yet neither provides much additional information on the function of gold money in the traffic.

120 *NA*, VOC 1549, Gamron to Batavia, 24 Oct. 1694, fols 600v-01r.

121 *NA*, VOC 1304, Isfahan to Batavia, 4 Sept. 1674, fol. 519v.

rather than of bullion. The ban was repealed in 1676 and the resulting resumption of bullion exports in turn led to a glut and a stagnation of demand in the East, with similar repercussions in Iran.[122]

War and political unrest were always a clear and immediate catalyst of higher gold prices. Most important in this regard was the political and economic state of the Ottoman Empire and particularly the eastern Anatolian border areas. Political turmoil or a surge in brigandage in unpacified parts of Anatolia or Mesopotamia were bound temporarily to interrupt caravan traffic and prevent considerable sums of gold and silver from reaching the Iranian borders, with subsequent repercussions for the state of Isfahan's money market. This is what happened in 1673 after some richly laden caravans had been held up by highway robbers near Tokat in Turkey.[123] Similarly, one of the alleged causes of the persistent scarcity and dearness of ducats and reals in the mid to late 1690s was the unrest and wars in the transit areas, the Ottoman Empire and parts of the Arabian Peninsula. Here, too, conditions further afield mattered. In 1703, during the war of the Spanish Succession in Europe, the price of ducats in Isfahan went up at the mere rumor that the export from Europe was about to be banned.[124]

Not surprisingly, export prohibitions, in Iran and elsewhere, as far as Japan, tended to influence bullion flows as well. They did not necessarily halt the traffic – porous borders and administrative graft militated against the effectiveness of bans and controls – but prices were usually not left unaffected. Thus the proclamation of the *Novotorgoviy Ustav* (New Trade Charter) in Russia in 1667, which taxed foreign merchants in silver and gold, encouraged them to import these precious metals into Russia rather than taking hem out of the country, slowed, though by no means halted, the flow of precious metal from Russia into Iran. Japan, from which the VOC received 40 per cent to 50 per cent of its annual demand for bullion, forbade the export of silver in 1668, making Iran an even more important source of bullion for the Indian market. Silver therefore became more profitable than anything else, whatever the profit on silk.[125]

Another example, more dramatic because of the larger volume involved, is the measures that the Ottomans took to counteract the currency outflow to Iran. Ottoman bullion export bans go back to the early sixteenth century, and were issued most frequently at times of war or tension with Iran.[126] At

122 Tucci, 'Emissioni monetarie', 284, 295.

123 *NA*, VOC 1291, Gamron to Heren XVII, 21 Mar. 1673, fol. 558r; VOC 1304, Gamron to Batavia, 24 May 1674, fol. 437r.

124 *NA*, VOC 1694, Isfahan to Gamron, 12 May 1703, fol. 71.

125 Ferrier, 'British-Persian Relations', 204.

126 Bacqué-Grammont, *Les Ottomans, les Safavides*, 55, 72; İnalcık, 'Ottoman Mind', 213.

the turn of the eighteenth century severe bullion shortages caused by the export of huge quantities of specie led Istanbul to take similar measures. The English representative in Aleppo in 1697 called the Armenian traders' practice to carry all lion dollars and Venetian ducats to Iran greatly prejudicial to the Ottoman economy, claiming that of late this had caused the coin to rise by 3 to 4 per cent in value.[127] In reaction, Ottoman vigilance increased and steps were taken to restrict bullion exports, presumably at the instigation of indigenous merchants. Jealous of the Iranian Armenians, these presumably informed the Porte about the damage done to the sultan's treasury by the steady export of gold and silver to Iran, petitioning for a ban on the outflow. A ban was issued forthwith, but for unclear reasons it soon had to be repealed. As an alternative, the English report relating this story continues, mints were set up in cities that served as entrepôts of trade with Iran, most notably Aleppo and Erzurum. Gold and silver could henceforth not be exported unless the coins bore a stamp from these mints. The charge, however, was so high, the English claimed, that it canceled all gain that could be made on bullion.[128]

On the external demand side, the most potent factor influencing the price of export money was the pull from India. In the case of the traffic with western India, the rhythm was even more season-bound and fluctuations were therefore more regular and predictable than in the Ottoman case. Shipping movements from and to India were determined by the monsoon winds. The pending departure of the fleet to India in the spring would invariably raise the level of competition for bullion and thus affect its price in Isfahan.[129] Conversely, prices would fall once the ships had left and none were to be expected until the following season.[130] Today's scarcity (toward the beginning of the monsoon) could therefore be tomorrow's glut (the end of the monsoon). The EIC agent wrote that in 1648 'soe full of money was Bandar [`Abbas] at the end of the monsoone' that a junk from Golconda had difficulty to gets its money accepted.[131]

127 PRO, State Papers, 110/20, Aleppo to Smirna, 17 Feb. 1697, fol. 99v. The lion dollar, called *esedi gurush* or *arslani* in Turkish, *abu kalb* in Arabic and *abuquel* in French, was a debased copy of the Dutch rix-dollar. These coins began appearing in large quantities in Turkey after 1669 and soon became so popular that Germany and Italy began manufacturing them in debased form. See Davis, *Aleppo and Devonshire Square*, 190.

128 IOR, E/53/6417, Isfahan to London, 15 July 1697. This can only have been a short-term arrangement, for no coins are available from these mints and otherwise no mints are known to have existed in Aleppo and Erzurum at this time.

129 Tavernier, *Les six voyages*, 1:136.

130 See, for example, *NA*, VOC 1694, Isfahan to Gamron, 8 June 1703, fol. 71, and VOC 1763, Isfahan to Gamron, 3 Mar. 1708, fol. 513.

131 Ferrier, 'British-Persian Relations', 258.

On the other hand, what was true for conditions along the western supply route equally obtained for the situation *en route* to India, where the vagaries of political conditions and commercial stability had an impact on prices as well. The demand from south Asia was constantly high but not without short-term oscillation. Illustrative of the precariousness of the equilibrium that determined prices is the reluctance of merchants to take money there after the death of the Mughal Shah Jahan in 1658. As reports spoke of unsafe roads around Agra, merchants were said to interrupt their journey to India and to try to rid themselves of the gold they were carrying.[132] The above-mentioned robbery of a caravan near Qandahar on the road to India had a contrary backlash effect on Isfahan's money market. The huge amount stolen in the incident alone was said to contribute to a scarcity of money and a lack of credit among the merchants in the Safavid capital.[133]

Internal and external factors intersected in their impact on the availability and price of gold ducats in Iran. Of these factors the annual pilgrimage appears a very potent one, given several examples of prices rising or falling according to the preparation for the journey or the caravan's departure – developments on which simultaneous bullion flows from Ottoman territory had no appreciable effect. The example from 1708, mentioned earlier, does not stand alone in this regard. Nor was the opposite case unheard of. Around 1690 the scarcity of the mahmudi coincided with a relatively low price for gold, occasioned by a large supply from Europe. Similarly, an increase in gold prices as a result of the pilgrimage season might be annulled by a fall once the caravans from Tabriz had arrived. In late 1703, when the pilgrims began to make preparations to leave on hajj, which that year drew a great number of high-ranking Safavid functionaries, the price of the ducat went up to 15¾ mahmudis. Rates fell again, however, with the arrival of caravans from Tabriz.[134] We also hear of contrary cases

132 *NA*, VOC 1226, Gamron to Batavia, 1 Mar. 1658, fol. 800v.; ibid., Surat to Batavia, 27 Feb. 1658, fol. 713.

133 *NA*, VOC 1291, Gamron to Heren XVII, 21 Mar. 1673, fol. 558r; VOC 1304, Gamron to Batavia, 24 May 1674, fol. 437r; Chardin, *Voyages*, 2:232–33.

134 *NA*, VOC 1694, Isfahan to Gamron, 23 Dec. 1703, fol. 183; ibid., Gamron to Batavia, 29 Mar. 1704, fol. 125. The frequent mention of the drain of money from Iran as a result of pilgrims suggests the growing numbers of prospective hajjis leaving for the holy places in Arabia every year and thus can be seen as numerical evidence of the growth of outward religious display under especially Shah Soltan Hoseyn. Judging by the references to high-ranking officials going to Mecca, the renewed popularity of the pilgrimage to the holy places in Arabia began as early as the latter part of Shah Soleyman's reign (1666–94). Under Shah Soltan Hoseyn the numbers seems to have increased dramatically. See Khatunabadi, *Vaqaye' al-sennin*, 55.

that suggest the same phenomenon, such as in 1714, when the ducat did not fall in price, despite the arrival of the Tabriz caravan because of the energy with which prospective pilgrims to Arabia collected the coin.[135]

Long-term Trends

Until the 1670s, information on gold and silver prices in Iran is scanty and intermittent. In 1585 the Italian Vechietti quoted 32,000 tumans as being equal to 700,000 ducats.[136] Since one tuman equaled 100 mahmudis, this would have given the ducat a value of 4.6 mahmudis. In 1619 Della Valle claimed that one tuman equaled ten (Venetian) ducats, thus suggesting that the ducat equaled 10 mahmudis.[137] In 1626 the Venetian ducat was said to be worth 12¼ mahmudis.[138] In 1629 its price had gone down to 11¼–11½ mahmudis,[139] and between 1630 and 1639 it does not seem to have exceeded 13 mahmudis.[140] In 1656, finally, its value was $13^{21}/_{40}$ mahmudis.[141] These figures appear to suggest a linear increase of gold in value against the Safavid silver currency but, given the possible impact of short-term factors outlined above, we should perhaps not read too much into these few references.

The sporadic reference to the ducat in the early maritime sources perhaps reflects the small proportion of gold in the commercial remittances to India until that period. The subsequent increased importance of gold in the transfers, in turn, may be related to the growing shortage of coinage in the Ottoman Empire toward the middle of the century.[142] Yet, the simultaneity of high gold prices in the Ottoman Empire throughout the 1670s and 1680s,[143] and the sudden drop in the value of gold in India in the mid 1670s, should alert us to the fact that neither conditions in Ottoman territory nor the Indian situation always worked in tandem with developments in Iran and that relative prices of gold and silver in the adjacent regions cannot automatically be taken as an index of those in the Safavid state. It can

135 *NA*, VOC 1856, Isfahan to Gamron, 27 Feb. 1714, fol. 675.
136 Browne, 'Report on the Condition of Persia', 319.
137 Della Valle, *Viaggi*, 358, 794.
138 IOR, E/3/11/1228, Isfahan to London, 14 June 1626, fol. 116; also in Sainsbury, *Calendar of State Papers 1625–29*, 211.
139 IOR, E/3/12/1300, Isfahan to London, 27 Feb. 1629, unfol.
140 IOR, E/3/13/1425, Gombroon to London, 22 Mar. 1631, fol. 182v.; Foster (ed.), *English Factories in India 1637–1641*, 251.
141 *NA*, VOC 1210, Invoice of goods sent to Surat, 6 Mar. 1655, fol. 822.
142 Pamuk, 'Money in the Ottoman Empire', 30.
143 Ibid., 28.

roughly be said that from approximately 1630 to the mid 1670s, gold, either in the form of gold ducats or in unminted gold bars, was the favored specie of import into most of India, where the south and in particular Coromandel was gold-based. This is reflected in the high silver value of gold until 1675.[144] In Iran, however, that was not necessarily the case.

A trend toward congruity between conditions in Iran and India is observable as of 1676–77, when the price of gold suddenly fell in India and silver prices began to increase relative to gold.[145] Whether the direct cause of this was a massive dethesaurization of gold stocks by the Emperor Aurangzeb, as Dutch resident merchants claimed,[146] or increased gold imports from Japan, the high valuation of silver continued in later years and was reflected in similarly high silver ratios in Iran and great quantities being transported to the subcontinent. An explanation for this development is found in part in changes in the political situation in southern India, where the kingdom of Golconda came under Mughal rule in the last third of the seventeenth century. Most important in this respect was the change from a traditionally gold-based economy into one where silver was more valued. As around the turn of the eighteenth century revenue and tribute payment in these areas was conducted mostly in silver, the price of this metal rose in relation to gold.[147] Another general development was the shift away from the gold-consuming and war-torn Coromandel Coast and, beginning in the 1680s, a growing Company involvement in silver-hungry Bengal.[148]

The relatively low price of gold seems to have bottomed out in about 1690, when an abundance of gold began to arrive from Europe. The cause of this surfeit is unclear, but it may have been related to the high proportion of gold that had been struck in the main European countries in the immediately preceding years.[149] As a result, the ducat became relatively cheap at Isfahan, where it now sold for 12 to 13 mahmudis. As was noted before, the Dutch took advantage of this situation and decided to minimize their dependence on the continually bad `abbasi and mahmudi by buying up large quantities of these ducats.[150] Despite the problems they

144 See the chart in Prakash, 'Precious Metal Flows', 63.

145 See IOR, E/3/37/4258, 22 Jan. 1677, unfol.; and, for a graph of gold–silver ratios, Moosvi, 'Silver Influx and Prices', 51.

146 *NA*, VOC 1226, Gamron to Batavia, 1 Mar. 1658, fol. 800v. This is also presented as the main cause by Chaudhuri, *Trading World of Asia*, 178.

147 Arasaratnam, *Merchants, Companies and Commerce*, 195.

148 Glamann, *Dutch-Asiatic Trade*, 69.

149 Morineau, *Incroyables gazettes et fabuleux métaux*, 304.

150 *NA*, VOC 1493, Gamron to Batavia, 13 Oct. 1691, fols. 281v-2v.

encountered with the Safavid mint farmers who, as soon as they found out, did their utmost to collect their fee on every ducat transported, the VOC factors from that time on managed to transport enormous quantities of ducats to Surat. Relatively low priced in Iran, gold was even lower in value in Mughal India, where state income was collected in silver and where silver at that time was said to be of much better quality than in Iran.[151] In 1691 the so-called 'Moorish' ducat (struck in the Ottoman Empire) sold at 12¼ mahmudis in Iran, while the European ducat was exchanged at 13¼ mahmudis. Even when the latter rose to 14 mahmudis in 1692 and 1693, they were still sent profitably to India.

Toward the end of the century, however, a swing back to gold is observable in a renewed increase in the silver value of gold specie in both Iran and India. The precise reasons for this are again far from clear. The disruption the Nine Year War caused in the Mediterranean trade was partly responsible for a diminishing influx. Within Iran, moreover, the accession of Shah Soltan Hoseyn in 1694 and the attendant demand for ceremonial gold, followed by the shah's imposition in 1695 of a 12½ qazbegi fee on every ducat exported, may have played a role. Already in 1694, ducats could no longer be obtained at their former price of 13½mahmudis and now were sold for no less than 14 mahmudis in Isfahan, whereas the ones that were brought down to Bandar `Abbas were said to be bought up at 15 mahmudis by Banyans who did not even bother to weigh or burn them for inspection. What is more, old ducats grew increasingly scarce and as of 1694 hardly any were bought at Bandar `Abbas, nor were any received as payment for merchandise. Gold prices went up accordingly. This was to be a long-term trend, for a slow rise in the price of the ducat in Isfahan is noticeable, from 14 mahmudis in 1694 to $14^{1}/_{4}$ mahmudis in 1699. In 1701 they had risen to ca. $14^{5}/_{8}$; in 1702 the trend was temporarily reversed, with the ducat falling to $14^{1}/_{20}$ mahmudis. In early 1703 the coin dropped even further in value to $14^{1}/_{40}$ mahmudis.[152] From then on prices went up again; in 1704, the ducat was valued at 15 mahmudis,[153] reaching a height in Isfahan of slightly over 15 mahmudis in 1708.[154]

151 *NA*, VOC 1476, Isfahan, to Batavia, 12 Aug. 1690, fol. 418r. According to this report, soldiers in India were paid in gold.

152 *NA*, VOC 1679, Isfahan to Gamron, 10 Feb. 1703, fol. 247.

153 The 1704 price is recorded in IOR, G/36/118, copy diary Isfahan, 29 June 1704, fol. 1704. See also Lockyer, *Account of Trade in India*, 241, who claimed that the ducat equaled 31 to 32 shahis, i.e., 152 to 16 mahmudis. Lockyer's information most likely refers to the price in Bandar `Abbas, where the ducat was always more expensive than in Isfahan.

154 *NA*, VOC 1779, Isfahan to Gamron, 24 May 1708, fol. 215; Ferrier, 'British-Persian Relations', 316.

Table 2.2: Export of gold ducats by the VOC from Bandar `Abbas (1701–12)

Year	Number of ducats	Value in guilders
1701/02	180,000	1,149,100
1702/03	162,000	1,034,494
1703/04	124,000	792,012
1704/05	172,000	1,098,395
1705/06	57,600	367,814
1706/07	270,000	1,724,120
1707/08	138,000	881,126
1708/09	129,000	823,734
1709/10	179,000	1,143,008
1710/11	97,000	619,429
1711/12	256,000	1,834,577
Total	1,764,600	11,267,814

Source: Floor, *Commercial Conflict between Persia and the Netherlands*, 35, based on *NA*, VOC 1812, fols. 1079–1113.

By this time, yet other developments contributed to the continually high gold price in Iran. The Nine Year War was followed, after an interval of a few years, by the War of the Spanish Succession (1702–13). This conflict affected the ultimate source of most bullion, the New World, and caused bullion supplies from the Americas to dwindle. In Iran this was perceived as the likely cause of the high price of ducats, which by late 1704 had risen to above 15 mahmudis in Isfahan and to 16 mahmudis in Bandar `Abbas.[155]

A second contributing factor must be sought in the Ottoman policy of overstriking gold (and silver) coins, which had been initiated in 1697.[156] The measure was repeated in 1707 when Istanbul outlawed the export of ducats

155 *NA*, VOC 1714, Gamron to Batavia, 20 Sept. 1704, fol. 29. For a similar situation in 1705, see VOC 1732, Isfahan to Heren XVII, 30 Sept. 1705, fol. 234.

156 Baladouni and Makepeace (eds), *Armenian Merchants*, 246–47.

and reissued an order to overstrike all that were found.[157] While these measures did not halt the bullion traffic across Anatolia, they did cause gold to become more expensive in Iran.

The third and final compounding factor was the hajj, whose effect on the price of ducats became most conspicuous in the time of the pious Shah Soltan Hoseyn, who encouraged members of his court to perform the pilgrimage. The European Company agents, always keen on keeping an eye on monetary developments, make no mention of the important phenomenon until the turn of the eighteenth century, when they begin to comment quite frequently on its effects on the availability and price of gold. Enormous sums were apparently involved – the *Vaqaye` al-sennin* in its reference to the money drain caused by the exodus of 1115/1703–04, gives an estimated 100,000 tumans as the amount the pilgrims carried with them – a huge sum given the Safavid crown's reported 600,000 tumans in annual income.[158] A Dutch report in 1705 notes that demand for ducats was high and that these coins were extremely scarce because of purchases by Mecca pilgrims.[159] In 1708, on the other hand, it was said that, in part as a result of the pending hajj season, ducats had gone up in price from $15\frac{3}{20}$ to $15\frac{9}{10}$ mahmudis.[160] After the hajj caravans had left in October of the same year, the price dropped to $15\frac{27}{40}$ mahmudis, despite the absence of new bullion-laden caravans from Tabriz.[161] The year 1709 saw a repetition of the previous year in the large numbers who left for Mecca, encouraged to do so by Shah Soltan Hoseyn himself, who allowed anyone to go and who appointed officials to accompany the travelers. Prices, which previously had fallen to $15\frac{3}{40}$ mahmudis, rose to $15\frac{17}{40}$ mahmudis in September.[162] This fluctuation following the hajj rhythm continued. In 1713 ducats went up to a maximum of 16 mahmudis, falling to $15\frac{7}{40}$ after the departure of the caravan.[163] The hajj of 1714 caused an unusually long period in which the ducat was expensive since the Safavid grand vizier, Shah Qoli Khan, who was scheduled to go on hajj himself, forbade the money-changers from selling the coins to anyone but him.[164] Agha Kamal, the royal Treasurer, in

157 *NA*, VOC 1763, Isfahan to Gamron, 21 Jan. 1708, fol. 494; ibid., Isfahan to Gamron, 23 Feb. 1708, fol. 502.

158 Khatunabadi, *Vaqaye` al-sennin*, 553.

159 *NA*, VOC 1732, Isfahan to Gamron, 23 July 1705, fol. 126.

160 *NA*, VOC 1737, Isfahan to Heren XVII, 20 Sept. 1708, fol. 120.

161 *NA*, VOC 1779, Isfahan to Gamron, 1 Nov. 1708, fol. 283.

162 *NA*, VOC 1798, Isfahan to Gamron, 4 Sept. 1709, fol. 222.

163 *NA*, VOC 1856, Isfahan to Gamron, 23 Nov. 1713, fol. 558.

164 *NA*, VOC 1856, Isfahan to Gamron, 14 Jan. 1714, fol. 625.

the summer of that year is said to have taken 200,000 ducats with him to Arabia.[165] In 1716 there were again reports of court eunuchs buying up all ducats available in the market.[166] In 1718, finally, the French envoy Gardane referred to the higher price of ducats in Isfahan due to the sale to India merchants and Mecca pilgrims.[167]

Clearly, by that time, Iran's internal chaos rather than any external circumstances accounted for the rising market value of the ducat. Desperately short on cash, the Safavid state at this time resorted to extraordinary measures to regain its solvency. In 1716 a (short-lived) ban was issued on the use of gold and silver thread in textile manufacturing.[168] Later that same year Shah Soltan Hoseyn, unable to pay his troops, devised ways to maximize the inflow of gold bullion into the royal treasury so he could issue a gold coin as 'pure as the Venetian ducat'.[169] The following year an order went out for gold from the shrine of Mashhad to be melted and minted into coinage. A reported 95,000 tumans worth of gold was brought to the royal treasury in this manner.[170] The shah even went so far as to remove the precious metals from his ancestors' graves in Qom.[171] The result was the issuance of the gold ashrafi, the first Safavid gold coin since the time of Shah `Abbas I. The measure did little to alleviate the problems, however, and gold prices continued to climb, until in the years directly preceding the fall of Isfahan they registered an unusually steep rise, hovering around 17 mahmudis in 1721, and reaching a level of almost 18 in 1722.[172] This trend continued, with the price reaching 20 mahmudis in 1728.[173]

Despite the high price of gold, the ducat remained very popular in the last decade of Safavid rule. The Ottoman ambassador who visited Iran in 1716 is said to have received 700 tumans in newly minted silver money and to have changed the entire amount into ducats.[174] The Dutch managed to

165 *NA*, VOC 1870, Isfahan to Gamron, 25 Aug. 1714, fol. 222.

166 *NA*, VOC 1879, Gamron to Batavia, 30 Jan. 1716, fol. 41.

167 AAE, Perse 5, 'Mémoire sur les monnoyes de Perse et autres qui y ont cours,' fols. 209–11. The drain of valuable currency through pilgrims continued to be a problem in later times as well, as is clear from references to the negative monetary effect of the pilgrimage to the `atabat during the Zand period. See Lorrimer (ed.), *Gazetteer*, 1/i, 164.

168 *NA*, VOC 1879, 4th fasc., Gamron to Batavia, 30 Nov. 1716, fol. 17.

169 *NA*, VOC 1897, Isfahan to Gamron, 14 Nov. 1716, fols 230–31.

170 Mostowfi, *Zobdat al-tavarikh*, 126; *NA*, VOC 1913, Gamron to Batavia, 31 Dec. 1717, fol. 49; and Bushev, *Posol'stvo Artemii Volynskogo*, 185.

171 Ibid., 257.

172 Coolhaas (ed.), *Generale missiven*, 7:506, 572, 628.

173 Chick (ed.), *Chronicle of the Carmelites*, 1:774–75.

174 *NA*, VOC 1877, Isfahan to Gamron, 14 Nov. 1716, fol. 236.

export the considerable quantity of 1,764,600 ducats – in addition to many silver `abbasis – to India in the first decade of the eighteenth century. Even during the turbulent decade preceding the fall of Isfahan, when gold became exceedingly scarce, the VOC exported ducats to the tune of 100,000 a year.[175]

175 *NA*, VOC 1857, 10 Dec. 1714, fol. 2317; VOC 1897, 30 Nov. 1716, fol. 49; VOC 1913, 13 Dec. 1717, fols. 38, 57–59.

3

Measures to Stem the Bullion Export

Introduction

In different countries and centuries, the most frequently employed method of stemming the outflow of coins and precious metal has been to prohibit the export of specie. The seventeenth century in Europe was the 'bullionist' age par excellence, an age in which various countries' emphasis on the amount of bullion in circulation occasionally verged on hysteria. The obsession with the volume of specie is easily dismissed in light of today's economic theory and practice. However, when placed in the context of a real existing scarcity of ready money and the deficient pre-modern understanding of monetary behavior, this obsession loses much of its irrational appearance.

What was true for mercantilist Europe was equally so for sixteenth and seventeenth-century West Asia, where the scarcity of ready money was even more endemic and financial dependence on outside sources of specie much greater. In the sixteenth century, Ottoman authorities imposed restrictions (so-called refontes), and sometimes outright bans, on the export of precious metals and coins, especially toward their eastern borders. The fact that these refontes had to be repeated regularly indicates that their effectiveness left much to be desired.[1] In 1539, for example, no merchants could leave for Iran without a special license from the Ottoman sultan. All travelers were stopped and searched.[2] For Iran no such early bans are recorded, although they almost certainly were in effect. In the second half of the seventeenth century the information about Iran greatly increases in volume and frequency. Isfahan at that time recurrently issued prohibitions on the export of bullion, suggesting a new seriousness that the problem of export had. By doing so, the government reacted to the working of Gresham's Law, which caused money with metallic value exceeding its monetary value to disappear from circulation. Great quantities, especially

1 Şahillioğlu, 'Role of International Monetary and Metal Movements', 276–77.
2 Membré, *Mission to the Lord Sophy*, 11.

of gold, must have been hoarded. As the official mint value of silver coin was lower than the price the market was willing to pay, and as Safavid Iran needed to export specie to pay for the deficit on its current account, huge amounts also disappeared to India via the mechanism of arbitrage. Safavid Iran allowed the free import and export of bullion and that the export of foreign coins was only subject to a fee.[3] These bullion shipments were naturally the subject of great government concern. Just as in Europe, the measures taken by the authorities in and of themselves bore more the character of a defense mechanism than of an aggressive hunt for treasure.[4] Given Iran's weak international commercial position, little alternative was available. The Safavids were greatly worried about the outflow of specie, in part on cash flow grounds and in part because of concerns about the effect on the domestic price level (the less specie, the lower the money supply and therefore the higher prices). The government, therefore, periodically tried to ban the export of specie from Iran. The authorities regularly issued edicts against the exportation of coin from the kingdom. Yet success was invariably partial and temporary at best, as these regulations could, without difficulty, be evaded indirectly by way of smuggling and concealment, or even directly, by bribing the authorities. The state's frequent attempts to control or even stop the outflow of specie thus invariably failed.

Government Policy until 1669

We have no record of Safavid export bans prior to the reign of Shah `Abbas I.[5] Shah `Abbas I is known to have decreed a ban on export of specie in 1618. The agents of the EIC in 1618 wrote of the 'Bannians in returne of their Linens carryinge of the Silver, and gould out of the country'. Merchants, they noted, 'at their comming into Persia [...] are used with great favour [...]

3 This is quite contrary to the suggestion of Simmons, 'Evolution of Persia's Monetary System', 167–69, who assumes that, generally, Safavid Iran allowed the free import and export of bullion and that the export of foreign coins was only subject to a fee. He attributes this freedom in part to the absence of a need to curtail exports in a situation where Gresham's Law did not operate because in Iran the monetary value of coins generally exceeded their bullion value.

4 Supple, *Commercial Crisis*, 194.

5 The statement of the Italian traveler D'Allesandri to the effect that 'the exportation of metals is forbidden' suggests Iran but in reality refers to the Ottoman Empire. This become clear from the Italian original, which states that it was forbidden to 'bring (precious) metals into the aforementioned country' (*nel predetto paese*), i.e., Iran. See Berchet (ed.), *La repubblica di Venezia e la Persia*, 180; and Grey (ed.), *Narrative of Italian Travels*, 226.

But at their going into India they use all extremitie, searching them to the skinne for gold, which to transport, or any coyne of silver out of Persia, but the King's, is death'.[6] EIC agents indeed reported the execution at Qazvin in 1618 of several Banyans who were accused of exporting bullion.[7] The effectiveness of controls on the export of bullion must have been aided by the fact that Shah `Abbas's court merchant, Molayem Beg, was also the mintmaster of Isfahan. The ban remained in force, because `Abbas I needed money for his wars. The Dutch and others therefore had to pay part of the purchases in cash rather than in barter. However, after `Abbas I's death, the ban was allowed to fade away.

`Abbas I's successors continued his attempt to keep as much bullion as possible inside the country. Part of the recurrent conflicts with the Dutch during the reign of Shah `Abbas involved the Safavid demand that one-third of the VOC imports into Iran be in precious metal.[8] Instead, as will be demonstrated later, the Dutch not only paid for most of the silk they exported in spices, but, after 1641, as silk deliveries decreased they began to export more and more bullion from Iran. In 1644, Isfahan issued a decree making it illegal to export reals of eight, gold ducats – the Hungarian and Venetian ones as well as the 'Moorish' (Ottoman) ones – or 'new money'; that is, new `abbasis, to India.[9] These severe restrictions made the transport of money at times problematic and risky. The merchants with whom the Dutch made an agreement in 1651 to transport 100,000 reals – at the merchants' own risk and expense – could not be convinced to hand over their money to the Dutch in Isfahan, as they were afraid of the stringent control system that had been put into place.[10] In 1652, in a period of great financial strain, the Safavid government tried to curb the Dutch export of bullion through a separate arrangement with the VOC. The new commercial treaty between the Iranians and the Dutch contained a clause that prohibited the Dutch from exporting Spanish money or 'Moorish' ducats (soltanis struck in the Ottoman Empire after the model of European ducats).[11]

These prohibitions had a noticeable effect on the trade in bullion. In the 1650s, VOC officials often voiced complaints such as 'at the moment no reals or rijksdaalders [rixdollars] are coming here',[12] or 'I begin to despair whether

6 Quoted in Ferrier, 'English View', 193.

7 Letter by Edward Pettus to the EIC, in Sainsbury (ed.), *Calendar of State Papers*, 199.

8 Meilink-Roelofsz, 'Earliest Relations', 35–56.

9 *NA*, VOC 1150, Gamron to Batavia, 10 Mar. 1644, fol. 136.

10 *NA*, VOC 1185, Gamron to Batavia, 25 Apr. 1651, fols. 574–89v; ibid., 18 May 1651, fols. 541–52v.

11 Speelman, *Journaal*, 235. 'Moorish' ducats are the soltanis that were struck in the Ottoman Empire in imitation of the Venetian ducat.

12 *NA*, VOC 1178, Gamron to Batavia, 15 May 1650, fol. 809v.

we will be able to change our proceeds into reals and rijksdaalders.'[13] However, and in spite of the admonition by the VOC director in Gamron to his colleague in Isfahan to strictly adhere to the clause that was part of the 1652 agreement, they never achieved their intended goal.[14] The VOC – and all other merchants – continued to export specie in defiance of the export ban. Its staff was creative in hiding gold and silver among the goods carried to Bandar `Abbas and hence to foreign destinations. Merchants always found ways to circumvent the regulations and were aided and abetted in their clandestine activities by officials who were eager to pocket bribes. How ineffective prohibitions were can be gauged from the fact that the Dutch, though impeded by the ban of 1644, managed to increase their remittances relative to the previous period, exporting an annual average of half a million guilders for the next few years.[15] As a result of the continuing bullion exports, by 1648 most of the 'old' `abbasis had been transported out of the country, so that only newly minted ones, which were 5 per cent lighter in weight, were still available.[16]

The prohibition on exporting gold continued throughout the 1650s or, at least, export prohibitions were periodically renewed. The year 1657, a year after Mohammad Beg, a former assayer of the mint, was appointed as chief minister, provides a good example. The campaign for increased revenue that was launched with his appointment included a reinstatement of the export ban on bullion. A royal decree specifically prohibited the export of gold. As with each such proclamation, restrictions on clandestine transports seem to have been fairly strictly enforced for some time. For example, the new assayer of the mint, Amin Beg, sent out spies to check on violators. The atmosphere of intimidation that ensued caused the moneychangers of Isfahan to close their shops. Feeling threatened, they also refused to assay coins any longer, either going into the mint or those given in payment. Everyone engaged in the gold business kept a low profile and, as a result, little gold could be obtained.[17] By May 1660, the demand for gold had gone up so much that the price of gold had risen from 14 to 14.5 mahmudis per European ducat.[18]

13 *NA*, VOC 1185, Gamron to Batavia, 25 Mar. 1651, fols. 596–603.

14 *NA*, VOC 1226, Gamron to Batavia, 1 Mar. 1658, fol. 800; Speelman, *Journaal*, 235.

15 Gaastra, 'Export of Precious Metals', Appendix 4; and Floor and Clawson, 'Safavid Iran's Search', 350, Table 1, which has slightly different figures.

16 *NA*, VOC 1170, Gamron to Batavia, 15 May 1648, fol. 738.

17 *NA*, VOC 1226, Gamron to Heren XVII, 16 Sept. 1658, fol. 800. See also ibid., Surat to Batavia, 16 Feb. 1658, fol. 864v.

18 *NA*, VOC 1233, Gamron to Batavia, 24 May 1660, fol. 95.

The length to which the inspectors would go to ferret out illegal shipments of bullion is exemplified by a case related in both the Dutch sources and by Tavernier. It involved a Dutch caravan that left Isfahan on 1 January1661 and was stopped near Abarquh, some 70 kilometers south of the city, by the inspectors of the mint. Eager to find if the Dutch were transporting money for Banyan merchants, these officials demanded to inspect the merchandise carried and, apparently, informed that the Dutch were secretly transporting gold, immediately went for the mattresses in which the gold was hidden. The gold, an amount of 30,300 ducats, was taken to the house of the sarraf-bashi, who put it in a chest and sealed it. He then handed the money chest over to the VOC agent in Isfahan to await the chancellor's decision. Privately, he advised the VOC agent to change the gold into silver `abbasis. As the coins were found to belong to the Dutch, they were released after being taken back to Isfahan for inspection. The VOC director immediately protested in outrage to the grand vizier, Mohammad Beg. Willems pointed out to the chancellor that while the export of gold had been forbidden, its transportation had not. The Dutch, he argued, every year bought ducats in Isfahan and subsequently transported these to Bandar `Abbas. The particular amount of money that had been apprehended by force had been the remainder of the funds that the VOC had sent to Isfahan to pay for the royal silk delivery. Because there was a shortfall in the supply of silk, and to prevent the money from lying uselessly there, it had been decided to send it back to Bandar `Abbas. The money was not destined for export but was meant to be used in trade with merchants there. Willems also drew the chancellor's attention to the fact that the Banyan merchants in Bandar `Abbas routinely exported specie, and that the Muslim merchant Mirza Mohsen Sarraf-bashi in Isfahan organized a similar trade with regards to the merchants who traveled overland to India via Qandahar. Willems finally asked the chancellor to see to it that such offense to the Company would not be repeated.[19]

Fortunately for the Dutch, shortly after they had been caught red-handed, Mohammad Beg fell from power. He was succeeded by Mirza Mohammad Mahdi, under whose rather weak governance control over trade and in particular over the export of specie became slack. Soon after the January incident, the Dutch had sent a second amount of specie to the coast. Because of the new and less strict situation the VOC agent was urged to remit as much capital as possible to Bandar `Abbas. If need be, he was permitted to ask the grand vizier permission to transport the specie to

19 *NA*, VOC 1232, Gamron to Heren XVII, 14 May 1661, fol. 666v; ibid., Request to E`temad al-dowleh Mohammad Beg, 31 Jan. 1661, fol. 682r.; VOC 1236, gGamron to Batavia, 12 Mar. 1661, fols. 312–15. See also Floor and Clawson, 'Safavid Iran's Search', 360.

Bandar `Abbas for trading purposes. The director would see to it that the money would be secretly brought aboard the Company's ships.[20]

Despite his bravura the Dutch Director temporarily decided to keep a low profile so as not to endanger the Company's profitable trade with Iran. Between June 1660 and the end of 1662, therefore, the VOC did not export any gold. By that time, however, the export ban on gold had been amended. The government had come to realize that gold continued to leave the country without yielding an export fee and, worse, that the merchants trading with Ottoman lands, the so-called 'Turkish' merchants, who normally brought gold and silver to Isfahan, now went to Basra. The VOC, therefore, decided to pay the export duty of 3.5 stuivers per gold ducat and resume their gold exports. The fact that the 'Turkish' merchants were coming to Isfahan again, as well as the higher profits on gold export of course, played a role in that decision. The sarraf-bashi received the right to inspect all caravans for clandestine transports.[21]

Regardless of bans and threats, therefore, the Dutch, forced to take out specie because this was the only way for the Company to remit the proceeds of its sales in Iran, did manage to export most of their bullion without incident throughout this entire period. The directors in Batavia, conforming the success of this turn of events, in 1658 showed themselves very content with the more than Dfl. 100,000 in gold shipped to Coromandel, and called Iran one of their most profitable factories.[22] In the period from 1642 to 1660 the VOC ferried the estimated equivalent of more than 9 million guilders from Iran. In the peak years 1649–50 and 1657 more than one million guilders were each year siphoned off to India.[23] In 1661 the VOC exported Dfl. 250,000 worth of gold and silver to Coromandel and Ceylon alone.[24]

Restrictive Measures in the Period 1669–84

The appointment of Sheykh `Ali Khan as grand vizier in 1669 occurred at a financially unpropitious time for Iran. Two years earlier Russia, in a measure designed to keep bullion inside its territory, had prohibited

20 *NA*, VOC 1236, Gamron to Batavia, 31 May 1661, fol. 630.

21 *NA*, VOC 1239, Gamron to Heren XVII, 31 Dec. 1662, fol. 1208v. In 1663, the export duty was raised to 4.5 stuiver or 2/5 mahmudi. See *NA*, VOC 1239, Gamron to Heren XVII, 13 Mar. 1663, fol. 1670.

22 *NA*, VOC 882, Batavia to Gamron, 21 Sept. 1658, fol. 482.

23 Gaastra, 'Exports of Precious Metals', 474; and Floor and Clawson, 'Safavid Iran's Search', 350, Table 1, which has a list with estimated bullion export figures from Iran.

24 *NA*, VOC 886, Batavia to Gamron, 18 Sept. 1662, fol. 474.

Iranian and other eastern traders from changing their money into ducats and rix-dollars for export.[25] The vizier's appointment also coincided with the ban Japan imposed on the export of silver. This ban, which had been instituted in 1668, affected Iran inasmuch as it further enhanced the role of the Safavid realm as a source of bullion for European and Asian merchants. To make matters worse, India in the 1670s became more silver-hungry than ever. In 1675–76, the price of gold suddenly fell in the Mughal Empire and silver became highly profitable.[26] In later years this trend continued. Changes in the political system in southern India were the main cause of monetary transformation in the subcontinent. The kingdom of Golconda in the Deccan, a traditionally gold-based economy, came under Mughal rule in the last third of the seventeenth century, and was thus incorporated into a monetary system based on silver. Revenue and tribute henceforth were mostly collected in coins of that metal.[27] The result of these changes is seen in unabated attempts by merchants to evade Safavid restrictions on bullion export. So great did this pull from India become that for foreign companies it more than compensated for the falling profitability of a commodity like silk.[28]

The measures Sheykh `Ali Khan took shortly after his appointment were precisely meant to thwart this opportunity. His aim was to make it less profitable for the foreign companies and private merchants alike to export their money out of the country. At the same time, however, his policy seems to have been informed by the awareness that money was going to be exported regardless of restrictions, and that it would be more profitable to tax this traffic than to outlaw it. A precedent for his policy had occurred already in 1662, when an important change took place in the rules governing the export of specie. The ban on the export of gold was lifted in that year and a fee of 3/5 mahmudi was imposed instead for every ducat that was transported from Isfahan. The sarraf-bashi received the right to inspect all caravans for clandestine transports. That move, the Dutch had plausibly anticipated, would benefit trade and contribute to its revival since it would lure to Isfahan the merchants from Turkey who for some time had been inclined to go to Basra with their gold reals and rix dollars.[29] The abolition of the ban was thus most likely meant to attract money to Iran that would otherwise have been diverted away from its borders.

25 Attman, *Russian and Polish Markets*, 192.
26 See IOR, E/3/37/4258, Swally to London, 22 Jan. 1677.
27 Arasaratnam, *Merchants, Companies, and Commerce*, 195.
28 Ferrier, 'British-Persian Relations', 204.
29 *NA*, VOC 1239, Gamron to Heren XVII, 31 Dec. 1662, fol. 1208v.

In 1670 Sheykh `Ali Khan launched his own restrictive initiative by instituting a 5 per cent tax on all silver money exports as well. The rationale for this measure presumably was that, if money was going to leave the country, it might as well yield some tax benefit for the government. Initially, the fee appears to have been payable in Bandar `Abbas. The Iranians continued to try and stop the flow of coins out of the country via the Gulf except 'what belongs to the English, Dutch and French ... without one Merza Mussey's leave, whose Deputy is now in towne hath given abonndance of trouble, threatening to open all chests and bales to seek for money, but the merchants at last made a general complaint and got leave for shipping their goods after he had searched all with running an Iron into both bales and chests, this new officer is absolute, receiving Comission imediately from the King.'[30] It was hoped that the shah would revoke this practice, fearing that it would hurt trade. The export levy was irregularly applied and the *kalantar* of Lar, Mirza Mosuum [Ma`sum?], was charged to correct the excesses. For instance, the *shahbandar* pretended that the levy had been abolished and then applied it.[31]

A little later, presumably in 1671, Isfahan became the site where merchandise was subjected to inspection. The opportunity for better control was undoubtedly the rationale for this change. Controls seem to have become more stringent as well. Chardin noted that, whereas formerly bales of wares had only been routinely opened for investigation at the country's borders, now all merchandise was subjected to scrutiny and taxation in the interior.[32] The VOC agent in Bandar `Abbas, while wishfully predicting that merchant opposition would eventually turn this new imposition into a dead letter, showed himself nonetheless worried about the consequences for trade, and particularly Dutch trade.[33]

The Dutch worries proved justified, for the 5 per cent imposition did have an immediate effect on trade in the southern ports. The first season after its introduction, VOC agents complained that very few merchants had come down to Bandar `Abbas and that those who did come brought little money in the expectation that the new fee would soon be abolished. The result was a drop in the volume of sales for the VOC.[34] A number of those who did come down from Isfahan tried to make their purchases on

30 Ferrier, 'British-Persian Relations', 287.

31 Ibid.

32 Chardin, *Voyages*, 8:194–95.

33 *NA*, VOC 1270, Gamron to Heren XVII, 24 Apr. 1670, fol. 892v.

34 *NA*, VOC 1274, Gamron to Heren XVII, 22 Apr. 1671, fol. 735r; ibid., Gamron to Heren XVII, 10 Sept. 1671, fol. 746r; VOC 1284, Gamron to Batavia, 15 May 1671, fols. 2353v-54r.

condition that they would be allowed to pay later in Isfahan. The Dutch factors in Bandar `Abbas, dreading bankruptcies and unpaid loans, refused this kind of credit arrangement, which was in any case prohibited by their superiors in Batavia.[35] In late 1671 the 5 per cent fee on money transports was reported by the English merchants to be 'strictly looked after, and paid at Spahan before permitted to come thence'.[36] Two years later, the Dutch complained that they were subjected to renewed checks on their shipments after the transfer to Isfahan.[37]

The ad-hoc trade tax did not fail to have a negative effect on trade activity. During the first year of implementation the new measure prompted local merchants, who anticipated that the imposition would soon be abolished, to hold back on selling their wares. As the tax farmers in Isfahan who oversaw the enforcement levied the 5 per cent also on bills of exchange drawn, no moneylender would issue a bill of exchange. The reason was simple: the new measure did away with one of the attractive features of bills of exchange, the possibility to transfer money to Bandar `Abbas anonymously and without having to pay dues.

More important, and of severe long-term consequence, the duty on silver did not prevent large quantities of this precious metal from being transported, either legally or illegally, to the coast, from where it was shipped to India. Following Gresham's Law, bad money continued to drive out good money regardless of government regulations. Just as the earlier lifting of the ban on gold export had done nothing to keep gold in the country, so too the new policy did not stop the best-quality money from leaving. Especially around 1676, when the price of gold fell in India and silver became highly profitable, the appeal of silver reached a peak. As no structural changes took place in the Safavid economy, the freedom to export gold and silver coin only contributed to the disappearance of currency from circulation. In fact, the restrictions on the export of precious metals mutually reinforced their price and availability. As a Dutch report in 1673 put it:

> The strict control that has been exercised on the export of silver for several years now is the cause that gold, of which a great capital is being carried down and transported, has become very expensive. The European ducats are now valued at $16^{2}/_{3}$ and $16^{1}/_{2}$ mahmudis, for which reason little silver and many ducats now arrive from the northern quarters of the

35 *NA*, VOC 1284, Gamron to Batavia, 15 May 1671, fols. 2353v-54r.
36 IOR, G/36/106, Gombroon to Surat, 13 Nov. 1671, fol. 51.
37 *NA*, VOC 1285, Gamron to Heren XVII, 17 Jan. 1673, fol. 1r.

country, and silver is very scarce, not only here but even in Isfahan, which is to the great disadvantage of the trade.[38]

The scarcity of silver, the irreplaceable metal through which trade was conducted, was the graver of the problems. One reason why little silver was brought in from Turkey in 1673 was the rumor that Iran and the Ottoman Empire were preparing for war. This apparently made the merchants coming from the Ottoman Empire reluctant to proceed to Isfahan with their money. As trade conditions in the Safavid Empire deteriorated, fewer merchants came from Turkey in any case.

The unavailability of silver in this period led to Dutch fears that eventually they might have to accept expensive gold ducats for their wares, ducats that would have to be changed at a loss in India. Before long, the toll collection on precious metal exports was moved back to Bandar `Abbas, and simultaneously the freedom of export without harassment was once again guaranteed so long as merchants could prove that their money had been ordered in Bandar `Abbas and provided they paid the 5 per cent tax on the coast. Yet, this did little to spur trade. Instead, local merchants became reluctant to entrust money to the foreign companies, preferring to keep their cash in Isfahan as interest-bearing capital as long as they possibly could.[39] In addition, much of the silver that would normally be carried to Isfahan now began to be taken to Basra. This remained a pattern for decades to come. The dearth of silver, in turn, led to the idleness of the mints on the borders with the Ottoman Empire, where most of the Safavid money was struck. Indeed, the only Safavid mints that thrived in this period were the ones located in Khuzestan, in the orbit of Basra. The most notable one of these, the mint of Hoveyzeh, in this period put out large quantities of mahmudis, which served as the workhorse currency of southern Iran and the Persian Gulf basin.[40]

The effect on trade of the 5 per cent toll imposed on silver had to be evaluated in conjunction with the role of gold, which circulated along silver. Merchants dealing in silver could always switch to gold if silver became unprofitable and provided enough gold was available. Wary of transporting silver, the local merchants as of 1672 indeed began to trade heavily in gold. As a result, a new ban was instituted on the export of gold, but apparently the prospect of good profits on this metal and the simultaneous fee on

38 Ibid.

39 *NA*, VOC 1285, Gamron to Heren XVII, 6 May 1673, fol. 385r.

40 See Matthee, 'Mint Consolidation'.

silver outweighed the risks of being caught while carrying gold. Local merchants also took to gold for logistical reasons: because of its value gold could be transported in relatively small quantities and was therefore easier for merchants to hide from inspection.[41] As soon as the 5 per cent fee on silver was instituted, the Armenian merchants trading with Europe seem to have ordered their factors to bring nothing but ducats back from Ottoman territory, and before long, the Turkish and Armenian merchants coming from the Levant through Tabriz and Baghdad brought mostly gold with them. In late 1672 ducats in Iran were valued at the extraordinarily high price of 16⅔ mahmudis each. As a natural consequence of this high price, merchants began to bring even large amounts of gold into the country. Silver suffered and little of it was imported at this time.[42]

Yet this spike in gold imports did little to increase the availability and circulation of cash in Safavid territory. Silver remained the principal trade metal. Dwindling imports notwithstanding, imported silver still allowed the border mints to strike large and small `abbasis, thus adding to the stock in circulation. Gold, by contrast, was purely a commodity metal; the bulk of it was either hoarded in the royal treasury or by the wealthy and the powerful, or taken directly to India, either via the sea route or via Qandahar.[43] Great profits could be made by selling gold specie to Indian merchants in the 1670s. The premium put on gold in this period is reflected by high prices for the ducat. Whereas the average price for the ducat hovered around 14 mahmudis in the middle of the seventeenth century, late 1676 saw a price of 15½ mahmudis.[44] Tavernier confirmed this state of affairs. Merchants, he noted, who managed to evade the minting requirement on the borders by hiding their gold made a good profit selling their specie to private traders.[45] Around 1674–75 the price of silver hit a low in India and the ratio to gold worsened to 1:17; it was, for a brief period at least, more profitable to export gold than silver from Iran.[46] Much of the gold appears to have been exported toll-free from the little-controlled small southern ports west of Bandar `Abbas. The ease with which gold could be hidden made illegally exporting it a relatively simple procedure and thus an attractive option.

41 *NA*, VOC 1349, Gamron to Batavia, 25 Nov. 1674, fol. 1712r.
42 *NA*, VOC 1285, Gamron to Heren XVII, 17 Jan. 1673, fol. 1r.
43 *NA*, VOC 1343, Resolution 13 Feb. 1680 concerning the state of trade in Persia, fol. 600r. A copy is contained in VOC 1360, fol. 1891r-v.
44 *NA*, VOC 1315, Gamron to Batavia, 5 Jan. 1677, fol. 728v.
45 Tavernier, *Les six voyages*, 1:136.
46 Chauduri, *Trading World of Asia*, 177–78. Also see, Matthee, 'Between Venice and Surat'.

Nor did this new preponderance of gold make the export of silver coins dry up. The VOC, for one, in 1674 managed to export Dfl. 500,000 worth of silver `abbasis to Ceylon.[47]

The Safavid government thought the worsening silver shortage was due to coin exports. VOC officials, howver, in one of their outbursts against what they saw as the short-sighted protectionist policy of Sheykh `Ali Khan, blamed the shortage on the restrictions imposed on the free movement of silver currency. Trade controls, they argued, were the greatest impediment to a flourishing trade. Aside from this, they contended, shortages were caused above all by the reluctance of the royal court to strike silver coins in adequate quantities. Matters would not improve, according to the Dutch director, as long as more silver money was exported from the country than was minted in new coins.[48]

Problems of lightweight coins, debasement and clipping made the ensuing period a trying one for money exporters. In this situation, the Dutch in 1679 decided that it would be less detrimental to acquire gold ducats and silver rix-dollars, despite the inevitability of having to acquire these coins at a premium, than to receive shoddy mahmudis.[49] As the `abbasis minted by Shah Soleyman in the period between 1679 and 1681 turned out to be lighter in weight than previously issued ones, all the available coins current in trade transactions, `abbasis and mahmudis alike, were unattractive. Yet, though the newly minted `abbasis were up to 24 per cent lighter than the old ones, they were still favored over the available mahmudis. That, at least, is implied in the advice the parting Dutch director Casembroot in 1682 gave to his successor van Heuvel to accept as few of the latter for VOC merchandise as he possibly could.[50] The VOC resident in Basra, where small quantities of ducats and reals continued to be available, was instructed in 1684 not to accept any `abbasis and mahmudis, but only the two former coins.[51]

Admonitions to avoid bad Iranian currency did have some effect on the specie exported from the southern ports. Yet, due to the limited availability of sound coins, adulterated mahmudis and `abbasis ended up in India in large quantities anyway. The Indian factories of the VOC repeatedly billed their colleagues in Bandar `Abbas for the losses sustained on bad coins received

47 *NA*, VOC 1297, Gamron to Heren XVII, 31 Jan. 1675, fol. 355v.

48 *NA*, VOC 1323, Gamron to Batavia, 12 Aug. 1677, fol. 675r. According to the Armenian merchant Zak`aria Agulis, the minting of 'panj shahi' `abbasis had begun in 1662. See Zak`aria of Agulis, *Journal*, 66.

49 *NA*, VOC 1332, Gamron to Batavia, 1 June 1679, fol. 917v.

50 *NA*, VOC 1364, Memorandum Casembroot to Van Heuvel, 14 June 1682, fol. 368v.

51 *NA*, VOC 1406, Gamron to Batavia, 28 Feb. 1684, fol. 1183v.

from Iran.[52] And even if the VOC did its best to limit the percentage of compromised coins in the total amount remitted, private traders continued to import bad specie. This caused the Dutch policy in the 1680s in Ceylon to differentiate between the mahmudis and `abbasis they themselves imported from Iran and the privately imported, adulterated ones, by overstriking the former with a VOC stamp.[53]

After the financial crisis of the early 1680s, the monetary 'reform' of 1684–85, which will be discussed in the next chapter, did little to alleviate the scarcity and adulteration of coin. The minting of only a small number of new `abbasis apparently did not noticeably increase the amount of money of good weight and alloy in circulation; instead, it caused much confusion among merchants. In anticipation of the working of Gresham's Law, the recoinage was accompanied by a renewed strengthening of control on bullion exports in Bandar `Abbas. Thus, in December 1684, the English mentioned that an order for the shahbandar had just arrived from the shah, 'not to let any money Gold or Silver be caried out of his Countrey by any person whatever and whoever it be and send the party prisoner up to court ...'.[54]

Sharpened control on the export of precious metals, meanwhile, was not confined to the Persian Gulf routes. The existence of control over overland routes is demonstrated by what happened to William Hedges when he passed through Kermanshah on his way to Baghdad in January of 1686. Shah Qoli Khan, the governor of the city and a son of Sheykh `Ali Khan, forced the caravan to open various bales looking for gold and silver. The authorities forced Hedges to pay a sum of 15 tumans in cash and goods to prevent further scrutiny.[55] This conclusion suggests that local officials benefited more than the central treasury from the inspections and export restrictions.

Developments after 1684

After 1684, badly adulterated coins continued to plague the Safavid government as well as those bent on exporting treasure. The Dutch, the

52 See, for example, VOC 1448, Gamron to Heren XVII, 16 July 1689, fol. 428v, which reports a bill for Dfl. 15,566.13.13 submitted by Malabar for adulterated coins from Iran for 1687–88, and a much higher one for Dfl. 101,315.17.2 for 1688–89.

53 *NA*, VOC 1644, 'Twee placcaten wegens het stempelen der persiaensche abasis en het billioen verklaren der valsche ditos,' Colombo, 7 Dec. 1688 and 27 Jan. 1691. See also Codrington, *Ceylon Coins and Currency*, 113, 164.

54 IOR, G/36/109, 2d sect., Gombroon to Surat, 9 Dec. 1684, fol. 73.

55 Hedges, *Diary*, 1:216.

biggest exporters, were reduced to idleness for a considerable period of time. A conflict over the silk contract with the Safavid crown escalated to the point where the VOC occupied the island of Qeshm off the coast of Bandar `Abbas in 1684. As long as the state of war with Isfahan lasted, the Dutch were naturally unable to operate in the Iranian market. In 1685, when the VOC surrendered the island and the conflict came to an end, the company immediately contemplated resuming its bullion transports to India. The Dutch, however, found themselves faced with a surfeit of bad coins that were bound to cause losses in the subcontinent. Their counter strategy was to try to avoid these coins by converting as much of their profits as possible into commodities. Silk, which was at a low price where it was to stay for another decade, was not a good option. Instead, over time, the VOC found a partial alternative in the export of goat's wool from Kerman. The company in 1685 also cast an eye on pearls from Bahrain as a way to profitably convert income earned from the sale of spices.[56] The Dutch were not alone in this predicament, for Banyan merchants, too, in the early 1690s converted their money into commodities such as pearls, madder, fruit and tobacco, instead of exportable coins.[57] None of these commodities was capable of absorbing the profits the VOC began to earn through its importing of enormous quantities of Indian textiles in the closing decade of the century. As a result, the company continued to remit most of its revenue in specie.

After the normalization of relations, only in 1687 was the VOC able to resume its shipments of bullion to India as part of renewed trade activities. However, of the specie the company had procured in the interim, many current `abbasis and mahmudis proved to be deficient in weight. Those struck in Tiflis, for instance, were 22.5 per cent below standard weight.[58] Ducats were only available for 16 mahmudis each; the only good `abbasis, those that had been struck under `Abbas II, had to be purchased at rates that exceeded their face value by up to 11.5 per cent.[59]

While informed about these extra costs yet not fully aware of the practical problems the currency situation presented in Iran, the Directors in the Netherlands in 1688 exhorted their agents in Bandar `Abbas either to demand good `abbasis and mahmudis for the goods sold or to sell the goods at prices high enough to compensate for the lower real value of the money received. The answer from the factors to the first option was that

56 See *NA*, VOC 1416, Gamron to Batavia, 16 July 1685, fol. 1726r; and VOC, Generale Missiven, 8 Jan. 1686, in Coolhaas (ed.), *Generale Missiven*, 5: 2–3.

57 *NA*, VOC 1559, Gamron to Batavia, 31 Oct. 1693, fols. 804–07.

58 *NA*, VOC 1434, Gamron to Batavia, 2 June 1688, fol. 555r.

59 *NA*, VOC 1425, Gamron to Batavia, 21 Aug. 1687, fol. 441r.

unadulterated `abbasis and mahmudis were rarely to be found and those few that did turn up were treated as a commodity. The second option, they said, would be workable if they were the only ones engaged in commerce on the coast and did not have any competitors. The only remedy to the situation, the director in Bandar `Abbas suggested, would be to try gradually to reduce the price of the ducats, the specie that was most readily available in Iran.[60]

The attention to the ducat in these considerations was understandable for, in light of the dismal state of the mahmudi, gold clearly was becoming the specie of choice. In order to keep the commercial risk involved in the possession of mahmudis at a minimum, the Dutch had adopted a policy of limiting the amount of mahmudis they received for their wares to the equivalent of the cash needed to buy goods, and to insist on ducats for payment of the remainder.[61]

Clearly, gold was on the upswing. To some extent, the working of Iran's bimetallic system acted to balance capital flight. The influx of gold compensated in some measure for the fall in the silver imports. However, not all gold this silver scarcity attracted was lured to Iran. Basra again reaped benefits from Iran's uncertain economic conditions. By 1690 merchants preferred to take not only their silver but even their gold to Basra rather than to unprofitable Iran, despite the fact that by then the city and its environs were in the throes of war and disease.[62]

The strategy proposed by the VOC factor proved more difficult to implement than was foreseen. The Dutch attempt to reduce the price of ducats was complicated, among other things, by the same phenomenon that prevented unilateral increases in the price of goods: the competition that existed between the various merchants, local and foreign, who were all equally keen on exporting specie. The Dutch complained that, quite simply, it was impossible to have the price of the ducat reduced further than 15 mahmudis because the English were willing to pay 15½ mahmudis.[63]

Nevertheless, around this time the Dutch began to send larger quantities of different coins, but especially gold ducats, to their various factories in India; in early 1690, for example, they managed to receive the payment for their spring sale in Bandar `Abbas two-thirds in heavy European ducats and one-third in current mahmudis.[64] Yet, this did not prevent them from incurring a loss on both the ducats and the reals they sent to Malabar. Thus

60 *NA*, VOC 1448, Gamron to Heren XVII, 16 July 1689, fol. 428v.
61 *NA*, VOC 1476, Gamron to Isfahan, 12 Aug. 1690, fols. 473r-74r.
62 *NA*, VOC 1476, Gamron to Batavia, 29 Apr. 1690, fols. 405–14.
63 *NA*, VOC 1476, Gamron to Isfahan, 8 July 1690, fol. 451v.
64 *NA*, VOC 1459, Isfahan to Heren XVII, 20 Dec. 1690, fol. 1017r.

in 1690, the ducat was valued at 6 guilders, 16 stuivers in Iran, in Ceylon at Dfl. 6.15, and in Malabar at only Dfl. 6.[65] Ultimately the Dutch factory in Iran had to pay for these losses. In 1688 and 1689, for example, the bill sent by Malabar for losses on specie remitted from Bandar `Abbas amounted to Dfl. 116,882.10.15.[66]

Control on the ban on export slackened after the death of Sheykh `Ali Khan in 1689. The following year saw the confiscation of 400,000 rix-dollars belonging to Armenians who were shipping this with Dutch ships, though lots of other smuggled specie belonging to Turks, Arabs and Indians was not found.[67] In 1691, after a vacancy of two years, a new grand vizier, Mirza Taher Vahid, was appointed. Shortly after his accession, Mirza Taher Vahid followed his predecessor by taking steps to tackle the symptoms of the economic malaise. Among his concerns was that so much money bypassed Iran by being taken to India via Basra. Having been told that the principal reason for this was that the mint price paid in Iran for silver did not match its market value, he decided to raise the price of Spanish reals of eight. Simultaneously, the ban on the export of reals from the southern ports was reaffirmed and inspectors stepped up their vigilance.[68] Moreover, one of the conditions the new vizier sought to impose on the Dutch, who were anxious to have their silk contract abolished, was that the VOC would prevent ships coming from India from proceeding to Basra.[69] As the Dutch envoy Van Leene was able to refuse this demand, nothing came of the suggestion. It was nevertheless clear to everyone that money exports had to be handled with the utmost secrecy and that great care had to be taken in transporting coins from Isfahan. One way of doing so was to send money only with large caravans. This, it was thought, would make inspection less easy.

Soon things began to change. Beginning in 1691, due to the abundance of coins brought from Europe, the ducat became relatively cheap at Isfahan, where the 'Moorish' ducat sold at 12½ and the European ducat at 13½ mahmudis. Given their relatively low price in Europe and Iran, ducats now began to be sold for profit in India. Even when their price went up to 14 mahmudis in 1692 and 1693, ducats were still sent profitably to India. The Dutch took advantage of this situation and decided further to minimize

65 *NA*, VOC 1476, Gamron to Batavia, 12 Aug. 1690, fol. 416r.

66 Ibid., fol. 429r.

67 *NA*, VOC 1476, Gamron to Isfahan, 20 Sept. 1690, fols. 479–83; Sanson, *Estat de Perse*, 14.

68 IOR, E/3/48/5760, Gombroon to London, 10 Mar. 1691; VOC 1501, Generale Missiven, 11 Dec. 1692, fol. 245r.

69 *NA*, VOC 1501, Notulen van Leene, 31 Mar. and 12 Apr. 1691, fols. 520, 524; IOR, E/3/49/5774, Gombroon to London, 18 July 1691, fols. 3–4.

their dependence on the continually untrustworthy `abbasi and mahmudi by buying up large quantities of these ducats.[70] Despite the problems they soon encountered with the mint farmers, who did their utmost to get a fee paid on every ducat transported, the VOC factors from that time on managed to transport enormous quantities to India.

As part of their new drive to obtain gold coin, the VOC in the early 1690s adopted the practice of sending most of their proceeds in Bandar `Abbas to Isfahan via bills of exchange, where they exchanged them for gold ducats. The latter, after all, could be obtained for one half to one mahmudi apiece less in Isfahan than on the coast. The procedure was to the mutual advantage of all parties, the Dutch claimed. They benefited by buying their ducats cheaper than on the coast, while the merchants were spared the effort of transporting specie from Isfahan to Bandar `Abbas. The VOC broker received 1 per cent for checking the coins for purity and in return assumed responsibility for any false specimens.[71]

In these circumstances, things seemed to be getting better for the foreign companies; the Dutch, for example, in mid-1692 reported a good return on their trade.[72] Soon, however, the price of gold ducats was on the rise again. No longer obtainable at 13½ mahmudis in late 1693, they now were valued on the coast at 14½.

The reason for this renewed appreciation in the price of the gold ducat was the decline of the availability and the circulation of silver specie. Not only did the anticipated surfeit of silver from Turkey not materialize, but trade in reals of eight was again strictly prohibited: all who dealt in coin were ordered to bring their reals to the royal mint.

The year 1691 was not the last time measures were taken to curtail the export of specie. Merchants continued to take specie out of the country at a fast clip. The EIC, for instance, in 1695 sent 23,000 ducats packed in galbanum; in 1697, some 17,000 in ammoniacum, and a total of 83,000 were sent to Bombay that year.[73] In 1699 the Ottoman authorities, faced with their own financial problems, took measure against the unfettered outflow of gold and silver from their realm. In that year Levant Company merchants, confronted with an Armenian refusal to buy their cloth, complained that the latter took their silk to Europe themselves and in return exported large amount of silver and gold to Iran. In response to a petition, the authorities first banned the export, but when disturbances broke out in Aleppo,

70 *NA*, VOC 1493, Gamron to Batavia, 13 Oct. 1691, fols. 281v-82v.
71 *NA*, VOC 1732, Instruction Casteleyn to Backer Jacobsz., 1705, fols. 30–33.
72 *NA*, VOC 1493, Gamron to Batavia, 12 July 1692, fol. 323r.
73 Lockyer, *Account of the Trade in India*, 241.

weakened the measure to the effect of mandating the overstriking of all coins designed for export.[74] It is not clear how much effect this had, and if the new ban that the Safavid authorities issued in the same in response to unabated money trafficking by merchants was in any way connected. In any event, in 1699, the Armenians exported 100,000 ducats on the English ship, *Hampshire*, while the customs of Bandar `Abbas were farmed for 23,500 tumans and expected to yield 40,000 tumans.[75] And because money goes where demand is the ban on export of bullion had to be repeated regularly and almost yearly until 1720.[76] The problem thus was not that there was no money; it just was not circulating inside Iran. After all, large sums of hoarded money were found after the Afghan occupation of the country.[77]

The prime targets of this incessant battle against currency flight continued to be the Dutch. Rightfully suspected of exporting huge sums of specie, they remained embroiled in conflict with Isfahan over the export of specie until the last days of Safavid rule. A quarrel between the VOC director Willem Backer Jacobsz and his deputy Pieter Macare in Isfahan in 1712 led to intense government interest in the issue of bullion export. The quarrel was caused by personal ambition and the gentlemen's private interest in the export of ducats. Macare accused his chief of having exported 188,000 golden ducats and a number of silver `abbasis since 1701. The government next demanded to examine the VOC accounts to establish the truth, which of course was rejected. Following these events the shah ordered a new ban on the export of bullion, to check caravans for the presence of specie and seal all bales and chests prior to their departure from Isfahan. The control on the export of ducats was intensified, for the supply of ducats had dwindled and they were hard to obtain in Isfahan. The purchase of ducats by pilgrims aggravated this situation. In August 1714 the government informed the VOC that it had revoked the commercial treaty. It offered new terms, including, among other things, an obligation to have VOC caravans examined and the payment of duties on the export of gold and silver. Fath `Ali Khan Daghestani, the new grand vizier, repeated these measures in September 1715. He intimated that he did not want to wait for the return of the Safavid ambassador who had been sent to Batavia to discuss the new terms. Neither subsequent discussions, nor the arrival of the Dutch ambassador, Johan Josua Ketelaar, in 1717, led to a resolution

74 Baladouni and Makepeace (eds), *Armenian Merchants*, 246–47.

75 Ferrier, 'British-Persian Relations', 317.

76 Ibid.; *NA*, VOC 1843, Isfahan to Gamron 6 Sept. 1712, fols. 92–93 with text of the farman; VOC 1947, 1 Nov. 1719, fol. 280; VOC 1875, Isfahan to Heren XVII, 19 Aug. 1721, fols. 169–74.

77 See Chapter 5.

of differences. Although accommodation was reached, discussions on the final and formal arrangements for the export of specie by the VOC dragged on until the Afghan invasion of Iran in 1722.[78] Under Nader Shah and his successors a ban on the export of specie also was ordered, similarly to be met with non-compliance.[79]

Conclusion

This chapter has marshaled additional evidence in support of the proposition that Iran's fundamental weakness in the late Safavid period resulted from the country's lack of exportable commodities and its inability (or unwillingness) to attune its consumption pattern to its economic means. With the Ottoman Empire and the Russian state a positive trade balance was maintained, but its volume was not sufficient to compensate for the enormous trade deficit with India. The result was a perennial outflow of bullion and minted coins through commercial channels. This pattern had been in place since the beginning of the Safavid period, but was greatly stimulated by the influx of New World bullion in the course of the sixteenth century and, above all, by the entry of the Western maritime companies into the Persian Gulf in the early seventeenth century.

All merchants, foreign as well as indigenous, seem to have exported of bullion, but the greatest sums were exported by those who were most successful in the Iranian market, the Dutch. They took out enormous sums of specie from the 1630s until 1660, after which amounts decreased. After 1690, when the VOC began to import large quantities of Indian textiles into Iran, Dutch bullion exports, this time almost exclusively in the form of ducats, resumed their former volume. The remittance of bullion to India had less to do with the profits that could be made – these were quite small and the export of specie was often unprofitable – than with the absence of a suitable and more profitable alternative. In most cases anything that was not too badly adulterated was sent, gold or silver, regardless of the profit or loss anticipated in India. As has been pointed out by Kristof Glamann, the transportation of gold and silver was largely dictated by the currents of the international trade.[80]

78 On this conflict and its aftermath see Floor, *Commercial Conflict*.

79 Perry, *Karim Khan Zand*, 260; and Floor, 'Dutch Trade in Afsharid Iran'.

80 Glamann, *Dutch-Asiatic Trade*, 67–68.

A persistent scarcity of cash money made bullion a commodity like any other, a fact that was expressed time and again by the foreign factors resident in Iran. This is seen most clearly in the various forces that determined the price and availability of gold, the specie that conformed most to the definition of a commodity. The actual volume and price of the specie exported to India was a function of a combination of interdependent internal and external circumstances. It is difficult to disentangle the various elements, which were not merely a function of the gold–silver ratio and the mechanism of arbitrage. The fact that the price of silver in India was high did not necessarily and directly translate into large shipments of silver from Iran. An increase in the remittance of silver to India did not automatically entail a decrease in the amount of gold exported. Certain trends can nevertheless be followed. Until the 1660s silver was the most common specie imported and exported thence. In the 1670s gold became more abundant in Iran as export restrictions on silver were instituted. Conditions in India and other parts of Asia, while not always working in tandem with developments in Iran, account for some of the changes in the export of bullion. Coromandel in southern India was a constant magnet for gold. Temporary swings in the Indian silver–gold ratio favored gold at times. The long-term trend, however, was for the silver–gold ratio to be higher east of Iran and lower west of Iran, in large part due to the continuing flood of silver from the New World. Furthermore, Japan's prohibition of silver exports and the emergence of Bengal as an important market for the maritime companies ensured a surge in the demand for silver in the later part of the seventeenth century. This situation continued into the early part of the eighteenth century when great quantities of silver were shipped to India.

The centerpiece of this chapter has been the reaction of the Safavid regime to this constant bullion flight. Even if they had no information about the precise volume exported, the authorities in Isfahan clearly realized the magnitude of the trade. Yet its ability to regulate the monetary system of the Iranian economy was extremely limited and was made worse by its hoarding of gold and silver. Whatever action the court at Isfahan undertook amounted to reactive attempts to affect processes that were insufficiently understood and beyond political control. Basra's role as an overflow for specie coming from Turkey illustrates that the availability and price of bullion responded to the exigencies of market forces rather than to government dictates. The prohibition of the export of treasure was the most consistently used device to prevent money from leaving the country in large amounts. This measure was by no means unique to

Iran. It was a common strategy in the early modern world. The Ottoman government occasionally attempted to halt the flow of money to Iran just as the Safavids tried to stem the drain of gold and silver to India. In several European countries, too, bans on the export of bullion were in place at this time.

The main reason why the prohibitive measures did not work is contained in the opening quote of this chapter, which underlines the intractability of private initiative in search of gain. No conclusive remedy existed for the constant flight of treasure that was the inevitable result of this situation. Export bans proved futile because they did not solve the real problem. Indeed, they exacerbated it by encouraging subterfuge and clandestine activity. To get a clearer picture of this situation, however, we need to take a closer look at the internal situation and particularly at the minting policy of the Safavid state in the face of worsening economic circumstances. This policy, its ramifications, and implications, will be discussed in the next chapter.

4

The Politics of Minting

Introduction

Chapter 3 explored some of the causes and effects of the silver shortages that plagued Iran throughout the Safavid period (and beyond). It was seen how the government attempted to manage its own coinage in interaction with international market forces, and how the circulation of a plethora of currencies, structural trade imbalances, and the activities of merchants exporting money, combined to make that endeavor exceedingly difficult. The limits of government policies were most conspicuously visible in its largely futile attempts to stem the outflow of specie and bullion.

This chapter seeks to probe deeper into the government monetary policy in response to a complex situation that combined systemic bullion scarcity and fiscal difficulties. These two are to be distinguished analytically, although in practice they often went hand in hand in the sense that cash shortfalls resulting from scarcity of metal coins tended to lead to low cash revenue; that then might necessitate official tampering with the value of the currency with the intent of enhancing state income. This was no lasting solution, however, because if the market value of the altered coins fell, for instance, more of the debased coins would be required in exchange for the foreign coins which circulated widely. This chapter, then, concentrates on the response by the state to the persisting shortfall in revenue and the bullion famine that struck Iran (and all of West Asia) in the second Safavid century, beyond the persistent attempt to keep precious metal from leaving the country. It examines the various currency reforms and adjustments undertaken by successive Safavid rulers against the backdrop of the economic crisis that befell their country in the course of the seventeenth century, and takes up the question of the consolidation of the mints in the same period, probing the motivation and causes – efforts at centralization and a diminishing flow of incoming bullion – as well as the effects of this important development.

Money Matters before Shah `Abbas II

In the face of financial difficulties, governments in all times and the world over have chosen to tamper with the currency. Two ways need to be distinguished: reducing the weight of the coinage and compromising the alloy of the metal currency. Only the latter can properly be called debasement. It is clear and recorded that over time the Safavid state frequently engaged in the first type of reform; that is, it reduced the weight of the circulating coins without changing their value in terms of the unit of account – the dinar – or the ghost money – the tuman. Despite the abundance of coins compromised in their precious metal content, it is less clear whether the Safavid authorities ever officially – that is, deliberately and systematically – reduced the silver content of their silver coinage. In the later part of this chapter we will attempt to find an answer to that question.

Since all of the silver and gold coins in Iran were made with imported metal, Iran could increase its supply of precious metals only by running sustained balance of payments surpluses, which would have been difficult for a country so poor, both in absolute terms and in relation to its neighbors. Given the difficulty of financing constant imports of silver and gold, the supply of precious metals was inelastic in the face of growing demand for such metals for monetary, artisanal and commercial purposes, as well as for financing the persistent balance of trade deficit with lands to the east of Iran. When the economy grows and the supply of precious metal shrinks, any state with a coinage stable in weight and alloy would be struck by deflation, except to the extent that its authorities might be able to increase the money supply by substituting coins made of something other than silver and gold – in Iran as in most other countries, copper coins were used for most petty trade, and their use would increase at times when silver and gold coins were scarce. Continuous weight reductions were a safety valve, temporarily increasing the money supply until traders adjusted to the lower metal content in the coins. Furthermore, weight reductions in each country enhanced the stability of exchange rates among international currencies.

Obviously, no one would have been fooled for long by such weight reductions even had they been executed by stealth. However, it is important to realize that there was nothing furtive about such measures. The new coins were clearly marked off from the old ones, and the latter would either be recalled or declared similar in value to the new ones. The new coins in turn, would be accepted for payment of taxes at the same value as the old ones. With more coins in circulation, the state could collect more tax revenue – indeed, addressing growing fiscal problems was a major reason for the weight reduction (the major fiscal advantage of the reduction was that the precious metal held by the state could be made into more coins at the reduced weight than at the higher, earlier weight). But a weight reduction only temporarily reduced the fiscal imbalance, because the prices the state had to pay would soon increase, leaving the state with much the same structural deficit it had before the currency adjustment.

Especially for the sixteenth century, the European sources are scarce and give different values for the coinage. The coins themselves therefore form the principal evidence for monetary conditions in the period. H.L. Rabino and, more recently, Stephen Album have estimated the silver content that should be assigned to various notional monetary units (ghost moneys), based on the silver content of surviving coins and on the value of those coins in terms of the ghost monies. Their work shows that the tuman went from 1,814 g of silver at the start of the sixteenth century to one-fourth that level by the middle of the same century. It then stayed more or less at that level until the beginning of the seventeenth century.

The actual information available on the various weight reductions is patchy. In fact, Album concludes that his categorization of Safavid coinage 'must be regarded as tentative, especially for the 16th century'. Album's findings are shown in Table 4.1, which shows that there were two separate silver standards for the period until 1576, one for western and one for eastern Iran, which covered the provinces of Khorasan, Quhestan, Sistan and Astarabad. This suggests that the former Aq-Qoyunlu and Timurid parts still were not integrated monetarily.

Initially, from 907/1501 to 923/1517, there was one silver standard all over Iran, based on a standard of 1 tuman = 9,600 nokhud, except for Mazandaran, which continued to use the tangeh and Larestan the lari until the early seventeenth century (see below). The uniform national silver standard was changed in 924/1518 when in the west a silver standard was adopted based on 1 tuman = 8,100 nokhud, a situation that lasted until the end of Esma`il I' reign in 930/1524. This and the following weight reductions were necessitated by the invasions of the Uzbegs (1524–26; 1526–28; 1529–31, 1531–34, 1535–36, 1536–38) and the Ottomans (1533, 1535, 1536, 1548, 1553) as well as by Ottoman trade restrictions, which had a devastating impact on trade, and thus on the shah's revenues. Therefore, Esma`il I and Tahmasp I were forced to devalue the coinage several times. In fact, they 'corrected' the weight of the coinage seven times (see Table 4.1) to increase revenues and make it less attractive to export it.

The first weight reduction in the western region in 1518 was in response to Soltan Selim's trade ban, which was imposed in 1514 and remained in effect until 1521.[1] Likewise in the east, a new silver standard of 1 tuman = ca. 14,400 nokhud was adopted during 924–27/1518–21. The rather delayed introduction of this higher weight was probably due to a weight increase of the Central Asian Sheybanid coinage in 913/1507, a policy that the Sheybanids abandoned in 924/1518.[2] The Sheybanid weight reduction in that year resulted in another downward weight adjustment of the silver standard in the eastern region of Iran, based on 1 tuman = 9,600 nokhud, which standard only lasted for two years during 927–28/1521–22. Thereafter, until 931/1525, the east had the same silver standard as the silver standard in the west (1 tuman = 8,100 nokhud), where it continued to be applied until 937/1530. The new weight reduction of the western coinage was probably due to the re-imposition of the Ottoman trade ban in the late 1520s, which was lifted in the early 1530s.[3] Throughout Tahmasb I's reign the two shahi coin was generally favored, though there were occasional geographic differences; for example, in Gilan and the Caucasus the small half- and quarter-shahis were preferred. As of 1530 a new silver standard was adopted in the west based on 1 tuman = 6,400 nokhud, which was maintained until 947/1540. In the year thereafter a new western silver standard was adopted based on 1 tuman = 5,400 nokhud, which lasted until 953/1546. This new weight reduction was occasioned by the fact that, after the devastating 1536 Ottoman invasion of Iran, a new Ottoman trade ban was in effect. No merchants could leave for Iran without a special license from the Ottoman soltan. All travelers were stopped and arrested if they had no travel permit.[4]

In the east, a silver standard based on 1 tuman = 5,700 nokhud was in force from 931/1525 until 954/1547. The early part of this period (1524–38) was dominated by the 16-year long battle for Khorasan between the Sheybanids and Safavids. Thereafter, both parties had to recuperate; the Safavids in addition suffered three invasions by the Ottomans during that same period. In 954/1547, both in western and eastern Iran the same silver standard was adopted, viz. one based on 1 tuman = 4,800 nokhud, which lasted until 959/1552. One of the reasons for this weight reduction was the 1546 Ottoman ban on the export of all metals to Iran, which once again put pressure on Iran's hard-pressed bullion resources.[5] The subsequent Ottoman invasion of Iran in

1 Don Juan, *Don Juan of Persia*, 116; Bacqué-Gramont, *Les Ottomans, les Safavides*, 53–54.
2 Khandamir, *Habib al-seyar*, 4:379; Album, *Checklist*, 300–01.
3 İnalcık, 'Ottoman Economic Mind', 213.
4 Membré, *Mission to the Lord Sophy*, 11.
5 İnalcık, 'Harir', 213–14.

1548 only made conditions worse. In 960/1553, the standard was again changed in both the west and east of Iran, to which weight reduction followed by another Ottoman invasion in 1553 certainly contributed. In both regions the standard was fixed at 1 tuman = 3,000 nokhud, which lasted until 971/1563 or later.

Although the main coins of the western silver standard between 954–71/1547–63 have the same weights, their values were adjusted. Likewise, although both the western and the eastern standards of the 960–71/1553–63 period adhered to same 1 tuman = 3,000 nokhud, in the east the shahi was 50 dinars and in the west 80 dinars.[6]

Album found no numismatic evidence for a further weight reduction by Tahmasp I after 907/1563, but that does not mean that there were no problems with his currency. Despite the 1555 Peace of Amasiyeh there seems to have been no 'peace dividend', for Iran's foreign trade did not thrive as much as was hoped. In 1564 there were trade problems with the Ottomans, for a year later the English merchant Edwards reported that 'the Turkes Ambassador the last yere, as divers have told me, did put the Shaugh in despaire, saying that the Turke would not permit any cloth to be brought into the countrey'.[7] This cloth import ban must have been a temporary measure and certainly not a comprehensive trade ban in view of the fact that both parties adhered to the Peace Treaty of 1555. This situation, nevertheless, may have contributed to a trade crisis in 1572, which in the words of Alessandri was worse in its effects than the war between Venice and the Ottoman Empire. 'Because where formerly 2 bales of silk cost 400 zecchini, these are now sold at 200. The spices that come via Ormuz, are kept by nobody, ..., because there is nothing to exchange it with, they remain abandoned.'[8] As a result, revenue dropped and the value of the coinage was tampered with, effectively depreciating Iran's currency. When, due to depreciation, a situation of money scarcity occurred, the price of specie rose relative to other markets. Exporters therefore found it worth their while to send specie to Iran, despite an Ottoman ban on this export.[9] The currency seems to have been so seriously compromised that Tahmasb I on his deathbed, sensing his impending end, in 984/1576 ordered the minting of 1,000-dinar gold coins of 10,000 hazar and of 100-dinar silver

6 Album, *Checklist*, 275.

7 Hakluyt, *Principal Navigations*, 3:56–57.

8 Berchet (ed.), *La repubblica di Venezia e la Persia*, 179.

9 Ibid., 180; Grey (ed.), *Narrative of Italian Travels*, 2: 226; Chick (ed.), *Chronicle of the Carmelites*, 1: 52.

ones because of the prevailing impurity of assay and counterfeiting, with 20 dinar in current use circulating as if it were 200 gold dinar.[10]

The reign of Shah Esma`il II (1576–77) might seem too short to bring about major changes in the monetary system; nevertheless, some occurred. In 985/1577 he reduced the weight of gold coins to 800 and of silver ones to 80 dinars, and new coins (*zar-e jadid*) were struck in the mint.[11] This contradicts Album's finding that under Esma`il II the silver standard was 1 tuman = 2,400 nokhud.[12] The shah also ordered a change in the legend on the coinage. Existing coins had the Shi`i credo (*shahada*) on one side, exposing them to the impure touch of unbelievers. He thus ordered the following text to be included on the coins:

ز مشرق تا به مغرب گر امام است
علی و آل او ما را تمام است

Though there be emams from east to west
`Ali and his family are sufficient for us

On the other side of the coins the shah's name was struck.[13] The reason for this change may have been to allay suspicions that Esma`il II had abandoned the Shi`i faith for Sunni Islam.[14] After his death the Shi`ite *shahada* was struck again on the reverse of the coins. This remained so until the end of Safavid reign.

The sorry state of finances, which had already become evident under Tahmasb I, worsened under his son Mohammad Khodabandeh (1577–88), who succeeded his brother Tahmasb II after the latter's assassination in 1577. The fact that immediately after the accession to the throne Mohammad Khodabandeh emptied his treasury to buy the loyalty of the Qezelbash military caste did not help matters much either. At the same time Mohammad Khodabandeh restored the weight of gold coins to 1000 and silver coins to 100 dinar,[15] and maintained a silver standard of 1 tuman = 2,400 nokhud. As of that time the silver coinage followed the same uniform sequential types throughout Iran, except in Mazandaran until the early

10 Qomi, *Kholasat al-tavarikh*, 1:610–11; 2:1002.
11 Ibid., 2:667.
12 Album, *Checklist*, 278.
13 Astarabadi, *Az Sheykh Safi*, 100; Natanzi, *Naqavat*, 40 (deh dang).
14 Monshi, *`Alamara-ye `Abbasi*, 1:217. Esma`il II was known for his pro-Sunni policies, as expressed, among other things, in his ban on the public denunciation of Sunnis in Iran.
15 Qomi, *Kholasat al-tavarikh*, 2:667.

1600s and Khuzestan until 1108/1697.[16] This means that henceforth the Safavid Shahs wielded full monetary control throughout their entire realm, a situation that had not fully existed prior to that time.

The shah's liberality with his treasury came at a cost. In 990/1582, when Mohammad Khodabandeh was preparing for a campaign to regain Khorasan, the only period of significant countermarking in Safavid coinage occurred. The surviving coins are our only witness; neither foreign accounts nor Persian-language sources mention this countermarking episode. Countermarking is a way, among other things, of revaluating an issue of coins or of limiting their use to a specific area with the intention to generate additional revenue. The countermark normally consisted of the phrase *`adl-e shahi* followed by the name of the mint, sometimes with the date. Examples are known from Khodabandeh's entire reign and from at least twenty mints. Otherwise few Safavid countermarks are known, with the exception of widespread countermarking under the early reign of Esma`il I of Aq-Qoyunlu, Timurid and Mamluk coins. Countermarks therefore seems to have been rare and generally a local phenomenon, limited to one or a few mints only.[17]

Under Mohammad Khodabandeh the designation *khodabandeh* or *mohammadi* for the 100 dinar or two shahi coin was introduced. It was also and better known as *mahmudi* as Europeans mistakenly called this coin. In 1640, VOC agent Geleynssen de Jongh claimed that 7 mahmudis was 'like the ryksdaalder here among the Europeans'[18] In Khuzestan, which had as many as six mints, these *mahmudi*s were struck in preference to *`abbasi*s, with designs different from those on coins from other regions from 996/1588 until l 1092/1681. Known as Hoveyzeh mahmudis among Europeans, these were used as trade coin in the Persian Gulf region.[19] The two-*shahi* coin of 100 dinars was known as *nim `abbasi* (half *`abbasi*), or in Turkish *yarim `abbasi*, and also as *sad dinar*, *sannar* and *sadi*, or in Turkish *yuz altun*. This name became soon obsolete and the coin became known as mohammadi, a term still used in Shiraz and surrounding area to refer to the two-shahi copper coin in the beginning of the twentieth century.[20]

16 Album, *Checklist*, 278.

17 Biddulph, 'Countermarked Coins'; Album, *Checklist*, 275.

18 *NA*, Coll. Gel. de Jongh, 147, unfol.

19 Olearius, *Vermehrte newe Beschreibung*, 294; Hinz, 'Value of the Toman', 92; Matthee, 'Mint Consolidation'; and Idem, 'Safavid Mint of Huwayzah'.

20 Olearius, *Vermehrte newe Beschreibung*, 560; Rabino, *Coins, Medals, and Seals*, 15.

Table 4.1: Official silver standard under the Safavid shahs (1501–1722)

	Coin types	Coin weights	Silver standard periods (hejri dates)	Tuman–Nokhud ratios
Esma`il I				
1st silver national standard	4, 2, 1, ½ shahi	37.60, 18.80, 9.40, 4.70 g	907–23	1 tuman = 9,600 nokhud
2nd western silver standard	1, ½, ¼ shahi	7.88, 3.94, 1.97 g	924–30	1 tuman = 8,100 nokhud
2nd eastern silver standard	1, ½, ¼ shahi	10.16, 5.08, 2.54 g	924–27	1 tuman = 10,440 nokhud
3rd eastern silver standard	½ shahi	4.67 g	927–28	1 tuman = 9,600 nokhud
4th eastern silver standard	1 shahi	7.88 g	928–30	1 tuman = 8,100 nokhud
Tahmasp I				
1st western silver standard	1, ½, ¼, ⅒ shahi	7.88, 3.94, 1.97, 0.79 g	930–37	1 tuman = 8,100 nokhud
2nd western silver standard	1, ½ shahi; 10 dinars	6.22, 3.11, 1.24 g	937–47	1 tuman = 6,400 nokhud
3rd western silver standard	1, ½ shahi	5.25, 2.62 g	948–53	1 tuman = 5,400 nokhud
4th western silver standard	1, ½ shahi	4.67, 2.33 g	954–59	1 tuman = 4,800 nokhud
5th western silver standard	4, 2,1 bisti; 10 dinar	4.67, 2.33, 1.17, 0.58 g	960–71 or later	1 tuman = 3,000 nokhud
6th western silver standard	2, 1, ½ shahi	4.67, 2.33, 1.17 g	975–84	1 tuman = 2,400 nokhud
1st eastern silver standard	1, ½ shahi	7.88, 3.94 g	930–31	1 tuman = 8,100 nokhud
2nd eastern silver standard	1, ½, ¼ shahi	5.54, 2.77, 1.38 g	932–54	1 tuman = 5,700 nokhud
3rd eastern silver standard	1 shahi	4.67 g	955–59	1 tuman = 4,800 nokhud
4th eastern silver standard	1 shahi; 1 bisti	2.92, 1.17 g	960–71 or later	1 tuman = 3,000 nokhud

Table 4.1 (continued)

Esma`il II				
	1 shahi	2.30 g	984–85	1 tuman = 2,400 nokhud
Khodabandeh				
	2, 1 shahi	4.61, 2.30 g	986–95	1 tuman = 2,400 nokhud
`Abbas I				
1st silver standard	4, 2, 1 shahi	9.22, 4.61, 2.30 g	996–1004	1 tuman = 2,400 nokhud
2nd silver standard	4, 2, 1, ½ shahi	7.68, 3.84, 1.92; 0.96 g	1005–38	1 tuman = 2,000 nokhud
Safi I				
	4, 2, 1 shahi	7.68, 3.84, 1.92 g	1038–52	1 tuman = 2,000 nokhud
`Abbas II				
1st silver standard	4, 2, 1 shahi	7.68, 3.84, 1.92 g	1052–54	1 tuman = 2,000 nokhud
2nd silver standard	20, 5, 4, 2, 1 shahi	36.96, 9.24, 7.39, 3.69, 1.84 g	1054–77	1 tuman = 1,925 nokhud
Safi II				
	20, 4, 2, 1 shahi	36.95 g, n.a.	1077–79	1 tuman = 1,925 nokhud
Soleyman				
	20, 10, 4, 2 shahi	36.90, 18.45, 7.39, 3.69 g	1079–1105	1 tuman = 1,925 nokhud
Soltan Hoseyn				
1st silver standard	4, 2, 1 shahi	7.39, 3.69, 1.84 g	1105–23	1 tuman = 1,925 nokhud
2nd silver standard	10, 5, 4, 2, 1 shahi	17.29, 8.64, 6.91, 3.45, 1.73 g	1123–29	1 tuman = 1,800 nokhud
3rd silver standard	4, 2, 1 shahi	5.34, 2.68, 1.34 g	1129–35	1 tuman = 1,400 nokhud
4th silver standard	1 `abbasi	4.62 g (Isfahan only)	1134	1 tuman = 1,200 nokhud

Source: Album, *Checklist*, 275–82, Safavid section.
Note: 1 `abassi = 4 shahi; or, said another way, 20 shahi = 5 `abbasi.

Shah `Abbas I introduced the `abbasi, a silver coin, which formally was called *shahi-ye `abbasi.*[21] Until 999/1591, the shah continued to strike coins on the one mesqal standard. Two-mesqal coins of 9.19 and 9.10 g are extant from 996/1587, the first year of his reign, and of 4.57 g from 999/1591.[22] Shah `Abbas's reform of 999–1003 involved the change from a one-mesqal standard to an `abbasi of 7.80 g or 1²/₃ mesqal.[23] This reform is only known from the coins that survive; no textual references to it have come to us. While Radzhabli and Rabino suggest that the reform took place in 1003/1595, Pakhomov puts the date a year later, in 1004/1596.[24] Radzhabli, who places the reform in the context of heightened economic activity causing an increase in the circulation of money which in turn necessitated a uniform solid currency, argues for 1003 as the most likely year because in that year the Safavids took all of Khorasan from the Uzbegs. The consolidation of the shah's power over Gilan and Mazandaran, the rich silk-producing provinces that had been incorporated into his realm in 1592, clearly played a facilitating role as well in this step. Regardless of the precise date, the accomplishment strengthened the shah's power base, creating the preconditions for a currency reform (as it did for a host of other reforms).[25] `Abbas's monetary reform established a firm consistency in weight and the principle of a single type. Also new was that freshly minted money received wide distribution and circulation. The principles of this reform endured until the end of the Safavid period.[26]

A three-fold motive underpinned the shah's establishment of a uniform currency. The first was the centralization of the currency as part of an overall centralizing policy. The second was a policy designed to increase the circulation of coinage and thus to facilitate commerce. The third one involved taxation. The old mohammadi equaled 100 dinars. The new `abbasi equaled 1²/₃ mesqal or 167 dinars, but counted as 200 dinars. Hence the state derived a 33-dinar profit from minting these new `abbasis.[27] Beyond that, the new `abbasis were supposed to weigh 7.80 g but in practice did not exceed 7.62 g.[28] Standardization seems to have been successful in that it made the `abbasi current throughout the Safavid realm.

Further change took place in and after 1616, a year of renewed fighting with the Ottomans. This led to a presumed loss of weight for the `abbasi,

21 Monshi, *`Alamara-ye `Abbasi*, 2: 709, 797. There also was a *shahi-ye `eraqi*, i.e., the standard shahi. Ibid., 2:721, 859.

22 Radzhabli, 'Iz istorii monetnogo dela', 47.

23 Ibid.

24 Pakhomov, *Monety Gruzii*, 217.

25 Radzhabli, 'Iz istorii monetnogo dela', 46–47.

26 Ibid., 52.

27 Ibid., 50–51.

28 Ibid., 48–49.

which dipped as low as or even below 7.50 g.[29] Another change that occurred in this period, though not necessarily in the same context, concerns the epigraphy of the Iranian coinage. After 1609/1618 the epigraphy changes from the cursive *nasta`liq* to a mixture of nasta`liq and the more angular *naskh* script. The quality of the legend suffers as well, and a tendency to a bold epigraphy becomes apparent. Russian numismatists have tended to see in the bold and allegedly less refined epigraphy of Safavid coins beginning in the second half of Shah `Abbas I's reign an expression of the economic problems which supposedly began to plague the Safavid state in this period. Markov more specifically surmised that this was related to a loss of craftsmanship due to the disappearance of expert engravers.[30] Radzhabli, however, reminds us that the late reign of Shah `Abbas I witnessed a return of high-quality engravings, so that the reasons must lie elsewhere. He suggests a shortage of silver, which in turn may have been related to the outbreak of the Ottoman–Safavid war of 1616. This would have acted as a double-edged sword, combining a need of silver to pay for the military and a lack of silver coming in due to hostilities.[31] A need for more rapid access to ready cash may, inter alia, also explain why in 1619 Shah `Abbas established a raw silk export monopoly.

The tendency toward a bold epigraphy continued under Shah Safi I. The coinage of that ruler is as yet little known or understood, mostly because no currency reforms were enacted during his reign. Extant specimens of coins struck under him are also relatively rare, though not as rare as is sometimes assumed. A low production, if that is the case, points to the continuation of economic problems, as does the contraction of mints during his reign, more about which later.

Money Matters under Shah `Abbas II

There is clear evidence that the early reign of Shah `Abbas II saw further currency problems. External factors played a role in these. During the reign of Shah `Abbas II, the Ottoman-Venetian wars meant that little money was carried between Aleppo and Baghdad to Isfahan. But the underlying causes also have to do with measures and developments that go back to the rule of Shah `Abbas I, who intensified the system of tax farming that over time showed itself to be extremely destructive to the productivity of the

29 Ibid., 55; Rabino, *Coins, Medals, and Seals*, 34; and Kuteliia, *Gruziia e sefevidskii Iran*, 28.

30 Markov, *Inventarniy catalog'*, 712.

31 Radzhabli, 'Iz istorii monetnogo dela', 54.

land.[32] After Shah `Abbas I's reign, territorial conquest also came to an end. Assuming that tax revenue from conquered territory outweighs the military expenditure required for acquiring and subsequently controlling it, this meant that tax revenue was no longer growing. With the loss of Qandahar in 1637 and the loss of Baghdad a year later, to the Ottomans and Mughals respectively, the Safavids gave up two important commercial transit centers and thus a great deal of revenue in taxation and commercial wealth.

Some attempts at change were made in this period. The need for cash money for the payment of troops presumably prompted Shah `Abbas II in 1054/1644 to engage in a reform whereby the standard of the tuman was reduced from 2,000 to 1,925 nokhud.[33] Various sources confirm this reduction, even if they differ in their information on the extent to which the `abbasi was reduced in weight. Both the Dutch and The English in 1644 refer to lighter coins.[34] A contemporary English source claimed that whereas the old `abbasis had weighed '10 grains' – presumably not referring to the usual English grain, since 10 of those would be 0.65 g whereas the old `abbasi was at least 7.5 g – the reduction amounted to 10 per cent, so that new ones weighed only 9 g.[35] In 1645 the Dutch report that 'the newly coined abbasies equal 2 mamoedies, but now they circulate at 5 sjahies or 3½ mamoedies' worth in Isfahan and Shiraz'.[36] This suggests that it was a four shahi coin that soon after its issuance depreciated in value, requiring a monetary adjustment later, as happened in fact late in Shah `Abbas II's reign. Three years later the Dutch reported that, the 'new' `abbasis were 5 per cent lighter than the old ones, which after all is approximately what a reduction from 2,000 nokhuds to 1,925 would entail.[37] This latter figure closely matches Stephen Album's estimate of this development.[38]

The realization that the monetary situation required attention evidently played a role in the appointment of Mohammad Beg as grand vizier in 1064/1654. An erstwhile assayer of the mint, this son of the court's chief tailor had further risen to the position of *nazer-e boyutat* (overseer of the

32 Persian-language as well as European sources attest to this. The author of the *Tarikh-e jahanara-ye `Abbasi* insists that tax income tended to decrease once state land was converted to crown land. See Vahid Qazvini, *Tarikh-e jahanara-ye `Abbasi*, 748. Of the European observers, Chardin is the most emphatic in his claim that crown land led to a decrease in revenue. See Chardin, *Voyages*, 5:387ff., 428, 551–53. In general, see Floor, *Fiscal History*, 108–14, 133–42, 223–27; and Matthee, *Persia in Crisis*, 148ff.

33 Album, *Checklist*, 279–80.

34 *NA*, VOC 1146, Gamron to Batavia, 24 May 1644, fol. 928v; and VOC 1185, Gamron to Batavia, 18 May 1651, fol. 546.

35 Foster (ed.), *English Factories in India, 1646-1650*, 123.

36 *NA*, Coll. Gel. de Jongh, 147, unfol. (Annex 3).

37 *NA*, VOC 1170, Gamron to Batavia, 15 May 1648, fol. 738.

38 See Album, 'Iranian Silver Denominational Names', 20.

royal workshops) in 1051/1651. The monetary experience gained during his years as assayer of the mint clearly played a role in his subsequent appointment as grand vizier, for part of his mandate was the reorganization of the country's finances. To this end Mohammad Beg took several measures. One of these was the exploration of mining silver and copper deposits in the country. These efforts came to nought, however, for the exploitation of the mines proved unprofitable.[39] Mohammad Beg set out to increase the revenue of the shah by other means as well. Chardin stated that one of his ideas was to sell off the numerous palaces that had fallen to the shah through confiscation. As these mansions found no buyers, this plan came to nothing, however.[40]

Financial problems must have accounted for the subsequent introduction of a new coin as well. Some confusion exists as to the precise date of the entry of these so-called *panj shahis*, which weighed 9.331 g and equaled 250 dinars, as opposed to the regular `abbasis which weighed 7.776 g and equaled four shahis or 200 dinars. The old ones became known as small `abbasis.[41] We can disregard the observations of Radzhabli, who erroneously attributes the introduction of the new coin to the last years of the reign of Shah `Abbas I. Kuteliia, on the other hand, who claims that panj shahis were around from the beginning of Shah `Abbas II's reign in 1642, may have been confused by that fact that the four shahi coin circulated as if being a panj shahis coin (see above). The contemporary Armenian, Zak`aria of Agulis, mentions 1662 as the year when 'Shah `Abbas [II] issued an order throughout his kingdom that all mints had to strike new `abbasi coins weighing two mishkal [of silver], which would be worth five shahis. The old `abbasis were worth four shahis.'[42] Kuteliia also reports that the mint of Tiflis struck panj-shahis from the end of the reign in Georgia of Rostam (1658) and that from that moment until the end of Shah `Abbas II's reign, the mint in fact produced nothing but panj-shahis.[43] This later date also squares with the information provided by Zak`ari of Agulis, who said of the mint of Yerevan that in 1667 – following the accession of Shah Soleyman – Agha Vali, the new mintmaster, received an order from the shah to 'strike `abbasis worth four shahis', as a result of which the panj shahis went out of circulation.[44]

39 See Tavernier, *Les six voyages*, 1:617–20.

40 Chardin, *Voyages*, 7:137. For a more detailed analysis of Mohammad Beg's economic measures and his overall career, see Matthee, 'Career of Mohammad Beg'.

41 Sparr de Homberg; quoted in Hinz, 'Value of the Toman', 94. For the 'small' and 'large' `abbasis, see also Avery et al., '`Abbasi', 86 and Floor, '`Abbasi'.

42 Zak`aria of Agulis, *Journal*, 66.

43 Kuteliia, *Gruziia e sefevidskii Iran*, 36.

44 Zak`aria of Agulis, *Journal*, 78.

Regardless of the exact timing involved, both the adjustment of 1644 and the introduction of the panj-shahi were in all likelihood fiscal measures. The weight of the panj shahi should have been 9.37 g = 7.50 g + 1.87 g. In reality the average weight of these new coins is 9.17 g. In light of this, Radzhabli's suggestion that that revenue enhancement was the chief motivation of the state sounds plausible indeed.

Table 4.2: Names and values in imaginary dinars assigned to the various silver coins by H.L. Rabino/Album

Shah	Year	---------- Name of coin struck ----------					
		tuman	`abbasi	mahmudi	shahi	nim-shahi	bisti
		---------- Value in dinars ----------					
		10,000	200	100	50	25	20
		---------- Weight in grams ----------					
Esma`il	1502–11	2,518		18.662	9.331	4.665	
	1516–21	1,050		10.197	5.249		
Tahmasb	1524–28	778		7.776	3.888		1.555
	1526–38	622		6.221	3.11		0.622
	1534–35	544		5.443			
	1528–74	467		4.665			
Esma`il II	1576–77	467		4.665			
Khodabandeh	1578–81	467		4.665	2.333		
`Abbas I	1584–1629						
A.		4,677	9.331	4.665			
B.		389	7.776	3.888	1.994	0.972	

Table 4.3: Weights of silver coins

Shah	---------- **Name of coin** ----------									
	tuman	do hazar	yek hazar	chahar `abbasi	pansad dinar	do `abbasi	`abbasi	mahmudi	shahi	bisti
	---------- **Value in dinars** ----------									
	10,000	2,000	1,000	800	500	400	200	100	50	20
	---------- **Weight in grams** ----------									
`Abbas I	467							4.665	2.333	
	467						9.331	4.665		
	389						7.776	3.888	1.994	
Safi I	389						7.776	3.888	1.994	
`Abbas II	467						9.331	4.655	2.333	
1642–53	389						7.776	3.888	1.994	0.778
1653–54	369		36.935		18.468		7.387	3.694	1.847	0.739
Soleyman	369		36.935		18.468		7.387	3.694	1.847	0.739
Soltan Hoseyn	369		36.935		18.468		7.387	3.694	1.847	0.739
1706–07	272	54.431					5.443	2.771		
1717–22	272		27.216							
1694–1721	233			18.662		9.331	4.665			
Tahmasb	272		27.216		13.608		5.443	2.721		

Table 4.4: Values and weights in grams of gold coins

Shah	ashrafi of 18 nokhud			ashrafi of 24 nokhud			`abbasi		
	1	0.5	0.25	1	0.5	0.25	1	0.5	0.25
Esma`il	3.499		0.875	4.666	2.333	1.166			
Tahmasb				4.666	2.333	1.166			
Esma`il II				4.666					
Khodabandeh				4.666	2.333				
`Abbas I					2.333	1.166	9.331		
							7.776	3.888	1.944

Despite its apparent stability and relative prosperity, the reign of Shah `Abbas II's reign was a period of serious monetary problems. Aside from the example given above, these show up in the tampering with the precious metal content of the currency that appears to have gone on in this period. The outward evidence, surviving coins issuing from hoards, points to a perceived purity of extant coins and thus has led some to argue that Safavid coins remained of sound alloy; however, it could be argued that those setting aside (hoarding) coins were likely to select the best coins.

We also have powerful textual evidence for this aspect of economic problems in this period. The *Tazkereh-ye Nasrabadi*, for instance, suggests the existence and circulation of large amounts of compromised silver money in 1064/1653–54, a year of harsh wintry weather.[45] Shah `Abbas II's court poet, Sa`eb of Tabriz, similarly captured the deplorable state of the currency succinctly when he said:

سکه سان رویی از آهن به کف آور صائب
کاین متا عی است که امروز به زر نز دیک است

Sa`eb, get yourself some iron object looking like a coin
because it's merchandise today that's close to gold[46]

Such references do not necessarily implicate the government in the form of the central mint as having struck and disseminated debased coins.

45 Nasrabadi, *Tazkereh-ye Nasrabadi*, 421.
46 This poem is found in Afshar, 'Enqelab-e deram', 273. For more information on this, see Matthee, *Persia in Crisis*, 90–92

They do point up the circulation of compromised currency, however, as well as the profound lack of trust in the system exemplified by the practice of shunning silver and dealing in gold on the part of those who could afford it.

More substantial evidence for the problems at the time is found in the contraction of a large number of mints. In the sixteenth century, Iran's mints numbered approximately seventy. Of these, no more than forty were operational at any given time, and many were ephemeral. The heaviest concentration is found. in the northwest, in the border area with the Ottoman Empire and Russia, through which most precious metal entered Safavid territory, and throughout the north and northeast as far as Khorasan. Toward the later part of the sixteenth century a large number of mints opened in Mazandaran and Gilan, due to the autonomy of these regions or at least their special status, having to do with the lucrative and fully monetized silk cultivation and trade.[47]

In the course of Shah `Abbas I's reign, the number of Safavid mints decreased to some forty, to drop to twenty-six under Shah Safi. The reasons for this contraction are complex, and we can only guess at their interplay. Conquest, incorporation and the reduced autonomy of provincial governors certainly had a role in this consolidation. The reduction in the number of mints in Khorasan and especially that of the many mints in the Caspian region came in the wake of Shah `Abbas's pacification of those regions. But a diminished inflow of bullion and specie also resulted from conditions in the Ottoman Empire, such as the outbreak of the Ottoman-Venetian war of 1570–73 and rebellions in Anatolia in the same period.[48] Shah Tahmasb did not pay his troops during the last 14 years of his reign, and no Safavid coinage exists for its last three years, the period 981–84/1573–76.[49] Problems continued after his death, when a new round of war erupted between the Safavids and the Ottomans that would last until 1590. The monetary difficulties the Ottomans experienced in the last quarter of the sixteenth century caused them to debase their coinage in 992 or 993/1584 or 1585, as well as to try and limit the outflow of silver to Iran.[50] Following the debasement of 992–93/1584–85 all Ottoman mints except for those at Istanbul and Cairo temporarily closed, and over time the number or working mints in Ottoman territory decreased from forty to some thirty

47 For this, see Matthee, *Persia in Crisis*, 83–85.

48 Matthee, *Politics of Trade*, 21.

49 For Tahmasb's inability to pay his troops, see Rumlu, *Ahsan al-tavarikh*, 635.

50 Pamuk, *Monetary History*, 135–39.

between the 1590s and the 1620s.[51] A similar reduction in minting activities is observable in India at the same period.

The consolidation of the Safavid mints continued under Shah `Abbas I's successors. By the time Shah `Abbas II came to the throne in 1642 their number had dropped to nineteen. During the last decade of his reign, only ten of those were still in operation.[52] But a continuing retrenchment coincided with relocation. While a number of mints in the northwest closed, new ones opened up in the southwest, in Khuzestan, called `Arabistan in the Safavid period. The origins of this intensified minting activity in `Arabistan remain obscure. A surge in regional economic activity, spurred on by increased trade and catalyzed by the entry of the European maritime companies in the Persian Gulf, may have been partly responsible. The mint of Hoveyzeh is the most noteworthy of these regional mints. Hoveyzeh mahmudis were struck in great quantities, especially during the reign of Shah Soleyman, and in the later Safavid period the Hoveyzeh mahmudi became the main currency of all of southern Iran and the Persian Gulf basin.

This very same period was also the time when the usual European complaint about a scarcity of silver money turned into a chronic jeremiad.[53] Some of the causes of this drying up of outside sources were external in nature. Warfare in Europe as well as rumors of an imminent war between Iran and the Ottomans diminished the volume of silver imports from the west. In the same period a number of spectacular caravan robberies and an overall deterioration in the country's political and economic situation made merchants reluctant to come to Iran through the Ottoman Empire.[54] Other factors include a Russian attempt to prevent bullion exports in the form of a decree, issued in 1667, that prohibited Iranian and other eastern traders from changing their money into ducats and rix-dollars for export purposes.[55] A year later Japan instituted a ban on silver exports. Silver from Japan had been a major source of cash for the VOC, which financed much of its Asian operations in this manner. This ban thus exacerbated

51 Şahillioğlu, 'Role of International Monetary and Metal Movements', 285; Pamuk, *Monetary History*, 135–39.

52 See Matthee, 'Mint Consolidation'. According to Chelebi, *Travels in Iran*, 44, who only visited northwestern Iran, under `Abbas II coins were struck at seven places: Ardabil, Hamadan, Baghdad, Isfahan, Tiflis, Nehavand and Tabriz.

53 See, for example, *NA*, VOC 1285, Gamron to Heren XVII, 6 May 1673, fol. 385r.

54 See *NA*, VOC 1291, Gamron to Heren XVII, 21 Mar. 1674, fol. 558r; and VOC 1304, Gamron to Batavia, 24 May 1674, fol. 437; ibid., Gamron to Batavia, 4 Sept. 1674, fol. 519v.; VOC 1343, Narrative of condition of trade in Persia, 13 Feb. 1680, fol. 600.

55 Attman, *Russian and Polish Markets*, 192.

the silver supply problem in Asia. Silver became higher valued in India as of mid 1670s, in part as a result of Japanese policy and in part following the expansion of the silver-based Mughal state towards the southern part of the subcontinent, which was traditionally gold-based.[56]

Internally, the principal factors contributing to the scarcity have to do with the policy the Safavid state adopted to combat the shortfall in the external supply of precious metal and the economic crisis that became acutely visible with the accession of Shah Soleyman in 1666 (and that was in part caused by the same shortfall). This included – aside from government hoarding, which is said to have intensified under the parsimonious Soleyman[57] – government decrees that imposed a 5 per cent fee on the export of all silver and that banned the export of gold ducats.[58] Paradoxically, these measures lessened the attractiveness of bringing silver into the country. Merchants coming from the Ottoman Empire now took much of their bullion and specie to freewheeling Basra, which presumably accounted in part for the increased activity of the nearby Hoveyzeh mint. Gold, which merchants found easier to conceal from the tax and toll inspectors because of its smaller volume, became more expensive. Attempts to channel greater amounts of the silver imported into the country to the mints had a similar counterproductive effect, for this policy merely served as another deterrent for Armenian merchants to bring silver into the country.[59]

All this seriously affected Iran's monetary system. The influx of silver into Iran from the northwest decreased. This, in addition to the export bans issued by the Safavids, slowed the transshipment to India as well, leading to a reduced mint output in Mughal territory.[60] Yet substantial amounts continued to be siphoned off to the subcontinent, via subterfuge and alternative channels, so that Iran suffered an acute silver famine.

This famine continued for the next fifteen years, a period during which few Safavid coins were minted. Least affected in Iran were, again, the mints of the northwest. Most continued to operate, albeit in reduced manner, because whatever quantity of silver continued to enter

56 See IOR, E/3/374258, Swally to Company, 22 Jan. 1677; Arasaratnam, *Merchants, Companies and Commerce*, 195.

57 *NA*, VOC 143, Narrative of conditions of trade in Persia, 13 Feb. 1680, fol. 600; and Kaempfer, *Am Hofe*, 124. Chardin claimed that Shah Soleyman spent one-twentieth of what he received in income and hoarded the rest in his treasury. See Chardin, *Voyages*, 5:414.

58 *NA*, VOC 1251, Gamron to Heren XVII, 6 Apr. 1666, fol. 1330.

59 Sanson, *Estat de Perse*, 12–13. For the overall policy, see Matthee, *Persia in Crisis*, ch. 5.

60 Moosvi, 'Silver Influx', 40, 41, 45, 53

the country still came through the Ottoman Empire.[61] In Iran, the total number of mints had decreased to fifteen by the time Shah Soleyman came to power.

Monetary Matters under Shah Soleyman

Although economic problems clearly preceded the reign of Shah Soleyman, his tenure saw a further intensification of the malaise. The period surrounding his accession in 1666 witnessed a particularly high incidence of bad harvests exacerbated by hoarding – and the result, famine followed by epidemics. Besides Isfahan, large parts of the Persian Gulf coast and possibly other regions of the country were afflicted by it.[62] The years that followed brought little relief. Thus, the winter of 1672 brought bitter cold and great snowfall to central Iran. Prices in Isfahan rose steeply, with bread going up to 6 shahis per man.[63] European travelers and residents are unanimous in suggesting that the Safavid coinage worsened between the 1660s and the 1680s. Chardin, whose travels to Iran span the first decade of Soleyman's rule, noted the difference for the worse between his first visit in the 1660s and his second in 1675. In 1677, the year he left Iran, he insists, the country's wealth seemed diminished by half and money itself had become altered to the point where one no longer saw good coins.[64] Thévenot and Tavernier noted the soundness of Iranian money in the 1660s.[65] A decade later the Safavid coinage had become so bad that sending it to India would result in a loss and sending to Isfahan meant losing five months' worth of interest. EIC Agent Petit in 1678 claimed that the shahi was 'an imaginary coin' and asked permission to keep the

61 *NA*, VOC 1304, Gamron to Batavia, 4 Sept. 1674, fol. 519v; VOC 1294, Gamron to Heren XVII, 5 Oct. 1674, fol. 32v.

62 See Chardin, *Voyages*, 9:571, 10:2–4; *NA*, VOC 1266, Surat to Heren XVII, 8 Nov. 1668, fols. 155, 941.

63 The harsh winter is mentioned in the margin of a drawing by Mo`in Mosavver in the collection of the Boston Museum of Fine Arts. The drawing and the translation of the marginal text are reproduced in Ettinghausen, 'Stylistic Tendencies'. According to this source, snow fell eighteen times in Isfahan between mid Sha`ban and 20 Shavval 1082, January to February 1672. The harsh weather in this period is confirmed in an EIC report from Isfahan, which mentioned great quantities of snow and many deaths between Isfahan and Shiraz. See IOR, G/36/106, Isfahan to Gombroon, 27 Jan. 1672, fol. 90.

64 Chardin, *Voyages*, 291–92.

65 Thévenot, *Relation*, vol. 2, *Suite du voyage de Levant*, 169; Tavernier, *Les six voyages*, 1:133–34. This argument is found, *inter alia*, in Rabino di Borgomale, *Coins, Medals, and Seals*, 4.

books in `abbasis at a 5 for 3 rupees.[66] Two years later the English were, in their own words, not 'able to procure 5 tomands in abasses in the whole Towne [Isfahan]'.[67] In 1672, a ban on the export of gold had been declared; however, gold, a high-value commodity, could more easily be transported and hidden than silver and therefore suffered less from the controls that were instituted.[68] With Ottoman caravans bringing more gold and less silver, Iran's money supply suffered, because, in contrast to silver, little of the gold was available for trading transactions: much of the gold that arrived in the country was either hoarded by its owners, kept in the royal treasury or exported to India.[69] A much quoted source on the bad state of affairs that had developed less than two decades later is Kaempfer, who in 1684 testified to the bad quality of currency in Isfahan, recounting how in February of that year Shah Soleyman inspected the funds kept for the maintenance of foreign envoys and found that out of 30,000 tumans only 300, or 1 per cent, were in good order.[70]

As said, the accession of Shah Soleyman occurred at an inauspicious time for Iran with regard to the international context. Russian and Japanese currency export bans combined with policies adopted in face of a continuing fiscal crisis made his reign one in which imports of bullion lagged and exports of specie soared. A decline, first in the quantity of precious metal available, followed by a decrease in the quality of minted coins, was the result. The number of mints also continued to decrease. For the period from 1075/1665 to 1092/1682 most of the centrally located mints ceased operation – only Qazvin and Isfahan are known to have produced coins in this period – and of the mints in the border areas, only the ones in Azerbaijan and Armenia continued their activities. The period from 1092/1682 to 1096/1685 saw a worsening of the situation and is marked by a virtual absence of all Safavid coins, with the exception of some activity at the mints of Tabriz and Tiflis, a rare representation piece struck at Isfahan and, presumably, a continuing production at Hoveyzeh.[71]

This development can be charted and demonstrated in some detail through the monetary policy of the period, beginning with the measures

66 IOR, G36/107, Gombroon to Surat, 24 Apr. 1678, fols. 85–86. That the shahi was 'but an imaginary coin' is gainsaid in IOR, E/3/37, Surat to Persia, 19 Oct. 1678, fol. 145: 'What you affirm about shahee is false; it being a reall coine and only the toman, lerree, bistee imaginary.'

67 Ferrier, 'British-Persian Relations', 289.

68 *NA*, VOC 1349, Gamron to Batavia, 25 Nov. 1679, fol. 1712r.

69 *NA*, VOC 1343, Resolution about the state of trade, 13 Feb. 1680, fol. 600r.

70 Kaempfer, *Am Hofe*, 71–72.

71 See Album, 'Iranian Silver Denominational Names', 20.

designed to enhance revenue taken by Sheykh `Ali Khan. Already in 1670, at the inception of his tenure as grand vizier, currency concerns were part of his energetic drive to harness resources for the shah's coffers. Kaempfer implicated Sheykh `Ali Khan as the official who was behind the decision to defray an Uzbeg envoy with bad money. It was the chief minister, he claimed, who failed to see why the envoy should be paid in good money from the state treasury. After consultation with the shah, it was secretly decided to pay him his 3,000 tumans in coins that were especially minted for the occasion and which contained only one-fourth of the silver of regular coins. The money received by the Uzbeg envoy eventually was distributed to merchants and thus found its way into the system, where it contributed to the deterioration of the currency.[72]

The effect of this one example is probably greatly exaggerated by the author – who was not in Iran at the time – and as an isolated example of deliberate policy it says more about the craftiness of Safavid authorities in dealing with gullible foreign envoys than about a deterioration of the currency. Nevertheless, in the late 1670s it was becoming abundantly clear that the deterioration of Safavid currency was not an isolated or passing phenomenon. Silver `abbasis became progressively less available; and especially those minted in Tabriz, by far everyone's favorite, were hard to come by. The shah's own parsimoniousness no doubt contributed to this. Sheykh `Ali Khan's various measures resulted in a substantial increase of the shah's own assets.[73] Meanwhile, rumor had it that Soleyman's eagerness to save money was the cause of his habit of leaving high administrative positions that fell vacant through attrition unfilled for long periods of time. Chardin, referring to Soleyman's habit of hoarding much of the revenue that flowed into the treasury, claimed that the shah spent no more than one-twentieth of what he received in income.[74]

The alternative coin, the mahmudi, in turn became more abundant, but over the course of time its quality suffered considerably – that is, the proportion of silver to base metal fell. The debasement of the mahmudi in this period is likely to have been the outcome of a variety of factors. One involved the relationship with a scarce `abbasi and lay in the opportunities the decentralized monetary system of Safavid Iran in times of scarcity offered for speculation and profit for those engaged in minting coin. Silver `abbasis became virtually impossible to obtain as a result of the general

72 Kaempfer, *Am Hofe*, 71–72.

73 *NA*, VOC 1379, Report Casembroot to Heren XVII, 25 Nov. 1682, fol. 2734. For details of Sheykh `Ali Khan's measures, see Matthee, *Persia in Crisis*, 64–65.

74 Chardin, *Voyages*, 5:414. See also Kaempfer, *Am Hofe*, 124.

silver scarcity in the late 1670s. The scant bullion supply from Turkey was one reason for this shortage. Another one was said to be the activity of the minters of Dowraq and Hoveyzeh in `Arabistan, which fell under Safavid suzerainty but preserved a considerable amount of autonomy.[75] These minters bought `abbasis but at prices above their intrinsic value that went up each year. The rising costs involved – in 1679 and 1680 the minters were changing `abbasis at a premium ranging from 10 to 19 per cent – they recouped by reminting the `abbasis into adulterated mahmudis. The mahmudis they struck also had to cover the increasing sums they had to pay to the rulers of their cities for the privilege of minting and the right of export and still leave room for the handsome seignoriage profit that the Dutch claimed they made on their operation. The decline of the coins they put out was not noticeable in depreciation through loss of weight – the mint officials made sure the weight was acceptable – but instead showed itself in a reduction of the proportion of precious metal.[76]

Until the mid 1670s the adulteration of coins seems to have been largely confined to the mahmudis struck in Hoveyzeh. In subsequent years it spread to the `abbasi as well. For years, `abbasis were coveted as the alternative to the debased mahmudis. `Abbasis minted in Tabriz were especially sought after. The latter may not have had the standard of the old 'large' ones minted under Shah `Abbas II, few of which were still available at that time, but they were certainly much better in quality than the regular small `abbasis that formed the majority of the coins minted during the reign of Soleyman.[77] By the late 1670s the `abbasis struck at most mints were compromised.[78] Government officials who collected tax revenues in debased `abbasis forced mint master to buy these above their intrinsic value. To recoup their losses, the mint masters melted the substandard `abbasis and reminted them into mahmudis of lower quality. The shah, the local governor and other magnates all turned a blind eye to this practice because they were collecting money – apparently in increasing amounts – from the mint masters. The minters continued to make a profit, too. In 1679–80, on reminting `abbasis they

75 The right of the ruler of Hoveyzeh to mint coins is indicated in Kasravi, *Tarikh-e pansad saleh-ye Khuzestan*, 87. For the mint of Hoveyzeh in the Safavid period, see Matthee, 'Safavid Mint of Huwayza'.

76 *NA*, VOC 1332, Gamron to Batavia, 1 June 1679, fol. 917v; ibid., Gamron to Isfahan, 1 June 1679, fol. 921v; VOC 1349, Gamron to Batavia, 25 Nov. 1679, fol. 1712r; VOC 1343, Basra to Heren XVII, 8 Aug. 680, fol. 619r. On the worsening of the Hoveyzeh coinage in this period, see Matthee, 'Mint Consolidation'.

77 *NA*, VOC 1323, Gamron to Batavia, 12 Aug. 1677, fol. 675r.

78 *NA*, VOC 1315, Gamron to Batavia, 5 June 1677, fol. 733r.

made 10–19 per cent iin seignorage. The result was an increasingly debased coinage, although the mint officials made sure the weight was proper.[79]

`Abbasis from Tabriz generally continued to be of good value. All other `abbasis, however, were swept up in the overall decline in currency quality. Already in 1676–77 the Dutch records provide evidence that the `abbasis which were struck at most mints were becoming deficient in quality.[80] As this development occurred in a period in which coin production seems to have been minimal, some consideration must be given to the possibility that an excessive hoarding of good coins caused visibly bad coins to be disproportionate in number, thus reinforcing the notion that all coins were compromised. The large sum in mahmudis hoarded by the shahbandar of Bandar `Abbas in 1694 reportedly consisted of mostly bad coins, but it nevertheless exemplified a general tendency among the rich and powerful to hoard their wealth.[81]

It might be objected that foreign merchants, forced to accept bad money for lack of exportable commodities, were easy targets for those who wanted to get rid of cash of dubious quality. The representatives of the Dutch and English Companies might have been led to believe that the great amount of bad money they unwittingly accepted was a true reflection of the state of the Safavid currency. The counterargument to this would be that merchants were different from Uzbeg envoys. A Company representative who had just arrived in the country was evidently ignorant of the ways in which commerce was conducted in Iran, but not for long. He was quickly instructed in commercial practice and its entanglement with politics, could fall back on a store of accumulated knowledge about conducting trade in Iran, and was ultimately able to rely on a network of indigenous brokers and middlemen who worked in the service of the Companies. Among them were financial specialists who certainly would not have been fooled by Iranian attempts to foist off money of questionable weight or purity on inexperienced foreign traders. Even allowing for the effect of hoarding and some success in deceptive techniques, however, it would be difficult to dispute the force of the evidence about subsequent developments. No relief was found in the issuance by Shah Soleyman of a series of new `abbasis in 1680. Far from improving on the overall quality of currency, these new coins were found to be both deficient in weight and faulty in their silver content. According to initial VOC reports, they differed 15 to 20 per cent in value

79 *NA*, VOC 1332, Gamron to Batavia,1 June 1679, fols. 917v, 921v; VOC 1349, Gamron to Batavia, 25 Nov. 1679, fol. 1712r; VOC 1343, Gamron to Batavia, 8 Aug. 1680, fol. 619r.

80 *NA*, VOC 1315, Gamron to Batavia, 5 June 1677, fol. 733r.

81 *NA*, VOC 1559, Gamron to Batavia, 8 July 1694, fols. 858–59.

with the old `abbasis.[82] In 1682 the Dutch could even be more precise. When they melted a number of the new `abbasis, a coin they said 'used to be of pure specie', these were found to differ 20 to 24 per cent in purity from the `abbasis struck under Shah `Abbas II. The new `abbasis were also 2 to 3 per cent worse in alloy than the ones that had been struck at the beginning of Soleyman's reign.[83] It is not altogether clear what triggered the issuance of 1680, though the Dutch suspected that the adulteration of the coin was part of a deliberate policy meant to prevent cash exports.[84] This suspicion was not entirely implausible. Concerns about cash exports to India loomed large in Sheykh `Ali Khan's preoccupations with the southern trade.

The worsening of the currency in the late 1670s and early 1680s put a severe strain on commercial relations. Merchants and bazaaris became increasingly reluctant to accept mahmudis. Some, such as the VOC agents, were in a position categorically to refuse being paid in these coins. Even officials became wary of accepting regular cash money and began to demand coins with a minimal guarantee of soundness. Thus in 1677, the treasurer in Isfahan responded to the monetary decline by refusing to accept anything but `abbasis minted in Tabriz and weighing 'noh dang nim' (9½ dang) in payment for the silk delivery to the Dutch.[85] The reason, the VOC factor commented, was that 'it had been found that the `abbasis minted in other cities were not of such good alloy'.[86]

The VOC merchants rejected that official request with the argument that it would be impossible for them to pay with coin other than that which was current among the local merchants and which the Dutch received as payment for their goods. They therefore continued to pay for their silk in mahmudis of bad alloy, wondering how long they would be able to continue their refusal to accept these coins in exchange for their merchandise. Foreign merchants who were at the debit end of transactions, or local merchants who lacked the clout of a large and powerful company such as the VOC, found it much more difficult to evade lightweight or debased cash money. The English, for example, had little choice with the toll money they each year tried to extract from unwilling harbor

82 *NA*, VOC 1355, Gamron to Batavia, 5 Mar. 1681, fol. 401r; ibid., Gamron to Batavia, 26 July 1681, fol. 431v; ibid., Gamron to Heren XVII, 21 Aug. 1681, fol. 426v.

83 *NA*, VOC 1364, Memorandum Casembroot to Van Heuvel, 14 June 1682, fol. 368r.

84 *NA*, VOC 908, Batavia to Gamron, 21 Oct. 1682, unfol.

85 There was a good explanation for the demand for a 9½ dang `abbasi by the court because the May 1652 silk contract with the Dutch stated explicitly that payment had to be made in this 'noh dang nim' coin. Speelman, *Journaal*, 240 ('in abacys nodonguim').

86 *NA*, VOC 1315, Gamron to Batavia, 5 June 1677, fol. 733r. The *dang* is a Persian weight equaling 0.768 grams or 11.84 troy grains.

masters in Bandar `Abbas who no doubt tried hard to get rid of the most undesirable coins by including them in such payments. The English called the debased mahmudis in which they were paid 'impossible to chainge except wee carry them up to Spahaun which will be at a loss of 5 months interest at least'.[87] A contrary example is the shahbandar of Bandar `Abbas who in 1683 would not take the `abbasis offered to him by the Armenian merchant Hovhannes. Heading for Surat, Hovhannes was only able to pay the requested sum at a great loss. His `abbasis apparently did not exceed 7 g in silver weight, falling .30 to .40 g short of the standard.[88]

The example of Hovhannes demonstrates that merchants, particularly indigenous ones, were among those hardest hit by the deterioration of the coins. Already in 1681 they complained to Sheykh `Ali Khan about the fact that the old `abbasis and the ducats had all been taken to India by Banyan traders and that given the bad and adulterated state of the new ones they would rather choose to lead an inactive life than continue their business. For the time being, however, their request for redress went unheeded.[89]

The Monetary Crisis of 1684–85

The merchants' call for redress in the monetary situation long went unheeded even as others joined in the clamor. In 1678 the common people of Isfahan rose in revolt against inflation and famine. It was, however, not until 1683 that rumors began to circulate that the shah intended to bring new money into circulation, and it was only a year later that the highest political authorities were willing to concede what poets, merchants and urban crowds had been trying to convey for years: that drastic action was needed.[90]

What triggered the monetary 'reform' of 1684 remains unclear. Developments immediately preceding the episode illustrate the extreme fragility of a monetary system in the throes of a crisis. A precarious balance of confidence and mistrust marked commercial dealings with money, be it cash or money of account, and uncertainty about imminent developments often was enough to turn confidence into mistrust. The mere rumor of impending reform caused a worsening of the opportunity to obtain credit in 1684; in anticipation of things to come, Iranian merchants refused to

87 IOR, G/36/107, Gombroon to Surat, 24 Apr. 1678, fol. 85.
88 Khachikian, 'Ledger of the Merchant Hovhannes Joughayetsi', 178.
89 *NA*, VOC 1355, Gamron to Batavia, 26 July 1681, fol. 431v.
90 *NA*, VOC 1373, Missive van den Heuvel, 31 July 1683, fol. 901v.; also in VOC 1388, fol. 2337r-v.

engage in bills of exchange. The Dutch, who conducted much of their trade on the basis of fiduciary money, shared in this refusal and demanded cash payment for their wares, only to find that of the `abbasis they received less than one-quarter was of acceptable standard. The remaining coins were found so debased that the VOC factors decided to send them back to their trading partners with the warning that they would have to stop distributing goods if no better money was forthcoming.[91]

In the period of idleness that followed, the VOC officials managed to garner only a small portion of the money owed from local merchants in good `abbasis. The Dutch soon realized that little more was to be expected, for the local merchants who were indebted to them asserted that they had been forced to change all good `abbasis in their possession at 2¼ to 2¾ mahmudis each (as opposed to the official ratio of 2 mahmudis per `abbasi), and that they would have to renounce the contracted goods if the VOC insisted on further cash payment on the spot. Just as dependent on the merchants as the latter were on them, the Dutch realized that the volume of their merchandise was too large to seek a different market in case the merchants turned their backs on them. The absence of an alternative made them therefore decide to consent to the usual procedure of letting the merchants pay part of what they owed via a bill of exchange drawn on Isfahan.[92]

From later reports it becomes evident that the Iranian merchants in this period had great difficulty meeting their commitment to pay their bills in Isfahan on the due date in proper coin.[93] That most nevertheless managed to do so was not seen as a sign that matters were about to improve. Merchants were in too somber a mood for easy optimism, and anticipated worse to come if the situation was left unchanged.

On the eve of the new trading season, that of 1684, it looked as if the problems with bills of exchange were about to be repeated. By then, many current `abbasis were found to contain little more than half of their supposed silver content and were accordingly valued at about 1¼ to 1½ mahmudis at the most. The English captured the seriousness of the problem in their observation that because of the 'bad money' there was in Isfahan 'neither buying nor selling, all the Bazars being shut up, and if you melt down one Tomand you will hardly find 5 abassis Silver in it, soe that Spahaune is now all in uproare ...'.[94]

91 *NA*, VOC 1373, Missive van den Heuvel, 31 July 1683, fol. 901v; also in VOC 1388, fol. 2337r-v.
92 Ibid., fols. 901v, and 2337v-38r, resp.
93 *NA*, VOC 1406, Gamron to Batavia, 28 Feb.1684, fol. 1182v.
94 IOR, G/36/109, 2d fasc., Isfahan to Surat, 13 Nov. 1684, fols. 74–75.

In the summer of that year expectations that the shah was about to undertake a recoinage turned into rumors that a beginning had already been made with the reminting.[95] It is unclear who was the driving force behind the project. According to Khatunabadi, it was the master of the mint, Saru Khan Sahandlu, who had ordered the 'reform' of the currency.[96] The Dutch, on their part, pointed their finger at his rival, Sheykh `Ali Khan, crediting Saru Khan Sahandlu not so much with the initiative as with the undermining of a successful outcome. Whoever was behind the move, the important news was not substantiated until the late summer and early fall, when the English averred that the shah had ordered new money to be struck. The actual recoinage, the EIC merchants cautioned, would not happen until Nowruz at the earliest.[97] Yet the Dutch, who seem to have been better informed, around the same time claimed that already 90,000 tumans had been minted. One of their reports said that the royal sarrafs were found in the bazaar offering the new coins for exchange against old `abbasis.[98] Everyone, another VOC report noted, was frantically trying to convert their old `abbasis into the new coins.[99] At the same time, in Zu'l hejjeh/Nov.-Dec. 1684, the shah is said to have issued a *farman* banning his subjects from visiting Ottoman territory in an attempt to prevent (the importation of) adulterated money.[100]

Hopes ran high but were soon to be dashed. The English anticipation that Nowruz would witness greater strides in the reform everyone had awaited for so long remained unfulfilled. When the New Year came, in March of 1685, the expectation of large quantities beyond the first coining had yet to be met. The Dutch put it this way:

> It is true that, according to rumor, the shah intends to mint large quantities of new `abbasis, and new ones have indeed been coined, but

95 *NA*, VOC 1383, Gamron to Batavia, 28 Aug. 1684, fol. 720; the same report is found in VOC 1406, fols. 1245r-47r.

96 Khatunabadi, *Vaqaye` al-senin*, 537.

97 IOR, G/36/109, 2nd fasc., Isfahan to Surat, 13 Nov. 1684, fols. 75–76.

98 *NA*, VOC 1416, Gamron (schip 'Blauwe Hulck') to Batavia, 20 Oct. 1684, fol. 1619v. Due to the occupation of Qeshm and the warlike state with Iran, the Dutch factor at this time did not reside in Bandar `Abbas but was aboard this ship which was anchored off the Persian Gulf coast.

99 *NA*, VOC 1398, Gamron (schip 'Blauwe Hulck') to Surat, 4 Dec. 1684, fol. 493v. According to the French cleric Sanson, the new coins were minted at various mints around the country, Isfahan, Yerevan, Dadiyan, Tabriz, Ardabil, Hamadan and Hoveyzeh. Dadiyan and Hamadan, however, are not known as mints in this period. See Sanson, *Estat de Perse*, 159–60.

100 Shubbar, *Tarikh al-Musha`sha`yin*, 155.

> this has been of so little significance that it is considered a curiosity if someone manages to lay his hands on one.[101]

The `abbasis that had been struck, the Dutch asserted, were equal in their fine silver content and weight to the ones produced under Shah `Abbas II. Director Casembroot in Bandar `Abbas claimed that the new `abbasis had suffered a weight reduction of 20 per cent or 2 dang.[102] A later report from Isfahan, dating from the fall of 1685, contradicted that assessment, however, and affirmed that the weight was the same as that of the old `abbasis, that is 9½ dang. Their silver alloy, on the other hand, the same report claimed, was ¼ dang less than the ones struck under `Abbas II. The silver content of the latter had been valued at 5¾ dang, only ¼ less than the full alloy of pure fine silver.[103] Despite the slight decrease in alloy, however, the VOC representatives saw neither the weight nor the silver content of the new `abbasis as the problem. The real problem, they asserted, involved the fact that so few of them had been minted and that after an initial issue the minting had stopped altogether.

The most convincing explanation for this suspension is found in the subsequent VOC sources. The one to blame for the lack of continuity in issuing new money, these asserted, was the grand vizier, who had dissuaded the shah from the plan to bring more money into circulation. Sheykh `Ali Khan's argument, director Casembroot insisted, had been that all unminted silver that used to be brought into the country from Anatolia and other areas was now being taken to Basra, and that if the ruler continued to put out new coins on a large scale he would ruin himself because his treasury would be depleted in a very short time. This apparently had convinced the shah of the need to discontinue striking new `abbasis.[104] Keen to have his treasury stocked with `abbasis, the monarch may have felt that the expense of striking new `abbasis would exceed his revenue because, whereas he might force people to accept the old `abbasis at a value above their metallic worth, that would no longer be possible if new `abbasis were issued, and so he would lose some of the value of his stock of old `abbasis. That little silver was indeed available because for some time most of it had been taken to Basra has already been noted. That fact was reiterated by the Dutch as being highly relevant to the crisis of 1684. Reals of eight, they said, were valued from 1 to 1¼ mahmudis higher in Basra than in Iran.

101 *NA*, VOC 1416, Gamron to Batavia, 9 Apr. 1685, fols. 1676v-77r.
102 *NA*, VOC 1416, Gamron to Batavia, 20 Oct. 1684, fols. 1619v-20r. In reality 2 dang is 33 per cent.
103 *NA*, VOC 1398, Isfahan to Batavia, 30 Sept. 1685, fol. 693v.
104 *NA*, VOC 1416, Gamron to Batavia, 9 Apr. 1685, fol. 1677r.

Nor, they asserted, was there much chance that conditions would change any time soon. Improvement would only come if Spanish reals, which were officially valued at 6¾ mahmudis, were raised to a price of 7 mahmudis.[105] The Iranian merchants, according to the Dutch, had pledged that in case of such a revaluation they would resume their silver transports to Isfahan. The desired increase, however, had not been approved in court circles. The reason for that decision, the VOC agent surmised, was that many state officials possessed fantastic amounts in old `abbasis and that they as well as the shah himself would sustain a significant loss in case more mahmudis were offered for the rival silver real.[106]

Instead of agreeing to an increase in the price of the real as a solution to the dearth of silver, the VOC agent continued, the shah, at the behest of Sheykh `Ali Khan, had issued an order to procure a few camel loads of silver from the mountains around Kermanshah in the western part of the country. From this silver a number of `abbasis had been struck at minimal cost, and these had all disappeared into the shah's treasury.

While this could be seen as logical from the court's perspective, its next step left observers puzzled. After minting a number of new `abbasis, the royal treasury proceeded to accept only mahmudis struck in Hoveyzeh and `abbasis minted in Yerevan, notwithstanding the fact, the Dutch report noted with surprise, that these coins were scarce and had to be bought at a premium. Moreover, it was reiterated by the Dutch, these coins were of lesser alloy than mahmudis and `abbasis minted elsewhere. That the treasury nonetheless insisted on stocking up on these coins was ostensibly explained by the fact that these were present in smaller numbers in the royal coffers than any other coins. The court concluded its series of steps by outlawing all coins but the mahmudis and `abbasis it was now soliciting. Before doing so, however, it had made sure to drain the central treasury of all other money.[107]

The shah's decision to declare invalid all but two types of money after ridding the treasury of other coin and securing a good supply of the new money for his own treasury remains puzzling. In the context of the prevailing monetary crisis, the measure gives the impression of a desperate

105 The text mentions 13½ and 14 mahmudis, but in light of the well-attested fluctuation of the riyal between 6 and 8 mahmudis, shahis, each worth half a mahmudi, must have been meant here. Instead of substituting shahis, we have chosen to halve the amounts.

106 *NA*, VOC 1398, Isfahan to Batavia, 30 Sept. 1685, fol. 640r.

107 Ibid., fols. 639v-40v. The date of this report, September 1685, contradicts the timing given by Kaempfer, *Am Hofe*, 71, who asserted that all money, with the exception of mahmudis from Hoveyzeh, was declared invalid in November of that year.

act after other salvaging efforts had been exhausted. The fundamental reason why the court appeared reluctant to mint as much new money as would be needed to restore monetary confidence and order was the mercantilist attitude – shared by all, Iranian and European at the time – that the import of goods in return for the export of cash was a bad thing. It was certainly true that minting more money – especially coins of a reliable quality – would lead to an immediate increase in export of whatever coin was released in the market. After all, precious metal, and particularly silver, was in high demand to pay for the goods the Iranian market wanted.[108] To the modern mind, it would seem strange not to facilitate such trade, from which Iran could profit, especially since some of the imports would in turn be re-exported at a profit. But at the time, it was taken for granted that the government's priority should be to accumulate more in the palace treasury and to impede cash exports. That this latter factor was undoubtedly a main concern of the attempted reform is reflected in the fact that the currency reform was accompanied by a renewal and strengthening of a prohibition to export bullion. In December 1684 the English reported from Bandar `Abbas that an order had arrived from the shah 'not to let any Money Gold or Silver be carried out of his Countrey'.[109]

The mint 'reform' of 1684–85 seems to have made a great impression on everyone. It is the only reference to monetary issues in late Safavid times in Khatunabadi's chronicle. The actual consequences of the measures that were taken were, however, entirely counterproductive. The process of reminting caused great consternation and brought many to destitution. How bewildering the result was is expressed by a resident European missionary who noted that 'for now, as new money has been coined, and the old coinage retouched, in part allowed to remain, there are three kinds of currency – of higher, medium, and lowest value ....'[110] For their part, the VOC agents predictably complained that the lack of continuity in issuing new money was highly detrimental to trade and commerce. The breakdown of the financial system was particularly devastating for commercial transactions since it had become extremely difficult to obtain credit. But the confusion caused by the half-hearted issuance of new coins followed by the prohibition of all but two types of currency was hardest

108 This is, after all, what happened in England, too, after the recoinage of the 1690s: money continued to be carried out and newly minted coin would disappear as soon as it came out of the mint. See Li, *Great Recoinage*, 143–50.

109 IOR, G/36/109, 2nd fasc., Gombroon to Surat, 9 Dec. 1684, fols. 72–73.

110 Chick (ed.), *Chronicle of the Carmelites*, 1:434, letter Fr. Elias, 16 Jan. 1688; based on Carmelite Archives, Rome, S.N.R., vol. 1, fol. 493.

on the common man. The lack of monetary stability, the Dutch claimed in mid 1686, had wreaked havoc among ordinary people. Everything had become extremely expensive and, moreover, little could be obtained for anything but the 'Havizeh' (Hoveyzeh) mahmudi. This would be tolerable, they contended, if only these coins circulated in sufficient amount. In reality, however, they were so scarce that people bought them at rates that exceeded their face value by 10 to 15 per cent. Gold was no alternative either, at least not for ordinary people, for how could they afford to pay the 17½ to 18 mahmudis for which each ducat was sold by speculators who took advantage of the confused circumstances?[111]

Developments after 1685

The uncertainty and lack of confidence in the soundness of money that had developed did not stop there. Even those who could afford to buy ducats as an alternative, the Dutch noted, found that the shopkeepers would not accept them. The owner was then forced to take them to the official mint, only to be paid in restruck new money worth a mere 14 to 14½ mahmudis. After all, it was court policy to have those who brought their specie to the mint and those who received their money from the mint bear the loss that accrued from melting specie and reminting it into new coinage. This, *inter alia*, was the reason, the same Dutch report noted, why in the circumstances no Armenian merchants were willing to bring gold ducats to Isfahan from the Ottoman Empire – or reals for that matter, the latter still being valued at no more than 6¾ to 6⁴/₅ mahmudis.[112]

The upshot of this dismal situation was that the collective merchants – including the foreign traders – no longer knew what kind of currency they should demand for their goods. By now good old `abbasis had ceased to circulate; they had either been siphoned off to India or were hoarded. New money, by contrast, continued to be so scarce that in the few commercial transactions still conducted it was reserved some eight to nine months in advance by merchants, in the anticipation that by that time the new coin might be more widely available.[113]

The decade after the dramatic events of 1684–85 saw no improvement in the Iranian monetary situation. Current `abbasis and mahmudis, received

111 For gold and its role in Safavid monetary matters, see Matthee, 'Between Venice and Surat'; and Floor-Clawson, 'Safavid Persia's Search for Gold'.

112 *NA*, VOC 1430, Isfahan to Batavia, 5 July 1686, fols. 1537v-40r.

113 Ibid.

in payment for goods, continued to be deficient in weight. `Abbasis and mahmudis struck in Tiflis, for instance, in 1688 were found to be 22.5 per cent below weight.[114] The royal treasury naturally was not unaware of the problem either: It reportedly refused to accept any `abbasis minted in Tiflis from merchants.[115] Ducats, meanwhile, were only available at 16 mahmudis each, and of the `abbasis the only good ones, those that had been minted under `Abbas II, had to be purchased at rates that exceeded their face value by up to 11.5 per cent.[116]

In 1690 conditions had grown even worse. `Abbasis received by the VOC registered a 40 per cent loss upon melting.[117] Most silver continued to be taken to Basra, despite the fact that the city and its environs were wracked by disease and war in the early 1690s. As was seen earlier, a dearth of silver and the theoretical result of a better price for gold did not even lead to a greater influx of the latter metal. The prospect of payments in silver of bad quality in Iran caused more and more merchants to take their silver as well as their gold down to Basra.[118]

At about this time the Dutch, wary of the debased Iranian coin, did make up their minds with regard to their coin of preference. In the spirit of Molla Qodrati's poem, they decided to sell their goods no longer for debased `abbasis or mahmudis but instead to command as many exportable gold ducats as they possibly could for their merchandise.

Contrary to appearances, the monetary situation continued to be a government preoccupation after the aborted recoinage of 1685. Asked in 1691 by the shah about the most pressing problems faced by the crown, the new grand vizier Mirza Taher Vahid listed monetary issues and the need for reform as one.[119] The scarcity of the reals of eight had never ceased to be a problem after 1685. Their extreme rarity in the Iranian market continued to be caused by the fact that at the royal mint they were still valued considerably lower than their market value and were therefore all taken to Basra to be carried from there to India. The undervaluation of silver clearly was a problem that had to be tackled first. That, at least, was the answer Jan van Leene, special Dutch envoy to the Safavid court in 1691, gave when asked by the newly appointed Mirza Taher Vahid for his opinion about the reason why so much silver in the form of Spanish reals was taken to Basra, from there to be siphoned off to India. The debased character of the silver coin,

114 *NA*, VOC 1434, Gamron to Batavia, 2 June 1688, fol. 555r.

115 *NA*, VOC 1448, Gamron to Batavia, 19 July 1688, fol. 422v.

116 *NA*, VOC 1425, Gamron to Heren XVII, 21 Aug. 1687, fol. 441r.

117 *NA*, VOC, Generale Missiven, 14 Mar. 1690, in Coolhaas (ed.), *Generale Missiven, 1686–1697*, 371.

118 *NA*, VOC 1476, Gamron to Batavia, 29 Apr. 1690, fols. 405–14.

119 Sanson, letter from Isfahan, 8 Apr. 1691, in Kroell (ed.), *Nouvelles d'Ispahan*, 30.

the VOC representative added, was a second reason why good money left the country in such large quantities. The remedy, van Leene suggested, would be to raise the mint price of the reals; that is, to pay for them according to their market value, to improve the quality of silver coin, and to leave the merchants free and undisturbed.[120]

Van Leene's first recommendation was heeded soon enough, for in 1692 it was announced that henceforth reals would be accepted in the royal treasury at 7 mahmudis as opposed to the former 6½. The Dutch anticipated that this augmentation would cause great sums of silver to enter Iran.[121] Their sources do not refer to the customary consequence of enhancing the value of silver, higher prices, and, in view of the scarcely increasing quantity of money, it remains unclear if higher prices in effect followed. A fall in the relative value of the gold ducat, on the other hand, was unquestionably related to the official appreciation of silver.

Matters finally seemed to turn around in 1692. With the ducat relatively low in price and the appointment as the new mo`ayyer al-mamalek of a renegade Armenian who was a merchant himself, expectations ran high for a real improvement of the mint and a revival of commerce. Hajji Piri, however, resigned his post as mint master in March of the following year, only to die a month later. When the *kalantar* (police prefect) and vizier of Isfahan succeeded him in his position, hopes were dashed that improvement was on the agenda.[122]

No improvement came with the passing of time. Neither the court nor commerce seems to have benefited much from the increase in the denominative value of silver coin. There is no record that more silver was brought to the mints as a result of the 1692 measure. Nor did the export of currency diminish. In 1694 newly struck `abbasis and mahmudis were bought by Banyan money-changers at a premium of 1 to 3 per cent, next to be sent to Surat. Throughout the country the mahmudi of Hoveyzeh continued to be the only current coin, notwithstanding the fact that half of these coins were false in silver alloy.[123]

The last years of Shah Soltan Hoseyn's rule, a period of severe shortages of currency in circulation, saw more reductions. In 1123/1711–12 a pentagonal and oval coinage made its appearance. The apparent aim of this issuance was to mask the significant lowering of weight that took place at

120 *NA*, VOC 1501, Notulen van Leene, 31 Mar. 1691, fol. 520.

121 *NA*, VOC 1493, Gamron to Batavia, 15 Mar. 1692, fol. 320v; VOC 1501, Generale Missiven, 11 Dec. 1692, fol. 245r-v.

122 *NA*, VOC 1507, Gamron to Heren XVII, 2 Aug. 1693, fol. 469r.

123 *NA*, VOC, Generale Missiven, 30 Nov. 1694, in Coolhaas, *Generale Missiven, 1686–1697*, 705.

the same time. Six years later, in 1129/1717, the government engaging in a devaluation by reducing the `abbasi from 7.62 to 7.50 g or even less.[124]

Conclusion

Following the assessment of the Russian historian Rakhmani, this chapter's principal conclusion is that the monetary crisis of late Safavid Iran and its chronic character must be considered in any analysis of the problems of the late Safavid state.[125] The fundamental question is: what came first: the scarcity and declining quality of money or the signs of economic distress?

Paraphrasing Pierre Vilar, monetary problems itself usually do not create a crisis, but merely signal it and mark its timing.[126] This certainly applies to Iran, where the economic retrenchment that became so abundantly visible around 1650 had deeper roots than mere monetary ones. Monetary problems did not create a crisis, yet certainly contributed to the weakening of structures in a process where cause and effect became blurred, interactive and mutually reinforcing.

This is precisely what happened in late Safavid Iran. Once the cycle of shortage and debasement was set into motion, it gained its own damaging momentum. Money was in short supply throughout the period. Some of the elements accounting for the absence of a natural expansion of money were systemic and endemic. In the absence of a banking system, there were few alternatives to holding large amounts of money both for trade and for liquid savings (partly as a precaution against bad times). This means that the velocity of money was low, and there was a widespread tendency to hoard. Furthermore, no precious metal was mined in Iran in any serious quantity, and Iran needed to export cash to pay for a chronic balance of trade deficit with the Indian subcontinent. More than either the state or trade as the force accounting for the quantity and the quality of available money, it appears that the interaction between forces, including trade, over which the state had scant control, and the state's reaction to these forces, determined the availability of bullion and the quality of coin minted from it. Precious metal and coin involved processes that were not easily regulated and harnessed for revenue purposes. This was as true for seventeenth-

124 Rabino, *Coins, Nedals, and Seals*, 40; Radhabli, 'Iz istorii monetnogo dela', 55; Kuteliian, *Gruzia i Sefevidskii Iran, 28.*

125 Rakhmani, 'Iz istorii monetnogo obrashcheniia', 261.

126 Vilar, *Or et monnaie dans l'histoire*, 20.

century Europe, where the issue of bullion, its behavior and ways to keep it within the system were the subject of heated public debate, as it was for Safavid Iran.

Maximizing revenue was the state's main preoccupation and the measures it took generally had an immediate fiscal objective. Tampering with the weight of coins was routinely part of these measures. There is much evidence for the circulations of money of lower alloy as well, even if it is not clear if this was part of official state policy. It was mostly local mints that were responsible for the output of compromised currency. The mint of Hoveyzeh, while not a typical one, is a good example of how the activity of a quasi-autonomous mint could upset monetary stability.

Tampering with the weight or quality of the currency increased the value of the state's considerable holdings of older high-quality coins, made available more currency which therefore allowed collection of more revenue, and prevented the flight of most current money. The price, however, was inflation and the upheaval of exchange relations. The various measures taken by successive rulers, from Shah `Abbas I to Shah Soleyman, bear this out. Short-term revenue enhancement may have been achieved, but the lasting effects, falling confidence in the realm's currency, a reluctance of merchants to bring cash to Iran, and increased exports of good coins, were all negative. Subsequent measures, culminating in the monetary 'reform' of 1684–85, only aggravated inflation and fueled suspicion regarding money.

The main obstacle to a sovereign monetary policy was the perennial threat that through the working of Gresham's Law all remaining good coin would be driven out by money thus manipulated. The nature of this cycle is clearly seen in the tendency of merchants to take silver to Basra, where silver obtained higher prices. This caused a shortage of silver in Iran, which would in turn weaken the prospects of sound payments for one's gold, and this, finally, led to a decrease in the influx of gold as well. Some of these factors were a function of domestic conditions. The more important ones, however, were regional and transregional in character and largely related to the nature and rhythm of long-distance trade. Notably beyond effective state control was the export of vast quantities of specie to India. This was a truly structural problem, rooted in Iran's unfavorable trade balance.

Trade was an important conduit for specie. The availability, nature, and price of specie, however, were also a function of political initiatives. The most important of these was the price paid for precious metal at the mint. A refusal to value silver at or near the current market price had immediate repercussions for the volume of silver and gold brought into the country. Throughout the late seventeenth century, an undervaluation of silver at the mint accounted for much of the export of silver, without, however, automatically leading to an influx of gold. Hardly less important for the nature and volume of monetary circulation were the periodic devaluations of the currency. These had the double objective of raising revenue for the treasury and of stemming the outflow of specie. The consequences of these measures, however, tended to be negative: they reduced an already low confidence in ready money and reinforced tendencies to hoard or to export the remaining good coins.

Part 2

THE AFSHARID AND ZAND PERIOD 1722–94

5

The Age of Copper

Introduction

The Safavids fell in 1722, yet their monetary policy was continued by their immediate successors, the Ghelza'i Afghans and Nader Shah, who between 1722 and 1740 maintained the same weight and assay for the coinage. Nader Shah made a break with the past, when in the latter year he decided to reform the currency. Instead of continuing the traditional Iranian standard, he introduced a new coinage based on the Indian standard, presumably to facilitate trade between the two countries. Thus, there were two standards for the coinage in Iran, in an arranged marriage that finally led to a divorce by the end of the eighteenth century. Yet all this was no more than a backdrop to the total disarray of the monetary system. Gold and silver became very scarce and expensive after 1730, leading to a flight into copper. As a result, copper became an important medium of payment in international trade, and the Iranian monetary system effectively became trimetallic system, with good, silver and copper circulating freely.

The Ghelza'i Afghan Period (1722–29)

The fall of the Safavid capital of Isfahan in October 1722 made the Afghan conquerors the owners of the riches they found in the royal palaces as well as in the homes of the wealthy. In addition to gold and silver vessels, there was jewelry, costly gold-threaded and silver-threaded robes as well as a large quantity of gems, gold and silver bullion and coins. Mirza Mohsen, who had been tasked to do a house-to-house search during the siege of Isfahan to locate food hoards, found fourteen large bags weighing each 100 Tabriz mans or more, thus in total more than 4,150 kg, hidden in the house of a rich merchant (*naqshineh-forush*) on the *Meydan-e Shah*. Each bag contained newly minted *`abbasis* representing a value of at least

1,792 tumans.[1] While this suggests the availability of substantial sums of money elsewhere in the city, Shah Soltan Hoseyn nevertheless pressed the VOC for a loan of the enormous sum of 70,000 tumans (or about 10 per cent of the shah's annual revenue) just one month prior to the fall of Isfahan.[3] All this ready cash, too, fell into the hands of the Afghans and their allies. Another important source of precious metal was the royal wardrobe of used clothes (*zobol-khaneh*). In 1716 when the country was in a deep economic crisis the grand vizier had forbidden the production of gold and silver wire, gold and silver brocades as well as the wearing of these textiles, including their use for horses. This ban did not last, for those in the gold crafts offered presents to the grand vizier, causing him to lift it; yet it suggests the importance of this this use of precious metals and the drain it was on the country's monetary resources.[3] Likewise, in January 1731, Shah Tahmasb II banned the production of gold- and silver-threaded clothes as well of female silver-gold jewelry, issuing orders to bring the gold and silver thus freed up into the Mint to strike coins.[4] Rostam al-Hokama, writing about a century later, claims that every seven years the Safavid court issued orders to make a heap of all the silver- and gold-threaded clothes and set fire to it. The gold and silver wire thus collected became available for other uses, including for monetary purposes. In fact, in 1750 the warlord `Ali Mardan Khan, after taking Isfahan, burned the royal wardrobe of used clothes. The yield in the form of gold and silver coins minted allegedly sufficed to finance the pay of an army of 25,000.[5] Like Soltan Hoseyn before him, Soltan Mahmud (r. Oct. 1723–Apr. 1725) confiscated money indiscriminately and imposed exactions on anyone suspected of harboring wealth, including foreign trading Companies. For example, in Isfahan, the VOC had to pay 20,000 tumans, while the Banyans furnished 9,000 tumans in 1723.[6] As a result, in the first two years of Afghan rule treasure-laden caravans were seen heading for Qandahar, some as large as 10,000 camels.[7] Many Afghan leaders became very rich

1 Mostowfi, *Zobdat al-tavarikh*, 134; Minorsky (ed.), *Tadhkirat al-Mulūk*, 20.

2 Floor (ed.), *Afghan Occupation*, 169. About the size of the shah's annual revenue see Minorsky (ed.), *Tadhkirat al-Mulūk*, 179–86 and Floor, *Fiscal History*, 67–68, 232–33.

3 *NA*, VOC 1897, Gamron to Batavia, 30 Nov. 1716, fol. 17.

4 *NA*, VOC 2255, Isfahan to Gamron, 28 Jan. 1731, fol. 2290. Whether this ban was executed is not clear, see *NA*, VOC 2255, Isfahan to Gamron, 21 Apr. 1731, fol. 2315–16. One year later Tahmasb Qoli Khan sold the entire contents of the royal palaces in Isfahan to raise money for his troops. *NA*, VOC 2322, Isfahan to Gamron, 28 Oct. 1732, fol. 205 v, 354.

5 Rostam al-Hokama, *Rostam al-tavarikh*, 89, 247–48.

6 In Floor (ed.), *Afghan Occupation*, 177–84, 192, 247 (booty taken from the Ottomans), 249–50, 254, 256.

7 Ibid., 224–26. Not all the goldware had been converted to bullion or coins. See ibid., 195.

in the process. An example is Amanollah Khan, the Afghan second-in-command under Shah Mahmud, who amassed so much booty that by 1725 his wealth was estimated at a staggering 300,000 tumans.[8]

The above suggests that in 1721 there was no shortage of bullion and thus no need to devaluate the `abbasi as Shah Soltan Hoseyn resolved to do. Similarly, so much gold and silver was available in 1723 that the new Afghan ruler had no problem striking coins, which he did. The Safavid coinage continued to be used, of course; in fact, it served as a model for the Afghan coinage which differed but little from it.[9] Mahmud initially continued to strike silver `abbasis of 4.61 g (based on a standard of 50 `abbasis, or 200 shahis, per tuman and 1,200 nokhud of 192 milligrams). In 1723 he ordered an increase in the weight of the `abbasis to 7.3 g. This implies that the `abbasi equaled 4 shahis, the normal standard, but that the new `abbasi was officially valued at 5 shahis. In line with Greshham's Law, a high demand developed for the heavier `abbasi. According to the *Tazkerat al-Moluk*, the five shahi coins became so popular that after being struck they were carried to the outlying provinces to the point of becoming current even in the towns which had not submitted to the Afghans. The author added that 'counterfeiting gives no profit if the coins are to be struck at this weight of metal'.[10] In addition, Mahmud had a silver rupee or 10 shahi of 11.52 g struck at Qandahar. And he issued gold coins or ashrafis (3.55 g) with varying texts.[11]

When Ashraf Shah (r. Apr. 1725–Dec. 1729) succeeded his cousin Mahmud in April 1725 he continued to strike coins of the same type and weight as his predecessor, although he reverted to the lighter, 4.6 g `abbasi. According to the *Tazkerat al-Moluk*,

> At present [1726] the coins of His Majesty are: the five *shahi*s weighing 9½ *dang*s, as at the time of Shah Mahmud, and gold *ashrafi*s struck according to the ancient norm of 4½ *dang*s, and God be praised, they enjoy great popularity and prestige in Isfahan and in all outlying provinces of the God-protected kingdom.[12]

8 Ibid., 236.

9 Mahmud Shah used Persian couplets on the obverse and the Sunnite form of the *shahada* on the reverse.

10 Minorsky (ed.), *Tadhkirat al-Mulūk*, 60.

11 For the numismatic information on Mahmud's coinage see Album, *Checklist*, 283–84. It is unclear why Mahmud did not adopt the 1,400 nokhud per tuman standard.

12 Minorsky (ed.), *Tadhkirat al-Mulūk*, 60.

The only difference with the coinage of Mahmud was the different Sunni legends struck on Ashraf's coins.[13] The one real exception to this was an `abbasi, struck at Isfahan in 1140–41/1727–28 by Ashraf, on which the shahada had been replaced by a formula giving the date and mint, which became a prototype for most post-Safavid coinage until the reforms of the 1870s.[14] Nothing is known about the output. The author of the *Tazkerat al-Moluk* suggests that Afghan coins were ready available and circulated everywhere. We have almost no other sources on this issue, and the total output of this coinage remains unknown, but it appears that Safavid coinage was still in circulation, to the extent that money continued to be used. The Dutch in Isfahan reported in 1728 that 'money had become so scarce that it was rarely seen'.[15]

The Afghan conquerors occupied most of central Iran, but not the entire Safavid realm. The Ottomans invaded the country as well in 1722, seizing Iran's Caucasian provinces (Armenia, Georgia, Shirvan, Darband and Daghestan), most of Azerbaijan, including Tabriz, as well as Kurdistan and Hamadan, all of which they held until 1735. The Russians occupied the eastern sea-board of the Caucasus, in particular Darband and Baku, as well as Gilan, which they held until 1732. In the northeast and east, Malek Mahmud Sistani took hold of Khorasan and Sistan. The occasional Safavid pretender rose up as well, invariably to be struck down. The most important of these pretenders was Sayyed Ahmad, who had a powerbase in Kerman from 1725 to 1728.

The coins minted by the Ottomans in occupied Iranian territory as well as by local warlords such as Malek Mahmud Sistani and Sayyed Ahmad were based on the pre-1721 Safavid 1,400 nokhud per tuman standard. This meant that the shahi was 7 nokhud (of 192 milligram each) and thus weighed 1.34 g, and that the 2 shahi weighed 2.67 g. In June 1722, Tahmasb Mirza, the third son of Shah Soltan Hoseyn, managed to escape from besieged Isfahan. At first, he tried to rally support for his father in Qazvin. He next moved to Tabriz and, being expelled from there by the Ottomans, he moved to Mazandaran and Astarabad, where he established a court in exile. In 1723 he acceded to the throne as Tahmasb II and struck coins mostly on the 1,400 nokhud standard. From Astarabad Tahmasb II did not

13 For particulars concerning the coins and the various Sunni legends on them, see Rabino 1945, 47–48; Album, *Checklist*. Album queries whether Ashraf's five- `abbasi coin is indeed such a coin. Given that it should weigh 9.5 dang (i.e., 38 nokhud of 193 milligrams each) or 7.29 g there can be no doubt about it that it is indeed a five-`abbasi coin.

14 Album et al., 'Coins and Coinage'.

15 Floor (ed.), *Afghan Occupation*, 250.

make much headway against the Afghans. Nor did he manage to expand his territory until the arrival of a young strongman from Khorasan in 1726. Nadr Qoli Beg, the individual in question, was able to convince Tahmasb II that he could change his fortune and defeat the Afghans, if given the chance to do so. After eliminating his main rival at court, he received the new name of Tahmasb Qoli Khan. He retook Khorasan and then set out to reconquer Iran.[16]

The Last Safavids (1722–36)

After the ouster of the Afghans at the end of 1729 and the entry of Tahmasb II (r. 1723–32) into Isfahan in December 1729, silver `abbasis (5.34 g), two-shahis (2.68 g) and shahis (1.34 g) were struck based on the standard of 1,400 nokhud of 192 milligrams per tuman of 200 shahis or 50 `abbasis as well as copper money. As before, silver coins were mainly used in long distance trade, to effect tax payments to the government and to finance the purchase of cash crops. Therefore, the return to the 1,400 nokhud standard probably was an effort to mint coins that imitated the value of the real of eight, an important medium of exchange in international trade. Gold ashrafis of 3.46 g were also struck, although, as in the pre-Afghan period, Safavid gold coins were much not used in circulation. It would appear that copper coins were struck only at the Isfahan mint, at least initially. This supposition is reinforced by the fact that there are no known copper coins for this period.[17] Tahmasb's II most common mints included Isfahan, Kerman and Yazd.[18]

Despite the striking of these new coins, the scarcity of specie, including that of copper money, began to be felt immediately after the defeat and ouster of the Afghans from Iran. In October 1730, the Dutch reported that there was no trade in ducats, because no merchants were coming from Tabriz, which at that time continued to be occupied by the Ottomans.[19]

As a result of Tahmasb II's inept rule and his own ambition, Tahmasb Qoli Khan deposed the shah on 1 September 1732 and thereafter ruled as regent for Tahmasb II's two-month old son `Abbas III (r. 1732–36). The coup d'état was not unexpected for it was Tahmasb Qoli Khan, not his nominal overlord Tahmasb II, who had defeated and expelled the Afghans from

16 Lockhart, *Nadir Shah*; Floor (ed.), *Afghan Occupation*.
17 Nasiri, *Titles and Emoluments*, 50–51; Kuteliia, *Catalogue of the Iranian Copper Coins*,
18 Album, *Checklist*, 282.
19 *NA*, VOC 2253, Isfahan to Gamron, 1 Oct. 1730, fol. 660.

Iran.[20] As a reward for Tahmasb Qoli Khan's vital role in re-establishing the dynasty, Shah Tahmasb II had effectively ceded control over Khorasan and Mazandaran to him, recognizing him as viceroy (*vali*) in 1729; later, Tahmasb Qoli Khan also gained control over Gilan and Kerman. In a reflection of the vali's far-reaching autonomy, Tahmasb II's decrees were not obeyed in Tahmasb Qoli Khan's territory unless he had them confirmed. Likewise, Tahmasb Qoli Khan only acknowledged Tahmasb II's decrees, even in the latter's territory, after approving them.[21]

The coinage, meanwhile, did not change. Although Tahmasb Qoli Khan was formally not a sovereign, he had, or at least exercised, the right to strike coins as viceroy in his territory. His coinage was semi-anonymous and was issued as if they were regular Safavid coins to the 1,400 nokhud standard, the legend on the coins being the only difference.[22] It would seem that Tahmasb Qoli Khan's role as quasi-independent viceroy in Khorasan had already started, for he began striking coins even before Isfahan had been retaken from the Afghans. According to a contemporary Persian source, Nadr Qoli Beg, on receiving his new name of Tahmasb Qoli Khan in September 1726, had coins struck, probably presentation silver, with the following text: *Shayad beh falak az eqbal rekabam - Tahmasb Qoli Khan shodeh az shah khetabam.*[23]

Already prior to the coup d'état of September 1732 there was a chronic need for money due to the military operations in eastern and western Iran. In 1735 the Dutch estimated that Tahmasb Qoli Khan needed 25,000 tumans or Dfl. 10.6 million each month to pay his 125,000 men strong army.[24] In 1734

20 For Nader's career, see Lockhart, *Nadir Shah*; Axworthy, *Sword of Persia*; Floor, *Rise and Fall of Nader Shah*. Already in May 1730, courtiers expected a showdown between Tahmasb II and Nader. *NA*, VOC 2168, Isfahan to Bandar `Abbas, 1 Jan. 1730, fol. 895.

21 *NA*, VOC 2255, Isfahan to Gamron, 3 Nov. 1731, fol. 1848 (We are not clear whether Tahmasb Qoli Khan is pro- or anti-shah; he has the title *Walie over Gorassoen*); Marvi, *`Alamara-ye Naderi*, 1:208; *NA*, VOC 2254, Kerman to Gamron, 23 Nov. 1731, fols. 1201–02; VOC 2254, Dagregister Gamron, 15 Sept. 1730, fol. 135. (The new governor of Kerman, Emamverdi Khan had publicly declared himself for Tahmasb Qoli Khan and against Tahmasb II); VOC 2255, Isfahan to Gamron, 20 Apr. 1731, fols. 2315–16 (allegedly Tahmasb Qoli Khan had given orders in Kerman not to name Tahmasb II but rather himself in the *khotbeh*; many believed that he wanted to become king, also because of a new seal that he had made); for the text of this new seal see Sha`bani, *Hadis-e Nader Shahi*, 12; and Rabino, *Coins, Medals, and Seals*, 53.

22 Sha`bani *Hadis-e Nader Shahi*, 11; Album *Checklist*, 285.

23 Sha`bani, *Hadis-e Nader Shahi*, 7.

24 VOC 2357, Gamron to Batavia, 24 Aug. 1735, fols. 282–83. Nader publicly stated that 'he could not care less if the whole country was ruined and whether there was trade or not, the only thing that interested him was to dress and maintain his troops'. VOC 2322, Isfahan to Gamron, 22 March, 1733, fol. 376vs. He usually paid his soldiers monthly in cash. VOC 2546, Relaes lopers, Sept. 1740, fol. 1700. The money had to be transported on mules. The official

Tahmasb Qoli Khan gave a present of 1,000 Shah Jahanabad ashrafis to the Usmi of the Qeytaqs, suggesting that there was a shortage of Safavid gold coins and that the payment was realized using Mughal gold coins from the royal treasury that had been received as a present.[25] Such lavish foreign presents were rare and, therefore, other venues had to be opened to find the necessary funds to pay the army.

At various times during this troubling period, governments in need of revenue used monetary manipulation of one kind or another for this purpose, or else demanded so much cash, usually from merchants and minorities, that the money supply was inadequate to carry on normal trade. Most of the Safavid coinage had already been exported by this time. Matters grew worse when in July 1731 the *mo`ayyer-bashi*, master of the mint, of Isfahan, who also served as the city's governor, announced that, henceforth, Afghan money would cease to be legal tender. What followed was a total standstill of the little trade that remained, causing many people to flee the city. Tahmasb I thereupon ordered the mo`ayyer-bashi to halt his exactions and allegedly arranged to have all revenue earmarked for mullahs sequestered, an estimated sum of 100,000 tumans per year. He further gave orders to collect the revenue of Qazvin, Saveh and Kashan.[26]

Another time-honored way of raising revenue through monetary manipulation was to tax the export of specie. In October 1732, Tahmasb Qoli Khan issued a decree stipulating that the export of (European) gold ducats was only allowed on payment of a duty of 5 per cent, to be paid in so-called white, i.e., silver money. Ducats had to declared and exported in bags which were inspected and then sealed by the agent of the mo`ayyer-bashi.[27]

On July 17, 1733 the Dutch reported how in Isfahan tax collectors had declared that one `abbasi silver money had to be accepted without any exchange discount (or 'agio,' the technical term) and that 10 paisas of copper money only valued four paisas. In other words, the government assigned some kind of face value to silver money, because it banned reducing its

charged with such money transport took the animals by force and paid for them a price fixed by himself. In 1744, a payment of 50,000 crowns or 5,000 tumans required 130 mules. Hanway *Historical Account*, 1:234–35.

25 Marvi, *`Alamara-ye Naderi*, 2:668. On the Usmi, see Floor, 'Who Were the Shamkhal and the Usmi?' On these events, see Bakikhanov, *Heavenly Rose-Garden*, 123–25.

26 *NA*, VOC 2255, Isfahan to Gamron, 3 Nov. 1731, fols. 1853–56, 1865.

27 *NA*, VOC 2322, Gamron to Batavia, 30 Sept. 1733, fols. 78–80. Calculations were made in purses. Rabino, *Coins, Medals, and Seals*, 17; Abraham of Erevan, *Chronicle*, 60, who further stipulates that 'some said that it cost 500 tomans, which is 200 kises;' Ibid, p. 113 [or 2,000], but on p. 133 he writes '500 [or 700] tomans, which makes 20 kises'. According to Marvi, *`Alamara-ye Naderi*, 2:540, one kiseh = 500 *tuman-e tabrizi-ye ashrafi*.

value by allowing for differences in weight and alloy. It also means that the government did not accept tax payments, which were calculated in silver money, in copper coins at the prevailing market rate, but announced an official exchange ratio between copper and silver in which 10 paisas were only valued at 4 paisas. Further, it was announced that bread could not be sold for more than one mahmudi. 'The authorities have gone mad', the Dutch commented, 'for everything is getting more expensive. For one `abbasi used to equal to 80 paisas but now is equal to 100 paisas. The price of bread increased by 10 paisas per man, for the *man-e shah* is bought for 40 paisas and because now 10 paisas have to be accepted at the value of 4 paisas the price of one man-e shah is 50 paisas.' This of course was impossible, and the money-changers immediately left Isfahan.[28]

This period saw a proliferation in the use of copper coins. As said, copper coins continued to be used as the medium of exchange for everyday transactions and low-income groups. The generic term used for copper coins remained folus or pul, and more in particular paisa and qazbegi, which was bastardized as goz by the English. Copper paisas came in two sizes: long and round. In 1733, according to the Dutch, Safavid copper coins were equal in quality and assay to Japanese copper.[29] In the 1730s, copper became equal to, if not more important than, silver in domestic and international trade.

This development was due to the particular characteristics of the Iranian economy. As before, Iran suffered from a lack of exportable commodities beside silk and some minor products. As the production of silk had gone down, the traditional export surplus and the corresponding inflow of specie with the Ottomans may have diminished. To some extent, this was offset by a larger trade surplus with Russia, as goods that normally would have been carried to the Levant were now exported via Russia. This held in particular for raw silk.[30] However, the trade surplus with the lands lying to the northwest appears to have been smaller than the trade deficit with India (and Asia in general). We lack definitive data, but the export of silver (and to some extent gold) to Asia unbalanced by an inflow from the north and west may well explain the sudden rise of the role of copper in

28 *NA*, VOC 2269, Dagregister Gamron, fol. 6608r-v.

29 *NA*, VOC 2322, Gamron to Batavia, 30 Sept. 1733, fols. 78, 138. Payments were in 'shahis and goz'. Saldanha, *Persian Gulf Précis*, 1:49.

30 Floor, *Economy of Safavid Persia*, 237–40; Kukanova, *Ocherki po istorii russko-iranskikh torgovykh otnoshenii*, ch. 3. The Russian merchants paid in goods, silver and copper. The presence of Russian troops in the Caspian provinces until 1732 also meant that additional bullion was available, in particular copper. VOC 2252, 11 Sept. 1729, fol. 695.

Table 5.1: Gold–silver ratio in the Ottoman Empire (1730–1800)

Year	Gold–silver ratio
1730	13.5
1740	15.0
1754	15.3
1757	12.5
1766	13.0
1774	12.7
1780	12.9
1788	14.6
1789	11.2
1794	11.6
1800	13.3

Source: Pamuk, *Monetary History*, 163 (Table 10.1)

international trade and the greater use of copper for domestic trade. In 1735 the government in Iran decreed the gold–silver ratio to be 1:11. This was much higher than in Europe (1:15), and, more importantly, higher than in the Ottoman Empire. Merchants in Iran who accepted silver therefore suffered a loss.[31]

The difference in gold–silver ratios between Iran and Ottoman Empire should have made the import of silver profitable. Ignoring transport costs, a merchant could have exchanged a pound of gold for 15 pounds of silver in Ottoman lands, exported that to Iran and exchange 11 pounds for a pound of gold, with a profit of 4 pounds of silver. However, that did not seem to happen; perhaps there was insufficient gold in Iran for such trade to occur on a large enough scale to affect the gold–silver ratio much. What did occur was that foreigners who exported silver received less for it than the official exchange rates in Iran would have suggested. In 1733, the Dutch observed

31 Marvi, *'Alamara-ye Naderi*, 1:377 (one mesqal, meaning 24 nokhud and therefore 4.61 g, of gold = 550 dinar; one mesqal of silver = 50 dinars). For Europe, see Braudel and Spooner, 'Prices in Europe', 459.

that for export purposes their financial loss was less on copper money than on silver `abbasis or gold ducats.[32]

The difference in loss between Bandar `Abbas and Batavia is due to the fact that these were two different money markets with different rates of exchange. VOC accounts provide a way to compare coin values in Bandar `Abbas to those in Batavia. However, a complication is that the VOC allowed each of their trading stations to calculate the various monies they received in fixed book values in Dutch guilders rather than in changing market values. In Iran's case, these book values were below the market price of the various coins. Also, the market price of a coin in Bandar `Abbas differed from the market value of the same coin in Batavia. So, in 1733, a European ducat was valued by the Bandar `Abbas trading station as being worth 2,040 penningen (converting from the original Dutch guilders, stuivers and penningen at the rate 1 guilder = 20 stuivers and 1 stuiver = 16 penningen), but the actual cost was 2,448 penningen, while in Batavia the European ducat's market cost was 2,160 penningen. This system meant that both Bandar `Abbas and Batavia calculated there was a 'loss' when purchasing foreign coins, in that the coins cost more penningen than the book rate, so contemporary VOC accounts refer to a financial loss from the currency trade. More important from our perspective, the data show for each coin the ratio of market prices in Bandar `Abbas relative to that in Batavia. Coins of all types for which data exist cost more in Bandar `Abbas than in Batavia. The extra value was greater for gold coins than for silver ones; that is, gold was more expensive and silver was cheaper in Bandar `Abbas than it was in Batavia. Moreover, the VOC allowed their trading stations to calculate the various monies they received in fixed book values rather than in changing market values. In the case of Iran these book values were below the market price of the various coins, as shown in Table 5.2.

In 1732, Tahmasb II ordered that silver and copper money had to be accepted 'as is' without the demand of any premium.[33] This decree represents a unique step in Iran's monetary history, even if the Dutch expected it to be revoked shortly, arguing that, otherwise, all trade would come to a halt. It meant, after all, that henceforth copper was not token money anymore, and that Iran implicitly had adopted a trimetallic system in the sense that gold, silver and copper coins had officially fixed rates of exchange. It appears that the decree was indeed rescinded, for nothing is reported about its application; yet it was a sign of things to come.

32 *NA*, VOC 2322, Gamron to Batavia, 30 Sept. 1733, fols. 79v-80.

33 *NA*, VOC 2255, Isfahan to Gamron, 30 May 1732, fols. 1991–92.

Table 5.2: Difference between market value in Bandar `Abbas and Batavia

Coin	Batavia market value relative to Bandar `Abbas market value	VOC book value in Bandar `Abbas compared to market value in Bandar `Abbas
Gold European ducat	.8868	.8333
Silver coins:		
Spanish reals	.9235	.7941
Old and new silver `abbasis	.8899	.8581
Whole and half silver *zolatas*	.9480	.8150
Leeuwendaalders	.9300	.7994

Source: *NA*, VOC 2322, Gamron to Batavia, 30 Sept. 1733, fol. 79. Note that the original also gives the underlying data for the prices of the European ducat in both places, from which the price in Batavia is 1.1176 times the price in Bandar `Abbas rather than the 1.1132 shown in the original.

In 1735 Tahmasb Qoli Khan ordered the striking of new copper coins of 5 mesqal, which were then passed off as paisas.[34] This marks the first time that the state effectively – as opposed to theoretically – backed the convertibility of copper coins with full-bodied silver coins throughout its territory. Tahmasb Qoli Khan also allowed other mints to be opened. For at the end of 1735, according to the Armenian Catholicos of Echmiadzin, Abraham of Crete, 'there were not enough coins and these were soon reduced further, became very scarce, and eventually disappeared altogether. Therefore, I asked the great and powerful Khan to order that a mint be established in Erevan [...] and the Khan immediately granted my request.'[35] Furthermore, Tahmasb Qoli Khan had given orders to begin mining operations at a silver mine situated at about 40 km distance from Kerman, which had been discovered at the beginning of the reign of Shah Soltan Hoseyn. The mine soon proved to be unprofitable.[36]

34 *NA*, VOC 2416, Isfahan to Gamron, 3 June 1735, fol. 1953.

35 Abraham of Crete, *Chronicle*, 49.

36 *NA*, VOC 2416, Isfahan to Gamron, 3 June 1735, fols. 1953–54. In 1736, the idea of extracting silver from this mine seems to have been revisited, since Tovakkel Beg Afshar, *ishik aghasi bashi* and supervisor of the silver mines, came to Kerman, probably to see whether it was worthwhile to start production again. He must have decided against it, because there is no report of new mining activity. VOC 2416, Resolution Gamron, 1 June 1736, fols. 1056–57.

Neither intervention brought relief. In fact, the monetary situation was made worse by the continued fiscal exactions that Tahmasb Qoli Khan imposed on Iran's population. For example, in 1734 Tahmasb Qoli Khan forced the people of Kerman to come up with two consecutive large quotas, to be paid in silver, as a result of which the value of the silver `abbasi rose to 4.5 mahmudis of copper money. At this price the VOC agent in Kerman could not afford to draw bills on Bandar `Abbas.[37] One year earlier, in April 1733, the `abbasi had been valued at 3.5 mahmudis and the ducat had only been worth 25–25.5 mahmudis in copper money.[38] The high price of `abbasis induced merchants from Isfahan, Khorasan and elsewhere to come with silver money to Kerman, so that its price there fell from 4.5 to 4 mahmudis.[39] In June 1735, the inhabitants of Kerman were faced with yet another extraordinary impost.[40] Other towns were targeted as well.

The Afsharid Period (1736–50)

Bolstered by his military successes, in March 1736 Tahmasb Qoli Khan deposed `Abbas III and declared himself king of Iran under the name of Nader Shah (r. 1736–47). He left the country's monetary policy unchanged. After his enthronement new silver `abbasis weighing 5.37 g and some lower fractions (of 1, 6, 10 and 20 shahis) were struck in Nader's name, based on a unit of account of one tuman of 1,400 nokhud – as before, the nokhud was 192 milligrams and the tuman was 50 `abbasis.[41] The ten shahi coin was called *naderi*. Twenty of these coins equaled one tuman.[42] According to the British, in 1736 an amount of 8,000 tumans equaled 160,000 rupees, or 1 silver tuman, and was equal to 20 Indian silver rupees of 1.52 g, or 30.4 g of silver.[43]

37 *NA*, VOC 2323, Kerman to Gamron, 1 May 1734, 1734, fol. 836; VOC 2323, Kerman to Gamron, 15 June 1734, fol. 843.

38 *NA*, VOC 2232, Isfahan to Gamron, 1 May 1733, fol. 401 vs.

39 *NA*, VOC 2323, Kerman to Gamron, 28 Aug. 1734, fol. 853.

40 *NA*, VOC 2416, Kerman to Gamron, 8 June 1735, fol. 1897; VOC 2537, Kerman to Gamron, 22 July 1735, fol. 911; VOC 2416, Kerman to Gamron, 22 July 1735, fol. 2108. Likewise in Isfahan. VOC 2357, Isfahan to Gamron, 4 Feb. 1735, fol. 1147. *NA*, VOC 2416, Kerman to Gamron, 22 July 1735, fol. 2109.

41 Marvi, *`Alamara-ye Naderi*, 2:457; Sha`bani, *Hadis-e Nader Shahi*, 15; Abraham of Crete, *Chronicle*, 144–45 (with the text of the inscription on the coin). For numismatic details about these coins, see Album, *Checklist*, 285.

42 Marvi, *`Alamara-ye Naderi*, 2:544. In 1736, 1,000 naderis equaled 50 tumans.

43 Saldanha, *Persian Gulf Précis*, 1:48.

Table 5.3: Silver coins and their weights during different rulers (1730–94)

	Mahmud	Ashraf	Tahmasb II	Nader 1736–40	Nader 1740–47	`Adel Shah-Ebrahim Shah	Karim Khan
1 tuman = 50 `abbasis = 200 shahis	tuman = 1,200 nokhud or 230.4 g	tuman = 1,200 nokhud	tuman = 1,400 nokhud or 268.8 g	tuman = 1,400 nokhud	tuman = 1,200 nokhud	tuman = 1,200 nokhud	tuman = 1,200 nokhud
double rupi	–	–	–	–	23.04 g	23.04 g	–
20 shahi or 5 `abbasi	–	–	26.88 g	–	–	–	–
16 shahi or 4 `abbasi	–	–	23.05 g	–	–	–	–
10 shahi or rupi	11.52 g	–	11.52 g	11.52 g	11.52 g	11.52 g	11.52 g[44]
double `abbasi	–	–	11.52 g	–	–	–	9.22 g
6 shahi	–	–	–	6.91 g	6.91 g	6.91	6.91 g
5 shahi	7.3–7.4 g	7.2 g	–	–	–	–	–
`abbasi or 4 shahi	4.61 g	4.61 g	5.34 g	5.37 g	4.61 g	4.61 g	4.61 g[45]
2 shahi	–	–	2.68 g	2.68 g	2.68 g	–	–
shahi	–		1.34 g	1.34 g	1.34 g	–	–
shahi	–	–	–	1.15 g	1.15 g	1.15 g	1.15 g
bisti or half shahi	–	–	0.53 and 0.67 g	0.67 g	0.67 g	–	–

Source: Album, *Checklist*, 283–90.

44 In 1768–77, the rupee was 12 shahis, and after 1777, it was 15 shahis.

45 In 1768–77, the `abbasi was 5 shahis; after 1777, it was 6 shahis

Since, according to a contemporary Persian-language chronicle, one mesqal, meaning 24 nokhod and therefore 4.61 g of gold, was equal to 550 dinars, and one mesqal of silver was equal to 50 dinars, this yields a gold–silver ratio of 1:11.[46] Nader Shah's new gold ducat or ashrafi weighed about 3.46 g and was heavier than the Venetian one, according to the Dutch, who bought 100 pieces at 17 silver mahmudis, i.e., 8.5 `abbasis or Dfl. 7:4:8 as a trial.[47] Nader Shah's most common mints were Isfahan, Mashhad and Tabriz, and to a lesser degree, Shiraz, Tiflis, Qazvin and Qandahar (Naderabad). Prior to 1734 his mints had been Mazandaran, Mashhad and Semnan. For the period after 1739, following Nader's invasion of India, there were also a number of Indian mints, including Bakhwar, Peshawar, Derajat, Kabul and Sind. Thus, Nader Shah's monetary policy initially was a continuation of that of the last Safavids, who had sought to strike coins of a weight which would accommodate trade and be compatible with the real of eight.

The new coins struck by Nader Shah did not address the problems that had caused the tightness in the money market, however, and in particular the adverse gold–silver ratio compared to conditions in the Ottoman Empire. Also, as always, a lack of bullion caused government revenue receipts in ready money to fall short. Therefore, Nader Shah again took to extracting cash money from the population. In October 1736, tax collectors were seen going about with sticks, swords and hatchets, tormenting and beating people to get the additional 12,000 tumans assigned to Isfahan and proportionally to other cities.[48] In addition, in 1735 Nader Shah temporarily devalued the copper money by declaring that, henceforth, the double paisa copper coin was worth a single paisa, involving a devaluation of 50 per cent. In early 1736 he rescinded that decree, and for a while the double paisa copper coin was counted at its normal value. This shows once again that there was an official rate of exchange between copper and silver. For although payments took place in copper money, the tax obligation was calculated in silver, and henceforth people had to come up with twice as much copper as before to meet the tax obligation. In Isfahan, in December 1736 the paisa decree of early 1736 was revoked, restoring the double paisa

46 Marvi, *`Alamara-ye Naderi*, 1:377.

47 *NA*, VOC 2417, Resolution Gamron, 9 Mar. 1737, fol. 3799. These were the older `abbasis of 4.61 g, in which case the silver weight (39.19 g) was 11.3 times the gold weight, which yields about the 1:11 gold–silver ratio said to be prevailing at that time. Had they been the new `abbasis of 5.37 g the ratio between the two metals would have been 1:13.2.

48 *NA*, VOC 2416, Isfahan to Gamron, 26 Oct. 1736, fols. 2539–40; VOC 2416, Isfahan to Gamron, 14 Apr. 1737, fol. 1315.

as a single one, and simultaneously a ban on the export of this coin was issued. Moreover, each Banyan and money-changer (sarraf) was permitted to keep no more than the value of 50 mahmudis in his shop or house on pain of a fine of 12 tumans.[49] Apparently, the decree concerning the paisas was being circumvented, for in June 1737 Nader Shah once again decreed that the double paisa henceforth was worth only one paisa.[50]

This devaluation of copper money may have improved Nader Shah's financial situation, but it created serious problems for trade. Because of the lack of silver, there was brisk buying of copper by English and French merchants in Bushire and consequently copper prices there rose sharply. Schoonderwoerd, the VOC agent at Bushire at that time, did not understand how they could make money on these purchases, for they bought copper at prices of 10.75 up to 13 silver mahmudis, although normally at 11¹/₅ mahmudis per man of 3.06 kg (6.75 lbs). But even that was not enough, for even copper money was in short supply. The EIC agents as well as other merchants therefore also practised barter trade. The VOC staff were not allowed to do so and had to accept copper at 10⁴/₅ mahmudis per 3.06 kg.[51] The situation in Bandar `Abbas was not much better. In December 1736, the EIC wanted sell all of its fabrics in Bandar `Abbas,

> [...] provided the money could be got for it in any reasonable time, which is impossible as Copper and Goz are so very scarce that neither the Broker or Merchants would be able to pay for the quantity now sent in those two species those two years. Nor would they obtain such prices to be paid in Abasse and Mahmoodies as would be equivalent to the difference of Exchange which is fifty per cent. & they are afraid should the King's Merchant return as expected he will offer to pay them in white money [silver] & expect the woolen goods cheaper than they formerly sold to the Broker.[52]

In March 1737, both copper and silver money were so scarce in Kerman that merchants did not care whether they were paid in silver (previously

49 *NA*, VOC 2417, Isfahan to Gamron, 26 Dec. 1736, fols. 3940–41

50 *NA*, VOC 2448, Isfahan to Gamron, 11 June 1737, fol. 1346.

51 *NA*, VOC 2416, Bushire to Gamron, 10 Dec. 1736, fols. 209–12. The price per 1 lb was 1 13/15 mahmudis. At 2.30 g per mahmudi (a half shahi), which is 30 g of silver for 3.06 kg of copper, or an exchange rate of about 1:100, which was the approximate rate prevailing in the two main centers of copper production and use at that time (Sweden and northeast Asia), see Treue, 'Copper Trade'.

52 Saldanha, *Persian Gulf Précis*, 1:50.

the preferred medium) or copper as long as they were paid.[51] This was an indication of a severe shortage of not only of silver but also of copper. It is, therefore, not surprising that in June 1737 Nader Shah issued orders that the road guards (*rahdars*) had to see to it that no copper was exported.[52] This had a negative impact on trade and, with most funds going to the army, ready money became very scarce.[53] This development resulted in higher prices for metals and coins. In Bushire, there was much old copperware for sale at 8.5 or 9 mahmudis silver money per man of 3.40 kg.[54] The little silver that still was to be had at Bushire was sold in small lots at a premium (at 15–16 mahmudis) or was exported to Basra, where higher prices were obtained.[55]

To fill his empty coffers Nader Shah needed additional funds. Therefore, in January 1738, if not earlier, Nader decided to devalue his currency. In early February 1738, a decree was made public in Bushire to the effect that henceforth all European and other gold ducats had to be valued at 18 silver mahmudis and that `abbasis could not be selected anymore by mint, but had to be accepted 'as is', irrespective of where they had been struck, on pain of confiscation and death.[56] The latter part of this decree received some attention in Gilan and quite likely elsewhere in Iran. In the 1740s, Hanway reported that the peasants in Gilan who sold silk checked the coins they received in return, for there was a problem 'of bad money, for they are often obliged to cut it through, in order to see that it is not copper silvered over. Their jealousy ran so high, that the governor of Ghilan once published an order, that whosoever refused any kind of money, except it was manifestly bad, his ears and nose should be cut off, and his estate confiscated: but I never heard that this order was carried into execution.'[57]

Nader's advisors, not satisfied with the devaluation, followed it up with more detailed instructions as well the announcement of the

53 *NA*, VOC 2417, Kerman to Gamron, 19 Mar. 1737, fol. 4170; Saldanha, *Persian Gulf Précis*, 1:51, 25 Feb. 1737. (In Kerman, 'silver money was at one hundred per cent. exchange'. ... old copper at Carmania was twenty nine Shahees that maund ... Abasses at five Shahees, or Black Money or old Copper.) See Marvi, *'Alamara-ye Naderi*, 2:664. (Nader's agents were buying ashrafis.)

54 *NA*, VOC 2448, Isfahan to Gamron, 11 June 1737, fol. 1346.

53 *NA*, VOC 2448, Isfahan to Gamron, 26 Oct. 1737, fol. 1423.

54 *NA*, VOC 2448, Bushire to Gamron, 24 Aug. 1737, fol. 1504.

55 *NA*, VOC 2448, Gamron to Batavia, 23 Nov. 1737, fol. 1511.

56 *NA*, VOC 2448, Bushire to Gamron, 18 Feb. 1738, fol. 2415. Given that ducats were 3.49 g that implies a gold-silver ratio of 1:11.9, assuming that the `abbasis (which were two mahmudis) were 4.61 g. It also means that the government insisted on the acceptance of a quasi face value of the `abbasi.

57 Hanway, *Historical Account*, 2:17.

issuance of new coins. To that end a royal decree was sent to all major towns in Iran. In Isfahan it was read in the main mosque on Zu'l Qa`deh 16, 1150/7 March 1738. From the text of the decree it is clear that the new measures aimed to 'correct' the weight and alloy of the coinage to make it less attractive for export. The royal message was that because money was being exported due to its good quality, assay and weight, the shah had decided to strike new `abbasis of 6 dang or 1 mesqal or 24 nokhud (4.6 g), instead of the previous ones of 7 dang or 1$^{1}/_{6}$ mesqal (5.37 g). Nader Shah further gave orders to strike six shahi coins of 9 dang or 1.5 mesqal (6.9 g), which would be passed off as if they had a value of 3 mahmudis. A number of these heavier six shahi coins had already been struck by the end of March 1738. No actual `abbasis were coined. Instead, coins of 1, 6 and 20 shahis were struck. Those in possession of old `abbasis of 7 dang could only spend them as if they weighed 6 dang. Bringing these coins to the mint to have them restruck required paying seignorage, but one would also receive the difference in value, or about 1.5 paisa. This decree was published all over Iran. In general, according to the Dutch, people were happy about the new measure, for they now expected money to remain in the country. However, they also feared that life necessities would rise in price, and that they would have to pay 7 instead of 6 dangs, because the shopkeepers would charge their wares at the old rate. The same held for debts which also would have to be paid in the old value, unless it was decreed that the old rule applied, so that this was a source of possible conflict.[58]

The new monetary regulations came into force about three weeks before Qandahar fell on 24 March 1738 after a one-year siege. With that conquest at least 300,000 tumans fell into Nader Shah's hands, a real windfall for his depleted treasury.[59] To commemorate this victorious event Nader had new silver coins struck at Qandahar and Isfahan, with orders to value them at 3$^{3}/_{5}$ mahmudis (3 mahmudis heavy or silver money) or Dfl. 1:10:9$^{3}/_{5}$. They were only allowed to be struck at these two towns.[60]

The new regulations caused `abbasis to become scarce. The Dutch, who were allowed to export specie, found it difficult to obtain cash. As soon as the governor of Bandar `Abbas learned that they were collecting small amounts of gold or silver, he would interfere. In addition, to buy a larger quantity of gold coins, they had to pay a higher unit price in silver. Van

58 *NA*, VOC 2448, Isfahan to Gamron, 7 Mar. 1738, fols. 2352–53; Album, *Checklist*, 285.

59 *NA*, VOC 2584, Beschrijvinge, fol. 2036.

60 *NA*, VOC 2448, Gamron to Batavia, 30 Apr. 1738, fol. 1805. These coins probably are the rare six shahi coins of 6.91 g. See Album, *Checklist*, 286.

Leypsigh, the Dutch agent in Isfahan, wrote that to get 5,000 tumans in `abbasis of seven dang or $1^1/_6$ mesqal he would have to pay in new coin and with a discount of 7 per cent. To this would be added administrative overhead of 12 per cent, because one had to appoint a special person to seek out and collect these coins.

Copperware at this point had become so prominent in the money markets that buyers even differentiated between the types of copper offered. There was Hamadani copper and Kermani copper, which was of almost the same quality as Qazvin copper. Hamadani copper was not always obtainable. It was of good quality, but it was higher in price due to the cost of its packing material.[61] Demand for copper was at times so brisk that it led to panic buying. In November 1738, Dutch agent Schoonderwoerd reported that in Bushire copper was bought at incredible price of 15 mahmudis per man. Buyers did not even look at the quality of the metal, but just put it into bags and weighed these on the local scale. The flabbergasted Dutchman wondered how these traders could make a profit.[62] Despite the fact that by then even long-distance trade was financed with copper money or copperware, Schoonderwoerd reported that 'one counts here never with black [copper], but always with white [silver] money at 50% agio [discount] for white money, so that 100 mahmudis in reality is 150 mahmudis copper money'.[63] As this example suggests, while there was one metallic standard (silver in this case) to value other commodities, at the same time other metals (and later also paper) circulated as well.[64]

The transport of copper coins was still not allowed without permission from the governor. Van Leypsigh therefore considered it best for the VOC to trade in used copper utensils rather than in new ones, because the former were cheaper and available in larger quantity. Merchants sold much used old copperware, but, according to the VOC broker (*dallal*), one might not collect more than 1,000 tumans in one year by purchasing it.[65] Writing from Isfahan, Van Leypsigh in December 1738 reported that he might be able to obtain a maximum of 2,000 tumans value in copper money in this manner. Although Batavia had instructed the Bandar `Abbas office to get as much

61 *NA*, VOC 2448, Gamron to Batavia, 30 Apr. 1738, fols. 1804–05, 1874.
62 *NA*, VOC 2476, Bushire to Gamron, 12 Nov. 1738, fols. 1091, 1095.
63 *NA*, VOC 2448, Bushire to Gamron, 21 Apr. 1738, fol. 2429.
64 On this issue, see Pamuk, *Monetary History*, 71.
65 *NA*, VOC 2476, Isfahan to Gamron, 21 Aug. 1738, fols. 898–900; VOC 2476, Isfahan to Gamron, 26 Dec. 1738, fol. 950. (Copper cost 10 4/5 mahmudis or Dfl. 4:11:12 4/5 per 6 lbs.)
66 *NA*, VOC 2510, Marginal note to Eis, Batavia, 15 Oct. 1738, fol. 1448.

purified copper as possible, the local agents had little success in doing so. The Dutch did not buy any old copperware, for it was mostly burned through and thus unprofitable.[66] Old copper pots, purified of its iron and rust by blacksmiths, were also offered for sale, but here, too, profits were not guaranteed.[67] Because Batavia had forbidden Bandar `Abbas to buy burned copper, it only wanted to have clean and refined copper, the same material of which copper paisas were made, the Dutch tried to smelt it in the form of Japanese copper. However this did not work out because the copper cakes cost too much.[68] By that time silver had become very rare, and at Bushire it was unobtainable even at a discount of 40 per cent.[69] Mattheus van Leijpsigh, the VOC agent in Isfahan, wrote in August 1739 to Carel Koenad, the director in Bandar `Abbas, asking him to send cash for his daily expenses, because it was very difficult to borrow money locally, even at 2.5 per cent monthly interest.[70] The Dutch were not only ones who suffered from the tight money supply; so did the viceroy, Nader Shah's oldest son. According to news from Kerman in November 1739, the viceroy had copper coins struck in Mashhad because of the scarcity of copper money. He put their value at three mesqals, which was a difference of one mesqal with the existing situation.[71]

Table 5.4: Difference in cost of copperware and copper coins between Bandar `Abbas and Bushire (May 1739)

Paisa	Gamron	Bushire	Paisa	Gamron	Bushire	Copper	Gamron	Bushire
cost per 6 lbs. excl. overhead	1,730	1,589	cost per 6 lbs. incl. overhead	1,747	1,606	per 6 lbs. refined excl. packaging	1469	1,160
difference with cost		141 or 9%			141 or 9%			309 or 26 ⅔%

Source: VOC 2477, Gamron to Batavia (14/05/1739), fol. 76–78. The original amounts were in Dutch guilders, stuivers and penningen, which have been converted into penningen. One Dutch guilder = 20 stuivers; 1 stuiver = 16 penningen.

67 *NA*, VOC 2476, Isfahan to Gamron, 26 Dec. 1738, fols. 949–50; Ibid., 25 Feb. 1739, fol. 51.
68 *NA*, VOC 2477, Gamron to Batavia, 14 May 1739, fols. 76, 79–80.
69 *NA*, VOC 2476, Bushire to Gamron, 12 Jan. 1739, fols 1100–01, 1104; VOC 2476, Gamron to Batavia, 25 Feb. 1739, fol. 90. (Dfl. 50,000 or 1,800 tumans copper or 1,200 tumans silver money.)
70 *NA*, VOC 2510, Isfahan to Gamron, 18 Aug. 1739, fol. 652.
71 *NA*, VOC 2510, Kerman to Gamron, 19 Nov. 1739, fol. 1357.

In March 1739, Nader Shah defeated the Mughal emperor Mohammad Shah and conquered his capital Delhi. As a result, Nader acquired an enormous booty, which he carried to Iran. The total estimated value of the spoils brought from India ranges from 30 million to 87 million pounds, with various sources claiming that half was in specie or coin.[72] However, one contemporary source states that the bullion part of the booty was much less. In a letter dated 12 June 1740, an unknown Iranian official to the Russian consul in Isfahan that the Mughal treasury, though invaluable, contained mainly precious stones. 'Current coins, both gold and silver were not found in great quantities.'[73] Keen to acquire as much as possible of the booty, Nader had his soldiers searched at river crossings and other transit points. Yet the resentment this caused made him decide to give each soldier 500 rupees in cash; officers received more. Assuming an army of 200,000, this translates into some 10 million pounds, or a sizeable part of the booty. Still, Nader Shah was able to amass much gold, silver and jewelry in his treasury at Kalat.[74]

Feeling militarily and financially secure after his Indian conquest, Nader Shah attempted to merge the monetary system of Iran with that of India to facilitate trade with Iran's main trading partner. Convinced that he had to play an historical role after his conquest of India in 1739, and further buoyed by that of Turkestan a year later, he resolved to establish an empire stretching from Delhi to Constantinople.[75] This intention was prefigured in the new legend that Nader Shah, in commemoration of his victory over Mohammad Shah at Delhi in March 1739, had put on his rupee:

72 Lockhart, *Nader Shah*, 152; Malcolm, *History of Persia*, 2:86–87; al-Esfahani, *Nesf-e jahan*, 263; Golestaneh, *Mojmal al-tavarikh*, 19–20 (in cash 15 *korur* or 7.5 million tumans). The booty did not only include the wealth he took in Delhi. His prior victories at Peshavar, Lahore, etc. also had yielded large treasures. For example, Marvi, *`Alamara-ye Naderi*, 2:760 (a hoard of 100,000 tumans and 500,000 *tuman-e ashrafi* was hidden in the castle of Amarkot).

73 Gopal, *Indians in Russia*, 197. Occasionally, Nader Shah was very liberal in giving extremely costly presents from his booty to those rulers whom he wanted to impress such as Abu'l-Feyz Khan of Bokhara. In 1740 he gave him 18 Arab pureblood horses with their jewel-studded accoutrements, which were valued at 60,000 tumans. Moreover, he presented him with a sword, dagger, armlets and jewelry valued at 100,000 tumans. See Marvi, *`Alamara-ye Naderi*, 2:795.

74 *NA*, VOC 2510, Gamron to Batavia, 25 Dec. 1739, fol. 102 (at the crossing of the Indus, Nader Shah had his soldiers take their clothes off one by one and took whatever valuables they had. These were registered, but so far he had only restituted 30 tumans to them; the remainder he took for himself. He promised to give them later 100 tumans); Lockhart, *Nader Shah*, 152; Malcolm, *History of Persia*, 2:86–87; al-Esfahani, *Nesf-e jahan*, 263.

75 Lockhart, *Nader Shah*, 123.

Obverse:

هست سطان بر سلاطین جهان　　　شاه شاهان نادر صا حبقر ان

The soltan of soltans, who is king of all the world, the shahenshah Nader, who has no equal

Reverse:

خلدالله ملکه ضر ب دار الخلافت شاه جهان آباد

God bless the country under his reign. Struck in the imperial residence Shah Jahanabad (in 1151).

The new rupee equaled other good rupees in price and value. Nader Shah also is reported to have struck a gold medal with a value of 100 tumans to pay his army. However, these coins could only be exchanged by presenting them to his treasurer, who charged a 10 per cent fee for this, thus further enriching Nader Shah's treasury.[76] In September 1740, he published a decree which stated that 'Because in Hindustan the coin is the rupee, in Turkey it is the qurush and sjalot [sic; *zolota*], and in Turkestan it is called aatje [sic; *aqcheh*], henceforth in Iran the coinage minted by weight and exchange will be of five mahmudis. These coins will be called naderis. It is forbidden to use the terms `abbasi, tuman, etc. The government officials etc. have to observe that the sum of the above mentioned 5 mahmudis is to be expressed in multiples of mahmudis, which equal so many naderis and dinars.'[77]

To integrate the Indian and the Iranian monetary system, the new Iranian monetary system adopted the Mughal gold *mohur*, known in Persian as *mohr-e ashrafi*, weighing almost exactly 11 g. This means that Nader abandoned the attempt to model the monetary system after the Spanish real of eight, widely used in long-distance trade at that time. Furthermore, the shah made one Iranian silver tuman equal to 20 silver rupees of 11.52 g

76 *NA*, VOC 2510, Kerman to Gamron, 16 Sept. 1739, fol. 1348; VOC 2510, Gamron to Batavia, 25 Dec. 1739, fols. 101–02; Sha`bani, *Hadis-e Nader Shahi*, 23.

77 *NA*, VOC 2546, Order by Welie Nemad (Vali-ye Ne`mat) concerning the coinage, received on 15 Sept. 1740, fols. 1841–42. The EIC records also report the proclamation that silver coinage (Abassees, Mamoodees and Nadirees) be called in and replaced with rupees – 'being of the same Value with those he [i.e., Nader] stamped in India ... which, if the exchange continues to fall here, ... must have a very good effect on the Trade carried into this country ...'. IOR, Gombroon Diary, G/29, 5 Feb. 1740 (i.e., 16 Feb., New Style). We thank Michael Axworthy for this reference.

each, or 230.5 g of silver. This is indeed the silver weight reported by Hanway around 1742 for all silver coins listed (see Table 4.6). It is also the ratio reported by contemporary Iranian sources.[78] Nader Shah also ordered that, for accounting purposes, the Indian term *korur* (*crore*, 10 million) and *lakh* (100,000) should be used. Given the fact that 20 silver rupees equaled one gold Iranian tuman in the new system, these two terms refer respectively to 500,000 and 5,000 Iranian gold tumans. However, Iranian clerks used the term *alf* (1,000) instead of lakh to refer to a sum of 5,000 tumans.[79] He also continued to strike 1, 6, 10 and 20 shahis. The latter was known as the double rupee. The ten shahi coin, the Iranian rupee or naderi, had a weight of 11.52 g, which was within the range of the various rupee denominations then current in India.[80] The `abbasi, which was no longer a coin but a unit of account, was kept at 4.61 g or one mesqal, based on standard of 1,200 nokhud (of each 192 milligram) per tuman of 50 `abbasis.

Although some ashrafis continued to be struck on the Venetian standard as late as 1165/1752, the principal coin after 1152/1739 was the Mughal mohur.[81] At the occasion of New Year 1747, Nader Shah gave 12,000 ashrafis to his courtiers and officers, suggesting that gold coins may have been struck in large numbers, at least for that occasion.[82] Half-, quarter-, and eighth-mohr-e ashrafis were added; the quarter ashrafi was the principal gold coin from about 1170/1757 until the extension of the tuman standard to gold in 1201/1787. Furthermore, in 1153/1740, according to numismatic evidence, all mints but Isfahan, Tabriz and Mashhad were closed.[83]

Whatever the goal of the monetary reform of 1740, it mattered little to the Iranian population or to those trading with Iran. Despite the enormous booty that Nader Shah had brought from India and the new coins that he had struck, commerce was still mostly carried on with copper. This reality

78 Astarabadi, *Tarikh-e jahangosha-ye Naderi*, 468 (200,000 rupees = 10,000 tumans).

79 al-Esfahani, *Nesf-e jahan*, 264; Marvi, *`Alamara-ye Naderi*, 3:1000, 1036, 1082, 1084-85, 1090, 1100, 1115, 1174, 1193 (alf =5,000 tumans = 100,000 naderis). According to Simmons, 'Evolution of Persia's Monetary System', 76, 'the word 'crore' came to mean 500,000 in Persia because of the failure of Nadir Shah's principal monetary reforms'. However, Simmons did not understand that *korur* meaning 500,000 tumans was correct, because he did not realize that to go from one tuman to rupees, one has to multiply that amount by 20. The Iranians knew very well that korur meant ten million. In 1738, the presents brought by an ambassador of the Mughal emperor had a value of 20 lakh of rupees or one million tumans, thus only 2 rupees per tuman. *NA*, VOC 2476, Isfahan to Gamron, 18 May 1738, fols. 888–89.

80 For numismatic information concerning these coins, see Album, *Checklist*, 286.

81 Album et al., 'Coins and Coinage.'

82 Marvi, *`Alamara-ye Naderi* , 3 :1088.

83 Album, *Checklist*, 285.

suggests that the basic parameters of Iran's monetary situation had not changed at all.

Given the new and large supply of bullion one would expect that Iran's problem of tight money supply was resolved, at least in the short, if not the medium term. However, that did not happen. For despite the major influx of booty into Iran after the conquest of India in 1739, much of that was hoarded by Nader Shah himself as well as his commanders. In fact, Nader Shah had instituted a policy whereby all gold and silver that he could lay his hands on was transferred to his treasury, or hoarded rather, in Kalat-e Naderi. According to Hanway, in the 1740s the army's wage bill alone amounted to 5 million pounds (2 million tumans) per year, while the annual revenues were supposed to yield a similar amount (5.7 million pounds or 2.3 million tumans), half of it from the conquered areas in India. However, except for the conquered parts of India and the provinces of Gilan and Mazandaran, the kingdom was so impoverished by rapine that, in Hanway's estimation, it might only pay one quarter of the normal revenues. These amounted to 2,387,000 pounds or 41 per cent of the total. Thus, if only one quarter of these would be paid, revenue would be about 590,000 pounds, with total revenue of 3.9 million pounds. This constituted a considerable shortfall of budgetary requirements, contributing to local rebellions, abandonment of land, further plunder and debasement of the currency.[84] Hence additional taxes were imposed on the population to cover the budgetary deficit.[85]

In another sign that the new policy had failed to address the underlying structural problems, debased coins continued to circulate in large quantities. Hanway reported that in the 1740s, Armenian merchants supplied the Lezghis with goods. They traded partly in barter, partly 'with false Persian money; for as the coin of this empire is made small and thick, it is counterfeited exactly with very little silver. It is said the Armenians accept of this counterfeit for a quarter part of its current value; however, this may be, it is certain there are great quantities of this money in Persia, not only silver, but gold also.'[86]

As a consequence, the specie which had to be exported to make up for the deficit on the trade balance continued to be composed of a great variety of domestic and foreign coins and metals. Precious metals, including Iranian struck silver and gold coins, became scarce, and copper, coins as well as metal, continued to make up the bulk of the specie that was exported (see

84 Hanway, *Account*, 2:26–27. According to Marvi, *'Alamara-ye Naderi*, 3:1088, in 1747 when Nader held court in Kabul, there were some 220,000 men in his army camp.

85 *NA*, VOC 2593, Gamron to Batavia, 31 Oct. 1742, fol. 1778.

86 Hanway, *Account*, 1:374–75.

Table 4.7). This may also explain why the considerable number of countermarked coins of the period from the reign of Nader Shah and his Zand successors consist of rupees and double rupees.[87]

Yet copper continued to hold its dominant place in the market. In Bushire, in April 1740, merchants greedily bought old copperware, even unpurified specimens. The market was spoiled when Banyans (who had come in an English ship) paid 12.5 mahmudis per man of 3.06 kg instead of 10 mahmudis.[88] At the end of 1740 they paid 13–13.5 silver mahmudis.[89] In March 1741, the English Captain Grant even paid the unprecedented price of 16 silver mahmudis for old copperware.[90] Assuming that these silver mahmudis weighed 2.3 g (either because they fell under the new rules, where 3 mahmudis equaled a 6.9 g `abbasi, or because they fell under the old system in which 2 mahmudis were equal to a 4.61 g `abbasi), the silver weight of 16 mahmudis was 36.8 g, which yields a ratio of 1.83 for a 3.06 kg man of copper, more or less in line with the prevailing world market average of 1:100.

Table 5.5: Coins in use in Iran – their weights and values in the 1740s

	Dinars	Nokhud and gram equivalent (note 24 nokhud = 1 mesqal = 4.6 g)
Gold		
Muhr ashraffie	6,000	57 nokhud or 10.94 g
Ashreffie, or old ducat (equal in fineness to Holland ducat)	1,800	18 nokhud or 3.46 g
Do. Shah nadir, or new ducat	1,800	18 nokhud or 3.46 g
Do. of mesched	1,800	18 nokhud or 3.46 g
Do. bokhara current at	1,800	17.75 nokhud or 3.41 g
Fonduckli, Turkish ducat, about	1,800	18 nokhud or 3.46 g
Venetian ducat	1,800	17.5 nokhud or 3.41 g
The common abbasie should be	2,000	24 nokhud or 4.61 g
Do. Shah sultan Hussein	5.44	28 nokhud or 5.38 g

87 Album, *Checklist*, 285.

88 *NA*, VOC 2511, Bushire to Gamron, 5 Apr. 1740, fols. 1094–95.

89 *NA*, VOC 2511, Bushire to Gamron, 16 May 1740, fol . 1107; VOC 2546, Bushire to Gamron, 9 Nov. 1740, fols. 1163–64.

90 *NA*, VOC 2546, Bushire to Gamron, 31 July 1741, fol. 1383.

Table 5.5 (continued)

	Dinars	Nokhud and gram equivalent (note 24 nokhud = 1 mesqal = 4.6 g)
Gold		
Do. Shah suliman	7.38	38 nokhud or 7.29 g
Do. Shah seffie	7.77	40 nokhud or 7.68
Silver		
One tuman [imaginary] is 10 hazardenaers	10,000	1,200 nokhud or 230.4 g
'It must be observed that the hazardenaer (which the English called mill denear, and the Russians a ruble) is computed by Europeans, and accounts kept in hundreds'	–	–
Peng sid denar, or rupie or nadirie	500	60 nokhud or 11.52 g
Sisid denaer, or shis shahie	300	36 nokhud or 6.91
Abbasie	200	24 nokhud or 4.61 g
Sid denaer, or mahmudie	100	12 nokhud or 2.30 g
Shahie, or sahie	50	6 nokhud or 1.15 g
Bistie [imaginary]3	20	
Copper		
Kazbekie	5	
'An English crown melted down in Reshd, produced at 17 denaers (the common price of silver) per muscal, only 95 denears; but we have always computed the mildenaer or 100 denears, equal to an English crown of 5 s.'[91]		

Source: Hanway, *Account*, 2:20–21 (weights in grains have been converted to grams); Lerch, *Nachricht von der zweiten Reise*, 401.

91 According to Simmons, 'Evolution of Persia's Monetary System', 310–11, 'The Europeans kept accounts in 100's, not 1,000's, and, in effect removed one zero from the tuman of 10,000 ghost dinars. This simply means that they made hazar, or 1,000 dinars the centerpiece of their system and called this mildinar. The English computed the mildinar as being worth an English crown of 5 shillings. This crown indicates a silver weight of about that of the piece of eight reals. Ten crowns give a silver weight for the tuman that is much higher than the 3.600 grains calculated from 20 rupees. The use of this unit by the Europeans in the 1740s confirms the trend towards the accommodation of the piece of eight reals.' It is more likely, however, given that the Russians still used the same system in the 1770s (see Table 4.9), that the British had adopted it from the Russians. The more so, since the mildinar was not only 10 crowns, but also equal to 10 rubles. It was more logical for the British to adopt an accounting system that accommodated the ruble, a currency that they also were trading in.

Table 5.6: VOC export of specie from Iran (1732–47)

Item / Year	1732	1733	1734	1735	1736	1739	1740
Spanish reals	9,000		3,148	645,342	103	1,025	84 1,870
Gold rupees	856		26			40	50
Gold ducats (some of which are 'Moorish')	21,000	7,014	100 637 9,500	5,070	1,175	300	1,066 1,500
Ducats melted	4,934	750	402	1,023		1,785 1,991 1,806	636
Imperial thalers				97	84		
Silver `abbasi	13,758 724	8,500		2,256			3,919
Zelotas	20,886	13,450		37,819	64,115	12,533 17,900	1,716
Zelotas light			17,000				
Zelotas heavy			3,419				
Lion dollars			929		10		625
Wellie mehmeds							82,000
Persian rupees							500
Reals silver		684				1,094 192 398	323
Rupees silver			100				
Piasters					14,095	5,600 9,500	2,751
Naderis silver							
Rupees Surat							
Paisas copper (in pounds)	6.5	81,880	53,280 107,280	140,382	67,950	30,500 20,000 9,988	9,860
Old copperware (in pounds)					60,622	21,729 35,970 40,466	7,702
Copper cakes (in pounds)						700	6,000
Unrefined copper							

Source: *NA*, VOC 2323, 22 Sept. 1734, fol. 248; VOC 2357, 24 Aug. 1735, fols. 442–45; VOC 2416, 10 Dec. 1736, fols. 448–49; VOC 2417, 4 Apr. 1737, fol. 3666; VOC 2476, 25 Feb. 1739, fols. 138–40; VOC 2477, 14 May 1739, fols. 164–65; VOC 2510, 25 Dec. 1739, fol. 173; VOC 2511, 31 July 1740, fols. 208–09; VOC 2511, 31 July 1740, fol. 210; VOC 2546, 15 Apr. 1741, fol. 150–53; VOC 2593, 22 Jan. 1742, fol.172; VOC 2705, 31 July 1746), fols. 147–48; VOC 2680, 10 Aug. 1745, fols. 191–92; VOC 2705 28 Feb. 1747, fol. 555.

Table 5.6 (continued)

Item \ Year	1741	1742	1743	1744	1745	1746	1747
Spanish reals		8,089				4,000	
Gold rupees	233	322			100	225 80	
Gold ducats (some of which are 'Moorish')	1,006 1,150 3,600	2,270 2,600			900	420 800	
Ducats melted							
Imperial thalers							
Silver `abbasis		1,582				300	
Zelotas	28,000	12,650				7,000	
Zelotas light							
Zelotas heavy							
Lion dollars							
Wellie mehmeds	40,000					49,200 2,800 doubles	
Persian rupees	1,500	13,500				5,000	
Reals silver	700 555*						
Rupees silver							2,823
Piasters	15,000	10,000				8,917	520 29,000
Naderis silver	4,584	110,672			20,835		
Rupees Surat					4,600		
Paisas copper							
Old copperware (in pounds)						60,509	62,501 Dfl. 36,173
Copper cakes (in pounds)	33,700						10,493
Unrefined copper	25,200				23,068		

Note: The *zolota*, originally a Polish coin (the zloty is still the Polish currency), was greatly used by the Ottomans after 1690. Originally, it was was $^{2}/_{3}$ of the weight of the *gurush*, later only $^{3}/_{4}$. It is also referred to as *isolott* and *sjalotte*.

Although the VOC lost on the export of copper, the English and French gladly bought it, even at those high prices, suggesting that there must have been a smaller loss on copper than on silver and gold coins. The governor-general of the VOC did not like copper. Hearing that the Bandar office traded in gold and silver coins, he pressed his director in Bandar `Abbas about this matter. In October 1742, Simon Clement, the new VOC director, called this rumor false. Reals and imperial thalers were not seen at all at Bandar `Abbas. Merchants sometimes offered Moorish ducats and rupees in secret in small lots of 100–200. But their number was too insignificant to be of use in trade. The problem was that Nader Shah claimed all gold for his Kalat treasure house. As the Dutch put it: 'The trade coin is the silver mahmudi of 10.5 and 3 mahmudis, which Nader struck. There are also Thatta, Delhi and Agra rupees, the latter being more numerous than naderis. They are all taken to India by the English and French, who find these to be more profitable.'[92]

Although prices fluctuated, copper money (paisas) and copperware remained expensive and scarce, so much so that in 1742 the Dutch reported that 'old copperware and paisa coins have totally disappeared ... so that we are sometimes in trouble when the ships have to depart, because we have to change the rupees into the said Persian [copper] coin. Moreover, traders do not like to transport it for you always lose money on it.'[93]

The cash scarcity formed another impediment to normal financial operations. To avoid sending cash, merchants made use of money drafts to facilitate trade. However, such transactions were not without problems either. For example, in December 1736 a draft was drawn by the VOC Isfahan office on its Bandar `Abbas office in an amount of 350 tumans in white money (i.e., silver) at 25 per cent premium, which means that the amount of silver to be received in Bandar `Abbas would be 25 per cent more than paid in Isfahan – which suggests high interests rates and a variation in the availability of cash from city to city. However, paying off that draft was no easy matter, since the only readily available money was copper, which at the market exchange rate meant that to pay off the note would require an amount of copper that, following the VOC's internal valuation system used for keeping its books, would be 50 per cent higher in value than the sum paid in Isfahan.[94]

92 *NA*, VOC 2593, Gamron to Batavia, 31 Oct. 1742, fol. 1622–23vs.

93 Ibid., fol. 1623vs.

94 *NA*, VOC 2417, Resolution Gamron, 19 Jan. 1737, fol. 3717. The same held for bills drawn in Kerman on Bandar `Abbas, where 100 tumans silver money were valued as being 142 tumans copper money. *NA*, VOC 2322, Kerman to Gamron, 30 July 1733, fol. 468r.

Sending drafts from Isfahan to Bandar `Abbas continued to be disadvantageous. In April 1739, the 'rate of exchange' for drafts from Bandar `Abbas to Isfahan was 12–15 per cent, yet from Isfahan to Bandar `Abbas the premium was 22.5 per cent.[95] This difference became more pronounced in the years that followed. For example, in Bandar `Abbas the discount on drafts was 25 per cent, while in Isfahan it was as high as 50–75 per cent for silver mahmudis in 1742. This meant that a holder of a draft of 100 silver mahmudis would receive the sum of 132.5 copper mahmudis at a 25 per cent discount in Bandar `Abbas, while in Isfahan he would get 150–75 copper mahmudis. This made it 15 per cent more profitable for merchants to transport copper from Isfahan to Bandar `Abbas rather than sending a draft. To resolve this problem Nader Shah gave orders that the value of the silver and copper mahmudi was the same, and that discounts were forbidden.[96] Increased oppression of the population and the incidence of rebellions by local governors prevented conditions from improving.[97] Everybody, therefore, breathed a sigh of relief when it was announced that Nader Shah had been assassinated in September 1747.

The Afsharid Successors (1747–50)

The twelve years following Nader Shah's death were marked by political chaos, leaving the currency situation confused. Nader's successors struck a whole range of denominations, although the `abbasi of 4.6 g and the rupee or naderi of 11.5 g tended to predominate. That Nader's successors continued to adhere to the Indian standard was most likely due to the dehoarding of the Kalat treasury by `Adel Shah in 1748.[98] Although the new authorities continued to strike coins using the Indian weight standard, they found it difficult to maintain a viable currency. Many local rulers struck their own coinage and fixed arbitrarily their accounting value. Both silver and gold were priced out of the market. This system prevailed until the introduction of the riyal by the Qajars in 1204/1790.

95 *NA*, VOC 2477, Isfahan to Gamron, 29 Apr. 1739, fol. 439.

96 *NA*, VOC 2593, Gamron to Batavia, 31 Oct. 1742, fol. 1628.

97 For a vivid description of the violence used by royal officials to collect money in 1746, see Lerch, 'Nachricht von der zweiten Reise', 432. Also, morals in the business community had reached a low. According to the Dutch, 'Sales are enforced here and they respect contracts as long as the ink is wet.' VOC 2593, Gamron to Batavia, 31 Oct. 1742, fol. 1625.

98 Golestaneh, *Mojmal al-tavarikh*, 20–21. `Adel Shah took all cash and jewels from Kalat to Mashhad, where he shared his wealth by practically giving it away to his army.

Nader Shah's nephews, `Adel Shah (r. 1747–48) and his brother Ebrahim Shah (r. 1748–50), made no changes in the coinage, nor did his grandson Shahrokh Mirza (r. 1748–50) in Khorasan.[99] Money continued to be scarce and changing it from one type of coin into the other remained problematic. Hanway related that in Gilan silver money was used to buy silk. Waiting for a payment from `Adel Shah, he worried that 'in case the shah pays us in gold, it will be difficult to get it exchanged for silver to purchase silk, and this commodity is chiefly purchased with silver, and very little gold can be put off that way. If he pays in silver, it will be difficult to get such a sum exchanged for gold without giving an advance thereon; and any of the merchants concerned chose to have their returns in specie.'[100]

The dehoarding of the Kalat treasury gave a short-lived boost to trade, yet money remained scarce and trade in the Persian Gulf was still dominated by barter and (partial) payment in copper and a variety of silver and gold coins, in particular after 1754. However, the lack of exportable commodities made barter a less attractive option for many merchants, and certainly for the VOC. The Dutch lost on such transactions, as they did on payments in copper. At times, money was so scarce that they had problems paying their daily expenses in Bandar `Abbas and Kerman.[101]

After the last Afsharids (except for Shahrokh Mirza in Khorasan) were eliminated from power in 1750, a nine-year struggle ensued between three new contenders: Mohammad Khan Qajar, Azad Khan Ghelza'i and Karim Khan Zand. The latter would prevail in 1759 over the other two, yet the former's son would oust the Zands in 1794. This was a period of continuous warfare, in which each of the three rivals had their ups and downs. Each struck his own coins, either anonymously or in the name of one or another Safavid scion, based on the standard of 1,200 nokhud.[102]

99 For numismatic information on their coinage, see Album, *Checklist*, 286-87. There existed already a coin with Shahrokh's name on the legend prior to his accession to the throne. In 1740, Nader Shah bestowed the governorship of Herat on Shahrokh Mirza and to commemorate this event he had coins struck with the text: 'amr shod az shahshahan nader sahebqeran – sekkeh bayad dar Herat az shahrokh nam va neshan'. Sha`bani, *Hadis-e Nader Shahi*, 36.

100 Hanway, *Account*, 2:94.

101 Floor, *Rise of the Gulf Arabs*, 87–90.

102 Album, *Checklist*, 288–89. In December 1756, Azad Khan had coins struck in Qazvin with the text: 'La allah illallah Mohammad Nabi Allah Ali Vali Allah'. See Gharavi, 'Un medecin des Lumières', 148.

Table 5.7: VOC export of specie and copper from Bandar `Abbas (1747–54)

Category	1747	1748	1749	1750	1752	1753	1754
Piasters	29	–	–	–	–	–	–
Copper	47,338	45,161	687	4,341	–	–	74,646
Copper cakes	7,065	4,839	–	–	–	–	1,673
Bullion	–	30,546	–	136,348	–	–	–
Silver riyals	–	–	140,000	–	32,000	92,000	–
Surat riyals	–	–	1,320	–	–	–	–
Iranian silver riyals	–	–	11,369	–	–	–	–
Gold riyals	–	–	–	–	–	208	–
Ducats, Turkish	–	–	–	–	–	1,700	–
Shahbumis	–	–	–	–	–	2,300	–
Ducats, Venetian	–	–	–	–	–	1,872	1,077
Gold riyals	–	–	–	–	–	116	1,211

Source: *NA*, VOC 2968, 26 Dec. 1758, fol. 5; VOC 2863, 20 Dec. 1754, fol. 61; VOC 2863, 13 Apr. 1755, fol. 73; VOC 2766, 10 May 1750, fol. 225; VOC 2766, 30 Dec. 1749, fol. 87; VOC 2748, 10 Oct. 1748, fol. 240; VOC 2843, 10 Oct. 1753, fol. 45; VOC 2863, 24 Nov. 1754, fol. 11; VOC 2804, 15 Feb. 1752, fol. 13; VOC 2724, 22 Dec. 1747, fol. 33. Copper and copper cakes are in lbs.; the coins indicate the number, while bullion is in Dutch guilders.

The Zand Period (1759–94)

By 1759 Karim Khan Zand (r. 1163–93/1750–79) had emerged as the victor in the struggle for the control over Iran, be it that some parts such as Khorasan were left under Afsharid authority (as vassals to the Dorranis), while other parts (the Caucasian provinces) remained semi-autonomous. Karim Khan Zand and his successors struck a whole range of anonymous or semi-anonymous denominations, although the `abbasi of 4.6 g and the rupee of 11.5 g tended to predominate. The standard of the coinage was 1200 nokhud per tuman until 1181/1767–68. According to Gmelin, writing in 1770, ‘Persian coins are partly gold, partly silver, and partly copper, both old and new, or rather both known under one name, but with different values. The tuman, bisti and dinar are units of account; the bisti was used as such for both silver and copper. One tuman consisted of 10 *hazar dinar* (hazardenaers) or equal to 10 Russian rubles.'[103] This system prevailed until the introduction of the riyal (Sp. real) in 1204/1790 by the Qajars.[104] The regular mints under Karim Khan were Tabriz, Qazvin, Rasht, Mazandaran, Isfahan, Kashan, Yazd, Shiraz and the court mint (*rekab*).[105] In Hanway and in Gmelin's time, the gold–silver ratio was 1:10 (1 ashrafi or 1 mesqal of gold is 250 kopecks, and 1 `abbasi or 1 mesqal of silver is 25 kopecks), whereas in India it was 1:14 to 1:15.

Although Karim Khan was recognized as overlord over most of Iran after 1763, with large parts independent or semi-autonomous, there was no monetary uniformity in the country. This was true in particular for Khorasan, which was under Dorrani and Afsharid control, as well as for the Caspian and Caucasian provinces, where semi-autonomous local khans held sway. Several of these khanates, especially Ganjeh, Shamakhi, Sheki, Darband, Qarabagh and Georgia, struck their own coins, initially in the name of Nader Shah and later in that of Karim Khan. By the end of the eighteenth century much of their coinage was completely anonymous. None of these local khans ever placed his own name on his coins, though a few rare issues of Darband bear an allusive reference to one of them.[106] These northern Iranian coins were entirely in silver and copper. The denominations of the silver coins remained the `abbasi and its fractions; those of the copper coins are not known. Gmelin observed in 1770 that the full value of a coin was only realized in the area where it had been issued and that one lost money by moving to another province. This meant that silver coins in these khanates were treated as tokens, as had been the case with copper money prior to the 1730s.

> Each khan strikes his own coins. He fixes a value, which about reflects the general pattern that has been briefly mentioned. Only the ducats that circulate in Gilan at two and a half rubles, obtain in Mazandaran only 2 or also only 180 kopecks. The Mazandaran one is not valid in Gilan, at Tabriz one looses on both and in one word as soon as one arrives from one khandom in another one looses money. I know that once it was made known to the Khan of Gilan that merchants had come to Resht with a considerable amount of money in gold to buy silk

103 Gmelin, *Travels through Northern Persia*, 78.

104 Album, *Checklist*, 288–89.

105 Ibid. Rekab means 'stirrup', and is metaphorically used as being 'in attendance to the ruler.

106 Bakikhanov, *Heavenly Rose-Garden*; Album, *Checklist*.

that the ducats would all at once fall to its old value by 25 kopecks, the merchants would buy silk for these prices and would immediately after their departure learn that the ducats once again had risen by 50 kopecks, i.e., to its previous value.[107]

Table 5.8: Coins in use in Iran, their weights and values in 1770

	Counted as	Cost	Verified coin weights
Gold			
Mohr-Ashrafi. Formerly this piece was counted as six hazar dinars, by the Russians computed at one hundred	six *hazar dinar*	6 rubles; now 10 rubles and 11 kopecks	11.00 g
Ashrafi or an old Shah Nader ducat; a new ducat, idem from Mashhad	–	180 kopecks; now 2 rubles 50 kopecks	3.55 g
Shah Safi ashrafi	–	formerly 210; now 314 kopecks	
Shah Soleyman ashrafi	–	formerly 210; now 314 kopecks	
Shah Soltan Hoseyn ashrafi	–	formerly 210; now 314 kopecks	
Silver			
One tuman, unit of account	10 hazar dinar	10 rubles	
Shesh shahi or *sehsad dinar*	300 dinar	30; now 37½ kopecks	6.91 g
`Abbasi	200 dinar	20; now 25	5.37 g
Sad dinar	100 dinar	10; now 12½.	2.68 g
Shahi	50 dinar	5; now 6½ kopecks	1.34 g 1.15 g
Bisti	20 dinar	2 kopecks	–
Qazbegi	5 dinar	½ kopeck	–

Source: Gmelin *Travels through Northern Persia*, p. 78; Album, *Checklist*.

107 Gmelin, *Travels through Northern Persia*, 78.

Traveling to Baku, Gmelin experienced that sometimes he could not even buy food for money.[108] This was partly due to the fact that most coins were adulterated.[109] According to Gmelin,

> In Shamakhi, Derbend and Baku things are even worse, because at these places one finds nothing else but totally adulterated money. The new *`abbassi* has itself an intrinsic silver value of barely 8 kopecks and a half ruble piece barely twenty two. Because all Persian gold and silver money is coined small and thick, therefore, a silver sliver applied on the obverse and the reverse side may hide the pure copper that is in the middle. During my presence in Shamakhi they had realized the damage that these kinds of money did to trade, and they were reduced to half of their previous value, so that I also was done the honor to loose 75 rubles.[110]

The situation in Khorasan was little better. Under Nader Shah's Dorrani successors in Khorasan and Afghanistan, the rupee continued to circulate, probably as the main trade coin. It was referred to as *rupiyeh-ye rayej*.[111] The use of the term *rayej* (current) may indicate that these were countermarked coins, a means to raise revenue.[112] Ahmad Shah Dorrani (r. 1747–72) also minted ashrafis.[113] When he struck new rupees (*rupiyeh-ye sekkeh-ye jadid-e Khorasan*) the old ones were referred to as *rupiyeh-e kohneh*.[114] The [old] rupee was equal to 2 dinar-e Tabriz in 1163/1750.[115] Prices, however, were expressed in the following units of account: tumans, dinars and derhams or derham-e safid.[116] There also was barter trade, in particular with the Turkmen.[117]

In the Persian Gulf region exports in this period mainly consisted of cash. Payments for imported goods were in principle accepted in all kinds of currencies, but in practice were restricted to only a few. The main currencies were the Indian gold rupee, the Iranian silver rupee and the silver naderis.

108 Ibid., 21.

109 Ibid., 11.

110 Ibid., 78–79.

111 al-Monshi, *Tarikh-e Ahmad Shahi*, fols. 71a, 72a, 304b.

112 Ahmad Dorrani principally countermarked rupees and double rupees. The countermark ordinarily consists of the word rayej (current) plus the hejri date. Numismatists believe that these countermarked coins mainly circulated in the Punjab part of the Dorrani kingdom; however, al-Monshi clearly shows that they may have been used in Afghanistan and Khorasan as well. See also Biddulph, 'Countermarked Mughal and Suri Coins', 44–45.

113 al-Monshi, *Tarikh-e Ahmad Shahi*, fols. 49b, 71b, 112a, 324b.

114 Ibid., fols. 72r, 170v;

115 Ibid., fols. 72r, 123r.

116 Ibid., fols. 25r, 117r, 324r, 339v, 360v.

117 Gmelin, *Travels through Northern Persia*, 283, 289.

By 1755 Venetian gold ducats became common in the Gulf. The Dutch at Khark preferred these at a 5 per cent premium to silver.[118] Nevertheless, silver payments were more important than gold, as gold became less and less available. Old copper remained an important form of payment for imported goods, but it is unknown how much copper was exported from the Persian Gulf, even by the VOC and EIC.[119] The VOC considered old copper undesirable, because it could only be disposed of in India with very little profit, and it was subject to underweight because it was delivered mostly in small chips. Although Von Kniphausen, the chief of the Dutch Khark trading station, would gladly have rid himself of copper payments – copper was cumbersome to collect, and it took merchants months to accumulate sufficient quantities – he advised strongly against this directive, arguing that by refusing to accept copper, the VOC might price itself out of the market.[120] This underlines the continued importance of copper in Iran without which international trade could not have operated. The relative importance of copper was further bolstered by the fact that many of the silver mahmudis were so bad that in India they suffered a loss so that in 1763 the EIC began sending them to Basra. Here the EIC lost about 7 per cent on silver money in 1767.[121]

Until the demise of the Khark factory in 1766, the VOC suffered considerable losses on the export of specie. That is, the specie the Company received for selling goods in Iran was not sufficient to recover the cash cost they had to pay abroad to buy those goods and to ship them to Iran – this despite the fact that the VOC laid down strict rules about how to value Iranian coins in terms of Dutch florins. In 1762, the Dutch calculated that from 1753–54 to 1761–62 the company had lost Dfl. 251,227:3:12 on the export of coins and specie, which represented 31 per cent of the total loss incurred by the operation of the Khark factory.[122]

Although he controlled much of Iran, Karim Khan ruled over a greatly impoverished country. Gmelin, describing the situation in the Caspian and Caspian provinces in 1770–73, stated that

> The Persians are less wealthy and impoverished because of oppression by Nadir Shah and even more so due to the revolts that followed his

118 *NA*, VOC 2864, Khark to Batavia, 31 May 1755, fol. 51.

119 *NA*, VOC 1009, Uitgaande brieven, Batavia to Khark, 27 June 1755, fol. 213.

120 *NA*, VOC 2885, Khark to Batavia, 27 Sept. 1755, fol. 17, 44.

121 Saldanha, *Persian Gulf Précis*, 1:159, 10 Mar. 1763; Amin, *British Interests*, 136.

122 *NA*, VOC 1015, Uitgaande brieven, Batavia to Khark, 31 Mar. 1761, fols. 75–76; Ibid., Batavia to Khark, 24 Nov. 1761, fol. 144; VOC 3003, Besogne Karreek, 11 Mar. 1762, fols. 1844vs-45vs. The EIC trading stations in the Persian Gulf (Basra, Bushire) also operated at a loss. See Amin, *British Interests*, 115.

> death as well as the internal wars. One could not trade goods without long and inconvenient credit, if merchants wanted silk to sell profitably in Russia. But apart from that, in comparison with the days of Nadir Shah, money circulation has decreased by more than ninety percent, so that silk cultivation also decreased.[125]

Gmelin's observation implies that the export of Iranian goods had declined.[126] As before, Iran's exportable commodities were limited in number and, apart from silk, small in volume. This was a severe constraint on imports. With silver cheaper in the Ottoman Empire (see Table 4.1), the import of silver into Iran was profitable, but Iran did not have an export surplus to pay for this, quite the contrary. The temptation for Karim Khan, as for past rulers, was to generate specie by debasing the currency or reducing its weight.

Faced with structurally tight money supply and widespread debasement of the coinage, in 1763 Karim Khan Zand first tried to alleviate this situation by having the British agree to a voluntary ban on the export of specie. In the agreement, which was drafted in Zu'l-Hejjeh 1176/July 1763, the British promised 'not to export from Persia the whole Amount of their sales in ready Money, as this will impoverish the Kingdoms [sic] and in the end prejudice Trade in general'.[127] This meant that part of British trade had to be in barter.

Events in India probably affected the monetary situation of Iran as well. In 1765 the EIC, acquiring control of the revenues of Bengal, changed the gold–silver ratio from 1:14 to 1:16.4, thus inflating the value of silver in India.[128] This may have contributed to the insignificant impact of the voluntary restraint in exporting specie from Iran. In 1766, to stop the

123 Gmelin, *Travels through Northern Persia*, 318.

124 For the trade with Russia see Kukanova, 'K voprosu o torgovle Rossii', 74–75; Kukanova, *Ocherki po istorii russko-iranskikh torgovykh otnoshenii*, 157–59; for the Persian Gulf trade, see above.

125 For the text of Karim Khan's decree, see Floor, *Rise of the Gulf Arabs*, 343–44; for a discussion of the negotiations, see ibid, 262–64.

126 Sircar, *Studies in Indian Coins*, 292–93. Shortly thereafter the EIC reduced the ratio to 1:15.

127 Amin, *British Interests*, 134–36. Another source of drainage of cash was the pilgrim trade. In the past pilgrims took merchandise with them to finance their travel expenses. However, 'towards the end of the eighteenth century the pilgrims brought almost nothing from Persia except specie to cover their expenses'. Ibid., 129.

128 Album, *Checklist*, 289. Minting technology remained unchanged, producing unmilled thick coins. In 1786, Francklin, *Observations*, 61, noted: 'There is a mint at Shirauz where money is coined in the name of Jaafar Khan, the present possessor, the process of which is very simple, like most in other places of the East, the gold and silver being laid in a dye fitted for the purpose, and struck with a large hammer, which completes the operation. Here also the public Serafs (or money-changers) set and regulate the exchange of gold and silver.'

continuing outflow of specie, and thus reduce the deficit on the current account, Karim Khan tried to ban the export of specie. He further decreed that henceforth all trade had to be in barter and that no cash should be paid for foreign goods. Naturally, this order was soon relaxed, because, like his predecessors, Karim Khan realized that such regulations could easily be evaded, indirectly, or even directly, by bribing the authorities. Nevertheless, market conditions were such that payments in cash only did not take place anyway. At best, exporters could hope for a partial payment in cash, albeit often in debased coins.[129]

Clearly the overwhelming balance against Iran could only be rectified by developing the export trade, or by reducing imports. As this was not possible in the short term, another way to deal with the problem was to 'correct' the weight and/or alloy of the coinage to make it less attractive for export. To that effect the government collected the old silver and copper money and struck new currency of less weight and/or alloy. Hard up, Karim Khan in 1181/1767–68 devaluated his currency in this manner. He increased the value of the existing coins against the tuman, the unit of account. The standard of the coinage, which until then had been 1,200 nokhud, was reduced to 960 nokhud, which meant that the old rupee had a value of 12.5 shahis. This measure may have had a positive short-term effect, but it did nothing to improve Iran's objective economic position vis-à-vis its trading partners. In 1190/1776, the Iranian coinage, therefore, was again devaluated, this time to 800 nokhud, increasing the value of the rupee 15 shahis.[130] This second devaluation of 33.5 per cent compared with 1766, likely followed Karim Khan's decision to invade and conquer Basra in 1775. The nearly year-long siege naturally was a serious drain on his exchequer. Mirza Mohammad in fact calls the entire operation, until the withdrawal of troops in 1779, a complete waste of money.[131]

The devaluation led to a great deal of illegal export of silver money from Russia into the Caucasus and the Caspian provinces, where the governors manipulated the market to their advantage by hoarding and/or speculating with Russian coins. According to Gmelin, 'The notables use force to get money or goods from them and are not worried about repayment. If the governor needs an amount of money he then increases its value and as soon

129 Mirza Mohammad, *Ruznameh*, 68.

130 Perry, *Karim Khan Zand*, 251; Kukanova, 'K voprosu o torgovle Rossii', 79–80; Kukanova, *Ocherki po istorii russko-iranskikh torgovykh otnoshenii*, 166–67; Markova, 'Russko-iranskaia torgovlia', 109–10; Gmelin, *Travels through Northern Iran*, 83, 323 ('Much Russian silver money is brought by these people from Kizlyar to Persia.').

131 Saldanha, *Persian Gulf Précis*, 1:314, 2 Feb. 1780. There was an 18 per cent rate of interest per month at that time indicating inflationary pressure.

as he has achieved this he lowers its value again.' The governors also re-issued Russian silver coins imprinted with the name of Karim Khan Zand. The Russians did not like Karim Khan's currency devaluations, since it encouraged these activities and undercut the profitability of their trade.[132]

Nor did Iran's shaky economic conditions improve under Karim Khan's successors. The ruler's death in 1779 unleashed a violent power struggle between the Zands and the Qajars, which lasted 15 years and resulted in ultimate victory for the latter. In 1780 the British reported that 105 Bombay rupees equaled 10,500 Iranian rupees, which meant a devaluation of the Iranian rupee by 50 per cent since 1760.[133] On the positive side, there was the traditional import of specie. The French traveler Olivier, who visited Iran in 1796, reported that the quantity of gold and silver pieces coming in from Turkey was so great that there was no other money than old Turkish piasters and old zecchini (ducats) from Constantinople. Venetian ducats, he explained in a refrain of earlier times, were scarce because they were the preferred money of export by merchants.[134] Because the value of Iran's exports remained insufficient to pay for its imports to thus make up for the current account deficit, in particular concerning trade with India, the country for the remainder of the century continued to export 'Venetian Sequins, and different sorts of Persian Silver Coin' to India. Because of the fluctuating rate of exchange exporters preferred to be paid in gold and silver bars.[133] This confused monetary situation lasted well in to the nineteenth century.

To conclude, the fall of the Safavid dynasty in 1722 was the end of an era. The Afghan conquerors followed the Safavid model and so did Tahmasb II, who was reinstated in 1729. Nader Shah reduced the weight of the coins, as did Karim Khan Zand (as of 1766), by increasing the value of the existing coins against the tuman, the unit of account. None of these measures was effective, owing to the difference in the gold–silver ratio between the Ottoman Empire and Iran, which made accepting silver more expensive than copper. As a result, there was a flight into copper and after 1734 copper coins were not used as tokens anymore, but as full bodied coins. Because of the small number of mints, which only struck coins intermittently, a shortage of copper coins developed as well, given the sudden huge demand. Consequently, copper in whatever form became also a major form of payment, while barter trade was widely practised as well to resolve the money crunch.

132 Olivier, *Voyage dans l'empire othomane*, 5:321. See also Lorimer, *Gazetteer of the Persian Gulf*, 163.
133 Saldanha, *Persian Gulf Précis* 1906, 1:423 (Report on the Commerce of Arabia and Persia by Samuel Manestry and Hardford Jones, 1790); Milburn, *Oriental Commerce*, 1:130–31.

Part 3

THE QAJAR PERIOD 1779–1925

6

Tradition and Change in the Use of Money

Introduction

Emerging in the late eighteenth century, the Qajar dynasty started with the same currency system as the Safavids. In brief, under that system, currency consisted of coins that were hand-struck at mints in all major cities, run by concession holders who paid for the privilege. The value of coins in theory was based on the precious metal content, certified by the government. Foreign coins were to be surrendered for reminting into Iranian coins. In practice, the system knew many imperfections. Coins, for instance, did not necessarily contain the requisite precious metal; foreign coins circulated widely; and merchants demanded differing discounts for particular types of coin. As before, three different types of metal – gold, silver and copper – were used for coins, while an imperfect system for adjusting to fluctuations in the price ratio among those metals remained in place. And Iran continued to adhere to the tuman-dinar accounting system (which had been temporarily replaced under Nader Shah and his successors with the silver rupees and golden mohurs of India), in which the coins actually in circulation corresponded loosely, at values that varied locally, to the theoretical accounting system.

The story of Qajar currency is that of slow and halting transition to a modern system. By the end of the dynasty, coins marked with a face value were produced mechanically in a central national mint run by the government, and paper currency had become common. But the transition was by no means complete: paper money was still seen as an imperfect substitute for metal, the three metals were still in use, and private businessmen still played a major role in issuing currency.

The study of the Qajar monetary system is rendered difficult by the paucity of numismatic studies which, among other things, would match coin types to specific mints and dates.[1] Therefore, this study will mainly rely on documentary sources, which may shed light on the hitherto murky situation.

This chapter discusses several major aspects of the Qajar monetary systems: the minting of coins, the transition from traditional, hammer-struck coinage to machine-striking, and the nature of the fragmented currency system.

Minting Coins

The Qajar state claimed the monopoly of the right of coinage and control over its fineness and weight. Its monetary policy had several objectives which were not fully consistent: to use mints as a source of revenue; to maintain a readily verifiable standard for measuring tax obligations and for making payments; and to promote trade, so as to maximize the income and power of the state.

Traditional Mints

In all, some 40 mints struck coins for the Qajars.[2] Under Agha Mohammad Shah, gold was minted in 13 cities and silver in 22, while under Fath Ali Shah, there were 25 gold mints and 31 silver mints.[3] After Fath `Ali Shah the number of mints was reduced so that in the 1850s only some 15 mints were operational in the Qajar realm. In 1866 only 13 mints, one for each province, were said to be active.[4] Furthermore, it would seem that not every mint had the right to coin gold or silver, and that most struck copper only.[5]

Running the Mints

The mints struck coins of a specific weight and fineness, for a fee, from bullion supplied by private individuals. 'There is no prohibition against the melting, or the exportation of the precious metals. Every one may convert his own bullion into any use. If he wishes to have his gold coin, he can send it to the mint to be struck into any piece of money.'[6]

1 Album, *Checklist*, 290.
2 For a complete list, see Album, *Checklist*, 291.
3 Rabino, *Coins, Medals, and Seals*, 62, 65.
4 Polak, *Persien*, 2:161; Lacy O'Brien, *Banking in Persia*, 66–67 quoting the *Money Market Review* of 24 Feb. 1866.
5 Polak, *Persien*, 2:161.
6 Morier, *Journey through Persia*, 237. See also `Eyn al-Saltaneh, *Ruznameh-ye khaterat*, 1:570; Southgate, *Narrative of a Tour*, 2:349.

The organization of the royal mints was based on the Safavid model. The supervisor of mints was the mo`ayyer al-mamalek, whose title and function remained in the same family from the days of Nader Shah until the end of the Qajar dynasty.[7] Brydges states that the shah 'had the good sense, or good fortune, never to allow either Jews or Armenians to have anything to do with [the] mint'.[8] This would have been a departure from the Safavid past, at least as far as Armenians are concerned, and it is anyhow gainsaid by various examples. Trezel, a French officer, talking about the mint of Shiraz in 1808, commented that it was run by Jews.[9] Jakob Polak confirmed the role of Jews in the minting business by stating that the technical staff of the mint consisted mainly of Jews, because they were good at assaying.[10]

It was the task of the *zarrab-bashi* to see to it that the fineness of the assay was respected. Accounts are inconsistent on how efficiently they performed their task. Strict procedures were used at the mints for verifying the quality of coins. According to Tahvildar, 'each group of the workers [of the mint] has a separate record. As for checking on debased or pure metal the rule has been that every piece is checked one time during the assaying process.'[11] In about 1808, a mint farmer in Yazd who increased the alloy of the coinage without royal approval was dismissed and fined 4,000 tumans, or almost seven times as much as he had paid for the Mint.[12] However, those with good connections were able to avoid punishment. In 1295/1878, the government ordered the mint of Shiraz to strike 2,500 tumans worth of *qrans*. Twenty bad coins – with a value of 10 shahis (500 dinars) instead of the requisite 20 – were found among the new qrans, and the culprits were identified but, because of their connections, they went scot-free.[13]

The mints were under the indirect control of the central or provincial government, for they were all farmed out to the highest bidder. Dupré, writing in ca. 1810, reported that in the early Qajar period the mint at Isfahan was farmed for 2,000 to 2,500 tumans per year, and at Yazd for 600 tumans. The latter decreased the precious metal content of coins by adding more base metal. He paid £600 a year for the mint but was dismissed and fined £4,000.[14] Of the mint in Astarabad, McKenzie wrote that 'last month [probably February–March 1857] it minted an average of 300 tumans and

7 Mo`tazed, *Hajj Amin ol-Darb*, 577; Momtahen al-Dowleh, *Khaterat*, 105.
8 Jones, *Account*, 433.
9 Trézel, 'Commerce in Shiraz', in AAE, MD, Perse 8.
10 Polak *Persien*, 2:163. See also E`temad al-Saltaneh, *Montazam-e Naseri*, 952–53.
11 Tahvildar, *Joghrafiya-ye Esfahan*, 123.
12 Dupré, *Voyage en Perse*, 2:475.
13 Sirjani, *Vaqaye`-ye Ettefaqiyeh*, 90.
14 Dupré, *Voyage en Perse*, 2:475; see also Bérézine, *Voyage*, 2 :127.

10 shahis per day [20 shahis made 1 tuman]. The Mintmaster, Hajji Molla Mohammad Baqer makes a profit of about 5%. He pays the government 400 tumans per year.'[15]

The cost of having bullion struck into coins at the mint was made up of several different types of fees and taxes, the sum of which makes up 'brassage' as distinct from seignorage, which is the tax component of what the mint charges.According to Tahvildar, writing in 1294/1871, the mint-related fees in Isfahan were as follows:

> The mint revenues [*vojuh-e zarrabkhaneh*] are of two kinds: The first is the assaying tax [*rosum-e mo`ayyeri*], which falls to the city assayer [*mo`ayyer-e balad*] and the state assayer [*mo`ayyer-e mamalek-e Iran*]. The second are the dues paid to the government, which form a part of the provincial taxes, which are collected by the governor, who has a separate controller appointed by the government [to do so]. For every weight of one thousand methqals [4.64 kg] of gold and silver a fixed tax is taken. The government and assaying fees and the hire for the [mint] staff etc. are paid out of these revenues. This is administrated by a separate inspector [moshref]. All the taxes and fees, the salaries and expenses are equivalent to 3 percent, which has been customary since old times.[16]

Polak also mentioned that brassage, *haqq-e sekkeh* was 3 per cent; however, Rabino estimated brassage at 2.5 per cent.[17] And Dupré reported that 'those who have gold or silver in ingots can take it to the mint to have it coined on paying an `abbasi for every gold coin and two for eight riyals or silver coins', i.e., a 200 dinar fee for 10,000 dinars minted, or per cent.[18] In any case, brassage seems to have been increased in the 1880s, when, as the value of silver went down, it went up, first to 5 per cent and then to 6 per cent.[19] It apparently dropped again around 1890, after which it rose steeply. The brassage rate for silver rose from 3.75 per cent in 1893 to 5 per cent in 1894, 6 per cent in 1897 and 8.5 per cent in 1898.[20]

15 McKenzie, *Safarnameh-ye Shomal*, 187–88.

16 Tahvildar, *Joghrafiya-ye Esfahan*, 123.

17 Polak, *Persien*, 2:163; Rabino, 'Banking in Persia', 1–55; Ibid., 'Economist's Notes on Persia', 265–82. According to the British Legation in 1862, 'The Persian Mint charges nothing for coining beyond giving for bullion an equal weight of coins.' See *NA*, FO 60/314, unfoliated. These coins were, of course, lower in value, which represented the mint master's fee.

18 Dupré, *Voyage en Perse* 2:475.

19 Simmons, 'Evolution of Persia's Monetary System', 94, n. 1, quoting *NA*/FO 248/146, 6.

20 Lorini, *La Persia economica contemporanea*, 313.

It is unclear how much income the mint managers earned and in what way they were compensated. In a royal decree, dated 1296/1879, appointing Hajj Mohammad Hasan Esfahani as Amin al-Zarb, the latter was awarded a salary of 300 tumans, from the 1,000 tumans accorded to the assayers of the mint.[21] Other sources report that Amin al-Zarb had to pay 25,000 tumans per year to farm the mint.[22]

The Production Process

Coins continued to be handmade and therefore lacked a uniform shape. A thin slice of metal was placed on an anvil which had one die engraved on its head, and the metal was then struck by a hammer that had the other die engraved on its striking surface. The coins were hammer-struck, though some of the heavier ones may have been cast. The dies, which were made of iron, varied in diameter and were irregular in shape. The same dies were used for gold and silver. The size and form of the coins varied, and no standard appears to have been adopted. Most coins were round, but some were oblong. Despite the skills demonstrated by the mint workers their output was not always quality work. The coins differed in thickness and in shape.[23] 'Old copper coins were still more unshapely than the silver ones'.[24] According to the British legation, in 1862 'the Tehran mint could hardly coin more than 5,000 Tomans a day'.[25]

This minting technique was used for most of Iran's coins into the 1870s.[26] By contrast, machine-struck coins with milled edges became common in Europe in the seventeenth century, and by the end of the century in the Ottoman Empire; steam-powered machinery was introduced from the late eighteenth century.

In Tabriz in the 1810s, the mint was located in the bazaar. Ouseley describes its operation as follows:

> [...] amidst crowds of people where two men sitting on the ground were employed in coining felus or copper money, with very simple instruments, and apparently with much ease; one man placed the unstamped piece of

21 Mahdavi, *For God, Mammon, and Country*, 79; Ardakani, *Tarikh-e mo'assasat*, 52.

22 Amin al-Dowleh, *Khaterat-e siyasi*, 61; Rabino, *Coins, Medals, and Seals*, 22.

23 Rabino, *Coins, Medals, and Seals*, 8; De Sercey, *Une Ambassade extraordinaire*, 197; Bérézine, *Voyage*, 2:127.

24 Wilson, *Persian Life and Customs*, 283.

25 *NA*, FO 60/314, unfoliated.

26 For descriptions by European visitors to mints, see Matthee, 'Changing the Mintmaster', 111. He also provides references on machine-minting in Europe, ibid., 110.

> metal on an iron die which he held, the broad or engraved face being uppermost. His companion holding the other die over this, the engraved face being downwards, struck on it violently with a hammer, and thus coin the felus most expeditiously.[27]

Melgunov, who in the 1860s visited the mint of Barforush, writes:

> The mint offers an odd spectacle, and it is difficult to understand, that here really the country's coins are being struck. Near the gate, for instance, which is usually open, the master or *ustad* is seated in front of a charcoal brazier, in which he heats gold or silver coins with one hand, whilst at the same time he, with the other hand, feeds bread and barley to the cow that stands next to him as well as to the roving chickens. In the free space before him stands another *ustad*, who in one hand holds a *qalyan* (water-pipe) from which he smokes, while with the other hand he presses the die on the round coins, which he then throws in a heap of sawdust beside him. In the latter the hands of the third ustad are hidden, whose task it is to take the struck coins out of there and to clean them. The striking of the coins is done quite mechanically; the ustad does not even look at the other two, or check the form of the coin. This is the reason why that among 100 coins one does not find one which is totally round and on which all the letters are uniformly imprinted. The mint is always open and anyone can have his good or silver coined here.[28]

The coining process in other towns appeared to have been equally informally organized and executed, despite the fact that the organization at, for example, the mint of Isfahan seems to have been quite structured, with a view to create an efficient and transparent production process. That said, the degree of control from Tehran is unclear. For instance, some coin designs were unique to the mint that issued them, but identical-appearing coins from mints as far apart as Yazd and Tehran 'suggest that by 1221/1806

27 Ouseley, *Travels in Various Countries of the East*, 3:409. In 1842, Bérézine, *Voyage*, 2 :126, described the Mint of Tabriz as being located in the bazaar, in a miserable non-descript building, that was divided into three sections. In the first section the metal was melted and turned into strips; in the second section the strips were cut into pieces the size of a saheb-qran, and in the third section the actual coins were struck. Gold, silver and copper coins were made here. The walls of the Mint were embellished with popular images of Fath `Ali Shah and others.

28 Melgunov, *Das Suedliche Ufer des Kaspischen Meeres*, 187. There was, however, a coin specialist (*sarraf*) present in the mint to verify the coins, but his probably was to look after the interest of the mint master not to that of the public. Momtahen al-Dowleh, *Khaterat*, 171.

both the obverse and reverse dies used in regional mints were centrally designed if not centrally produced'.[29] Mirza Hoseyn Khan Tahvildar wrote in 1877 a description of the royal mint in Isfahan:

> It has seven workshops (*dastgah*) and to each workshop many workers were attached; all of them are under the authority of the assayer (*mo`ayyer*):
>
> 1. The melting workshop (*dastgah-e godazandeh*); here gold and silver is melted. Putting the silver into crucibles (*qal gozashtan*) and purifying the gold (*khalas gozashtan*) is part of the melting-process.
> 2. The smithery (*ahangari*); here the ingots (*shomsh*) of gold and silver are shaped into round thin [bars].
> 3. The turnery (*charkh keshi*); here the ready-made gold and silver from the smithery is pressed through holes [using a steel plate?] and ejected by rotation from the holes. The metal has now become round, flat and smooth.
> 4. The punching workshop (*qatta`i*). After the completion of the previous operations [the gold and silver] is punched here to the size and weight of *ashrafi*s and qrans with the punching wheel (*beh charkh-e qatta`*).
> 5. The silver pounder workshop (*kahleh kubi*). Here every piece of punched metal is put on the anvil and is flattened with the hammer (*potk-e ahan*).
> 6. The minting workshop (*dastgah-e sekkeh zadan*). Here the flattened pieces of gold and silver are put on the anvil between two coin-molds (*sekkeh-ye zir va ru*), being pounded with a hammer (*chakush*) until they have the right imprint.
> 7. The blanching workshop (*dastgah-e safidgari*). Here the brass worker cleans the money, which has become black and dirty.[30]

This structured system, in principle, was also applied in other Mints, but in a less organized way, as the Isfahan case seems to imply. The Kerman Mint, as described in 1878, probably reflects the reality of an average well run Qajar Mint:

> The Khan buys up dollars and all krans of other mints than his own, and melts and restamps them. The mint was in full blast when I saw it. On

29 Soucek, 'Coinage of the Qajars', 74; see also, Bérézine, *Voyage*, 2:127.

30 Tahvildar, *Joghrafiya-ye Esfahan*, 123. It appears that the organization of the mint in Isfahan was almost unchanged from the Safavid period. See Chapter 2.

> one side the silver was being drawn into a thick wire by a clumsy wooden apparatus. On another, a man was chopping it into short lengths, with a rapidity and exactness that could only have been acquired by long practice. The next process was weighing the lengths (and nearly all were right). They were then thrown into a charcoal brazier near the dice-cutting anvil, and here was the smartest operation of all. The anvil itself was a hard steel pike bearing one face of the die. One man stood by with a pair of tongs, a second with a small hammer bearing the second face of the die, and a third with a huge hammer. The first seized a 'dab' of silver from the brazier, and with unerring certainty placed it on the center of the narrow anvil. Almost at the same time number two placed his hammer exactly on it, and thump came number three with a blow which flattened it and imprinted the die on both sides. They struck thirty-three or thirty-eight per minute, I am not sure which as the second figure has become blurred in my notebook.[31]

The minting in Kerman probably still took place in the Mint built by Ganj `Ali Khan, governor of Kerman in 1596–1624, which measured 18.5 x 5.7 meters.[32]

The mint was a symbol of imperial rule. Indeed, mints sometimes played a boundary-setting role. For instance, a set of coins bearing the inscription Kermanshah 1271/1855 may have been actually struck in Tehran, with the false location being 'a symbolic gesture to stress the Shah's commitment to maintaining Iran's western border'.[33] There also were mobile mints. In 1856 an Iranian army, in preparation for an attack on Herat, was raised and drilled in Sistan. Its commander left Tehran with, among other things, 'tools for coining money', and during his stay in Sistan, 'money [was] coined in the name of the Shah of Persia'.[34]

Modern machine minting in Iran is mentioned as early as 1806, with coins produced at Tabriz (and by some accounts Tehran and Isfahan) 'with full, even pressure and reeded edges similar to those found on

31 Floyer, *Unexplored Baluchistan*, 323–24. In Tehran in 1840, the mint consisted 'of five to six small bare rooms, where some workers, in squatting position, cut and beat in molds the different pieces of silver and gold, wich constitute the currency of the country. All this is undoubtedly done rapidly, but you understand how poor a country must be in coins, if such a situation suffices.' De Sercey, *Une Ambassade extraordinaire*, 197. For the mint in Shiraz, see Binning, *Journal of Two Years' Travel*, 1:276.

32 Bastani Parizi, *Ganj `Ali Khan*, 83.

33 Soucek, 'Coinage of the Qajars', 63.

34 MacGregor, *Narrative of a Journey*, 2:152. When the shah was present in the army camp the coins would be struck with the place of issuance as *rekab* (at the [royal] stirrup).

contemporary British Indian coins'.[35] However, 'most Persian mints continued to produce hammer-struck coins for another seventy years', because 'the machine-made coins produced at Tabriz and Tehran [before the 1870s were experiments] to produce a small number of beautifully executed specimens', especially for ceremonial purposes.[36] Crown Prince `Abbas Mirza b. Fath `Ali Shah, the governor of Tabriz from 1220/1805 to 1247/1831, was evidently instrumental in the production of these early mechanical produced coin.[37] By contrast, Fath `Ali Shah's grandson and successor, Mohammad Shah b. `Abbas Mirza (r. 1250–64/1834–48), appears to have been little interested, for only a few coins struck during his rule were mechanically produced and those only in Tehran.[38] Soucek states that under Naser al-Din Shah (r. 1848–96), 'some mints, such as Tehran, produced hammer-struck and machine-made coins concurrently'.[39] Modern minting only became common after the establishment of the national mint in 1877, described below.

Reducing the Metal Content of Coins

In the early 1800s, Brydges argued that Persian silver coins were as pure as any silver coinage could be:

> When I left Persia in 1811, the coin of the Empire was quite pure, and there was less alloy in the Persian gold tomaun, than there is in our coin called the sovereign; their silver rupee was as pure as silver could be; at least the coinage of Tauris was so. The contrast between Turkey and Persia, in this respect, affords matters for reflection. Persia has seldom attempted to debase her coin; and if, under particular Princes, she has attempted to do it, the mischief has not continued long before she returned to a healthful currency.[40]

However, this situation seems to have changed considerably by the late 1800s. The reasons are not hard to understand. Like their predecessors, Qajar

35 Album et al., 'Coins and Coinage', 37. They say these coins were produced at Isfahan but make no mention of Tehran; Soucek, 'Coinage of the Qajars' refers to Tehran but makes no reference to Isfahan.

36 Soucek, 'Coinage of the Qajars', 82.

37 Ibid., 66.

38 Ibid., 71.

39 Ibid., 74.

40 Jones, *Account of the Transaction*, 432–33; see also Bérézine, *Voyage*, 2:126 who praised the quality of the metal of Iranian coins in 1842

rulers viewed coins as a commodity and taxed them accordingly. It would seem that one of the ways of securing revenue from coins was by charging hefty fees to the mint managers for the privilege of running the mint. The mint farmers, in return, were given some latitude by the government about ways to increase revenue from the mint.

The mint farmer, who was often the local governor, had three ways of making a profit on minting coins. The first, most obviously, consisted of seignorage fees. This gave the mint farmer an incentive to try to enforce the legal requirement that foreign coins be handed over to the mint to be melted down and recast as Iranian coins.

The second revenue source was recalling money. This sounds like a peculiar procedure to modern ears. It meant that the populace had to hand in old coins and receive in return newly minted coins. This required paying the seignorage fee. As described below, it appears to have been done most often with copper currency.

The third revenue source was reducing the metal content of coins, which was facilitated when the coins were recalled. Because a new mint farmer typically had paid a hefty sum up-front to get his function, he had a strong incentive to start out in his new post by recalling the coins to strike new coins of less than the official weight.

An example of how the mint farmer combined these techniques occurs in a British report from the 1860s:

> Russian currency [...] is rendered scarce by the Directors of the Persian Mint who collect silver roubles and convert them into Persian Kerans and Panabats, which are issued at the same amount of alloy as is contained in the Russian roubles, though, according to the standard, the alloy in Persian coins, whether gold or silver, should not exceed 3 per cent. At Shiraz, the Mint authorities purchase silver rupees at 223 kerans per 100. These are melted down and recoined in 240 kerans by which process the Mint makes a profit, or rather defrauds the public of about 8 per cent on the value of the currency.[41]

The culprit, the Comte de Gobineau, writing in the late 1850s, claimed, was Hajji Qavvam, the governor of Shiraz, and the result was that people in and around Shiraz treated all gold and silver money with suspicion.[42]

The result of such policies was a continuing reduction in the metal content of coins. Under Fath `Ali Shah the weight of the gold tuman had

41 *AP* 1865, 209; and Bérézine, *Voyage*, 2:127.
42 Gobineau, *Trois ans en Asie*, 152. Thanks to Daniel Potts for alerting us to this reference.

fallen from 6.14 g on his accession to 4.61 in 1818; while the silver riyal dropped in weight from 10.36 g to 9.21 g, falling further to 6.91 g by 1834. Under Mohammad Shah the qran fell further to 5.34 g by 1848.[43] In 1857, the silver qran coins were collected and reissued as one-eighth lighter coins, with the grand vizier and his finance minister pocketing the difference. As a result, Indian merchants refused the Iranian silver coins which were discounted at 7.5 per cent in changing silver into gold.[44]

In 1866, according to a British report, 'The continually increasing depreciation in the value of the native coinage leave merchant with no basis on which to calculate the probable result of his commercial operations. The silver coin especially has been tampered with, and the sahibqran, which three years since was reckoned at 10,5 d. has been found, by assays made in France, to vary far below this figure, and to be reduced in some cases as low as 85 centimes of 81/6 d.'[45] Meanwhile, some of the gold tuman coins were in fact made of gilded silver.[46] Such practices had a negative impact on the development of trade, but despite frequent protests from the merchant community the government rarely took corrective steps.

The methods used to reduce the metal value of coins were similar. Aside from clipping coins with scissors, various methods used to check the nature of the metal, such as black stone and acid, were also employed to reduce the weight of the coins as well. The lack of milled edges on coins facilitated this practice. Morier, visiting Iran in 1812, wrote, 'Most of the gold is clipped, as every Jew pares a little off. The shopkeepers also contrive to rub the coin on a black stone to try the purity of the metal; by this operation small particles remain on the stone, which are extracted with care, and reserved till a sufficient quantity for a coin be collected.'[47]

Accounts differ on how common counterfeit coins were. Conolly in 1832 claimed that the eldest son of the 'high priest of Mashad, had long been in the habit of coining false money, and passing it in spite of the Vuzzur [vizier], who indeed could not, with any grace, prohibit him, seeing that he himself had made a large sum a few years before, by coining many thousand bad Heraut reals, and circulating them over Khorrassaun'.[48] Half a century later Stewart called the Tekke Turkmen 'very clever in manufacturing false

43 Album, *Checklist*, 293–95.
44 Polak, *Persien*, 2:163.
45 DCR 3953, Tabreez, 1867–68, 60.
46 Polak, *Persien*, 1:161.
47 Morier, *Journey through Persia*, 237; for similar remarks, see Lacy O'Brien, *Banking in Persia*, 66–67.
48 Conolly, *Journey to the North of India*, 1:265.

Persian money'.[49] The coins that circulated were 'often counterfeit, worn, punched, or *tezabi* (reduced in weight by acid), and subject to discount according to their condition'.[50] Kerr Porter called counterfeiters 'sure of death, while clippers are punished by mutilation', although he also claimed that much clipped and counterfeit money was found and permitted to pass.[51] Polak insisted that counterfeiters were punished by having both hands cut, adding that he had never had heard about even one case, even though false coins did circulate.[52]

Given such practices, merchants engaged in exchange always checked the weight and fineness of coins. They always carefully weighed gold and silver coins with a balance, which each tradesman had, or tested to see if they could be bent. The difference was made up by adding what was missing to get the proper theoretical weight.[53] Merchants also wrote up agreements stipulating payment in a specific coinage – for instance, in tumans of 18 nokhud struck under Nasir al-Din Shah.[54] In fact, in the late nineteenth century, Rabino scoffed at the idea that silver qrans could be used as means of payment by weight.[55]

The Creation of a Modern National Mint

In 1863, Naser al-Din Shah, 'having been persuaded by some interested individual to recoin the currency on the European system, instructed his minister at Paris to purchase the necessary machinery and to engage

49 Stewart, *Through Persia in Disguise*, 402; see also O'Donovan, *Merv Oasis*, 1:249 ('those manufactured by the Turcomans themselves, out of sufficient pure silver, but with the inscription in intaglio instead of relievo').

50 Wilson, *Persian Life and Customs*, 282; Basir al-Molk, *Ruznameh-ye khaterat*, 181, related attending a meeting where somebody came with implements to counterfeit copper coins.

51 Porter, *Travels in Georgia*, 1:251.

52 Polak, *Persien*, 2:163.

53 Southgate, *Narrative of a Tour*, 2:349; Polak, *Persien*, 2:160–61.

54 Polak, *Persien*, 2:161. To be sure that one was not short-changed in a commercial deal contracts would usually if not invariably state the nature of the coin in which payment had to take place. For example, a contract dated 1306/1888–89 states that payment will take place to the amount of '*panj hazar tuman-e rayej-e tabrizi*, 5 *manat*, 15 pieces of which are 1 tuman'. See Beygdeli, *Tarikh-e Beygdeli*, 46. Another one mentions payment in 'tuman-e rayej-e qeran-e jadid al-zarb-e amin al-soltani'; in ibid., 47; in 1307: '500 tuman-e rayej-e qeran-e 24 nokhudi-ye jadid al-zarb-e amin al-soltani'; in ibid., 49, 52; or payment of '75 tuman va naqd-e rayej-e divan -e a`la az jens-e qeran-e mozaffar al-din shahi'; in Ibid., 58; see also p. 76, 1326 H; '150 tuman-e rayej-e divan-e a`la be qarar-e 2.000 sarfan va 48 nokhud vaznan'; in Ibid., 77; also 78 in 1327. Ettehadiyeh and Sa`dvandiyan *Siyaq-e ma`shiyat*, 1:46–47, 49, 52, 58, 76–78.

55 Rabino, 'Banking in Persia', 37.

French engineers'. Father and two sons Davoust were contracted to operate the machinery.[56] Minting equipment – presumably a Thonnelier press – was ordered. But the French team was not able to accomplish much at all before it departed in 1867. Part of the problem was the bad state of the Iranian road system. 'The machinery, the packing-cases of which had already been consumed as fuel for the steamer that brought it, was deposited upon the sand at Enzeli, where it lay and rotted, no beasts of burden strong enough to carry the big boilers and wheels, and the Shah's elephant being even found unequal to the task.'[57] To move the mint machinery from the Caspian port of Enzeli to Tehran took three years, by which time much of the machinery had been damaged or lost. But the main problem was the bitter opposition by local officials, especially the mint master (mo`ayyer al-mamalek) Dust `Ali Khan and treasurer (*mostowfi al-mamalek*) Mirza Yusof Khan, who each assumed office in 1866. The proposed mint reform went against the private interests of those operating the mint who were issuing debased coinage.[58]

The plans to modernize the mint were not abandoned, though. During Naser al-Din Shah's visit to Europe in 1873, he was shown the mints in St. Petersburg and Paris. This led to a request for Austrian assistance to reform the currency system which was initiated by Mirza Hoseyn Khan, the grand vizier during the shah's first visit to Europe.[59] Following a formal request for assistance with the improvement of the mint and lengthy negotiations, Franz Pechan von Prägenberg, a high official of the Austrian mint, and a mechanic named Obonya on 13 November 1874 left Vienna for Tehran, where they arrived on 24 January 1875. 'The problems encountered by the Austrians were not confined to a rusty machine, missing parts, and a lack of technical back-up. The cooperation they received from Iranian authorities other than Mirza `Ali Khan seems to have been minimal at best.'[60] This is unsurprising. Pechan's proposal to create one national mint meant doing away with a situation where each mint had its own standard and where artisanal hammer-struck coining and mint farming created ample opportunity to make money through cheating. The new regime would also mean using modern machinery to produce milled coins of one national standard, with regard to weight (4.6 g per qran), alloy (90 per cent), appearance – involving the striking of coins with a clear face value – and

56 Matthee, 'Changing the Mintmater', 113–16.

57 Curzon, *Persia*, 1:472, who took this from Mounsey, *Journey*, 324–25; see also Ballantine, *Midnight Marches through Persia*, 9, 212; Slaby, *Bindenschild und Sonnenlöwe*, 137.

58 *AP* 3262, 301, Dickson on the trade and commerce of Tehran for the year 1866.

59 Adamiyat, *Andisheh-ye taraqqi*, 315.

60 Matthee, 'Changing the Mintmaster', 120.

control of the money supply, especially of copper. Mirza `Ali Khan (later known as Amin al-Dowleh), who received the concession for the mint in 1874, adopted these ideas and submitted them to the royal council.[61] The shah and the court rejected the proposals, the former because of high cost and reduced revenue; the latter because of a prospective loss of income. However, the shah agreed to the idea of reform, including the ordering of new equipment.[62] The government approved Pechan's proposal to produce gold tumans of 3.22 g, silver qrans of 5.0 g and copper shahis of 5.0 g.[63]

Although the idea of the currency reform was accepted there were no funds to buy new equipment. The mint, located in an old cotton factory, also provided housing for the two Austrians and the old French minting machinery – with its missing and rusty parts. Fortunately, Obonya was an able and inventive man, and with the help of three other European mechanics passing through Tehran in 1876 he managed to revive the machinery. As a result, the new mint was able to strike new qrans and medals to commemorate the thirty-year jubilee of Naser al-Din Shah in 1876. The official, festive inauguration of the Mint took place a year later, on 14 June 1877, when it was officially opened by the shah. The first year, political pressures limited production almost exclusively to copper coins. Between July 1877 and March 1878, some 6 million copper coins were struck. As raw material Pechan had to use old scrap copper and copper household utensils.[64] This was the first time that Iran put a face value on its coins. The word tuman with subdivisions was struck on the few gold coins that were produced; and the words 1,000 dinars were struck on the few silver qrans.[65]

Resistance against the standardized operation quickly mounted. 'When he [Pechan] attempted to coin a standard silver kran, and asked for the funds necessary for raising the quality of the piece, he was met by a refusal, and by a suggestion as to alloy which it was impossible for him, as an Austrian official, to accept.'[66] According to Arnold, writing in 1877:

61 Slaby, *Bindenschild und Sonnenlöwe*, 139; Lorini, *La Persia economica*, 300; Amin al-Dowleh, *Khaterat-e siyasi*, 58ff., 86.

62 Amin al-Dowleh, *Khaterat-e siyasi*, 86.

63 Rabino, *Coins, Medals, and Seals*, 71–72; Stolze and Andreas, 'Handelsverhältnisse Persiens', 35, agree about the qran, but on p. 36 say that the tuman was 3.206 g of 90.55 per cent gold, such that its value would be exactly 10 francs.

64 Slaby, *Bindenschild und Sonnenlöwe*, 138–39; Amin al-Dowleh, *Khaterat-e siyasi*, 86.

65 Matthee, 'Changing the Mintmaster', 120–25.

66 Rabino, 'Banking in Persia', 37; E`temad al-Saltaneh, *Montazam-e Naseri*, 2:352, and 3:355, 357, 375 give the fineness and weight of the new coins.

> During our stay in Persia, the Shah had two Austrian officials, who were engaged, to the disgust of the court, in arranging for the issue of money. They had been a year in the country, and were so successfully thwarted that nothing had been accomplished by these detested Europeans. A clever khan, whose acquaintance we made in the capital, had a coining machine sent from Paris at his own expense; and with the aid of this he last year presented the Shah with some specimen coins, remarking at the same time upon the dilatoriness of the Austrians. The consequence was that he received orders to proceed with his manufacture; and now new krans and penabats are occasionally to be seen. But base money is becoming more and more common. People who effect to know, and who are certainly in a position to be well informed declare that most of the bad money comes from the imperial mints; and if, say, a master of a mint has a salary of a thousand tomauns, and is able and willing, in order to retain his office, to give presents to the value of twenty thousand tomauns – which I am assured is the case with at least one of these officers – the fact would, to say the least, throw much suspicion upon this issue.[67]

To be sure, some progress was made. The twelve provincial mints were ordered shut on 14 June 1877, and Curzon writes that they were in fact closed as of 1878.[68] 'A large building on the northern outskirts of Teheran, which had been unsuccessfully tried as a cotton factory, having been converted into the Royal Mint. This establishment, which possesses a German overseer and French dies, is under the control of the Amin-es-Sultan, is now the sole mint in Persia.'[69] While agreeing that this mint used modern automatic machinery which produced milled coins, sources differ on whether this new machinery had newly arrived from Europe or was the old French machinery.[70]

67 Arnold, *Through Persia by Caravan*, 135–36.

68 Lorini, *La Persia economica*, 300; he lists the closed mints as Hamadan, Tabriz, Kashan, Isfahan, Kerman, Mashad, Kermanshah, Resht, Astrabad, Qom, Mazandaran and Sistan. Also see Curzon, *Persia*, 1:512–13.

69 Ibid., 1:472. The mint was located next to the Baharestan, the new of the village of Chalehraz. See Ehtesham al-Saltaneh, *Khaterat-e Ehtesham al-Saltaneh*, 220; E`temad al-Saltaneh, *Montazam-e Naseri*, 22. In 1884, M. Botin, a Frenchman, was in charge of the Mint. See Orsolle, *Le Caucase et la Perse*, 208.

70 Mostowfi, *Sharh-e zendegani-ye man*, 1:397; Amin al-Dowleh, *Khaterat-e siyasi*, 51–52. In 1876, the equipment ordered in 1860's was still lying on 'heavy drays, apparently abandoned, sunken in deep ruts', near Sonqorabad, and other drays at Rostamabad. See Ballantine, *Midnight marches*, 212.

The old hammered coinage, known as *pul-e kohneh* or old money, continued in circulation through the end of the Qajar period.[71] While the population preferred the pre-1870 qran, the new coins were readily accepted.[72] Their design, which remained essentially unchanged until 1978, was standardized. The name and titles of the shah were on the obverse; the reverse showed the portrait of the shah for gold coins and the lion and sun for silver.

But the success of the mint reform was very mixed. Ebrahim Khan, the Amin al-Soltan, wanted his protégé Hajj Mohammad Hasan (named Amin al-Zarb in 1878) to be appointed as mint director. The long and frequent absences of Amin al-Dowleh gave them a chance to convince the shah about the large profits of coining copper as compared with the seignorage. Amin al-Soltan and Amin al-Zarb offered the ruler to manage the mint for 25,000 tumans, on condition that they would be allowed to reduce the fineness of the qran and coin more copper. Amin al-Dowleh failed to convince the shah of the drawbacks of this proposal. The shah told him either to implement the proposal, or return the mint farming monopoly, and thus he did the latter in 1879.[73] The mint was then farmed for 25,000 tumans a year to Hakim al-Molk, who subcontracted it to Amin al-Zarb with the right to coin as many gold ashrafis weighing 2.87811 g (i.e., 15 nokhuds), as he wanted, silver qrans weighing 4.6 g (i.e., one mesqal, equal to 24 nokhuds), and copper shahis weighing 4.9 g (i.e., 26 nokhuds), all 90 per cent pure metal.[74] Note that these are only slightly lighter than what Pechan had wanted; furthermore, as Rabino noted, these coins were based on traditional Persian weights rather than on the metric system.[75]

When Pechan was told to strike new qrans with less silver, he was not ready to do so. According to Andreas and Stolze, Amin al-Soltan proposed a qran weighing 4.2 g with 77–83 per cent metal, i.e., 23–28 per cent less pure silver than the 5.0 g, 90 per cent metal standard.[76] Pechan asked the Austrian government for support for his attitude against what he saw as counterfeiting. As a result, Amin al-Soltan had Pechan dismissed using as an

71 Album et al., 'Coins and Coinage', 37; the description of the new coins is from the same source.

72 Wills, *In the Land of the Lion and the Sun*, 371.

73 Amin al-Dowleh, *Khaterat-e siyasi*, 69–70; von Riederer, *Aus Persien*, 149–51; Slaby, *Bindenschild und Sonnenlöwe*, 139. Some sources cite the change as being as early in 1878, but this seems to be wrong.

74 Lorini, *La Persia economica*, 301, 307; he lists the tuman as 17 nokhuds, but the weights in grams and grains he gives there and on p. 426 show it was 15 nokhuds. See also Yakta'i, *Tarikh-e dara'i-ye Iran*, 297–98; and E`temad al-Saltaneh, *Montazam-e Naseri*, 94, 378. In general, see Floor, 'Weights and Measures'.

75 Rabino, *Coins, Medals, and Seals*, 72.

76 Stolze and Andreas, 'Handelsverhältnisse Persiens', 35.

excuse an article in the Viennese press which attacked the new depreciation of the Persian qran. He further had the mint occupied by military troops and had guards posted. Pechan was forced to submit a detailed accounting of his activities. Though the records were all in order the objective had been achieved: Pechan left Iran (Obonya had already left with Riederer in April 1878 at the end of his contract). Therefore, new silver coins were struck, which were 4 shahis less worth than the old qran.[77]

The silver content of the qran gradually declined – exacerbating a steep decline in the purchasing power of Iran's silver coins caused by the falling price of silver, discussed below. By Lorini's description, by 1889 the reduction in weight and fineness had reduced the metal content by less than 10 per cent.[78] Indeed, the table he gives of the 1890–92 assay of two qran coins by three British firms shows the silver content tested to have been on average more than 95 per cent of the legal standard: the ten coins tested by the Royal Mint on average fell short by 1.5 per cent; the ten specimens tested by Sharps and Wilkins, 3.8 per cent on average; and the 30 coins tested by Johnson and Son, 2.8 per cent on average.[79]

Upon becoming mint master in 1879, Amin al-Zarb paid annually 5,000 tumans rent for the mint and 20,000 tumans from the minting charges.[80] He was able to make a profit by recoining the old heavier qrans into lighter new ones. Lorini describes how Amin al-Zarb converted qrans weighing 28 nokhud into ones weighing 24 nokhuds, pocketing the difference in weight as profit.[81] By 1881, the old qrans still available were not heavy enough to yield much profit. Amin al-Zarb imported silver bars from Britain, making a profit on the slight premium qrans commanded over the value of their silver content.[82] The whole operation seems to have worked on rather slim margins, given the costs of transport and fluctuations in prices. It is by no means clear how profitable the mint was. Amin al-Dowleh claimed Amin al-Zarb made an annual profit of 2,500 tumans after payments to the government.[83] In 1893, Rabino called it 'highly improbable that [illegible] in a year the Mint will coin a sum exceeding Tomans 1,500,000 upon which the profit would be about Tomans 30,000', from which the mint master had to pay his fee to the government.[84]

77 Slaby, *Bindenschild und Sonnenlöwe*, 135, 139; Issawi, *Economic History of Iran*, 389.
78 Lorini, *La Persia economica*, 308–09.
79 Ibid., 428–29.
80 Mahdavi, *For God, Mamon and Country*, 142.
81 Lorini, *La Persia economica*, 309–10.
82 Ibid., 310–14.
83 Amin al-Dowleh, *Khaterat-e siyasi*, 128.
84 As quoted by Lascelles in a report of 31 January 1893, FO 60/542, cited in Mahdavi, *For God, Mammon and Country*, 143.

However, as the case of Tabriz in 1882 demonstrates, operating the mint could be a very profitable business indeed.

> It appears that large remittances have to be made from Tabreez to Tehran in order to obtain bills of exchange and otherwise to balance accounts with Europe. But the Currency of Tabreez consists principally of Russian 20 Kopek pieces, and the Sarrafs or petty bankers are in the habit of charging an arbitrary Agio [discount] on all payments made by them in Persian Kerans. The Master of the Mint, on the other hand, encourages the evil by his own proceedings. He pays one Keran for every Miscal of pure Silver and, being entitled to add 10 parts of alloy to 90 parts of fineness, he gains about 11 per cent, out of which he has to defray the cost of minting, which can hardly exceed one per cent, as in Europe the cost of minting 100 francs is said to be not more than 65 centimes.
>
> The Mint, therefore, makes a net profit of about 10 per cent, supposing the legal standard of alloy is strictly adhered to, which appears doubtful from assays made both in Europe and at Tabreez. If the Mint were satisfied with a moderate profit, merchants at Tabreez would be spared the imposition of the Agio [discount] demanded by the Serrafs.
>
> The Russian 20 kopek piece contains 3 parts pure silver and 1 alloy, and there is no reason why the Mint should not accept these coins as the Tabreez market value; that is, 15 twenty-kopek pieces to represent the Persian Toman or 10 kerans. Fifteen of these Russian coins weigh 13 miscals, and the following calculation shows that by converting them, at the above rate, into Persian currency, the Mint would still derive a profit of more than 8 per cent, minus the cost of minting.
>
> 270 Roubles or 1,350 twenty Kopek pieces worth 90 Tomans
> weight 1,170 miscals
> deduct ¼ alloy 292½ miscals
> pure silver 887½ miscals
>
> By adding 11 per cent for alloy and converting into Persian Kerans, the result would be 97½ Tomans. The Persian keran weighs one miscal. it has been suggested, therefore, that the Persian Government should take steps to put a stop to the Agio [discount] system at Tabreez; that fifteen 20 kopek pieces should be officially recognized as representing the value of one Toman or ten kerans and that they should compel the Mint to content itself with a nett profit of 4 per cent, plus 1 to 1½ per cent to

> cover the cost of converting foreign coins or bullion into Persian kerans of the standard or 90 parts fineness and 10 alloy.
>
> Another grievance of the merchants at Tabrees is that the Persian Authorities, by attempting to fix the price of Russian gold Half Imperials under their intrinsic value, prevent to a great extent the importation of a valuable medium of exchange.[85]

Moreover, Rabino left out profits from copper coinage, which was the major source of profit. In 1879, copper coins were for the first time given a face value in terms of silver. As discussed below, the copper coins contained less copper than their face value indicated, and so the mint master could profit by minting more copper coins. Amin al-Zarb, the mint master, had bought copper at 8 to 10 qrans per man, had mixed it with an alloy, and after coining it, sold the copper for 32 qrans per man, thus making a profit of more than 300 per cent. At the same time he fixed the value of the qran at 25 instead of 20 shahis, which, according to Kosogovski, meant a profit of 6 million tumans for Amin al-Zarb.[86] Despite loud complaints about excessive copper coinage and adulterated coins, Amin al-Zarb remained in office until January 1893, when he was replaced by a syndicate of merchants led by Mohammad Vali Khan Nasr al-Saltaneh, who offered an initial payment to the shah of 50,000 tumans plus annual payments of 120,000 tumans to him, 12,000 tumans to Kamran Mirza, and a further sum to Amin al-Soltan.[87] The bad condition of the Mint only grew worse. In 1894, Rabino evaluated the situation as follows: 'The absence of any scientific supervision, chemical or mechanical, the employment of ignorant and unskilled labourers and the fact that the machinery is not only incomplete but old and worn out, are sufficient to account for the wretched pieces daily turned out by the Mint-master.' He argued that 'As Egypt had all its silver currency struck in Berlin, so it is very desirable that Persia should have its coins manufactured by the mint of one of the Great Powers.'[88]

In the winter of 1894/5, trade in the Tehran bazaar fell off sharply; the dissatisfaction with the state of the currency was so great that it was feared there could be another popular uprising similar to that against

85 *NA*, FO 60/456, Commercial Report, Dickson, Tehran, 17 Sept. 1882, unfol.

86 Kasakufski, *Khaterat*, 49, 156.

87 Mahdavi, *For God, Mammon and Country*, 138–45; E`temad al-Saltaneh, *Montazam-e Naseri*, 973, 1057, 1061–62, 1066.

88 Rabino, 'Report on the Possibility of the Reform of the Currency, 19 June 1894'. FO 248/586, Secret, No. 146, 2–3.

the tobacco concession.[89] Gordon wrote, 'Copper is at a discount in the bazaar, so much so that, when a purchase is beyond question above a kran in amount, an agreement as to payment in silver or copper is first made, and then the bargaining begins.'[90] As the year wore on the situation grew worse rather than better and the government did not know what to do, the more so as different factions held opposing views on this issue.[91] On 26 March 1896, public criers made it known that the shah 'had decreed that the going rate of black money should be 30 pieces per one qran white money. In reality, they cost five thousand per tuman. People are very upset and furious. Those shops that were still open closed.' People went quickly to try and change their copper into silver coin before it went at forty, for they expected that in two, three days the cost would rise beyond 45. 'In Shiraz the cost of black money is six thousand, in Kerman eight thousand, and Qom and Kashan also six thousand. Through investigation they say that 20 crore [10 million] tuman of black money was struck in Iran, which now all is held by the people, apart from that which Hajji Mohammad Hasan has hidden and stored.'[92] On 1 April 1896, Gordon wrote:

> yesterday the public criers again made it known that the rate of black money is again as it was before, i.e. 2 riyals per tuman. If it were not the thirteenth the merchants and artisans rightly would have rioted. The last four days has really hurt people and everybody only talked about money. Now it is the same. There is no conversation but for the story about money. The shah is a bit afraid, he does not know what to do. In no other era a shah has ever been so cowardly. It is a pity that the people are even more cowardly than he is.[93]

Clearly, the government did not consistently intervene to support the face value of its copper coins. Following Gresham's Law – bad money drives out good money – the result was that copper coins were available everywhere and silver ones were scarce. This was a recurring problem. Government measures fell short and came too late, as the mintmaster refused to issue silver coins in sufficient numbers. 'This is the Mint-master's excuse for

89 E`temad al-Saltaneh, *Montazam-e Naseri*, 1070.

90 Gordon, *Persia Revisited*, 75; E`temad al-Saltaneh, *Montazam-e Naseri*, 1188; `Eyn al-Saltaneh, *Ruznameh-ye khaterat*, 1:683.

91 Amin al-Dowleh, *Khaterat-e siyasi*, 184, 194–205; `Eyn al-Saltaneh, *Ruznameh-ye khaterat*, 1:861–63, 865–66, 893.

92 `Eyn al-Saltaneh, *Ruznameh-ye khaterat*, 1:916.

93 Ibid., 1:918.

sending out copper in great quantities to take the place of silver.'[94] People called the debased money *pul-e qalb* or *qollabi*.[95]

Three weeks prior to his assassination on 1 May 1896, Naser al-Din Shah issued a decree that copper should not be struck for a five-year period, and government agencies such as customs farmers, telegraph and post office, were urged, but not ordered, to accept copper at fixed rates for certain amounts.[96] This decree did not solve the problem immediately, if only because the shah was assassinated shortly thereafter. The day after the Naser al-Din Shah's assassination, `Eyn al-Saltaneh reported that, following the shah's death, the IBP refused to accept copper money. The price of silver, as expressed in copper coins, skyrocketed. In Kashan one tuman of silver cost 2.5 tuman in copper money. Each qran had risen to 45 shahis and nobody accepted these coins. It was said that 'In Hamadan, Malayer and Kermanshah two tuman is one tuman.'[97]

Taking advantage of the dissatisfaction, Amin al-Zarb and his friend `Ali Amin al-Soltan managed to reassert control over the mint, though this control was at first contested by reformers led by Amin al-Dowleh, who in 1897/98 briefly served the new Shah, Mozaffar al-Din Shah, as prime minister. Amin al-Zarb and his son in 1896 were arrested and fined 800,000 tumans, but in October of the following year got the mint back, in conjunction with a group of merchants and moneylenders.[98] Amin al-Soltan also held the farm for the customs; his brother Amin al-Molk headed the treasury. Since Amin al-Soltan had to pay even slightly more for the mint farm than had Nasr al-Saltaneh, it is not surprising that the quality of the currency continued to suffer and that the mint functioned poorly. After Amin al-Zarb's death in 1898, the problems at the mint persisted. In 1901,

94 Gordon, *Persia Revisited*, 75.

95 Mostowfi, *Sharh-e zendegani-ye man*, 3:419.

96 Gordon, *Persia Revisited*, 74–76. According to `Eyn al-Saltaneh, *Ruznameh-ye khaterat*, government agencies were not urged, but would accept payment of one-third in copper money. On 16 April 1896, 'They made an announcement about black money. First, as of now no black money will be struck. Two, everybody may bring up to twenty tumans in black money to the Imperial Bank and will receive silver money at the rate of two riyal per tuman. Three, government offices such as post, telegraph, customs, and the like will accept payments in one-third of black money at [the rate of] two riyal.' `Eyn al-Saltaneh, *Ruznameh-ye khaterat*, 1:926.

97 Ibid., 952.

98 The complex machinations are described in Bakhash, *Iran: Monarchy*, 21–22. `Eyn al-Saltaneh, *Ruznameh-ye khaterat*, 2:1104 (arrest of 'the cursed hajji'), 1109, 1111–12. Nezam al-Saltaneh Mafi, *Khaterat va asnad*, 1:208, in addition to information on the arrest and fine of Amin al-Zarb, reports that it was decided to melt much gold ware from the Museum and coin it to pay off the Tobacco Regie debt. Likewise, the 10 and 20 tuman coins minted by Hesam al-Saltaneh at the occasion of the victory at Herat would be melted and coined.

Rabino estimated that the mint's output was at most 3 million to 4 million tumans annually.[99]

In that year, the custom of farming the Mint was discontinued, and its operation was entrusted to Belgian advisors, who also managed the postal, customs and other fiscal services. They found that, although the minting machinery was modern, weighing metals was still done with traditional methods; dried peas and grains of wheat were being used as the units for weight standards, with 4 *gandoms* (grain of wheat) being equal to 1 nokhud (pea), while 6 nokhuds made up 1 dang, and 4 dangs were 1 mesqal.[100]

The 1880s and 1890s saw great monetary turmoil in Iran. The collapsing value of silver on the world market forced a substantial loss in the value of Iran's qran relative to the pound sterling; driven by greed, mintmasters had so many copper coins struck that they lost most of their value relative to silver; the traditional mints in provincial cities were closed while the Tehran mint came under great pressure to adulterate coins so it could meet the payments due the shah; and modern milled coins replaced the traditional hammered coins. Yet these were hardly auspicious circumstances for the acceptance of the new milled coins. Not surprisingly, many Iranians would fondly remember the monetary system of the old days, viewing all the changes between 1880 and 1900 as somehow linked. For instance, `Abdollah Mostowfi, scion of a prominent family, in his 1943 memoir waxes lyrical about the glories of Iran's currency prior to 1300/1882–83, as he blames the new modern coins for the collapse in the currency's value by stating that, 'the mint factories of Amin al-Soltan totally broke up this sound currency'.[101]

The Tehran mint continued to experience problems up to the very end of the Qajar dynasty. In 1929, for instatnce, the IBP, rather than importing silver in bars for the Tehran mint to turn into coins, used a British mint to produce silver coins which it then imported, to the constant complaint of Tehran mint officials (the IBP's authority to do this was not entirely clear; it misled the British mint into thinking it was acting at the direction of the Iranian government).[102]

99 Rabino, 'Economist's Notes on Persia', 273.

100 Rabino, *Coins, Medals, and Seals*, 7.

101 Mostowfi, *Sharh-e zendegani-ye man*, 1:396–98. Mostowfi goes to great length insisting that before 1300/1882–83, Iran had managed official bimetallism quite well, and that the new monetary system broke with the wise practices of the past.

102 The use of the Birmingham mint seems to have been motivated by the inability of the Tehran mint to produce coins in sufficient numbers. The 20 March 1929 'Tehran Report on Progress' notes that in the previous half-year, £450,000 in silver had been purchased for minting in Iran, while £524,566 in minted coin had been shipped from Birmingham and £233,902 was still at the Birmingham mint. The Iranian complaints about the minting of coins in Birmingham make up much of the BBME 602 files.

A Fragmented Currency System

Local Currencies other than the Official Standard

To the modern mind, Iran's early modern monetary system, with its host of moneys and money units that might vary substantially from place to place and from time to time, was bizarre. One way that Iranians adapted to this situation was to calculate and keep records, to the extent they did, in a ghost money. As before, the tuman served this purpose, but the qran, equal to 1,000 dinars or one-tenth of a tuman, was used as well. Arnold described it this way: 'Everybody talks of "tomans", which are gold coins of the nominal value of ten krans. But the small remnant of this gold coinage is sold as a curiosity in the bazaars at twelve or thirteen krans for each gold toman. Virtually, there are but three coins in the currency of Persia: the silver kran, the half kran, or penabat, and the shihee.' [103] Wills wrote,

> Prices are given indiscriminately in tomauns or kerans; the price in kerans as five hundred kerans being mostly spoken of and always written as kerans and not fifty tomauns. Till lately the tomaun has been only a name. I on arrival took my servants' accounts in tomauns and kerans, afterwards in kerans and shaies, and at last in kerans and puls; while an English merchant friend actually wrote his house accounts in dinars, and said it awed his servants! one thousand dinars make a keran, so one dinar is the 1/1000 of 9d.[104]

As was true in earlier times, the Qajar monetary sytem was fragmented and decentralized. Two types of ghost money existed, an Iraqi or Tabrizi tuman (used in most of Iran) as well as a Khorasani tuman (used in the eastern part of Iran).[105] This was but a reflection of the existence of local currencies with their own ghost tumans, as shown in Table 5.1. According to Dupré, there were not less than sixteen local systems of currency in Qajar Iran in the early nineteenth century.[106] The local moneys were called

103 Arnold, *Through Persia*, 134.

104 Wills, *In the Land of the Lion and the Sun*, 63.

105 Monshi, *'Alamara-ye 'Abbasi*, 1: 605 (10.000 dinar-e 'eraqi which in the custom of the *ahl-e 'ajam* or Iranians is one tuman-e Tabrizi), 2:721, 849 (shahi-ye 'Eraqi); Fraser, *Narrative of a Journey into Khorasan*, 455, 468 (One Khorasani tuman was equal to 20 riyals, while an Iraqi tuman was equal to 8 riyals); Forbes, 'Route from Turbat Haideri', 152 (30 Khorasan = 70 Irak tumans).

106 Dupré, *Voyage en Perse*, 2:477–81; Waring, *Tour to Sheeraz*, 134; Simmons, 'Evolution of Persia's Monetary System', 78–79.

pul-e mordeh or dead currency, in contrast to *pul-e divani* (official currency), or *pul-e zendeh* (live currency), which was used in a number of large towns, but not in Yerevan, Khoy, Lahijan, Qazvin, Qom, Rasht, Shiraz, Tehran and Zanjan, which kept to the official system.[107] The variation is illustrated in the following table.

Table 6.1: The value of local copper and gold coins relative to official standards

Town	Number of shahis to the official riyal	Number of official shahis to the local tuman	Number of official dinars to the local tuman	Weight of silver in a local tuman, in grams
Kerman	35	$142\frac{6}{7}$	$7{,}142\frac{6}{7}$	60.16
Kashan	32	$156\frac{3}{16}$	7,812½	65.78
Tabriz	31¼	$156\frac{3}{10}$	8,000	66.69
Maragheh	31	$161\frac{9}{10}$	$8{,}064\frac{16}{31}$	68.19
Yazd	27½	$181\frac{9}{10}$	$9{,}090\frac{10}{11}$	76.64
Isfahan	26	$129\frac{2}{10}$	9,615	54.41
Official (Tehran, Qom, Khoy, Zanjan, Shiraz, Qazvin, Resht, Lahijan, Yerevan)	25	200	10,000	84.24
Hamadan/Orumi	22	$227\frac{3}{11}$	$11{,}363\frac{7}{11}$	95.68
Kermanshah*/Semnan	20	250	12,500	105.30
Kermanshah*/Mazandaran/ Persian Gulf	16	312½	15,625	131.63
Mashhad#/Herat/Bandar `Abbas	12	$416\frac{2}{5}$	$20{,}832\frac{2}{5}$	179.40
Mashhad#/Tabas	10	500	25,000	210.60

Source: Dupré, 2:477–80, using the method of presentation developed by Rabino di Borgomale, *Coins, Medals, and Seals*, 13.

*Kermanshah is given a different currency in Dupré's tables.
#Mashhad is given two different currencies in Dupré's tables.

107 However, in 1305/1887–88, Basir al-Molk, *Ruznameh-ye khaterat*, 345, relates that he paid workers the value of a *lu'i* (louis d'or?), which was equal to 18 qrans in Tehran money.

Thus, in each major town, copper coins were first computed as shahis, then via ghost dinars converted into the local ghost tuman. This means that copper coins had a value in dinars, although neither the government nor the bazaar needed to respect this value. This, however, made it easy for the authorities, usually the local mintmaster, to tax copper by reducing the accountancy value of coins made of that metal.

Consequently, many European travelers commented on the variation of local moneys. Waring in 1802 put it this way: 'Indeed monies which are current in one city, will probably not pass at the next; and, excepting the Qooroosh and the Tooman, I know of no coin which you can receive but to considerable disadvantage. The current coins are the following; besides which are a number of others, not however so common or so generally received.'[108] In 1809, Dupré wrote, 'The number of abbassees in a real differ in different provinces, but are in general from five to six, and there are about as many pool-e-siahs in each abbassee; the former, when found, for it is not current every where, is of silver; the latter are lumps of copper, heavy and shapeless, with a few letters stamped on one side.'[109] Stocqueler, traveling in Iran around 1830, reported that 'It was pretended between Doodhekh and Zunjoon, that the money in use at Isfahan and Tabrees was not current at half its value, and I found myself considerable looser in all pecuniary transactions.'[110] Abbott observed that many towns had their own currency standards, though he pointed out that the usual standard of value in trade was the official one. For instance, he wrote that Yazd, in 1849–50 had a currency of its own, 'different from that of other places, there being 25 Shahees reckoned to the Sahib Keran, 12,5 Kerans pay or currency of the place are equal to one Toman. This currency is generally adopted in small dealings; in commerce the Sahib Keran of 20 Shahees is the standard.' In Kerman, he said, 'The money of the place is the Keran of 28 Shahees and 3,5 Punabads and 2 Shahees of Kirman make one Keran of Standard Coin.' Isfahan's currency, the ray, was 'of 23 Shaees to the SahibKeran, but the common currency of Persia is frequently adopted in mercantile transactions'.[111] In the 1880s, consul Preece noted that 'At Bandar `Abbas and about here [Ziyarat] the current coin is the rupee. At the former place they would only take the krans at 27 pul instead of 40, and here they would not take them at all.'[112] The governor's (or the

108 Waring, *Tour to Sheeraz*, 128.
109 Fraser, *Narrative of a Journey into Khorasan*, 74.
110 Stocqueler, *Fifteen Months' Pilgrimage*, 1:149.
111 Amanat, *Cities & Trade*, 82 (Yazd); 85 (Kerman); 104, 117 (Kashan, Isfahan).
112 Preece, 'Journey from Shiraz to Jashk', 422.

mintmaster's) need for money as well as external factors determined the rates of exchange. Fraser noted that it was not easy 'to state the exact value of these coins, because it is disturbed by the state of exchange between India and Europe'.[113]

Part of the reason for the existence of these variations, at least until the establishment of the national mint in 1877, was that the local mints simply did not stick to the official standards for weight and fineness. Pechan examined a sample of coins from the local mints. Rabino summarized the survey, 'These figures give some idea of the irregularity of the Persian Currency. Between krans of Hamadan and those of Teheran, there is a difference in value of no less than 17 per cent; between those of other towns and of the capital the difference is very considerable from a monetary point of view, although less than in the extreme case quoted.'[114]

But even when one national mint had begun to strike coins of the same weight and fineness the regional monetary systems continued to function. Traveling in Iran in 1901, Landor observed that he 'never knew exactly what a kran was worth, and almost in every province I received a different exchange of shais for my krans'.[115] Bradley-Birt in 1910 complained,

> The variations of the Persian bank rate must surely remain a mystery to any but a bank manager. All I was able to discover about it was that it steadily fell as I advanced across Persia. Whereas I received fifty-one krans for every fifteen rupees or English sovereign at Bushire, I got only forty-seven by the time I reached Teheran, where not long before I was told the rate had stood as huge as sixty krans.[116]

The situation was partly caused by the lack of a sufficient number of coins available to the public at large. For example, Stotherd in May 1893 noted that, 'Many of the coins which pass in Bushire are not accepted in the districts, as they become so defaced as to resemble nothing but a smooth round piece of silver without mark or inscription. The new coinage in use up-country is scarcely procurable in Bushire.'[117] No change had occurred in 1901, when Landor noted that in villages 'no one would have anything to do with them [nickel coins] as they were absolutely unknown'.[118] Even ten years later, the same basket of coins was not necessarily circulating in every city.

113 Fraser, *Narrative of a Journey into Khorasan*, 74, n.
114 Rabino, 'Banking in Persia', 37.
115 Landor, *Across Coveted Lands*, 1:131.
116 Bradley-Birt, *Persia*, 52–53.

Table 6.2: Sample of silver qrans from regional mints, by weight and fineness

Mint	Year	Weight in grams	Fineness per mille	Value in francs
Hamadan	1293/1877	4.95	760	0.836
Tabriz	1290/1874	4.90	820	0.893
Kashan	1282/1865	5.03	820	0.917
Isfahan	1293/1877	5.02	840	0.937
Kerman	1293/1877	4.90	840	0.915
Mazandaran	1292/1876	4.97	840	0.928
Mashhad	1293/1877	4.90	840	0.91
Kermanshah	1282/1866	4.97	880	0.972
Resht	1280/1864	4.80	890	0.949
Tehran	1292/1876	5.02	900	1.004
Shiraz	1291/1875	4.90	900	0.98
Yazd	1278/1862	4.97	900	0.994
Herat	1277/1861	4.90	900	0.98

Source: Rabino, 'Banking in Persia', 37, which states the table was furnished by Pechan.

The situation in the various major cities as shown in Table 6.3 represents the reality until the end of the Qajar dynasty. Gold coins were no longer in circulation in the provincial centers. There was some slight variation in the basket of coins in use. The 3-shahis coins did not circulate much. In 1911 the 2-pul copper coin and the silver two shahi coins were no longer listed as being in circulation. Whereas in Yazd the half qran silver coins were no longer used in 1911, the half qran, an 'old hammered coin struck in the provincial mints, of varying degrees of fineness, was probably more current locally than the modern minted one. A premium was changed for the new one.'[119] Copper was disappearing from circulation. In Isfahan the 4 pul was still in use, though it had completely disappeared in Yazd by 1912.

117 Stotherd, *South-West Persia*, 2.

118 Landor, *Across Coveted Lands*, 1:133.

119 DCR 5048 (1912), 43. According to the *Military Report on Persia*, 4 vols. Simla, 1924, vol. 4/2, 142, the 'favourite coin is the silver 2 qran, often called *gudgari* by Afghans and Baluchis, this being their pronunciation of Qajari, a name given on account of the image of the Shah on the coin.'

Table 6.3: Coins in use by 1911, in a number of cities

Coin type	Tabriz	Isfahan	Yazd	Kermanshah	Mashhad	Bandar `Abbas
Copper						
1 pul	–	–	–	–	X	–
2 pul (shahi siyah)	–	–	–	–	X	–
4 pul (sannar siyah)	–	X	–	2 shahi (24 per qran)	X	–
4 shahi	–	–	–		X	–
Nickel						
1 shahi safid	X	X	X	–	–	X
2 shahi (sannar safid)	X	X	X	X	–	X
Silver						
half shahi	–	–	X*	–	–	–
1 shahi	–	–	–	–	–	–
2 shahi	–	–	–	–	–	–
3 shahi	–	X (scarce)	–	–	–	–
5 shahi	–	X (scarce)	–	–	X	–
10 shahi	–	X	–	–	X	–
1 qran	X	X	X	X	X	X (scarce)
2 qran	X	X	X	X	X	X (scarce)
5 qran	X	X	X	X	X	X (scarce)
Gold		not in circulation	not in circulation	not in circulation	not in circulation	–

Source: DCR 4994 (Kermanshah, 1912), 3; DCR 4794 (Khorasan, 1911), 4; DCR 4811 (Bunder `Abbas, 1911), 2 (IBP notes very scarce; Indian rupees and rupee notes are plentiful and freely used); DCR 5048 (Isfahan-Yazd 1912), pp. 3, 43 (* old hammered coins probably more current than the modern minted coin, for which a premium is charged); DCR 5088 (Azerbaijan, 1912), p. 3 (plus the notes issued by the IBP). There were undoubtedly other coins circulating as well, but these were the most common ones.

To complicate the monetary situation even further, foreign currencies were still widely used. In 1796, Olivier called the quantity of foreign coins, gold and silver, entering Iran via Istanbul so great that there were no other coins in Iran.[120] In 1802, Waring wrote, 'Few of the coins which are current in Persia are coined in that Empire; those of the most general circulation are the Qooroosh, or Piastre of the Turks, and the Mujjur or Dutch ducat. The consequence of this want of standard coins of the empire, and the introduction in their stead of foreign coins, is a constant fluctuation in their value: so much so, that it is impossible to form a notion of the value of the gold coins for any length of time.'[121] Seven years later, Dupré reported that the official hazar was represented by an Ottoman coin, a piece of 60 paras called *qorush-e `eyn* (old piaster), struck in 1187/1773–74. It circulated freely and widely in Azerbaijan, Iraq-e Ajam (western Iran) and the Persian Gulf.[122] Writing in 1829, Sir John Malcolm commented, 'It is remarkable that among a people, whose sovereign deems the right of coining the highest privilege, foreign coins should form a considerable part of the economy.'[123] Fraser, describing the inflow of foreign currency into Iran from the north and west, wrote, 'Much of the gold remains current under its original form of ducats; the rest is coined into tomans; the silver is all coined into reals; the manets being only current in the western parts of the kingdom bordering on Turkey and the Russia territories.'[124] The type of foreign currency used in a region was determined by the local import–export trade. Thus, in northwest Iran Russian coins were of major importance, while in southeast Iran, Indian currency prevailed. Burgess, writing in 1846, claimed that 'There is more Russian money in circulation at Khoee [Khoy] than Persian'.[125] Twenty years later, the British reported that in Tabriz, 'Russian silver coins of 10, 15, and 20 c.' were the principal circulating medium, outstripping the 'new krans, called "Ameeni sultans", coined at the Tehran mint', in quantity as well as in quality. [126]

The value of the foreign coins varied from region to region. Zarrabi noted that the exchange rate of the Russian Imperial, which played such

120 Olivier, *Voyage*, 3:180.

121 Waring, *Tour to Sheeraz*, 128–29.

122 Dupré, *Voyage en Perse*, 2:478.

123 Malcolm, *History of Persia*, 2:515.

124 Fraser, *Travels and Adventures*, 1:372.

125 Schwarz, *Letters from Persia*, 85; Momtahen al-Dowleh, *Khaterat*, 157 (*bajoqli*; a Polish or Swedish gold coin); Basir al-Molk, *Ruznameh-ye khaterat*, 47 (*baqlicheh*; *baghlicheh*). According to Ferrier, *Caravan Journeys*, 121, n. 'The Bajoglee or the Belgian ducat, which is universally current there to the exclusion of almost all other gold coins.' Stirling, *Journals*, 343 called it the 'abjughi, the European ducat, also called majar.'

126 DCR 445 (1888 – Tabriz), 3, claiming that, upon inspection, the Iranian qran contained 'only 64% silver, against 72 per cent of the same metal in the old Russian silver coins in vogue here'. See also Wilson, *Persian Life and Customs*, 282.

an important role in the trade of Tabriz, was much lower in Shiraz than in Tabriz.[127] In other regions a Russian coin might not be accepted all. In 1904 the Belgian customs official at Nasratabad in Sistan 'asked us to give him Persian silver in exchange for a Russian gold rouble piece which he could not change in the village'.[128] Similarly, Stocqueler traveling in Khuzestan in 1828 related that 'all my money was in Persian coin, and the inhabitants refused any but the Turkish piaster'.[129] In the Bandar `Abbas area in 1884, the current coin was the Indian rupee.[130] Even in Tehran payments might take place in foreign coin.[131]

In sum, Qajar Iran had local currencies more than a national currency. Before 1877 each major town had its own mint and the coins produced there could vary 10 per cent or more in weight from the national standard, and in any case, varying discount rates were demanded by merchants. In addition, foreign coins were widely used at exchange rates that varied from city to city. Arbitrage was limited by the heavy weight of the coins and the high cost of transport. Many aspects of this system persisted until into the twentieth century. The difficulties of establishing a truly national monetary system mirrored the general shortcomings in creating a national economy in Iran. Well into the twentieth century, the Iranian economy was actually a series of regional economies, each consisting of a major commercial center with its own hinterland.

The tuman/dinar system was not the only ghost money used. In 1864, a time of monetary scarcity, 'goods were sold and accounts kept by merchants on the basis rightly called churuk or "rotten", and payments were made by drafts cashed at the above discount. Cash when obtained, was a rare and curious spectacle.'[132] The Qajar government promoted this fictitious currency, which also existed in some parts of Turkey. It was momentarily abandoned in the mid 1860s,[133] but soon thereafter was widely adopted again, and this time it became a necessary fixture of commercial practice. MacLean in 1904 insisted that, 'This system was born out of necessity, since Persian bookkeeping does not lend itself to changes of interest on daily balances, consequently when cash was scarce in the bazaars the banker, instead of altering his rate of interest, made a distinction between book transfers and cash payments, charging an agio [discount] on the

127 *AP* 3653, Report by Consul-General Jones, Tabriz, Nov. 1872, 371–72.
128 Benn, *Overland Trek*, 208.
129 Stocqueler, *Fifteen Months' Pilgrimage*, 1:82 (in the village of Gadee, near Bandar-e Mash`ur).
130 Preece, 'Journey from Shiraz to Jashk', 422.
131 Basir al-Molk, *Ruznameh-ye khaterat*, 14 (*imperial*).
132 DCR 318, Tabriz 1864 and 1865, 268.
133 DCR 3729, 1866, 476.

latter.'[134] The discount rates differed per article, often even per banker. For example, the discount for German yarn was 16 per cent and for English white shirting 4 per cent. According to MacLean, the Stamboulchis only used this form of quotation. British and Continental piece-goods were often quoted on the basis of *havaleh-ye sarraf*, or only 4 per cent discount, while Russian goods were quoted in qrans. Silk and woolen goods were quoted in *choruk* money (see below). In fact the discount system was charged on all manufactories, but metals and sugar were paid for in cash. Somewhere in the 1880s the discount was fixed at 7 per cent for cash money versus choruk money, and later another 4 per cent was added. At the end of the 1890s a further 4 per cent under the heading of banker's transfer (havaleh-ye sarraf) was added.[135]

This intricate system of calculation was used to fix the prices, which were paid for with havaleh at 10 to 15 days' sight, with the amount of value cash at due date. The sarraf received no cash guarantee from the drawee, but he in turn was paid with the drawee's havalehs on smaller traders, and the banker would charge a discount on paying the havaleh in cash money. This method was applied to book transfers as well as cash payments.

The following example illustrates the working of the system; note that the method used to calculate the discount (technically, the 'agio') is different from the usual modern way to calculate a discount.

> The cash price for an article sold at 200 qrans choruk money is:[136]
> I. On the price of 200, a 7% discount is applied: (200 x .07) / 1.07 = 13.1. So now the price is 200–13.1 = 186.9.
> II. A further 4% discount is applied: (186.9 x .04) / 1.04 = 7.1. So now the price is 186.9–7.1 = 179.8.
> III. A further 4% discount is applied: (179.8 x .04) / 1.04 = 6.9. So now the price is 179.8 - 6.9 = 172.9.

This means that a book money price of 200 qrans, when paid for in cash, amounted to 172.9 qrans only. In reality, the system was even more intricate. We have seen that there were two kinds of money, book money and cash money, but in fact book money was again subdivided in three separate monies, differing in discount only.[137]

134 MacLean, *Report on the Conditions*, 61.
135 Ibid., 61; *Berichte* 1910, 314.
136 *Berichte* 1910, 314; MacLean, *Report on the Conditions*, 61.
137 DCR 445 (Tabreez; 1888), 4; Lorini, *La Persia economica*, 334; see also Wilson, *Persian Life and Customs*, 282.

1. 'Raidj divan' [*rayej-e divan*] or government rate by which 15 pieces of 20 c. plus 2 shahees are the countervalue for a toman. This rate is used in paying the army, official salaries, pensions; also in payments to custom house, telegraph and pensions.
2. 'Raidj bazaar' [*rayej-e bazar*] or market rate by which 15 pieces of 20 c. we equal to 1 toman, three pieces of 20 c. making 2 krans. Servant's wages, bazaar purchases, household expenses, &c., are paid at this rate.
3. Lastly, 'Raidj toojar' [*rayej-e tojjar*] or merchants' rate, adopted in mercantile transactions, by which 15 pieces of 20 c. are equivalent to 1 toman and 10 shahees. Money paid at this rate is termed 'Poul tchourouk' [*pul-e choruk*] or rotten money (litt. filthy lucre) in contradiction to 'Poul saf' [*pul-e saf*] or pure money, which is another name for 'Raidj divan'.

As for the actual Iranian coins, they came in three metals: gold, silver and copper. It is unclear if this constituted official trimetallism, since we do not know if there was a legal requirement that the coins be exchanged at fixed ratios.[138] It seems that the value of coins continued to be determined in the traditional manner, on the basis of metal content coupled with societal expectations about the normal value, reinforced by sporadic government action. The concept of a normal rate of exchange is referred to time and again by those describing the system, as is the pre-eminence of silver. Consider just one such account, a very lengthy 1834 report on Iran's trade by the British official James Brandt. He explained the monetary system as:[139]

> 20 Shahees = 1 Sahib Koraun
> 10 Sahib Koraun = 1 Tomaun
>
> [...] The Tauman has become only a money of account having been withdrawn from circulation and replaced by Persian Ducats nominally of the same value as Dutch or Russian Ducats but intrinsically worth a trifle less. The Sahib Koraun is a Silver Coin equal to about a Shilling Sterling. The Shahee is a copper money. As the silver coinage has never been altered it is considered more sure.

138 Mostowfi, *Sharh-e zendegani-ye man*, 1:399, claims that until 1300/1884, the government kept the silver/gold ratio stable with gold being the standard and the weight of silver coins being adjusted (e.g., if silver became cheaper, the coins became heavier). There is little evidence to support this claim.

139 For the full text of Brandt's report, see Floor, *Textile Imports*, 190.

In 1858, Blau cited the coins in use as: 'In gold, Toman = 10 Keran = equivalent to 50 Turkish piasters ... In silver, Keran = 20 Schahis or 5 Turkish piasters. In copper, Schahi = 2 nimschahi = 10 Turkish piasters,' explaining that in the bazaar, silver was used most.[140]

Many travelers' accounts offer the same account of 20 copper shahis for 1 silver qran and 10 silver qrans for 1 gold tuman.[141] But it is by no means clear how much legal basis there was for a fixed exchange rate. Album et al. refer to an early Qajar minting of both gold and silver tumans. They read this as 'an attempt at bimetallism, that is, at fixing the ratio between the two metals', contrasting it with the older system under which the 'ratio [between gold and silver] had traditionally fluctuated in response to market conditions'.[142] According to them, it is 'doubtful that this experiment with bimetallism was successful'. This account may well over-simplify a situation in which there was an expectation, backed by tradition, about what constituted a normal exchange rate among the three currency metals, with the actual rate then fluctuating based on local demand and supply conditions and the quality of the various coins.

The ratios at which the coins of different metals circulated could fluctuate from month to month. Sirjani reports the value of copper relative to the silver qran on various dates. In December 1893 one silver qran bought only 15 copper shahis compared to the official rate of 20.[143] But the rate fell quickly thereafter: in April 1894, the rate was 30 shahis; in August 1894, 35; in December 1898, 40; in September 1900, 50.

The universal practice of applying discounts to particular coins shows that the government did not or could not completely impose fiat values for the coins. It similarly failed to control the widespread use of foreign coins, despite the theoretical requirement to surrender these to the mint for recoinage into Iranian coins.

Besides the lack of a firmly enforced legal ratio among the three types of coins, another reason why the Iranian system of three metals was rather stable, despite considerable fluctuations in the prices of the metals, was that, as before, the coins were largely separated by their uses: copper coins were mostly for local trade; silver coins were for government use and long distance trade; while some gold was for long distance trade but most was for hoarding and luxury items.

140 Blau, *Commerzielle Zustände Persiens*, 171.

141 E.g., Marsh, *Ride through Islam*, 75.

142 Album et al., 'Coins and Coinage', 36.

143 Sirjani, *Vaqaye`-ye Ettefaqiyeh*, 445 (Dec. 1893), 455 (Apr. 1894), 461 (Aug. 1894), 557 (Dec. 1898), and 557 (Sept. 1900). At some points in between these dates, the rates were even higher.

Furthermore, it would have been unrealistic to expect the value of coins to have been determined solely on the basis of world market prices for the metals: markets in Iran did not operate smoothly, the cost of transporting large amounts of metal might create significant variation in prices between individual Iranian cities, and the government had various means to press for the acceptance of coins at a nominal value that varied from the value of the metal.

There was nevertheless some arbitrage, the movement of specie to capture differences in price ratios – typically when the gold/silver price in one city was higher than in another. For example, Zarrabi describes how gold ashrafis disappeared from Kashan leaving only silver *sahebqerans* and copper shahis/*pul-e siyah*: 'A few years ago, gold became expensive. One ashrafi of 18 nokhuds of 10 sahebqrans reached a value of 14–15 sahebqrans. The merchants who traded with the outside, before the people [of Kashan] learnt about this, bought the ashrafis first at the old price, then at 5, 10 shahis, or 1 to 2 hazar premium. When people learned about the real value of the ashrafi, there was not one ashrafi in Kashan anymore. Now, apart from the sahebqran, panabad and pul-e siyah, there is no [money] in people's hands.'[144]

However, arbitrage was no easy matter since coins were heavy and transport was costly. Rabino has left us a graphic description of the logistics and cost of the transport of cash in the late nineteenth century:

> A street porter will carry about £300 in silver, an ass load is about £600 in silver; a mule load is about £800 in silver and a camel load about £900; consequently, to bring in to a bank a sum of £25,000 [which was a very large sum in those days], would take 83 men, or 41 donkeys, or 31 mules or 28 camels, and to count and scrutinize it, an expert money changer would take about 16 days.

Add to this the length of travel time and security isues. The journey between Tabriz and Tehran, for instance, would be at least seventeen days by caravan or four days by post, and travelers everywhere risked being despoiled by highway robbers.[145]

144 Zarrabi, *Tarikh-e Kashan*, 275.

145 Rabino, 'Banking in Persia,'39; the time required comes from a table on p. 34 which warns, 'during winter and bad weather, times much in excess for letters, and in caravan column, days of stoppage not added.'

In sum, this chapter has shown how much Iran's long-standing pre-modern monetary system persisted well into the nineteenth century. To the modern mind, the advantages of a common national currency and standard coins seem obvious. Not so to Iranians under the Qajar dynasty, who were quite accustomed to a fragmented monetary system, using foreign coins and coins hand-made by local craftsmen. Indeed, modernization when it came at the end of the nineteenth century was not particularly welcome, in no small part because the milled coins from the new national mint in Tehran began to circulate at a time of great monetary turmoil as the world market price of silver (the most common monetary metal in Iran) was dropping relative to that of gold (the basis of the pound sterling and most other European currencies). The next chapter analyzes in more detail the Qajar system of coins in three metals and the gradual transition to paper money.

7

The Politics of Money Supply under Modernizing Conditions

The previous chapter began the analysis of the Qajar monetary systems by looking at the minting of coins, the transition from traditional, hammer-struck coinage to machine-striking, and the nature of the fragmented currency system. This chapter extends that analysis by discussing the role of copper, silver and gold coins; the supply of bullion and specie; silver's declining value relative to gold; and the transition to paper money.

Copper, Silver and Gold Coins

As had been the case earlier, Qajar Iran had coins of three metals: copper, silver and gold. Copper was the main currency for everyday life, but silver was seen as 'real' money: copper was not as readily accepted, especially for large or long-distance transactions, as silver. Gold was rarely used, being largely confined to ceremonial purposes. There was a popular expectation, more or less reflected in law, about the relative value of coins in the three metals, but in practice, there was considerable variation depending on market conditions, such as how many coins of each type were available. Meanwhile, large parts of the Iranian economy functioned with little if any use of money; barter was quite common, especial in rural areas.

Copper Coins

In nineteenth-century Iran, copper was as the main currency for every-day life. Retail prices were in copper and laborers were paid were in copper coins. Copper provided poor people with circulating coins in a cost-effective way, and it served as an effective means of additional exploitation. Used by the poor, in small quantities and slow in velocity, copper was too marginal to enter into normal monetary discourse.[1]

Copper coins generally circulated at a value that exceeded their metallic worth; that is, they were token money with a value established by the state rather than determined by their metallic content. In a situation that went back to pre-Qajar times, copper coins only had their full value in the area of the governor who had issued the coins. In 1809, Dupré observed that copper coins were only accepted in the city where they were struck. Those produced in Khoy were not accepted in Tabriz or Maragheh and vice-versa.[2] Likewise in 1840, Mitford remarked that 'It is a curious peculiarity that the copper money in almost every town in Persia is different, the money of one town not circulating in the next: this is a great drawback to local trade and intercourse, the only people who gain by the impolitic arrangement being the money-changers.'[3] The fact that some legal documents explicitly state that payment had to be in the copper coins of Qom (*pul-e siyah-e Qomi*) or of Tehran implies that copper coins outside their legal jurisdiction had less value.[4]

A major reason why such local petty coins could have different values was that, as in previous times, the Qajar economy did not constitute a national market, but rather consisted of a number of regional markets made up of commercial centers and their hinterland. Each major town continued to have a mint and its own currency system to accommodate local commerce. Until the establishment of the national mint, the copper coins differed in size, weight and value by area, with the local governor having much power about whether to coin copper and what value to assign to coins. Both the output of the local mint as well as the local 'exchange rate' were often markedly different from conditions in other regions, or from the formal national standard. There were twenty-four known copper striking mints: Astarabad, Yerevan, Hamadan, Herat, Isfahan, Kerman, Maragheh, Nishapur, Qazvin, Shabankareh, Shiraz, Soltaniyeh, Tabriz, Yazd, Isfahan, Kashan, Kazerun, Kerman, Lahijan, Mashhad, Qazvin, Rasht, Tabriz and Tehran.

Some contemporary observers write that governors had much leeway in reducing the metal content of copper coins. Waring, referring to the situation in 1804, notes that 'the governors of districts will alter the standard value of

1 Perlin, 'Money-use in Late Pre-colonial India', 237.

2 Dupré, *Voyage*, 2:480.

3 Mitford, *Land March*, 2:10.

4 Beygdeli, *Tarikh-e Beygdeli*, 66, 116; see also Bérézine, *Voyage*, 2 :127 about the difference in the quality of copper coins in different cities.

coins without assigning the smallest reason'.[5] Isa Khan, the governor in Resht in 1856, made a fortune, by changing the value of copper every month![6]

As an example of how localized the various parts of the Iranian economy were consider Sirjani's report that on 20 February 1884, a large quantity of coined (from Tehran) and uncoined copper (from Bombay) arrived in Shiraz.[7] Since there was a surplus of copper coins in Shiraz, it was decided not to unpack the copper without orders from Tehran.[8] Amin al-Zarb sent for the uncoined copper – not surprisingly, since he could make a nice profit from coining it – at which point the merchants in Shiraz petitioned Tehran not to allow it to be coined, because it would hurt trade.[9] The value of copper in one city, this example shows, depended on local supply and demand conditions much more than on developments in the world market.

We have limited data about the weight and denomination of copper coins. 'These coins were struck in multiple denominations, but the weight standard and the preferred denomination varied from mint to mint. Typical weights vary from less than 4 to more than 20 grams ....'[10] Until the Qajars minted their own copper coins, the qazbaki of 5 dinars circulated in Iran. This coin remained in circulation until the introduction of the copper half shahi by Fath `Ali Shah. During the rule of the latter, a period when copper was scarce, Russian two kopeck pieces were used. These were given a countermark or restruck, with date and place of minting. Copper coins of the EIC were treated that way as well.[11]

Copper coins were generally referred to as folus, pul, and generically as pul-e siyah or *qara pul* or black money, to distinguish it from *pul-e safid* or silver money.[12] The indiscriminate use of the word shahi or pul or any of the other terms is probably due to the fact that Europeans hardly ever dealt in low-value copper money. Also, its fluctuating price as a raw material made it an interesting source of additional income for the servants. As Arnold put it,

> There is a copper coinage, the shihee, of which twenty make a kran. But there are no shihees, there are only half-shihees; and it seems to be the abiding and unvarying conviction of Persian servants that this

5 Waring, *Tour to Sheeraz*, 128, n.
6 MacKenzie, *Safarnameh-ye Shomal*, 214; Lacy O'Brien, *Banking in Persia*, 66; Rabino, *Coins, Medals, and Seals*, 20; Adamiyat, *Amir Kabir va Iran*, 274.
7 Sirjani, *Vaqaye`-ye Ettefaqiyeh*, 109.
8 Ibid., 210.
9 Ibid., 232.
10 Album, *Checklist*, 316.
11 Rabino, *Coins, Medals, and Seals*, 21.
12 Basir al-Molk *Ruznameh-ye khaterat*, 48.

coinage, which is for the most part stamped with the well-known Persian combination of the lion and sun, is not sufficiently valuable for Europeans to handle. The odd shihees in any purchase or any settlement of expenditure are never forthcoming; the real value is much greater than the nominal worth, and perhaps Persian servants do not like to see the premium lost by unthrifty masters. Possibly this is why they collect and sell them wholesale for their private advantage, at about twenty-five per cent. increase upon the nominal value of the coins.[13]

Table 7.1: Local names of copper coins

Dinar value	Shahi value	Name					
5	rob` shahi	nim pul	qara pul kuchek	jandak (Khorasan)	qazbegi	qaz	
10	nim shahi	pul-e siyah or pul	qara pul bozorg	kalwar (Borujerd)	papati (Tehran)	bisti (Shiraz)	qapak (Tabriz)
20	–	bisti (unit of account)	–	–	–	–	–
33.3	–	tambal	pul-e siyah	–	–	–	–
20 or 50?	yak shahi			–	–	–	–
200	–	`abbasi (unit of account)	qamari (Khuzestan)	–	–	–	–
40 or 100?	du shahi	sannar	yuzaltun	mohammadi	–	–	–

Source: Waring, *A Tour to Sheeraz*, 128; Dupré, *Voyage*, 2:482; Bournoutian, *Eastern Armenia*, 69; Southgate, *Narrative of a Tour*, 2:349; Polak, *Persien*, 2:162–63; Binning, *Journal*, 1:168; Blau, *Die commerzielle Zustände*, 171; see also Haentzsche, 'Spezialstatistik von Persien', ', 36; Mostowfi, *Sharh-e Zendegani*, 51; Rabino, *Coins, Medals, and Seals*, 17; Farahani, *Tarikh-e Sekkeh*, 76 (*bash achiq*), 77 (*papashi*); Bérézine, *Voyage*, 2:127.

13 Arnold, *Through Persia by Caravan*, 136.

Prior to the establishment of the national mint, the names used for coins varied by region. Some of the coin sizes and names are shown below. The list is by no means exhaustive; for instance, the term *qapak*, from the Russian kopeck, was also in use in Tabriz as a unit of account referring to 10 dinars,[14] while the same city also used as a money of account the *tanbal* equal to 2/3 shahi or 33.3 dinars.

Zarrabi mentions that copper money was stamped on both sides. By one account, the coins were embellished with calligraphy and/or eponymous animals on one side, while on the other there was the name of the city and the minting date. By another account, on one side there was the sun-lion and date, and on the other *folus rayej-e mamalek-e mahruseh-ye Iran*. By a third account, the coins showed the Persian sun and lion; the Shah had wanted his portrait, but artists were unable to make good ones.[15]

After the establishment of the national mint, copper coins were standardized. Lorini listed five copper coins, with their equivalents in silver qrans and their legal weight in copper:[16]

4 shahi or 4 abbasi coin, worth 1/5 qran, with a legal weight of 20.0 grams;
2 shahi or sanar or dinar coin, worth 1/10 qran, with a legal weight of 10.0 grams;
1 shahi or abbasi coin, worth 1/20 qran, with a legal weight of 2.5 grams;
½ shahi or pul coin, worth 1/40 qran, with a legal weight of 1.25 grams; and
½ pul coin, known in Khorasan as jekdek, worth 1/80 qran, with a legal weight of 0.6 grams.

Note the peculiarity that the shahi is one-fourth the weight of the two shahi coin and one-eight the weight of the four shahi coin, and that one qran bought 100 g of coin for the four shahi or two shahi coin but only 50 g of coin for the shahi or one-half shahi coin. All this illustrates that the metal content was much less important for the value of copper coins than for gold and silver coins. As Album et al. note, 'European travelers regularly reported that the copper coins were officially rated against silver at a substantial premium over their metal value, as was quite normal for base metal currencies in most parts

14 Rabino, *Coins, Medals, and Seals*, 17. Some copper coins were issued by the royal mint; `Ala' al-Dini, *Sekkehha-ye mesi-ye Iran*, 18, has a photo of a copper coin stamped '*ordu*', suggesting that the royal minit at times issued copper coins for the ordu.

15 Dupré, *Voyage*, 2:476–77; Zarrabi, *Tarikh-e Kashan*, 275; Olivier *Voyage*, 5:322; Polak, *Persien*, 2:163.

16 Lorini, *La Persia economica*, 426.

of the world.'[17] One indication of this was the profits made on the operation of the mint, which came primarily from copper coins, thanks to the greater value of coins compared to their metal value.[18] Describing an 1886 cabinet meeting, Amin al-Zarb wrote, 'His Excellency Amin al-Dawla said ["black money"] in the end is nothing but copper and if the appellation of money is taken away from it, it is copper and worth little.'[19]

A further indication of the low esteem in which copper coins were held was that the Qajar government did little to support the face value of the copper coins when the their real value dropped relative to silver coins. Eventually, government agencies such as customs farmers, telegraph and post offices, were urged to accept copper as legal tender at a fixed rate up to certain amounts.[20] It is clear the government never anticipated that it would have to accept copper in payment at the face value on the coins. Nor was the state the only one unwilling to accept copper as payment. People just did not consider copper coins legal tender.[21]

But the copper coins were no less susceptible to fluctuations in value than silver or gold. The main factor for copper appears to have been the amount of coin produced. After Amin al-Zarb took over the mint in 1879, copper coins fell sharply in value relative to silver (followed soon by the collapse in value of silver relative to gold, caused by the world market decline in the price of silver).[22] Sarrafs insisted on an increasing number of copper coins for each silver coin given in exchange. Rabino was trenchant in his complaint about how the government made a mess of the copper coins, which he called 'the whole fortune of the poor'.[23] He observed that 'copper nominally issued at 20 shahis per kran was current at 30, 40, 50, or even 80 shahis per kran' – a clear indication that people expected copper coins not to fluctuate but, like the shahi, have fixed conversion rate to silver coins such as the qran. Lorini also describes the qran as typically being worth at least 30 shahis, adding

17 Album et al., 'Coins and Coinage', 38.

18 Rabino, 'Report on the Possibility', 2.

19 As given in Mahdavi, *For God, Mammon, and Country*, 139. Amin al-Zarb's response to this jibe at him was to defend copper coins as 'not worse than paper money or paper stamps', demonstrating the contempt for paper money.

20 Gordon, *Persia Revisited*, 74–76; Simmons, 'Evolution of Persia's Monetary System', 124–25.

21 Rabino, 'Economist's Notes on Persia', 279.

22 Mahdavi, *For God, Mammon, and Country*, 138–39, presents this episode in the best possible light for Amin al-Zarb; many other accounts describe him as responsible for flooding the country with copper coins in order to increase his profits as mintmaster.

23 This paragraph and its quotes are drawn from Rabino, 'Economist's Notes on Persia', 278. `Ala' al-Dini, *Sekkehhha-ye mesi-ye Iran*, 104,108,119,129,133, and 160 has photos of coins with countermarks.

that it reached 50 shahis in March 1899.[24] Rabino ascribed the drop in the value of the copper coins to 'the excessive over-issue of copper coins, due to the iniquitous system of farming, the ignorance of the authorities, and to the corruption of officials' – all indications that the value of the copper coins depended in part on the mint master, not solely on the metal contained in the coin valued at market prices.

At times, the government acted to reduce the supply of copper coins, so as to increase their value. In 1885, for instance, the shah forced the mint farmer to withdraw 50,000 tuman and in 1886 100,000 tuman in copper money.[25] The British consul in Shiraz in 1894, commenting on the recent departure of the governor, refers to a local copper coin repurchase: 'The steps taken by the Nizam es Saltaneh for the reduction of the agio [discount] on silver from 18½ per cent by collecting and storing 30,000 tomans worth of copper coin [...] have led people to regard him as a successful and beneficent ruler and he seemed much regretted by all classes'.[26] In other words, rapacious officials issued too much copper coin, thereby depressing its value, while virtuous officials ensured that copper coins were close to their 'normal' rate relative to silver. Rabino in 1894 warned, 'It is difficult to suppose that this oppression of the lower classes [due to over-issuance of copper coins] will not have to be paid for, sooner or later, by the Shah himself or by his immediate successor.'[27]

Because people had lost faith in the value of copper, its circulation dropped sharply and, as a result, 'cardboard tokens were widely used as coin'.[28] After the troubles caused by the mint's excessive issuance of copper coins in the mid-1890s, the IBP was charged to repurchase a large amount of the coins. As usual, this led to a continuing dispute with the government about reimbursement. In April 1897, of the 587,504 tumans in copper coins the Bank was holding, the government had paid for only 100,000 tumans.[29] Rabino noted, 'The Shah sent his written promise [...] it was intended to give us out of the large sums paid over by Hajji Mohamed Hassan Amin es Zarb as smart money for the copper inequities.' However, the latter paid 275,000 tumans in gold and 500,000 tumans 'in claims and assets of various kinds', – rather different than the 800,000 tumans he is usually said to have paid.[30] There followed a long and acrimonious dispute with Sani` al-Dowleh about selling the gold – seen as a commodity – to the Bank.

24 Lorini, *La Persia economica*, 363–66.
25 Greenfield, *Verfassung*, 328.
26 *NA*, FO 248, Persia, 586, No 125, 28 May 1894, Mr. Crowe's Report on Shiraz for 1892–93, 23 May 1894.
27 Rabino, 'Report on the Possibility', 3.
28 Jones, *Banking and Empire*, 1:81.
29 Report on the Working of the Bank, marked 'Rec'd 9 April 1897', BBME 594.3.
30 Letter of 25 Jan. 1897 by Rabino the Secretary of the IBP, BBME 594.3.

Nor was this the only time when the government took action to reduce the gap between the nominal and actual value of copper coins. Rabino mentions the repurchase in the late 1890s of about 200 million shahis (720,000 tomans nominal of the copper coins at 25 shahis per kran', presumably at 10 qran per tuman). Lorini describes the repurchase in detail, explaining that the rate at which the shahi was repurchased was set at different rates: 25 per qran in Tehran and Tabriz, 27 in Rasht, 28 in Hamadan and 30 in Isfahan, Kermanshah, Shiraz, Yazd and Bushehr. Since the actual market rate was higher – e.g., 40 in Isfahan – the merchants could make a killing from selling to the IBP; they could also profit from shipping the copper from Tehran to Isfahan, in contravention of the ban on shipping copper coins between cities imposed by the government on 31 August 1898.[31]

Nickel coins, which were said to wear better, were scheduled to be introduced in April 1896, but Naser al-Din Shah's assassination in May 1896 delayed the project.[32] The IBP raised the issue again under his successor, Mozaffar al-Din Shah. As a result, in November 1899, the government of Iran and the IBP agreed to a complete reform of the currency system. It was also agreed upon to demonetize all 'copper' coins, and to replace them with 'nickel' coins, which the IBP would distribute throughout the country. Those terms are placed in quotes because in fact both coins were alloys of copper and nickel; indeed, the 'nickel' coins were, according to the contract for their minting, 25 per cent nickel and 75 per cent copper.[33] As noted earlier, the 1878 assay of the new National Mint had found that the 'copper' coins were 90 per cent copper, which was considered a sign of their high quality; presumably the other 10 per cent was nickel, the metal usually added so that copper coins wear better, or iron. In other words, the 'nickel' coins would have differed some, but not that much, in metal composition from the previous 'copper' coins. Reflecting the

31 Lorini, *La Persia economica*, 367–69. Because of the rise of silver money, in Isfahan sarrafs and shopkeepers refused to accept copper. Business in the bazaar came to a halt, bread became scarce, and the government to prevent riots imposed a new rate of 40 shahis per silver qran. 'However, because all wages are in copper, the people are sorely effected by these changes. People never know its value, and the government's orders are so often varying, nothing will give them confidence until radical change is made in the coinage.' DCR 2260 (Isfahan, 1879–98), 7.

32 Lorini, *La Persia economica*, 367–69.

33 Jones, *Banking and Empire*, 1:81–82. Paragraph 7 of the 23 Feb. 1900 contract among the Imperial Persian Legation in Brussels, the Imperial Bank, and the Directeur de la Monnaie of the Belgian Government, BBME 798. Rabino, *Coins, Medals, and Seals*, 74, also lists them as 75 per cent copper. Intriguingly, when listing on p. 81 the copper coins still in circulation under Reza Shah (r. 1926–41), he lists the 10 shahi, 25 dinar, and 10 dinar copper coins as 100 per cent copper, whereas few countries have ever issued pure copper coins. He lists the 2 dinar and 1 dinar copper coins as 95 per cent copper, 4 per cent tin, and 1 per cent zinc, which is more like the copper coins of other countries.

continuing preoccupation with metallic value, the weight of the nickel coins was set so that the value of the metal (nickel plus copper) would equal the face of the value of the coin. At the same time, in keeping with the social norm about a fixed ratio among the different metals, the value of the nickel coins in terms of silver coins was set in law.[34] But the prescribed value of the nickel coins in terms of silver was not consistent with the prescribed weight of the nickel coins if the silver price changed relative to that of the metal (nickel and copper) in the new coins, which of course it did. Just to add to the confusion, the one shahi pieces were 3 g in weight while the two shahi pieces were 4.5 g.[35]

The coins were struck in Belgium, after initial attempts to do so in Tehran were unsuccessful – yet another indication of continuing problems at the mint even after the mint farming was ended and the Belgians took over.[36]

Some reports indicate that nickel coins were initially not readily accepted outside of the capital. Landor reported that in 1901 the nickel coins circulated freely in Tehran, Qavzin and Resht, but 'In other cities I did not see any, nor would people accept mine in payment, and in villages no one would have anything to do with them as they were absolutely unknown.'[37] In Kermanshah, 'there are now some 10,000 tomans of copper coin still in circulation. Of nickel coin in 1900, 3,000 tomans were put in circulation and readily accepted and in the villages preferred to copper.'[38] In 1909, the British consul-general in Mashhad reported, 'The old copper coin continues in general use, nickel coin making practically no headway in Meshed.'[39] Küss wrote that people in Khorasan refused the nickel coins, and only accepted the old, larger copper coins.[40] Mostowfi regarded the exchange of copper coins for nickel as one of the foul deeds of Amin al-Soltan.[41]

The evolution of copper coins in Iran was little affected by world market developments regarding copper. The nineteenth century saw dramatic

34 'Le shahi en nickel devra en tout temps être accepté au cours invariable de Vingt shahis en nickel pour un Kran d'argent', according to the 28 October 1899 draft contract between IBP and the government represented by 'le Sadrazam Amine Sultan et Hakim ul Mulk, Ministre de la Monnaie', BBME 594.5. A 3 April 1900 'Memo: Nickel Contract' from Maclean refers to the contract having been signed, implying the draft was the final.

35 The 1900 contract with the Belgian mint. Ten million of each of the two coins were to be minted.

36 Rabino, *Coins, Medals, and Seals*, 77. The BBME archives have extensive correspondence about the dealings with the Belgian mint.

37 Landor, *Across Coveted Lands*, 1:132.

38 DCR 590 (Kermanshah, 1903), 25.

39 E.g., DCR 4376, 5, Report for 1908–09 on the Trade of Khorasan, which states, 'The old copper coin continues in general use, nickel coin making practically no headway in Meshed.'

40 Küss, *Handelsratgeber für Persien*, 163.

41 Mostowfi, *Sharh-e zendegani-ye man*, 1:399.

changes in the world market for copper. Production rose from an average of 16.5 thousand metric tons in 1801–10 to 376.5 thousand in 1891–1900, while the price, in pounds sterling per long ton, dropped from £151 in 1800 to £78 in 1900.[42] Then by 1914 production tripled and prices fell to £60, fed by demand for electric wires and production from the massive Minnesota and Chile deposits. Copper became a widely used industrial metal, the price of which had little to do with monetary conditions even though many countries continued to use copper for base currency – with the role of copper perhaps greatest in East Asia, but also seen in coins such as the U.S. penny.

Silver Coins

Silver was the main currency for tax, administrative and large-scale or long-distance trading purposes. Throughout the nineteenth century, silver was seen as the real currency in Iran, unlike in Europe where increasingly gold was king. A telling example of this came during the 1897 run on the Imperial Bank of Persia in Tehran. Rabino made great efforts to exchange IBP's paper currency notes for silver, but after several days had to give up. 'Up to Tuesday we managed to pay silver to everyone but on that day we had to pay in gold for all but small amounts. Gold being not a coin but a merchandize [sic] we fixed the price at Krs: 19½ per ashrafi but gave our engagement to redeem them in a fortnight at the same rate. Comparatively little gold has been paid out.'[43]

In the beginning of his reign, from 1194/1780 until 1201/1786-87, the first Qajar ruler, Mohammad Agha Khan (r. 1779–97) issued rupees of 11.52 g, of one tuman of 800 nokhud (1 rupi = 15 shahis), the standard adopted by Karim Khan in 1190/1776. From 1201–04/1786–90, the tuman was revalued to 600 nokhud (1 rupi = 20 shahis). From 1204/1789–90 to 1211/1796–97, the tuman was reduced to 528 nokhud. In 1206/1792, instead of the rupee he adopted the riyal of 1,250 dinars (1 rupi = $^{10}/_{11}$ of a riyal) as the main silver coin, weighing 12.67 g. Its value was fixed at 25 shahis, yielding a rupi worth of a little over 22 shahis. From 1211–12/1796–98, the riyal became identical to the rupi (1 riyal = 1 rupi 25 shahis), with the tuman reduced to 480 nokhud. This type was used for the final issues

42 Ketzer, 'Copper from a Statistical Viewpoint', 106, 115. On the early twentieth century and the use of copper as coins, cf. Treue, 'Copper Trade', 103–04. The main silver/copper money system was that of Manchu China; cf. Sandrock, *Copper Cash*, 1995.

43 Rabino to Secretary IBP, 2 Sept. 1897, BBME 594.3. The Persian Foreign Office account of this episode described IBP's offer to pay in gold as an 'excuse' (Translation of an account received by the Persian Legation in London from the Imperial Foreign Office Date Rabi` II, H. 1315, 2 Sept.; BBME 651.1 Folder 6).

Table 7.2: Silver coins struck by Qajar shahs (1779–1877)

Reign	Name of coin	Weight/ grams	Ghost value	Tuman weight in nokhud	Period
Agha Mohammad	Rupee	11.52	15 shahi	800	1194–1201/1780–86
	Rupee	11.52	20 shahi	600	1201–04/1787–89
	Rupee	11.52	25 shahi	528	1204–11/1790–96
	Riyal	12.67	1,250 dinars	528	1206–11/1791–96
	Riyal	11.52	1,250 dinars	480	1211–12/1796–97
Fath `Ali Shah	Riyal	11.52	1,250 dinars	480	1212–13/1797–98
	Riyal	10.36	1,250 dinars	432	1213–32/1799–1816
	Riyal	9.21	1,250 dinars	384	1232–41/1816–26
	Qran	6.91	1,000 dinars	360	1241–50/1826–34
Mohammad Shah	Qran	6.91	1,000 dinars	360	1250–51/1834–35
	Qran	6.33	1,000 dinars	330	1251–52/1835–36
	Qran	5.76	1,000 dinars	300	1252–54/1837–38
	Qran	5.37	1,000 dinars	280	1254–64/1838–48
Naser al-Din Shah	Qran	5.37	1,000 dinars	280	1264–74/1848–57
	Qran	4.99	1,000 dinars	260	1271–96/1858–79

Source: Album, *Checklist*, 291–96.

of Agha Mohammad, as well as all early issues of his nephew and successor, Fath `Ali Shah.[44]

Under Fath `Ali Shah (r. 1212–50/1797–1834) the standard of 1 tuman was 480 nokhud (1 riyal = 11.52 g) in 1212–13. The riyal was reckoned as 1250 dinars. From 1213–18 the standard of 432 nokhud was used for the

44 Album, *Checklist*, 292–93. The term rupee continued to be used in documents. One *rupiyeh* of 1.5 mesqal equaled 1,000 dinars in 1243/1827–28. Further, a *rupiyeh-e Naser al-Din Shahi* of 28 nokhud of 1,000 dinars is mentioned in 1266/1849–50. The term *rupiyeh-ye saheb-qrani* is also met. See Beygdeli, *Tarikh-e Beygdeli*, 53, 59, 70, 74.

tuman (1 riyal = 10.36 g). In the period 1232–40 the standard was reduced to 384 nokhud for the tuman (1 riyal = 9.21 g). Until 1826, the coinage of the reign was based on 1 tuman equals 8 riyals, of 1,250 dinars. The standard was further reduced to 360 nokhud in March 1826, when the qran made its appearance. It would become the principal coin of 1,000 dinars weighing 6.91 g; hence if was also called hazar or hazar dinar. Its issue was discontinued in 1932, when it was replaced by an equivalent riyal.[45]

Under Mohammad Shah (r. 1834–48), the standard remained 360 nokhud for the tuman (qran = 6.91 g) until 1250–51/1834–36. In that point the standard was reduced to 330 nokhud (qran = 6.33 g); it remained in use during 1251–52. From 1252 to 1254, the standard was at the reduced rate of 300 nokhud (qran = 5.76 g), while a further reduced rate of 280 nokhud (qran = 5.37 g) was used during the period 1254–64/1838–48. Under Naser al Din Shah (r. 1848–96), the standard of 1 tuman remained at 280 nokhud (1 qran = 5.37 g), between 1264–74/1848–58. The standard was then reduced to 260 nokhud (1 qran = 4.99 g). This standard applied between 1271/1857–58 and 1296/1878–79. The transition from the 5.37 g to the lighter 4.99 g standard took place gradually at the various mints between 1271 and 1274, reflecting the local nature of the 'currency' used in different cities. By 1275/1858–59, the lighter standard had been universally adopted, with the exception of Herat, which was under Iranian occupation for a number of years. Of course, coins of both standards continued to circulate together at different values.[46]

Although after 1826 the qran was the standard silver coin, the term riyal continued to be used. For instance, in Isfahan the qran was called a riyal and a riyal was called *riyal-e kohneh*, or old riyal.[47] In Tehran, around 1900, Mostowfi's servant called 1 qran and 5 shahi always yak riyal-e kohneh, 1 old riyal.[48]

45 Album, *Checklist*, 293; Dupré, *Voyage*, 2:476; Rabino, *Coins, Medals, and Seals*, 16. In 1809, the silver riyal weighed 2 mesqal and 6 nokhud (10.37 g) pure silver without alloy. The fractions of the riyal (half, quarter and one-eighth riyal) circulated in small numbers only. In 1826, Col. Stannus, the Bushire Resident wrote to John Wedderburn (Bombay 27 Apr. 1826), that 'instead of the real or new Persian Rupee, which is abolished, a new coin Hazar Dinar takes its place. The purity of silver is said to remain unchanged.' IOR, R/15/1/43, unfol.

46 Album, *Checklist*, 295. In 1857, according to the British, 10 hazar dinar (one tuman) contained 1011.55 grains of pure silver, while one tuman contained 71 grains of pure gold, or a gold to silver ratio of 1:14.247. B. Noton to J. Wedderburn (Bombay, 27 May 1857), IOR, R/15/1/43, unfol. In Rajab 1303, Ketabchi proposed to devaluate the qran. E`temad al-Saltaneh, *Ruznameh*, 448.

47 Stolze and Andreas, 'Handelsverhältnisse Persiens', 36.

48 Mostowfi, *Sharh-e zendegani-ye man*, 1:396.

Tables 7.3: Names for silver coins in the mid-nineteenth century

Dinar value	Shahi value	Name	Other name	Observations	Other name
1,250	25	riyal (-e kohneh)	rupee	–	–
1,000	20	qran	yak hazar	–	–
1,000	10	riyal (Nishapur)	(Astarabad)	hesab-e qadim	–
500	10	dah shahi	panabad	–	nimqran
250	5	panj shahi	–	–	–
125	1	shahi-ye safid	aq-shahi	–	–

Source: Mostowfi, *Sharh-e Zendegani-ye man*, 1:398; Rabino, *Coins, Medals, and Seals*, 16; Stolze and Andreas, 'Die Handelsverhältnisse', 36.

In documents of a legal nature as well in wage lists, the term riyal was used well into the twentieth century.[49]

While old names remained in use, other silver coins were issued. The ten-shahi piece, which fell into disuse with the introduction of the riyal, was first re-issued under Fath `Ali Shah by Ebrahim Khan Javanshir, governor of Panahabad in Shusheh (Nagorno-Karabakh). As a result, the coin was called *panahabad*, later shortened to panabad.[50] Other silver coins were the half, fourth and one-seventh of a yak hazar; they were called *dah shahi*, panj shahi and *shahi-ye safid*.[51] In addition, there were ceremonial silver coins. On the occasion of Nowruz, the Qajars issued silver shahis

49 Beygdeli, *Tarikh-e Beygdeli*, 35 (166 riyal-e Fath `Ali Shah = 20 tuman-e tabrizi of 32 nokhud), 43 (riyal-e naseriyeh-e methqaliyeh of 24 nokhud = 1,000 dinar-e ravaj-e jadid al-zarb), 45 (riyal-e Naser al-Din Shah of 25 nokhud), 61 (riyal-e saheb qrani), 83, 87 (riyal of 26 nokhud = 1,000 dinar-e ravaj-e Irani), 103, 146, 162, 188, 195, 201, 651 (riyal-e Mozaffariyeh); Rashvand, *Mojmal-e Rashvand*, 95 (Rudbar and Alamut); Basir al-Molk, *Ruznameh-ye khaterat*, 131; `Eyn al-Saltaneh, *Ruznameh-ye khaterat*, 1:575.

50 Rabino, *Coins, Medals, and Seals*, 16. It was also coined in Ganjeh and Sheki, see Album, *Checklist*, nrs. 2900 and 2901. A panahabadi of 13 nokhud of 500 *dinar-e ravaj* mentioned in 1277/1860–61 and 1292/1875. Beygdeli, *Tarikh-e Beygdeli*, 38–39, 79.

51 Mostowfi, *Sharh-e zendegani-ye man*, 1:396; E`temad al-Saltaneh, *Montazam-e Naseri*, 175, 555, 587, 721, 789, 849, 917, 985, 1079, 1213.

called shahi-ye safid or *aq shahi*.[52] They were usually struck on one side only. These coins were also kept as *tah-kiseh* [bottom of the purse] for luck. The sarrafs collected these shahis after the Nowruz ceremony, keeping them for the next Nowruz.[53]

The qran was the basis for the currency system under the new national mint which started operation in 1877. As noted, its silver qrans were supposed to be 4.99 g, but few were minted at that weight before the standard was changed in 1879 to 4.6 g. The new, lighter qrans were variously known as *pul-e tazeh* (new coin), *tazeh-qran*, *pul-e jadid al-darb* (newly minted coins), *pul-e charkhi* (milled coin) and *pul-e Amin al-Soltani*, after the minister who introduced the new currency.[54] The pieces struck were:

0.25 qran or panj shahi or in Turkish besh shahi, or rob` qran or rob`i
0.5 qran, dah-shahi or pansad dinar or panabat

1 qran (yak qran, yak hazar, yak hazar dinar)
2 qrans (du qran)
5 qran (panj qran).

As noted earlier, the mint master had a strong incentive to issue copper coins rather than silver one. On the other hand, the IBP made a considerable profit from importing silver to be minted into coins. The first such contract between the IBP and the government came in July 1896 and was followed by several more contracts between 1897 and 1899.[55] These contracts specified that the Mint was to coin the IBP silver 'as soon as delivered to the exclusion of all other coinage operations', which effectively gave IBP a monopoly of

52 Polak, *Persien*, 2:161. The Nowruz coins were kept in 'little silken bags containing silver coins about the thickness and size of ordinary wafers'. Mounsey, *Journey through the Caucasus*, 162, 166 (trays of coins); `Eyn al-Saltaneh, *Ruznameh-ye khaterat*, 1:350, 520, 579, 589, 913 (with facsimile of invitation note for the Nowruz audience). At Nowruz, 'Luck-money, coined with the name of the shah, is distributed to all. Some of these gold and silver tokens are sent to the mujtehid and other ecclesiastics. They presage a fortunate year for the recipient, because the king thus indicates a royal favor.' The soldiers who passed in review each received 'a token of fourteen shahis in value'. In Wilson, *Persian Life and Customs*, 246.

53 In 1819, this shahi was struck in gold and silver, Dupré, *Voyage*, 2:475, n.

54 Rabino, *Coins, Medals, and Seals*, 16; also the source for the types of coins struck. According to E`temad al-Saltaneh, *Ruznameh*, 93 'the shah gave three persons a tip of two hazar, so that each person received three `abbasi, in the past the tip was never less than one tuman, but now it has come down to three `abbasi'.

55 Jones, *Banking and Empire*, 1:80–81.

56 'Contract for the supply of five millions of miscals of silver to the Imperial Bank of Persia' 5

access to the mint, though the Bank vigorously denied that this was the case.[56] The contract with the mint was very favorable to IBP; that is, the value of the qrans it received was higher than the value of the silver it provided.[57] Although in 1900 IBP lost its de facto monopoly to the mint in response to Russian pressure, silver imports provided the Bank with 35 per cent of its published profits for 1900–02. In addition, for many years after 1900, the Bank imported silver on behalf of the government at favorable rates.[58]

It would seem fair to read this record as saying that, after the currency crisis of 1894–95 caused by the mint master's over-issuance of copper coins and under-issuance of silver coins, the problem of how to guarantee sufficient silver coins was solved by letting the IBP assure the supply. This arrangement was to the mint master's loss and the IBP's profit. Not surprisingly, the mint master complained about the IBP's activities while the IBP regarded the mint as badly run: they were in effect competitors.

Gold Coins

Gold was not particularly important in Iran at this time. Gold coins rarely circulated among the people. De Bode recounted in 1845, 'When the time came to renumerate my Illiyat guides, for their troubles and exertion, with gold coin, I found they were ignorant of the value of that metal, and preferred a few silver sahib-corans, which I had about me, though greatly inferior in amount.'[59] There may have been some exceptions, in particular

July 1896. BBME 594.2. However, an addition to Article III stated, 'In case the Mint is unable to strike Tomans 10.000 per day, it will strike in 24 hours as much as it can and will not be bound to 10.000' –a figure not cited elsewhere in the contract. To a question by the Russian Legation, 'Was it true that Bank had obtained a monopoly of Mint', Rabino responded, 'Nothing of the sort but Bank has contracted to import Tms500000– when no one else would bring in anything and of course asked that this should be coined before outsiders' parcels on the principle First come, First served' (Chief Manager's Notes for 28, 29, 30 Aug. 1896, BBME 594.2).

57 For instance, the 10 April 1902 contract specified that for each 100 mesqals of pure silver (which the contract specified was equal to 14.8 troy ounces, which is 460.3 g), IBP would get 105 qrans (BBME 671). This contract specified that the Mint had to produce from the Bank's silver 4,000 tumans of coins per day (Fridays and holidays excepted) if the Mint's production remained at its then current level of 14,000 tumans daily, or 5,000 tumans if the Mint's production rose to 16,000 tumans daily.

58 The Finance Committee report for the year to 20 March 1910 states, 'The arrangement for importing silver to be coined on Government Account is of the greatest importance, enabling the Chief Manager to gauge the position of Foreign Exchange and every nerve should be strained to make it work smoothly' (BBME 290.3).

59 De Bode, *Travels in Luristan*, 2:233.

in the case of financing foreign trade; Fraser describes the sale of horses for gold coins in the 1830s.[60] In 1836, Burgess sent payment to Istanbul in ducats and gold tumans.[61] By one account, in 1847 the Turkmen were paying as taxes one Torkoman tela or three sahebqrans per family – though it seems doubtful that the payments were actually in the gold coin in which they were denominated.[62] The British legation in 1862 reported that 'gold coins are hardly at present in circulation, the Persian Currency consisting almost entirely of Silver Kerans and Half Keran pieces, and of copper pieces called "Pool."'[63] In 1880, O'Donovan reported that in Sabzavar, people 'did not understand gold'.[64] Wills claimed that in 1883 gold coins had not seen for the previous fifteen years; the gold coin 'is merely nominal, or old coins hoarded for the sake of its purity'.[65] Soon thereafter, Stolze and Andreas stated that the gold coin did not circulate anymore, adding that because of their high fineness they were exported.[66]

In reality, the Qajar Shahs coined gold, but, as before, the coins served primarily for special uses – for instance, as presents in particular for Nowruz. Polak remarked that in the 1860s small gold coins did not circulate much, for they were usually used for handouts and presentations.[67] These coins were also kept as tah-kiseh (bottom of the purse) for luck. As they did with shahis, the sarrafs collected these coins after the Nowruz ceremony, keeping them for the next Nowruz.[68] The price varied considerably, rising toward Nowruz, when many ashrafis were given as presents to servants and others.[69]

Each Qajar shah struck gold coins, often minted from foreign coin such as Russian imperials and Turkish pounds. Until 1877, the coins were struck in various mints. According to Ouseley the gold tumans of Isfahan and Tabriz

60 Fraser, *Winter's Journey*, 2:326.

61 Schwartz, *Letters from Persia*, 35.

62 Amanat, *Cities and Trade*, 61; O'Donovan, *Merv Oasis*, 1:249. (The coins struck by the national mint after 1877 were accepted by the Turkoman; 'but there are also places up the country where the Turcomans will have nothing to do with them, and will accept only the old fashioned kran and toman. Even the toman is not always willingly received, for as a rule the Turcomans have little or no gold, and do not understand it.')

63 *NA*, FO/60 341, unfoliated.

64 O'Donovan, *Merv Oasis*, 1:426.

65 Wills, *In the Land of the Lion and the Sun*, 63.

66 Stolze and Andreas, 'Handelsverhältnisse Persiens', 34.

67 Polak, *Persien*, 2:161. The governor of Mashhad sent Wolff 'sweetmeats, and gold and silver *pence*, -which are considered *blessed* pence,- to the value of five tomauns sterling, according to the Persian custom'. See Wolff, *Narrative of a Mission*, 155.

68 Dupré, *Voyage*, 2:475, n.

69 DCR 1671, 1896, 7–8.

were commoner than those of Tehran.[70] The formal term for the gold coins was tuman, but they were often referred to as ashrafi or gold shahi. Each Qajar shah issued one tuman coins and some large coin or coins; most also half-tuman and quarter-tuman coins.[71] The *shahi-ye ashrafi* or *shahi-ye tela* were gold shahis issued by the Qajars for distribution during Nowruz. They were struck usually on one side only.[72] Ouseley wrote that the coin was very thin, and often exceeded in diameter the quarter riyal or gold half tuman.[73] Besides these, two gold coins were used, 'one a little more, and the other a little less than a tuman, which last is, in fact, only a nominal value'.[74] Gold coins also served as presents to the shah, to brides and others. Whenever the shah honored one of his courtiers with a visit, those attending this event had to present the ruler with gold coins.[75] When in 1812 a Qajar princess married, 'the room in which the bridegroom received his bride, was ornamented by large gold coins (five tomaun pieces), 500 of which were arranged on the shelves'.[76]

The weight of the tuman declined steadily until the national mint system was fully functioning in 1879, when it stabilized at 2.92 g (see Table 5.7).

Limited Use of Money in Trade

There is considerable evidence that the Qajar period resembled earlier times in that many transactions took place without involving money. Lorini wrote, 'a large part of the population lives almost completely in a barter system, which reduces to a minimum the demand not only for the principal money [i.e., silver] but also for the auxiliary money [i.e., copper]'.[77]

70 Ouseley, *Travels in Various Countries*, 2:490; Bérézine, *Voyage*, 2:126. In 1809, a gold tuman weighed 28 nokhud or 1 1/6 mesqal (5.37 g) of pure gold. It had been reduced in weight from 32 and then to 30 nokhud. The gold shahi weighed 7 nokhud and had a value of 2 riyals. Dupré*Voyage*, 2:475. One ashrafi = 1 tuman = 1 mesqal in 1202. One *ashrafi-ye Fath `Ali Shahi* of 32 nokhud in 1219. Beygdeli, *Tarikh-e Beygdeli*, 27, 45.

71 Rabino, *Coins, Medals, and Seals*, Table 1 (page not numbered). Album, *Checklist*. In 1857, B. Noton wrote to J. Wedderburn (Bombay, 27 July 1857) that the 'gold toman is 24 grains and the new one 22½ or a depreciation of 6¼ %. Assuming the gold coin at 22½ qran yields a ratio of 1:15 with silver. The real was 2 mithqal, but the hazaar dinar is ½ mithqal; at the established exchange of 8 reaal and 10 of hazaar to 1 toman gives a depreciation of silver currency as in gold.' IOR, R/15/1/43, unfol.

72 Dupré, *Voyage*, 2:476–77.

73 Ouseley, *Travels in Various Countries*, 2:493.

74 Southgate, *Narrative of a Tour*, 2:349.

75 `Eyn al-Saltaneh, *Ruznameh-ye khaterat*, 1:671.

76 Morier, *Second Journey through Persia*, 392.

77 Lorini, *La Persia economica*, 357.

Table 7.4: Gold coins struck by Qajar shahs (1779–1879)

Reign	Weight in grams	Ghost value	Period
Agha Mohammad	8.2*	1 tuman	1193–1212/1779–97
Fath `Ali Shah	6.14	1 tuman	1212–21/1797–1806
	5.76	1 tuman	1222–24/1798–1809
	5.37	1 tuman	1224–30/1809–15
	4.61	1 tuman	1230–40/1815–24
Mohammad Shah	4.61	1 tuman	1240–50/1825–34
	3.85	1 tuman	1250–54/1834–38
	3.45	1 tuman	1255–65/1839–48
Naser al-Din Shah	3.45	1 tuman	1254–79/1848–79

Source: Album, *Checklist*, 291–96.

* Agha Mohammad did not strike a one tuman gold coin, but multiples and fractions thereof.

This was particularly true for the substantial nomadic population; for example, among the Turkmen Tekke copper coins did not circulate at all; they used barter for those transactions whose value did not exceed one qran.[78] In isolated Lurestan, barter was still common in the early twentieth century.[79] But money was not always used even in sophisticated Tehran circles in the 1880s: physicians in Tehran were paid by the female members of the Shah's harem in 'small articles of embroidery, and cakes of sugar-candy'.[80] Even where money was used an element of barter might be involved. In Bint (Iranian Baluchistan), Floyer in 1876 noted that 'Money-dollars, rupees, krans, half-krans, and floss silk', were used as currencies.[81]

While payments to the state were supposed to take place in official silver coin, these often actually took place in-kind. The tas`ir system of fixed annual conversion rates between produce and its value in coin, facilitated

78 De Bloqueville, quoted by Lorini, *La Persia economica*, 357; see also Curzon, *Persia*, 2:299; de Morgan, *Feudalism in Persia*, 598 (the Lurs 'are very poor in actual money, so that the possession of a few krans (about 10 cents) is their constant thought'.)

79 Grothe, *Wanderungen in Persien*, 57. In parts of Sistan people 'would understand neither the nature of money nor the value or appearance of a *kran*'. Goldsmidt, *Eastern Persia*, 1:262.

80 O'Donovan, *Merv Oasis*, 1:19.

81 Floyer, 'Journal of a Route from Jask', 193.

such payment in-kind. The tas`ir rates were adjusted at least once a year to reflect the local supply–demand situation of a particular commodity that served as a means of exchange. This also offered an opportunity to those in charge of fixing these rates to enrich themselves at the expense of the peasants.[82] Also, the state paid many of its officials in-kind through assignments on the produce of land, though their salaries were expressed in monetary units of account.

There were good reasons to avoid using coins. For one thing, coins were often under-weight, and thus had to be counted, which was time-consuming and irksome. To accommodate this activity there were 1,189 counting houses in Tabriz alone in the mid-nineteenth century.[83] Paying out the salary of the Austrian mint master, Pechan, and his assistant, disbursed in qrans and half-qrans, would take an entire day.[84] This counting business therefore required a method to avoid mistakes and the chance of being shortchanged. Wilson describes the process:

> The Persian sits on the floor, counts in handfuls of three or five coins each, setting aside one coin as a counter when the fiftieth hand is reached, and finally reckoning up the counters. On reaching thirteen, the unlucky number, he is accustomed to say, 'It is not thirteen,' and complacently throws down the next hand. He keeps repeating the previous number, lest it slip from his memory.[85]

Arnold described the hard work of counting money:

> It is a hard morning's work to count one hundred pounds sterling in the silver currency of Persia. The labor is generally shunned by employers, and trusty servants become skilled in the business. The method is always the same. The money-changer and the receiver sit upon the floor; the changer throws down from his hand the krans by fives, and both payer and payee keep in mind the number of tomans by repeating it all the while in an audible mutter. Thus, while the first ten krans are being poured out, they say 'yek [one] yek - yek - yek;' then, while the 'ties' are mounting to twenty, they say 'du[two] du-du-du', and so on. It is very rarely that such as servant as Houssein makes an error in counting.[86]

82 Floor, *Fiscal History*, 189, 265, 342.
83 Tabriz 1859, *AP* 30, LXIII, DCR 2896, 60–61.
84 Slaby, *Bindenschild und Sonnenlöwe*, 131–32.
85 Wilson, *Persian Life and Customs*, 282.
86 Arnold, *Through Persia by Caravan*, 135.

In addition, as always, coins were scarce and often not available at all. Olivier, visiting Iran in 1798, called `abbasis and other Persian coins, whether in gold or silver, extremely scarce, adding that, in fact, 'there was no money but old Turkish piasters and old sequins of Constantinople'.[87] In 1834, Conolly was unable to obtain cash in Mashhad even when the governor wrote a note to the high priest to ask for some. This prompted him to comment that, 'In this country, cash is like Oonka, a bird which flies to fast that it is not seen.'[88] Two years later, Fraser had this to say about the desperate shortage of cash in Mashhad: 'I have a credit on a merchant here, who admits the validity of the bill, but adds, that though I am welcome to a thousand tomauns in goods, he cannot furnish me with *ten* in coin; and what are goods to me?'[89] Nor did the problem get better over time. In 1862, 'the state of the finances of the province [of Khorasan] may be inferred from the fact that Dolmage having presented an order on the local government for fifty tomans, the utmost that could be scraped together to meet the demand was twelve tomans, and while that sum was being collected, several other claims were absolutely repudiated on the ground of "no effects"'.[90] In the countryside such shortages persisted into the twentieth century. Floyer said of Baluchistan that, 'there is no coin in the country less than half a kran'.[91] Tate, discussing the same region, wrote, 'Previous to the Mission of 1903 a large proportion of the people had never even handled silver money. In 1899 I was compelled to send to the village of Chilling in order to change a few rupees of Indian currency into Persian coin.'[92] Likewise, the Yakut Turkmen had no change. 'The smallest coin in the country was the kran. They had no copper, and refused to take them even as a present. The consequence was that a kran was the minimum charge for even the smallest things.'[93]

Even when coins were available, paying with them was a time consuming affair. O'Donovan reported that in 1881 when in Sabzavar 'All the money I had was perfectly good in the capital and the surrounding districts, but, for some not very easily understood reason, the people in this place objected to a very large proportion. The lengths to which people here will go for the sake of a few pence must be seen to be appreciated fully.'[94] Among the Turkmen, for

87 Olivier, *Voyage*, 5:321–22.

88 Conolly, *Journey to the North of India*, 1:363; his travails are described on 364–65.

89 Fraser, *Winter's Journey*, 2:241, 250.

90 Eastwick *Journal*, 2:274–75. This not only happened to foreign officials, but also to Iranian ones. See E`tesam al-Molk, *Safarnameh*, 212.

91 Floyer, *Unexplored Baluchistan*, 54.

92 Tate, *Frontiers of Baluchistain*, 227.

93 Yate, *Khurasan and Seistan*, 243.

94 O'Donovan, *Merv Oasis*, 2:426.

example, a qran struck in Hamadan would only be accepted at a discount of about 10 per cent, with people giving contradictory reasons for their refusal to accept the coin at face value. Even less estimated was the so-called Queen Mother qran, which bore the impress of a lion an sun, a crown, and a wreath of laurel leaves. As result of such perceptions about certain coins as well as the need to check coins for false and clipped ones, 'if you have to pay away in *krans* a sum equal to five pounds sterling, the best part of a day is wasted in examining the coins one by one, and in hearing the arguments *pro* and *con* as to the relative merit of each'.[95]

And it made good economic sense for people to hold on to what coins they could collect, rather than using them for trade purposes. Hoarding was – and is – easily misunderstood. Too often, rather than recognizing its economic rationality, Western observers attributed hoarding to backward attitudes. A good example is this observation by Stirling: 'The nature of the government, the prevalent insecurity, the consternation of society and certain religious tenets, seem all to concur in favoring avarice, repressing the spirit of spending and indulging the rise of hoarding and committing their wealth to the bowels of the earth.'[96] In a modern economy with a developed banking system, cash can be put into bank accounts with ready assurance that the funds will be available in the event of urgent need or during times of year when income is low, such as before the harvest in the case of farmers, with the bank offering safety from robbery and interest income as well. None of this was the case in Qajar and Safavid) Iran. Hoarding cash was the only way of securing funds to meet needs during slow periods or in the face of a crisis; hence its practice by the rich as well as the poor. According to Binning, 'the practice of burying money is as common here as in India'.[97] In 1828, Stirling noted that in Mashhad the system of hoarding was 'carried on to a prodigious extent and not least among the *moolahs*'.[98] Finally, there were the needs of the gold and silversmiths, who absorbed precious metals for the production of gold and silver ware, gold and silver wire for the making of costly textiles, as well as for jewelry.[99] For most farmers, precious metal and copper was the only liquid asset, and they held on to cash to meet needs in the low season: 'From June to September, the opium crop absorbs all the floating capital of the provinces, of which Isfahan and Yezd are the centres; the money goes into the villages, to the great inconvenience of

95 Ibid., 1:249–50; see also Baker, *Clouds in the East*, 188.
96 Stirling, *Journals*, 183, see also p. 169.
97 Binning, *Journal of Two Years' Travel*, 2:152.
98 Stirling, *Journals*, 169; see also Dickson, *East Persia*, 152.
99 Mostowfi, *Sharh-e zendegani-ye man*, 1:396.

those towns.'[100] And many farmers held their 'liquid' savings in the form of copper vessels and other copper household utensils. This is clear from Tahvildar's reports in 1871 that 'some years ago when [the price of] cotton rose, the peasants became active again and bought back the copper which they had sold before'.[101] Even Fath `Ali Shah was aware of this structural phenomenon. During a discussion about lending money, Grand vizier Mirza Shafi` told the shah, 'You know I have no money, but I am always ready to sell my pots and pans for Your Majesty's service.'[102]

Supply of Bullion and Specie

Qajar Iran had no gold or silver mines, and limited copper production. Nevertheless, it had a negative trade balance with India, which difference had to paid for in specie. Also, Iran needed bullion to provide for coins for domestic trade, hoarding and luxury goods. Where did this bullion come from?

Local Production of Bullion

No gold mines existed in Iran. Of a district known as Zarshuran, 'gold washers', on the slopes of the Kafitan Mountains, it was said that in the dim past gold had been washed in the river.[103] Ferrier refers to Jews in Hamadan who worked in the stream around town, where they 'collected gold in skins by washing, but in a clumsy manner. They earn about a shilling a day, but with a better system could no doubt earn more'.[104] The same author claims to have seen a white gold mine near Damghan. He also insists that there were gold mines near Soltanabad and Hamadan, but he is the only one to do so. Ferrier refers to the Kuh-e- telleh-noqreh (the gold and silver mountains) on the side of the Derrood, which were not worked because they were not profitable to do.[105] There was periodical excitement about gold having been found, followed by careful exploration.[106] Stewart recounts how Houtum-Schindler went out to check a story about gold at Kavend, near Zanjan, accompanied by four professional gold washers from Hamadan. However, no gold was found. Naser

100 Rabino, 'Banking in Persia', 35.
101 Tahvildar, *Joghrafiya-ye Esfahan*, 107; see also Höltzer, *Persien vor 113 Jahren*, 57.
102 Jones, *Account of the Transaction*, 288.
103 Blau, *Commerzielle Zustände Persiens*, 92.
104 Ferrier, *Caravan Journeys*, 38.
105 Ibid., 117.
106 Bassett, *Persia, the Land of the Imams*, 255.

al-Din Shah, angry, had the man who had found the alleged gold nugget that started the rumor, flogged and his house pulled down.[107] On the road to Rasht, Stewart met a Persian engineer sent by the shah to verify the presence of gold in abandoned mines near Semnan. He had not found anything either. Stewart only knew of three places where gold was formerly worked: near Zanjan, near Mashhad, and at a place called Khuzir.[108] Naser al-Din Shah in 1873 asked the Austrians to assist him in finding gold and diamonds. The Austrians sent the geologist Tietze as someone who would be able to assess Iran's resources, but he did not find gold or diamonds. Tietze was followed by Huebel, who cheated by stating that he had found oriferous ores, whereas he only found abandoned and well known mines near Sabzavar.[109] Even in 1899, Amin al-Soltan told the ulama not to worry because the gold mine at Kaval yielded 1 mesqal of gold from 500 mesqal of ore.[110]

Some of the silver in circulation under Fath `Ali Shah is said to have originated from a silver mine near Bokhara in Central Asia. Yet there were also silver mines in Iran proper, in Azerbaijan, and another one near Shiraz, which was abandoned for lack of profitability.[111] Important silver mines were located in the Sahand Mountains, south of Tabriz. These were owned by Malek Qasem Mirza, a princely entrepreneur, who tried without much success or profit to mine these sites. He had fourteen kilns in production. As a yardstick the normal production of one kharvar of ore should yield 100 tumans of pure silver, or a silver ratio of 1.82 per cent, which is not very much. It was also reported that some silver was produced at Rayy, near Tehran.[112] Jamalzadeh claimed a silver mine near Saruq with 0.68 per cent silver ore.[113]

Whereas gold and silver were non-existent or very elusive metals, Iran abounded in copper ore. According to Polak, almost every district had a copper mine. The most productive mine was at Qaradagh near Tabriz, but there were 20 mines on the northern slopes of the Elburz near Tehran, and many more in the vicinity of Qazvin.[114] Abdullaev cites a report – undated but evidently from shortly before the First World War – by A. Kassis, the Loan and Discount Bank representative in Sabzavar about the copper mines of Khorasan, which had been leased to Mohammad Ismail Arbab in the late

107 Stewart, *Through Persia in Disguise*, 210–13.
108 Ibid., 294–95.
109 Slaby, *Bindenschild und Sonnenlöwe*, 128–29.
110 Nezam Mafi, *Khaterat va asnad*, 1:246.
111 Morier, *Journey through Persia*, 238.
112 Blau, *Commerzielle Zustände Persiens*, 92.
113 Jamalzadeh, *Ganj- e Shayegan*, 76.
114 Polak, *Persien*, 2:174.
115 Abdullaev, *Promyshlennost*, as translated and printed in Issawi, *Economic History*, 299.

nineteenth century.[115] The main mine, near the Dagan Siyah mountain, had 250–300 workers mining ore that was between 20 and 30 per cent copper until 1910 (after a flood in 1912–13, production was limited to the upper parts where the ore contained 5–7 per cent copper). Altogether, Arbab's mines – including one at Kuh Goma'i which employed 50 in 1900, as well as a mine at Chund employing ten, and one at Rivand – were producing 54 mans of pure copper a day. Blau wrote, 'copper is to be found in large quantity', referring to mines in several places besides Khorasan, e.g., Gilan, Qaradagh (near Seijan), in Kafiladagh (near Terabad) and near Jenichah.[116] Melgunov wrote that there was a copper mine near Astarabad (at 28 *farsakh*).[117] Sheil wrote that copper in Kashan came from the nearby the Sivas mountains: 'It is only lately that they ceased to import copper from Turkey, when they started to mine Qaradagh mines.[118] Other reports speak of copper production in Kerman, with ore containing 7–8 per cent copper.[119]

However, it is not clear whether the indigenous copper was much used in coinage. Copper was certainly imported, as discussed below. And several authors suggest that imported copper was of higher quality and so better suited for use in final products, presumably including coins. Höltzer, for instance, claims that there were no copper presses at all in Isfahan in the 1870s and through the 1890s.[120]

Importing Bullion and Specie

All three monetary metals were imported regularly throughout the Qajar period. Not only was monetary metal needed to replace that worn out and, occasionally, to meet demand in an expanding economy, but in addition Iran needed gold and silver to settle its large balance of trade deficits with India. Until the late Qajar period, all such deficits triggered an immediate counterbalancing flow of monetary metal in the opposite direction.[121] Like the Safavids before them, the Qajars were unhappy about this outflow of specie and sought to prevent it by occasionally issuing bans. Yet this export was a long-standing and structural part of Iran's trade with India.[122] 'About 1790, it was reported that nine-tenths of the merchandise imported into Iran from

116 Blau, *Commerzielle Zustände Persiens*, 93.
117 Melgunov, *Das Suedliche Ufer des Kaspischen Meeres*,
118 Sheil, *Glimpses of Life*, 96.
119 Schlimmer, *Terminologie Médico-Pharmaceutique*, 173–74.
120 Höltzer, *Persien vor 113 Jahren*, 57.
121 Fraser, *Travels and Adventures*, 372.
122 On the specie export ban of 1866, see DCR 3953 VIII, 1867–68, 499 (1867); on that of 1873, *AP* 27, LXV, Tabriz, 1873, 968.

India were paid for in specie.'[123] This situation remained unchanged after the Qajars had established their hold over the entire territory of Iran. Malcolm, in 1800, estimated the portion paid for by Iran in specie or bullion to be at only eight lakhs of rupees, or four-tenths of the whole. He placed the annual export of specie and bullion from Basra at ten lakhs of rupees out of a total exports worth 30 lakhs.[124]

It would appear that the Safavid pattern – a trade surplus with the north and west, a trade deficit with the east and south – continued well into the nineteenth century. A good summary of how Iran faced this situation is provided by Fraser, describing the situation in 1822:

> French and German crowns and Spanish dollars are brought in large quantities from Baghdad, but seldom pass into circulation, being for the most part transmitted by sea to India. Golden ducats and silver manêts (roubles), which form the medium of traffic on the frontiers with Turkey and Georgia, are poured in from those quarters ... A large current of the precious metals flows annually into Persia, and though the greater proportion passes on to the eastward, there still remains a sufficient quantity to form the currency of the country, the treasury of the king, and the hoards of a few rich individuals in the kingdom ...
>
> [Iran's] silk, her cotton, her grain, and her manufactures, form an aggregate of great value, for the greater part of which she is paid in specie by the consumers at Bagdad, Aleppo, Constantinople, and the other cities of the Turkish empire, as well by the Russians from Astracan and Teflis. It must also be remembered, that a large proportion of the valuable Indian produce which enters Persia, is re-exported to the countries west of it, and thus returns with interest the specie of which it drained the kingdom for a time.[125]

Brandt in 1834 makes the same point, offering a more quantitative analysis:

> It is a well authenticated fact that large sums of bullion are annually exported to India by Bushire, as well as to Constantinople from Tabreez, and it is equally certain that this constant drain of specie has not hitherto occasioned any perceptible scarcity in the current coin of the Kingdom ... Persia has neither gold nor silver Mines, it is therefore evident that she

123 Lorimer, *Gazetteer*, 163.
124 Ibid.
125 Fraser, *Travels and Adventures*, 372.

> must give a large quantity of her production to those who pay for them in bullion.[126]

Brandt estimated that 'the exports of specie in 1830 must have been about £500,000 Sterling and since that period they have probably increased'. That is no small sum, since his summary of exports of all types led him to conclude 'Persia has the means of purchasing from Foreign Nations to the extent of two million Sterling' a year.[127] Brandt's account suggests how Iran managed to export such a significant amount of precious metal without losing its currency base: the country ran a large trade surplus with some countries, most notably Russia, which shipped substantial amounts of precious metal to Iran. His detailed list of which commodities were exported and to where indicates that Russia was a major market for exports, including re-exports from India. As he observed, Russia sent gold in return:

> The export of Russian Ducats being so considerable the import annually must be so too, for it is a common remark that nearly all the Ducats to be seen are new in appearance and bear a recent date and consequently cannot have long been in the country.

A similar account was offered for 1846 by Burgess:

> Perhaps about one third of the import of European manufactures may be paid by raw silk and other Persian produce and the rest in Russian gold and silver ... The returns from this country are made in a great measure in Russian gold and silver coin which comes into pay for Persian silk (raw), dried fruits, and other merchandise.[128]

In 1857, Blau estimated that Iran exported 21 million thalers a year and imported 20.95 million. It ran a balance of trade surplus with Russia of 5.3 million thalers and 2 million thalers with 'Tartary, Bukhara, and other lands of Inner Asia', while running a trade deficit of 6.3 million thalers with 'Europe through Trebizond'.[129] However, Blau based his estimates on observations

126 Floor, *Textile Imports*, 152–53 (Brandt, fols. 211–12).

127 Ibid., 152–53 (Brandt, fol. 211v). The following paragraph draws on his account in Ibid., 152–55 (Brandt, fols. 211v-14), with the quote about Russian ducats on p. 153 (fol. 212).

128 Schwarz, *Letters from Persia*, 85. Stocqueler, *Fifteen Month's Pilgrimage*, 1:155, also reports that payments in foreign trade were 'in most cases in specie'.

129 Blau, *Commerzielle Zustände Persiens*, 164–68 (also excerpted in Issawi, *Economic History*, 132–34). He calculated a 50,000 thaler annual balance of trade surplus, factoring in a 2.2 million thaler deficit with 'the East Indies' and a 1.5 million surplus with 'Turkey in Asia'.

Table 7.5: Russo–Persian trade
(annual average, millions of 1896 gold rubles)

Year	Trade (exports plus imports)	Persia's surplus
1830–34	6.4	1.2
1835–39	4.9	2.3
1840–44	5.9	3.5
1845–49	6.2	4.4
1850–54	6.3	3.8
1855–59	7.2	4.3
1860–64	7.6	4.4
1865–69	7.6	4.0
1870–74	7.8	3.5
1875–79	9.0	3.6
1880–84	11.3	2.9
1885–89	15.9	2.9
1890–94	22.4	3.7
1895–99	35.7	3.7
1900–04	48.5	-0.6
1905–09	55.4	-2.6
1910–14	87.7	-10.7

Source: Enter, *Russo-Persian Commercial Relations*, 5–6.

made during one trip plus heroic assumptions which he presents with little if any supporting evidence. There are also some serious peculiarities in his data, such as the small role assigned to trade via the Gulf.

The truth is that neither the Russian nor the Iranian government produced reliable data in the nineteenth century. The two countries' data on trade, to the extent that they exist, also differ substantially, with Russia reporting sharply lower Iranian exports for Russian markets. However, even the Russian data show a substantial trade surplus in Iran's favor during the mid-nineteenth century.[130] These data seem to confirm the many travelers' reports that substantial amounts of Russian bullion were being shipped into Iran.

One point on which the various sources agree is that Iran, as in previous centuries, was running a substantial trade surplus with some regions and a substantial trade deficit with others, at a time when the only way such imbalances were settled were by shipments of precious metal and coin.

The amount of the trade imbalance appears to have varied considerably from year to year, depending on the ups and downs of cash crops. An important factor was the quality of the harvest. In 1867, Abbott reported from Tabriz that the scarcity of money there was due to the failure of the silk harvest in Gilan during the past two seasons, which, he said, had 'in a great measure deprived the country of the supply of foreign coin usually brought for the purchase of that article'.[131] This naturally affected other cash crops as well, from wool to cotton to fruit, because agricultural products were Iran's main export commodities.

Global bullion flows provide a further reason to believe that early Qajar Iran experienced considerable bullion shipments. Barrett's estimates that in the late eighteenth century, Western Europe, benefiting from 600 tons a year of silver from the Americas, exported about 200 tons of silver per year to cover a chronic trade deficit, with 70 tons going to the Baltic and 50 tons to the Levant – such that the amounts re-exported from Russia and the Ottoman Empire to Qajar Iran would have been a small portion of the flow coming into those areas.[132]

From this scattered evidence, it seems reasonable to conclude that Iran saw substantial shipments of precious metal and coin moving into and out of the country during the early Qajar years. At the same time, additional research will have to establish how much bullion was flowing and in which direction. Certainly the continuing need for monetary metal – if for nothing else, to replace coins being worn out – would suggest that Iran may have run an overall balance of payments surplus which financed the inflows of monetary metal.

By the late Qajar period, Iran's foreign exchange transactions appear to have undergone considerable change. For one thing, the country seems

130 Entner, *Russo-Persian Commercial Relations*, 8–9. Entner summarizes at length the work of Russian scholars on the differences in Russian and Persian trade data.

131 *AP* 29 (1867–68), 499.

132 Barrett, 'World Bullion Flows', 224–54, especially 243 and 251.

to have had consistent trade deficits in the late nineteenth century. In 1885, Stolze and Andreas compiled data from various (mostly British) reports on exports and imports through Bushire, Lengeh, Tabriz, Rasht, Astarabad and Trabzon in the late 1870s and early 1880s.[133] While the data are not necessarily comprehensive, they strongly suggest a large trade deficit. Rabino cited the data for 1898–99 at the Persian Gulf ports as showing a trade deficit, with imports into Persia being £5,239,169 and exports from Persia being £4,403,275 (both figures excluding specie).[134] The data from the Customs Administration also show substantial trade deficits until after the First World War; indeed, the deficit for the period 1901–02 through 1919–20 was more than one-fourth of the total import bill (2.1 billion qrans compared to 8.0 billion qrans). Perhaps the recorded deficits reflect better reporting on trade through the southern ports than through the northern trade routes, which is where Iran traditionally enjoyed a trade surplus.

But the trade imbalances may also reflect a growth in invisible items, namely, services and debt. It would seem that Iran experienced a substantial inflow from these invisible items. Service income would have included remittances from the increasing number of Iranians working in pre-revolutionary Russia, royalty payments by the Anglo-Persian Oil Company, and expenditures by foreigners in Iran – a major item during the First World War – counterbalanced to some extent by service expenditures by pilgrims to Iraq, and debt service.[135] On the foreign debt account, inflows from new borrowings certainly exceeded repayment of debt. Further research would be needed to establish exactly the sum total of these items, but it is hard to escape the conclusion that they grew considerably in late Qajar times; and several of these items sky-rocketed.

In this changed atmosphere of trade imbalances and increasing invisibles and loans, the impact of specie flows on the economy surely declined, to the point where financing bullion flows no longer required a trade surplus. Other developments in the monetary sphere meanwhile broke the link between bullion flows and the money supply. An example is the growing role of paper currency, to be discussed below. As a result, bullion inflows became a shrinking part of total imports. In 1901/02–

133 Stolze and Andreas, 'Handelsverhältnisse Persiens', 69–85. On pp. 44–46, they describe and analyze various estimates of overall Persian trade, with particular criticism of Blau.

134 Rabino, 'Economist's Notes on Persia', 267, citing Russian government data, and 271.

135 Yaganegi, *Recent Financial and Monetary History*, 100–11; and Issawi, *Economic History*, 128–29.

19/20, bullion accounted for 5.4 per cent of imports, and the net trade (imports less exports) in bullion was more than 10 per cent of the trade deficit: 219 million qrans compared to 2,112 million qrans (although this calculation may overstate bullion imports, as it includes 22 million qrans in imports of bar copper and nickel, when it is not clear if such imports were used to produce coins). By contrast, in 1920/21–26/27, bullion accounted for only 2.2 per cent of imports. The value of bullion imports per annum fell from 22.8 million qrans in 1901/02–19/20 to 15.5 million qrans in 1920/21–26/27, even though in the latter period the economy grew much more rapidly, and so presumably the demand for money was on the increase. It seems reasonable to conclude that by the late Qajar period, Iran had shifted from a traditional balance of payments-cum monetary pattern to the modern system. That is, Iran had gone from settling its trade accounts with bullion – with a surplus in trade to the north more than offsetting a deficit to the south and east, thereby producing the net bullion imports needed to sustain and expand the money supply – to relying on bank transactions to settle trade imbalances, with bullion flows taking a back seat to paper currency as a means of expanding the money supply. In the realm of foreign trade and finance, therefore, unlike in most monetary realms, the Qajar period witnessed a transition from tradition to modernization.

Silver's Loss of Value

The second half of the nineteenth century was a time of great turmoil in world silver markets and of great change in the role of silver as a monetary metal. Iran did not adjust well to this period.

Adjusting Ratios among Coins

At first, Iran managed its silver and gold coins relatively well. Until 1857, Iranian silver was undervalued relative to gold; that is, at international market prices the gold content of an ashrafi was worth less than the silver content of 10 qrans (theoretically equal to one ashrafi). This led to export of Iranian silver coins until there were too few silver coins and too many gold coins relative to domestic demand – although the process proceeded slowly because the ratio between the coins was not rigidly enforced (in particular, the coins had no face value) and so merchants could exchange qrans and ashrafis by weight, not necessarily at 10 qran per tuman.

Table 7.6: Customs administration data on trade of Persia (in million qrans)

Year	Import excess		Total trade		Trade in gold and silver					Trade in copper and nickel				
	Total	Bullion	Imports	Exports	Import	Imports		Exports		Import	Imports		Exports	
					Excess	Money	Metal	Money	Metal	Excess	Money	Metal	Money	Metal
1901–02	148.0		298.6	150.6										
1902–03	84.2		273.4	189.2										
1903–04	130.2	32.3	385.0	254.8	27.50	4.65	25.09	2.24	0	4.79	.16	4.63	0	0
1904–05	101.9	7.9	349.9	248.0	4.94	4.65	5.01	4.72	0	2.97	.18	2.80	0	.01
1905–06	93.4	6.3	386.5	293.1	6.28	9.35	5.71	8.78	0	0	0	0	0	0
1906–07	77.6	-11.6	431.0	353.4	-11.60	6.09	.15	17.29	.55	0	0	0	0	0
1907–08	91.3	3.9	408.4	317.1	3.87	9.05	9.94	15.11	.01	0	0	0	0	0
1908–09	46.3		372.5	326.2										
1909–10	70.9	23.5	442.4	371.5	21.25	14.58	40.68	34.01	0	2.28	.30	2.05	0	.07
1910–11	109.1	26.9	484.5	375.4	21.32	11.93	42.47	33.08	0	5.58	.07	5.59	.03	.05
1911–12	149.4	46.1	570.2	420.8	41.41	12.86	66.20	37.65	0	4.73	0	4.90	0	.17
1912–13	131.3	-8.8	567.6	436.3	-9.73	12.15	5.55	27.43	0	.98	0	1.06	0	.08
1914–15	133.2	13.1	499.3	366.1	13.08	3.92	22.70	13.54						
1915–16	87.0	7.4	464.1	377.1	7.41	3.38	9.08	5.05	0					

1916–17	60.9	28.5	494.8	433.9	28.49	11.61	19.06	2.18	0				
1917–18	129.4	16.7	468.1	338.7	16.46	15.30	8.64	7.48	0	.23	0	.23	0	0
1918–19	205.4	5.3	476.3	270.9	4.98	3.14	3.14	1.30	0	.34	0	.34	0	0
1919–20	262.0	21.1	629.8	367.8	20.33	23.32	0	2.98	.01	.80	.80			
TOTAL	2,111.5	218.6	8,002.4	5,890.9	195.99	145.98	263.42	212.84	.57	22.70	1.51	21.60	.03	.38

Total bullion imports were 432.6 million qrans, or 5.4% of imports; total bullion exports were 213.8 million qrans, or 3.6% of exports.

1920–21	111.2	4.3	482.4	371.2	2.25	5.25	0	2.98	.02	2.06	.05	2.01	0	0
1921–22	107.8	3.8	609.8	502.0	3.00	8.72	.04	5.76	0	.76	0	.81	0	.05
1922–23	-114.8	-.7	619.2	734.0	-1.93	10.00	.22	12.15	0	1.21	0	1.24	0	.03
1923–24	-87.1	-12.7	681.3	768.4	-12.66			12.66						
1924–25	-228.8	10.4	771.4	1,000.2	6.71	10.79	8.56	12.64		3.73		3.73		
1925–26	-178.4	40.5	881.0	1,059.4	37.30	28.87	17.15	8.72		3.25		3.25		
1926–27	-316.7	-1.1	787.4	1,104.1	-1.09	7.56		8.65						
TOTAL	-706.8	44.5	4,832.5	5,539.3	33.58	71.19	25.97	63.56	.02	11.01	.05	11.04	0	.08

Total bullion imports were 108.2 millions qrans, or 2.2% of imports; total bullion exports were 63.7 million qrans, or 1.1% of exports.

Source: Adminstration des Douanes, *Statistique Commerciale de la Perse*: Tableau Général du Commerce avec les Pays Etrangers, annual series. 'Metal' is 'cuivre, nickel, et leur alliages en barres, plaques, feuilles, ou fils' and 'or, argent, et platine en lingots;' it excludes 'ouvrages en cuivre on en alliage de cuivre' and similar items in silver and gold. Blank entries indicate missing data. Total excludes blank entries.

However, in 1857, the Qajar government reduced the weight of the qran to 5.0 g, while the weight of the ashrafi as presented by Lorini remained 3.24 g, both being 90 per cent pure metal. This differs slightly from the 3.45 g claimed for the same coin in the same period by Album; cf. table 7.4. The reason for this discrepancy remains unclear. With 10 qrans containing 50 g of silver and one tuman 3.24 g, the silver to gold ratio was 1:15.4, which was essentially the international market ratio. A further complicating factor of note is that the official ratios and weights were not always fully reflected in the reality of the various mint outputs.[136] In fact, by 1860, the (silver) qran did not reflect its official standard, for it had a fineness of 82.0 per cent, i.e., it contained 4.1 g of silver. In practice, 11 qrans were exchanged for one tuman. Since 11 qrans had 45.0 g of silver while a tuman 2.92 g of gold that meant a gold–silver ratio of 1:15.4, again essentially the ratio on international markets.

However, the management of the silver currency became more complicated as countries began to abandon silver as a monetary coin. Whereas until 1850 most nations had been on a bimetallic silver and gold standard, thereafter most began to move towards a gold standard, with a result that the international demand curve for silver shifted inward at the same time that new discoveries (primarily in Nevada) shifted the supply curve outwards. Under pressure from silver producers, the U.S. government from 1873 to 1893 sought to maintain the gold–silver ratio. Nevertheless, the value of silver dropped 30 per cent, from 1:14 in the late 1860s to roughly 1:18 by 1889, with a brief stabilization (or even rise) in 1889 following enactment of the U.S. Sherman Silver Purchase Act mandating massive purchases designed to stabilize the ratio at 1:16. But silver's decline accelerated in the early 1890s, after the failure of the international monetary conference of 1893, the repeal of the Sherman Act in 1893, and the abandonment of the silver standard by nearly all countries except Iran and China. Iran's two major trading partners, Russia and India, ceased minting silver coins at this time. Silver fell by 1898 to roughly 1:27, at which point the ratio stabilized, with silver gaining a little at times.

As the value of silver fell relative to gold, Iran made some adjustments in the weight of coins, but not enough. The 1879 mint reform, described above, had established the gold ashrafi at 2.878 g and the silver qran at 4.6 g, both 90 per cent pure metal, meaning the ratio was 1:16.0. But further adjustments were not made, as the value of silver relative to gold internationally fell to 1:27. This meant that Iranian gold coins were worth more than their theoretical equivalent in silver coins. As predicted by Gresham's Law – bad

136 Lorini, *La Persia contemporanea*, 296.

money drives out good – this caused gold coins to disappear. The traditional adjustment mechanism for changes in the relative value of gold and silver was to apply a discount – at the extreme, for merchants to insist on weighing the coins and valuing the silver at its international market price relative to gold. But that was hard to do because after the 1877 mint reform described above, Iranian coins now had a face value on them. With the transition to a semi-modern system in which the value of coins was dictated by the state rather than being determined by the metal content, Iran fell under the sway of Gresham's Law; that is, Iran was drained of gold as the value of gold rose relative to that of silver and the major economic powers shifted from silver to gold (e.g., Germany in 1871, Austro-Hungary in 1892 and Russia in 1897) – a trend not replicated in Qajar Iran.[137]

There is only scattered evidence about official efforts to preserve the official silver to gold ratio in the face of changing world market prices. Presumably such an effort is what lay behind the 1882 report of attempts to fix the price of gold: 'Another grievance of the merchants at Tabrees is that the Persian Authorities, by attempting to fix the price of Russian gold Half Imperials under their intrinsic value, prevent to a great extent the importation of a valuable medium of exchange.'[138]

Silver's loss in value would be expected to drive up the prices of goods expressed in silver qrans. On 17 March 1896, `Eyn al-Saltaneh writes in his diary:

> The cost of white money has gone up much. They pay two riyals and three thousand [dinars]. Trading has stopped. Every hour they quote a new price. Everybody is perplexed and does not know what to do. They said that the price of white money in Kerman is one tuman for eight thousand, that is, the price of one silver tuman of ten thousand is eighteen thousand in black money. In Shiraz it is six thousand. May God make it all end well. I do not know where it all will end.[139]

Unfortunately, there is no meaningful way to compare prices of goods over time in Qajar Iran prior to 1881. The most systematic and detailed attempt at this is Migeod's twenty-page essay, citing many, many contemporary accounts of the prices of some basic standardized foodstuffs – e.g., rice and bread – over the forty-eight-year reign of Naser al-Din Shah (r. 1848–96).[140]

137 Avery and Simmons, 'Persia on a Cross of Silver', 16, make this argument, with but little supporting evidence.

138 *NA*, FO 60/456, Commercial Report by W. J. Dickson. Tehran, 17 Sept. 1882, unfoliated.

139 `Eyn al-Saltaneh, *Ruznameh-ye khaterat*, 1:911.

140 Migeod, *Persische Gesellschaft*, 345–65.

He found that prices were so highly localized that there was no meaning to any sort of Iran-wide price index. For instance, in 1877, the price of bread in Shiraz was two and a half times higher than the price on the same date in towns 70 km away. The principal differences in prices over time were the spectacular increases in years of penury or famine.

Fortunately, as of 1881 British consuls provided annual data on prices of a variety of goods, including foodstuffs data that were not available to Migeod. Although these data do not reflect seasonal differences, they constitute the closest figures available for the late nineteenth century that may be called times series. These data were analyzed by Gad Gilbar, who indeed noted that the price increase of goods was enormous. A food basket costing 3 tumans in 1881 would cost 15 tumans in 1898. However, this phenomenon was not universal in the country, reflecting its persistent regional economies. In Rasht, Tabriz and Tehran there was a high rate of inflation during the 1880s and 1890s. However, in Mashhad and Nasratabad prices remained stable until 1879 and 1906, respectively. Then these towns were also hit by inflation, though it was much weaker than in the aforementioned cities. Bushire, Isfahan and Shiraz, too, felt inflationary pressure, but it remained moderate, while in Yazd prices remained stable throughout. The three northern towns, Tehran, Tabriz and Rasht, were the ones most affected by inflation. Interestingly, the cities most active in the 1906 revolution were the ones hardest hit by deflation following unemployment and a general economic downturn, in the years preceding the revolution.[141]

Switching to a Gold Standard?

During the Qajar years, there were many proposals to switch to a gold standard. For instance, the 1889 IBP concession's Article 3 reads,

> The Imperial Bank shall, as State Bank, have the exclusive right of issuing notes to bearer, payable at sight. In order to promote the development of public credit, to place a limit on the circulation of silver money and increase that of gold, the Imperial Bank accepts in principle the introduction of a single standard on the basis of the gold Toman; during the 10 years which follow the formation of the Bank, the Government of His Imperial Majesty

141 Gilbar, 'Demographic Developments', 177–98. Money was so scarce that `Eyn al-Saltaneh, *Ruznameh-ye khaterat*, 1:575, reports that the government wanted to pay his wages half in copper money and further to reduce the value of the tuman by two riyals. He further mentions the rise in food prices as well as of foreign gold coins, of which he provides details. Ibid., vol. 1, 671–72, 683 (further rise in the price of gold coins), 861, 892–93 (rise in food prices).

> and the Directors of the Bank will common to an understanding as to the means and measures most favourable to attain this end. At the same time, taking into account the exigencies of the actual monetary situation, the issue of Bank notes will at first be on the basis of the silver Kran.[142]

British and IPB officials were unhappy that Iran remained on a silver standard. The IBP's Rawlinson wrote in an internal memo in 1902, 'Silver has been discarded as a medium of exchange by the whole civilized world, and its general demonetization renders it utterly preposterous that any civilized Government should continue to hamper its commerce, and inconvenience its administration, by retaining a standard of value other than that practically universal.'[143] In 1902, IPB Manager and Secretary George Newell came to Tehran expressly for the purpose of pressing the government to abandon the silver standard. He argued for adoption of the Indian solution, namely, 'a silver currency on a gold standard.'[144] The traditional silver coins would continue to be used, satisfying the public insistence on silver currency, but the actual value of the coins would become greater than the metal content contained in them thanks to government policies which fixed the qran relative to the pound (and therefore relative to gold). To make this system work, the government would assume the monopoly of coinage of silver, prohibit the import of silver, and give up silver reserves. And the state could reduce the quantity of silver coins in circulation to keep the value at the target level, as had been done in India.[145] The IBP argued that by stabilizing the value of the qran relative to the pound, the Iranian government would more easily service the external debt; the debt was denominated in gold currencies such as pounds sterling, whereas government revenue was in the silver currency of the qran, so each fall in the value of silver relative to gold raised the burden of the debt service.[146]

142 *NA*, FO 881/5808; also printed in Jones 1986, vol. 1, 341.

143 Albert Rawlinson, 13 Oct. 1902, BBME 798.

144 'Memorandum on the Currency Question and the establishment of a gold standard in Persia', attached to a 28 Oct. 1902 letter from IBP General Secretary and Manager Newell to Attabeg-i A`zam Mirza `Ali Ashgar Khan, BBME 798.

145 The Question of Exchange in Persia, attached to an undated letter to the Atabeg-e A`zam (evidently translated into French before being delivered, as there is both a typed and a longhand copy in the archives, with the latter bearing various notations about how to translate phrases), BBME 798.

146 Rawlinson's 13 October 1902 memo spells out in detail how the government would benefit from the switch, including the revenue it would earn from minting silver coins worth more than the silver content.

One reason why the Iranian government never implemented these suggestions was, as the Atabeg al-A`zam (the new title of Amin al-Soltan) put it, 'unfortunately owing to the rivalry which exists in this country the Government cannot put the management of the scheme in the hands of the Imperial Bank because the Russian Bank would certainly object'.[147] In addition, the Atabeg 'seemed to think that the question of profit to the Bank was the prime factor in [the gold currency] proposal to him, not the good of the country'.[148] Indeed, the Bank was acutely conscious that its proposals might be seen as self-serving. The IBP Board discussed recommending that a neutral commission supervise the transition, saying 'the Board must disclaim any intention of benefiting the Bank by an commission to be obtained on the business ... they are persuaded that the permanent interests of the Bank can more surely be secured by assisting in establishing financial stability for the Persian Govt. than by obtaining temporary commissions for themselves'.[149]

The failure to implement this switch means that the value of Iran's money supply as measured in European gold currencies steadily dropped, because the late nineteenth century was a period of declining value of silver relative to gold. Rabino calculated that the legal intrinsic value of the qran declined from 25.05 qran per pound sterling (a gold-based currency) in 1863 to 38.85 in 1889.[150] The actual exchange rate of the qran on the London market was usually somewhat higher than the metal value would indicate, which was normal for metal-based currencies (that is, the market valued the ability to use qrans as currency in Iran). Based on references in British records to the value of the qran, Issawi calculates that the value of the qran fell from 11 per pound sterling in 1809 to 55 per pound in 1914, with most of the drop coming between 1881 and 1894, during the years of the silver crisis.[151] Had Iran converted from silver to gold at any point, it would have been better off, as Avery and Simmons argue.[152] The losses from its decision to remain on the silver standard persisted to the very end of the Qajar dynasty. At that

147 'Extract of letter from Mr. Newell to the Chairman, dated Teheran, 6 Nov. 1902' about a meeting Newell had with the Atabeg, BBME 798.

148 'Extract of letter from Mr Dalton to Mr Newell, dated Teheran, 14 Nov. 1902', recounting Mirza Aboul Hassan Khan's description of his meeting with the Atabeg the day before, BBME 798.

149 'Memo on a Gold Standard for Persia, by Mr. Coke', undated but evidently 1902, BBME 798.

150 Rabino, 'Banking in Persia', 31. This table and the associated graph have been widely reproduced, e.g., Avery and Simmons, 'Persia on a Cross of Silver'; Issawi, *Economic History of Iran*, 350.

151 Issawi, *Economic History of Iran*, 343–45 presents a table on the value of the qran in pound sterling from 1809 to 1914, based on his combing of the British archives for references to the value of the qran.

152 Avery and Simmons, 'Persia on a Cross of Silver'.

time, Iran and China were the only economies of any size left on the silver standards.

Paper Currency

Prior to the late nineteenth century, Iran had only one brief experience with paper currency. The Mongol khan Geykhatu introduced paper notes as *chav* in September 1294, with the death penalty decreed for anyone who failed to exchange coins for paper or refused to accept the paper currency. The result was dramatic: the bazaar came to a complete standstill, and prices rose more than ten-fold. By spring 1295, Geykhatu had been overthrown, the paper currency recalled, and the machinery which made it burned.[153] This was not an auspicious precedent. During the Qajar period, paper currency became common, but it was only slowly accepted and it continued to suffer from considerable limitations. At first glance this is odd, for Iran would seem a natural place for the rapid spread of paper currency for several reasons. First, paper currency is much less subject to quality problems than are coins; paper currency could not be adulterated by reducing the precious metal content. That was no small factor in a country with such problems with the mint. Second, paper currency weighs much less than coin. That is of obvious convenience when carrying or shipping a substantial sum. The lesser weight should have been a considerable factor in a country with as poor transport conditions as Iran. To some extent, the problem of transferring currency over long distances could be met by the buying and selling of letters promising payment in foreign trading centers. While such bills were the main business of the well-established local money-lenders, or sarrafs, the bills offered little advantage over the transport of coin: the bills carried high charges and were not necessarily easily converted into coin in the city of destination.[154] Indeed, the difficulty of arranging for long-distance payment is a steady theme of Europeans analyzing trade with Iran.[155]

Third, paper currency is easier to produce than coins, which require access to precious metals. Precisely the difficulty in assuring sufficient metal,

153 Jackson, 'Čav'.

154 Floor, *Guilds, Merchants & Ulama*, 53–68. Note that despite this translation of sarraf as banker, the sarrafs did not typically take deposits, which is often seen as an essential characteristic of commercial banking. The evaluation of the utility of bills is from Ibid.

155 E.g., in E.F. Law's 6 Dec. 1888 report 'British Trade and Foreign Competition in North Persia', he writes, 'One of the great difficulties which meets the foreign importer is the finding of a steady and safe medium for making his remittances to Europe.' In *NA*, FO 881/5728.

combined with the problems in arranging shipments, were major factors behind the currency shortages that left merchants complaining and travelers wondering. In 1892, Rabino wrote to his English audience, 'It is scarcely possible to conceive the difficulty of working in a country where exchange may for months be unobtainable, whilst at other times money cannot be procured, no matter at what sacrifice. Forecasts of movements, based as elsewhere upon general causes, become consequently valueless.'[156]

Given these factors, Rabino was confident,

> When the country has been sufficiently educated to understand the theory of a sound paper currency and when, therefore, it has acquired a little of that confidence in a bank note, which two centuries of good government, financial security and progress have given to the Bank of England notes, Teheran notes will circulate everywhere, and trading transactions will be greatly facilitated and hastened.[157]

In reality, the universal acceptance of paper money in Iran took far less than two centuries, although the time necessary extended beyond the Qajar dynasty's days.

The history of paper currency in Iran is intimately associated with that of the IBP. Although there were several earlier tries at starting modern banks operating on a scale that would permit currency issue, the IBP totally dominated the banking scene in Iran almost until the end the Qajar dynasty.[158] As in most countries during the nineteenth century, paper currency issue was carried out by a state-licensed commercial bank – recall that the Bank of England was still a privately owned commercial bank during that period. It would be tempting to regard the undoubtedly cautious practices of the IBP as the major reason for the slow acceptance of paper currency in Iran, but more fundamental problems existed as well.

IBP's Practices

The IBP adopted extraordinarily cautious practices in its note issuance – not only by the standards of modern practice but even by those of British nineteenth-century colonial banks. In some regards, this was to be expected:

156 Rabino, 'Banking in Persia', 36.
157 Ibid., 38.
158 For a summary of these early efforts at establishing a bank, see Basseer, 'Role of Financial Intermediaries', 81–112. In addition, see Matthee, 'Changing the Mintmaster', 113 about an Austrian effort in the 1860s.

Iran not being a colony, the British government was not as committed to the success of the IBP as it was to analogous banks in its colonies. In addition to which, Iran had such a poorly functioning transportation and communication network that the IBP was vulnerable to runs on its bank branches (that is, transporting coin from one branch to another was hard to arrange).

The most striking example, but hardly the only one, of the conservative practices was the extent of the reserve in coin and metal relative to the volume of notes issued. The initial 30 January 1889 concession was rather ordinary by the standards of the day, providing,

> In order to guarantee this payment of notes [in metal coins upon demand], the Bank expressly binds itself to hold cover in specie equal to at least half the value of the notes in circulation for a period of two years from commencing operations, and to at least one-third after the lapse of the said period two years. The difference between this reserve fund in specie and the value of the notes issues shall be covered by securities for realty or personality belonging to the Bank, and deposited in its coffers in Persia.[159]

Had this provision been put into effect, the IBP could have lent out at interest two-thirds of the value of the paper money it issued. The profit from this operation would be 'seignorage', which, when referring to paper notes, is the term for the profits from issuing currency. However, immediately after the signing of the concession, the government became dissatisfied with the reserve requirement clause. After months of negotiations, an appendix was signed on 27 July 1889, with Article 4 reading,

> The following shall be the guarantee for the repayment of notes viz: the Bank is bound to hold a metallic reserve equal to at least one third of the amount of its notes in circulation. The metallic reserve to the extent of two thirds thereof may be in bullion [i.e., not in coin]. The difference between this metallic reserve and the amount of the notes in circulation shall not at any one time be more than the amount of the paid up Capital.[160]

159 *NA*, FO 881/5808; also printed in Jones, *Banking and Empire*, 1:342.

160 *NA*, FO 60/507; also printed in Jones, *Banking and Empire*, 1:346. Interestingly, the Bank's Charter of Incorporation from Queen Victoria, issued 2 September 1889 (printed in Jones 1986, 1:349–53), is more restrictive about the metal reserve. The reserve has to be the capital less the fee paid for the concession, and it cannot be mortgaged or pledged ('charged') in any way. Furthermore, if Persia converts to a single metal standard (be it gold or silver), four-fifths of the reserve must be in that metal.

In other words, the Bank had to hold paid-up capital equal to the value of the difference between its metallic reserve and the notes in circulation – capital on which it had to pay the shareholders dividends. This severely limited IBP's seignorage profits.

In addition, the Bank's charter from the British government, issued on 2 September 1889, muddied the waters with its provision,

> The Company shall keep, at their principal and branch banks in Persia, a metallic reserve equal to at least one-third of the total amount of such notes issued by the principal and branch banks of the Company in Persia and in circulation.[161]

The Iranian government read the charter to say that each IBP branch had to keep in metal one-third of the notes in circulation from that branch, while another one-third had to be kept in metal at the office in Tehran.[162] In fact, IBP kept at each branch more cash – that is, silver and gold – than the notes in circulation, as Rabino assured the Board in 1896.

Table 7.7: Cash and notes in circulation by IBP branch, 20 February 1896 (in tumans)

	Cash (i.e., silver and gold)	Notes
Tehran	296,477	290,766
Tabriz	73,616	1,922
Isfahan	32,809	25,951
Bushire	99,500	41,790
Yazd	8,717	12,968
en route to Yazd by post		9,000
Mashhad	19,061	3,599
Shiraz	87,110	68,190
Total	617,290	454,186

Source: Rabino to Secretary IBP, 24 February1896, BBME 594.2

161 Jones, *Banking and Empire*, 1, gives the entire Charter; this provision from Article 3 is on p. 350.

162 Rabino to Secretary IBP, 24 Feb. 1896, BBME 594.2. This is also the source for the data on notes compared to reserves.

Because of the very conservative reserve in coin, Rabino may well have been correct to say that note issuance was not directly profitable. That said, the note issuance put the IBP in a good position to argue that it should be allowed to import silver for the Mint to turn into coin, an operation that was quite profitable. The Bank archives show Rabino and the IBP Board were intensely interested in the silver import business, frequently haggling with the government about the terms to ensure that the IBP made a handsome profit from the various fees it charged.[163]

One indication that the IBP had good reason to hold such large reserves in coin was the value of notes fluctuated considerably. Rabino listed the value of outstanding notes for each year from 1890 to 1900.[164]

Table 7.8: Value of IBP notes outstanding 1890–1900 (in thousands of tumans, as of 20 September each year)

Year	Notes outstanding
1890	29
1891	99
1892	194
1893	207
1894	334
1895	254
1896	415
1897	203
1898	365
1899	589
1990	1,058

Source: Rabino, 'An Economist's Notes on Persia', 279.

163 For instance, letter of 22 Feb. 1897 by Rabino to the IBP Secretary (i.e., the Board). The IBP bought silver in London , had it shipped to Tehran where it was then minted into coins 90 per cent pure for a fee, typically 4.5 per cent of the value of the coins. The coins had a face value as if they were 100 per cent silver. So once source of the profit was the difference between the face value and the metal content. In their correspondence about the transactions, Rabino and the Secretary clearly see the imports – and the Bank in general – as a trading operation. The Bank did not see itself as primarily a lending institution.

164 Rabino, 'Economist's Notes on Persia', 279.

In 1904, the value rose 61 per cent, only to fall 24 per cent in 1905. It then rose 63 per cent in 1906, and fell 51 per cent in 1907. And the value of notes issues at each branch was subject to even more dramatic short-term changes. For instance, the note issue at the Tehran branch rose from 1,402,148 tumans in September 1908 to 2,269,831 tumans in September 1909.[165] The start of the First World War saw a general abandonment of notes for the safe refuge of silver coins. At Tabriz, notes in circulation fell from 651,000 tumans in March 1915 to 155,000 tumans in September 1915; at Hamadan, from 324,812 tumans in March 1915 to 42,000 in September 1915; and in Tehran, from 2,201,176 tumans in April 1915 to 673,261 tumans in June 1915.

Table 7.9: Distribution of notes outstanding on 30 September 1898 (per cent)

Note (in tumans)	Per cent of notes	Per cent of value of money issued
1	18.04	1.15
2	13.64	1.75
3	5.17	1.00
5	39.42	12.61
10	8.97	5.74
20	5.47	7.00
25	3.57	5.71
50	1.02	3.26
100	3.46	22.13
500	1.24	39.66
Total	**100.00**	**100.00**

Source: Lorini, *La Persia contemporanea*, 435 and authors' calculation, on the assumption Lorini's 'cifre percentuali dell'ammontare complessivo' is the per cent of notes issued rather than the per cent of the value of the money issued.

165 Finance Committee Report for 20 Sept. 1909, BBME 290.3. Finance Committee Reports are the source for the figures cited for the First World War as well.

The 1889 concession provided, 'The Imperial Bank shall be bound to pay its notes at sight at the place of issue; nevertheless, the notes of the branch offices shall be payable also at Tehran.'[166] In practice, notes issued at one branch were generally accepted at other branches, but at a discount. Indeed, Rabino complained in 1896 that some branches were in the 'piratical business' of financing speculation against the currency notes issued by other branches.[167] Only in the 1920s did the Iranian government force IBP to accept at each branch notes irrespective of branch of issuance. One Bank report described the government's requirement as 'a blessing in disguise' – yet another indication that the Bank's practices were ultra-cautious and that more vigorous promotion of banking and modern currency might have served well not only Iran but the Bank.[168]

The bank notes were designed and printed in Britain, with the Shah's portrait on the side with Persian writing and the lion and sword shield seal on the side with English writing. They came in denominations of 1, 2, 3, 5, 10, 20, 25, 50, 100, 500 and 1,000 tumans.[169] In 1898, the 5-tuman notes were the most common note, but more than 60 per cent of the value of the notes was in the relatively small number of 100 and 500-toman notes.

At first, each bank note had to be signed by the Chief Manager, the Cashier and the Persian High Commissioner of the Bank. But after Rabino complained in April 1896 that, 'I have signed nearly 60,000 notes a great part during the last 6 weeks', the Bank Board permitted use of a stamped signature by the Chief Manager on the 1, 2 and 3 tuman notes, but the Cashier and Persian High Commissioner still had to sign those while those two gentlemen and the Chief Manager had to sign the larger denomination notes.[170] In 1924, the Bank had printed up new bank notes with watermarks to replace the old ones, which were exchanged with little difficulty.

Limits to Acceptance of Paper Currency

The IBP faced difficulties in getting its paper currency accepted as fully equivalent to silver. Lorini reports the sarrafs typically required a discount to convert the banknotes into silver. More serious were the periodic runs on IBP branches. Sarrafs had an obvious interest in organizing a run on their

166 *NA*, FO 881/5808; also printed in Jones, *Banking and Empire*, 1:342.

167 Rabino to IBP, 21 Oct. 1896, BBME 594.2.

168 Jones, *Banking and Empire*, 1:202; the quote is from The 20 March 1929 Tehran Report on Progress, BBME 101.

169 Letter of H. W. Maclean to Credit Lyonnais, 11 Jan. 1900, BBME 798. Maclean noted the 100, 500, and 1000 tuman notes were 'not much asked for except for hoarding'.

170 Jones, *Banking and Empire*, 1: 79.

competitor, the IBP, but also benefiting were authorities looking for handouts from the Bank. As Dunlop explained in 1912, during a run 'the olama vilified the infidel foreigners and had to be quieted with presents. The local governor, of course, also [would volunteer] to make things all right (*eslah*)' for the right price.[171] Writing about the 1897 run, Rabino described the role of the olama and the police:

> On Friday and Saturday last Notes were presented in large amounts by the most improbable persons, Seyeds who came noisily and made a disturbance and ill-dressed men who could not be the owners of the sums they held ... During three or four days we had a terrible tumult but the Bank was guarded inside and out by about sixty police besides our usual guards, and better than all a most influential Seyed was seated in the office and prevented any disorderly person from sheltering himself behind the green turban.[172]

Runs on the IBP were at times quite successful at preventing regular conversion of notes into silver. The worst experience came early in the First World War, when nervousness about German advances and British losses led to encashment of most outstanding notes, as discussed above. The IBP had to delay payment of silver for notes: 'During this time [Branch Manager] Mr. Wood had to call on the Government to come to his assistance until Silver could be imported, and a moratorium was granted for two months, the Bank being called upon to pay in Coin against Notes Ts. 10,000 per diem.'[173]

The run in late August and early September 1897 was the worst peace-time run.[174] This run occurred soon in the midst of intense political intrigue following the May 1896 accession of Mozaffar al-Din Shah: the March 1897 appointment of the pro-British reformer Amin al-Dowleh as prime minister, and the scheming about the return of the mint to the old guard under Amin al-Zarb against Amin al-Dowleh's protests (which happened after the run, on 24 October 1897). In this context, there is good reason to credit the suggestion that the enemies of Amin al-Dowleh, including the powerful governor of Tehran, Farmanfarma, organized the run, presumably with assistance from Russia and the Russian-owned Loan and Discount Bank.[175]

On the other hand, Entner cites Russian sources claiming that the Loan and Discount Bank had about 700,000 rubles of IBP notes in its vault during an 1898 run, which bank manager E.K. Grube refused to release because

171 Dunlop, *Perzië*, 419.

172 Rabino to Secretary IBP, 2 Sept. 1897, BBME 594.3.

173 Finance Committee Report, 20 Sept. 1915, BBME 290.3, 2.

Russia needed the IBP, as it was the principal facilitator of money transfers by Russian merchants.[176] Indeed, these sources claim that Grube lent the IBP specie to tide it through its crisis. This account is implausible, if for no other reason than that 700,000 rubles was the equivalent of 238,000 tuman, whereas the total value of notes outstanding in Tehran was 410,000 tuman after the 1897 run. Even assuming the Russian sources are referring to the September 1897 run, the total note issue before that run was 732,000 tuman. More plausible about what happened during runs is Rabino's account in his letters to the London IBP management about the 1897 run, namely:

> we arranged with the Banque de Prêts [i.e., the Loan and Discount Bank] to withdraw all Notes in their hands and have made a deposit of our surplus silver [that is, 150,000 toman in bar silver, rather than the coins which were in great demand] with them not only to cover these Notes but also the total of their deposits with us as it of the utmost important that we would show the State Bank of Russia that we do not require the smallest sum upon our simple signature.[177]

As an indication of just how poor were the relations between IBP and their Russian colleagues, consider that in November 1914 – when Britain and Russia were war allies:

> the Qazvin Branch of the Russian [Loan and Discount] Bank posted notices in the bazaars of our town to the effect that "Until further orders they would refuse all Imperial Bank of Persia Notes." ... The only explanation we can give for the Russian Bank's action is that it was done out of sheer animosity and jealousy.[178]

While paper currency faced many problems in gaining acceptance in Qajar Iran, there are also indications that as it spread, it came to be seen as quite useful. One sign of this is the competing paper currencies issued by Iranian merchants. The IBP objected, noting that the Bank's concession included the

174 Jones, *Banking and Empire*, 1:80.

175 The politics of the moment are explained in Bakhash, 'Failure of Reform', 21–22.

176 Entner, *Russo-Persian Commercial Relations*, 44–45, citing Lomnitskii, *Persiia y Persy* (SPB, 1902).

177 Letter of Rabino to the Secretary of the IBP, 2 Sept. 1897, BBME 594.3. The Persian government account agreed, 'I heard that the Russian Bank had taken away all the silver bars that the Imperial Bank possessed on account of the notes which they held' (Translation of an account received by the Persian Legation in London from the Imperial Foreign Office Date Rabi` II, H. 1315, 2 Sept.1897; BBME 651.1 Folder 6).

178 A report from Mr. Goodwin at the IBP Qazvin branch quoted in the March 20, 1915 Finance Committee Report, BBME 290.3.

provision, 'The Government of His Imperial Majesty the Shah binds itself not to issue any kind of paper money during the terms of this Concession, nor to authorise the creation of any other Bank or other Institution possessing a like privilege.'[179] But complaints about the enforcement of this provision are a persistent theme in the IBP archives. For instance, the 1897 'Report on the Working of the Bank' complained, 'The Concession is being constantly violated by the illegal issue of Notes principally in Shiraz without any guarantee or profit to the State and by means of private arrangements we are told with the Governors who disobey Imperial orders'.[180] The Bushire branch reported on 28 May 1900, 'During the past half year the condition of the branch bank has much changed for the better. Illegal notes have been abolished. The serafi krans have disappeared and the Bank Notes are now readily negotiated in the place.'[181] The Isfahan branch in 1909 noted with satisfaction, 'an agreement has been made with the Massoudieh Co. [to] withdraw their illegal notes before the 1st May and that they seem to be carrying out the agreement'.[182] The Fars Trading Company issued 300,000 tumans of currency notes in 1, 5, 10, 25 and 50 tuman denominations, which looked like the IBP notes.[183] The Russian Bank also issued paper currency at various times.[184]

The paper currencies issued by merchants were in many ways a further development of the system of *bijaks* or *barats*, which were credit certificates issued by sarrafs, or money-lenders (as well as by the large merchants, especially in cities without specialized sarrafs). In practice, it was not always clear what was the distinction between various credit instruments, such as a tamassok or simple I.O.U., a havaleh or money-order on a third party with whom one had a credit balance, and a bijak or barat.[185] The bijaks were not a true form of money, in that they were only payable at a future date and to a specific person.[186] Great delays in cashing these credit certificates were common; creditors were often willing to accept a 10–30 per cent discount for prompt payment.[187] The bijak trade was lively, accounting for 60 per cent of

179 *NA*, FO 881/5808; also printed in Jones, *Banking and Empire*, 1:342.

180 Report on the Working of the Bank marked 'Rec'd 9 Apr. 1897', BBME 594.3.

181 I.B.P. Inspection Committee notes, BBME 290.1.

182 'The Finance Committee's Report of the Account at 20th March 1909, adopted by the Board at their Meeting of 30th June, 1909', BBME 290.3.

183 *Berichte über Handel und Industrie* 1910, Band 14, Heft 7, 358.

184 Ronall, 'Beginnings of Modern Banking,' 260.

185 Floor, *Guilds, Merchants & Ulama*, ch. 4.

186 Floor, Ibid., explains the mechanism by which the barats circulated.

187 Bakhash, 'Failure of Reform'. 275, citing 'Memorandum by Sir M. Durand on the Situation in Persia', *NA*, FO 60/581 (1894), 21. Bakhash surely exaggerates how readily the bijaks were accepted when he writes (p. 22), 'Known as bijacks, the bills passed as money;' there was almost certainly a discount applied to bijaks compared to coin, and there may have been a reluctance to accept them.

the volume of bazaar trade in the late nineteenth century.[188] Furthermore, bijaks became more and more money-like, in that they would be frequently endorsed from one creditor to another for an discount – typically 0.1 per cent to 2 per cent but higher during times of tight money.[189] Floor attributes the increasingly attractive terms for use of bijaks as a consequence of the competition with the developing modern banking system.

The experience with bijaks could hardly have helped the IBP in its efforts to secure acceptance of its credit certificates – for that after all is what paper currency consists of – as a ready equivalent for hard coin. To make matters worse, the government frequently made payments by means of barats – the term bijak apparently being seldom used for government credit certificates – which were little more than forced loans. During the tenure of Amin al-Molk as treasurer after 1883 (especially when his brother Amin al-Soltan was mint master and customs-master in the 1890s), barats were left unpaid for eight or nine months, while the treasurer were lent out government funds at high interest for his own benefit.[190] Not that the situation had been that much better earlier in the nineteenth century. Writing about the 1840s, Lambton argues:

> The salaries of government servants and other government expenses were largely paid by drafts (barats) on the revenue. Thus, someone having a claim on the government would be given a draft, or payment-order, on the governor of the province, and this would be noted in the central government register against the revenue due from that province. The issue of barats under Muhammad Shah far exceeded the total revenues of the kingdom. Their value was therefore nominal and the holders, unless they were persons of influence and able to insist on payment of their claims before those of other persons, were glad to sell them at a discount of 70 or 80%. The principal governors had their agents in Tehran to purchase the barats drawn on their provinces. The full amount of them was afterwards charged in their accounts with the government although only a small part of them may in reality have been paid.[191]

188 Lorini, *La Persia contemporanea*, 336.

189 DCR 241, 2; DCR 4179, 89.

190 Bakhash, 'Failure of Reform', 275.

191 Lambton, *Qajar Persia*, 165, citing as source Sheil to Palmerston, No. 117, 20 November 1846, *NA*, FO 60/125. Sir Justin Sheil, the British minister in Tehran, was describing the demands for repayment of barats being made by rich merchant Hajji `Abd al-Karim, who claimed British citizenship by virtue of his birth in India. The dispute dragged on for years. Palmerston's attitude was, to quote Lambton, 'that it was objectionable to encourage British subjects in so corrupt a country as Persia to enter into complicated pecuniary transactions with local people and to expect the British government to step in and help them in their difficulties'. (Lambton, *Qajar Persia*, 175, citing Palmerston to Sheil, No. 130, 18 Dec. 1851, FO 60:157). For background, see Floor, *Fiscal History*, 450–51, 455–56, 463–64, 466.

In short, Iranians had many reasons to regard with suspicion paper promises to pay in coin, so it is hardly surprising that the IBP faced reluctance to accept at face value its claim that its paper could be readily converted into hard coin. And it was hardly surprising that sarrafs, angered that the IBP was taking over from them the business of lending to the government, would periodically organize runs on the IBP.

Money at the End of the Qajar Dynasty

The decade after the 1926 founding of the Pahlavi dynasty saw accelerated change in Iran's monetary system. The new ruler wanted to move to the modern system of gold-backed paper currency issued by a government-owned national bank, with coins having accepted for the face value stamped on them.

The early years of the Pahlavi dynasty experienced a serious monetary crisis as the value of silver collapsed in the late 1920s and early 1930s. The Pahlavis tried at first to shift to a gold standard, with the Persian Monetary Unit Act of 28 March 1930.[192] But faced with difficulties, they adopted the same short-sighted approach as the Qajars, namely, to stay on the silver standard. The Act of 22 Esfand 1310 (13 March 1932) specified, 'pending return to a normal economic situation and reestablishment of the liability to pay in gold or in foreign exchange based on gold, suspended owing to the economic crisis, the National Bank is authorized not to redeem by the payment of gold (coin, bullion or foreign exchange) any silver coins or notes in circulation which may be presented. The National Bank, however, shall pay silver Rials on demand, without delay, against notes and nickel coins presented, without restriction of any coin as regards Teheran, and, as regards the provinces, to the extent of its reserves of silver currency.'

More successful was the switch to paper currency issued by a government-owned national bank. The Bank-e Melli (National Bank) was established and on 13 May 1930, the IBP and the government signed an agreement providing,

> The Bank renounces the right to issue Bank Notes. [The Bank shall repay the notes no later than 20 June 1931]. At the expiration of the said period the Bank will pay to the Government the amount required for the repayment of such of the Notes as shall not then have been presented ... In consideration of the renunciation by the Bank of the right to issue

192 Both this and the 1932 act are, in translation, in BBME 398.

> Bank Notes, the Government shall pay to the Bank, in London, on the 20th March, 1931, the sum of £200,000 (two hundred thousand pounds sterling) in cash.[193]

Note that the IBP had to pay in foreign exchange for any currency notes not presented, including any notes that had been destroyed or lost over the years. When the Note Department closed its account, 164,630 tumans had not been presented; IBP paid the government this sum without the government having to issue new currency for this amount.[194] The government's profit from this transaction was in a way somewhat reminiscent of how older dynasties used currency exchanges to reap revenue.

While paper currency was making great inroads under Reza Shah, still older attitudes lingered on. For instance, the notion that metal is the real basis for money can be found in the legal requirement that paper currency be backed 100 per cent by gold or foreign exchange, with many being scandalized when the Bank-e Melli raised the declared value of the crown jewels to meet the cover requirement. Still, the transition to a modern currency system was one of the accomplishments of Reza Shah's reign.

193 As printed in Jones, *Banking and Empire*, 1:348.

194 Report on Progress, 20 Mar. 1933 by Mr. Williamson, BBME 101, 51.

Afterword

The monetary history of Iran between 1500 and the advent of a modern financial system in the early twentieth century has been poorly known, certainly in comparison to conditions in comparable states such as the Ottoman Empire, Mughal India and Qing China. This study has tried to fill that gap. To do so, it has drawn on numismatic evidence as well as sources in ten languages, ranging from newly published primary Persian-language material to Russian narratives, from traveler accounts to the eyewitness reports of Dutch and English East India Company agents and the archives of the Imperial Bank of Persia.

The Iranian monetary system of this period was much more complicated than modern monetary arrangements. The value of coins was based in theory on the precious metal content, certified by the government. Foreign coins were to be surrendered for reminting into Iranian coins. In practice, the system had many imperfections, e.g., coins did not necessarily contain the requisite precious metal and foreign coins circulated widely. But the main complication was that Iran had coins of three metals: copper, silver and gold. Silver was considered 'real' money: The state typically kept its accounts and levied its taxes in silver, which was the main coin used in large and long-distance trade. Gold coins were primarily for ceremonial occasions. Most ordinary transactions were done with copper coins which were often issued by provincial governors. Meanwhile, large parts of the Iranian economy functioned with little if any use of money; barter was quite common, especial in rural areas. Another wrinkle was that accounts were often kept using 'ghost moneys' – that is, units which did not correspond to any actual coin.

The system was not fully a 'trimetallic' system in which the value of coins of each metal is fixed relative to coins in the other two metals. To be sure, there was a popular expectation, more or less reflected in law, about the relative value of coins in the three metals, but in practice, there was considerable variation depending on market conditions, such as how many coins of each type were available. Also, until the 1870s, the coins from each of the many mints were handmade and were not uniform. A thin slice of metal was placed on an anvil which had one die engraved on its head, and the metal was then struck by a hammer that had the other die engraved on its striking surface. The size and form of the coins varied, and no standard appears to have been adopted. Because the coins from one mint were not necessarily equal to the coins from another mint, merchants and money-traders often demanded a discount to convert the coins from another mint into the local coins – the technical term is 'agio'. Differences in the relative value of different coins – for instance, in the ratio between copper and silver coins – from one area to another led to the shipment of coins from to capture the difference in their value. The relative value was monitored closely in each city by the sarrafs whose business it was to move metal and bullion.

The monetary policy of the Safavid and Qajar states had several objectives which were not fully consistent with each other: To use mints as a source of revenue; to maintain a readily verifiable standard for measuring tax obligations and for making payments; and to promote trade, so as to maximize income and power of the state. To achieve these objectives, the state established mints as its main executive agency in the field of monetary policy and laid down rules for their operation. Although shahs set up mints, they did not have full control over them. The mints were typically farmed out, and the farmers were under varying degrees of control by the ruler.

The state's main preoccupation was often maximizing revenue. So it took measures with an immediate fiscal objective such as tampering with the weight or quality of coins. The result, however, was inflation and the upheaval of exchange relations. Short-term revenue enhancement may have been achieved, but the lasting effects, a lack in confidence in the realm's currency, a reluctance of merchants to bring cash to Iran, and increased exports of good coins, were all negative.

At many intervals during the period 1500 to 1925, Iran faced a complex situation that combined system bullion scarcity and fiscal difficulties. Although these two are to be distinguished analytically, in practice they often went hand in hand: Scarcity of metal coins tended to lead to low tax revenue (because taxes were paid with coins), and that led to official tampering with the value of the currency with the intent of enhancing state income. This was no lasting solution, however, because the purchasing power of the altered coins fell. In late Safavid Iran, such a cycle of shortage and debasement gained a damaging momentum, which arguably was a significant contributor to undermining that dynasty.

Iranian merchants and rulers chronically complained about a shortage of currency. Expanding the supply of money required (1) production of metal from mines; (2) acquisition of booty through conquest; or (3) a positive trade balance. Neither of the first two factors was particularly important during this time. Throughout this period, Iran, benefiting from its large exports of raw silk, apparently had a positive trade balance with Russia and the Ottoman Empire. On the other hand, Iran had a trade deficit with the Indian Ocean lands, such as Mughal India, and this had to be paid for in precious metal. The two trade deficits – positive with the lands north and west of Iran, negative with the lands south and east of Iran – meant that large amounts of coin or bullion was flowing into and out of Iran. Another way to describe the trade pattern of the centuries in question is that the West received large amounts of silver and gold from the Americas, and that precious metal was being used in part to finance the West's persistent balance of trade deficit with South and East Asia. Such a description highlights the intermediary role Iran was playing.

The large-scale shipments to and from Iran of specie and bullion made the money supply dependent on factors over which the state had little control. War outside the borders would keep the caravans from the north and west away and thus raise the price, for example. Like many other governments of the day, Iran's rulers at regular intervals tried to control or even stop the export of silver, gold or both. Those prohibitive measures did not work well, given the weakness of the state and the intractability of private initiative in search of gain. Such bans were particularly common in the seventeenth century, which in Iran as in Europe was the 'bullionist' age par excellence. The obsession with the volume of bullion and specie reflected both the metal-based monetary system and the deficient premodern understanding of monetary behavior.

Besides the trade deficit with India and the needs of trade, the demand for money was also a function of the amount of 'hoarding'. While the term implies irrational behavior, in fact holding and hiding coins was one of the few secure ways to have liquid savings in an economy without a banking system. And such liquid savings were useful for large purchases or as a fallback in the event of hard times in the form of unrest, crop failure or epidemics.

The monetary systems of the Safavids and early Qajars, as well as the Afsharids and Zands in between those two long-lasting dynasties, were largely similar. The biggest change in Iran monetary system came in the late Qajar from the mid-nineteenth century. This period saw a slow and halting transition to a modern system. First came changes in the minting of coins, which shifted from traditional, hammer-struck coinage at a multiplicity of local mints run by mint farmers, to machine-striking at one national mint of coins marked with a face value. Then came the introduction of paper money. But at the dynasty's end in 1925, the transition was by no means complete: Paper money was still seen as an imperfect substitute for metal; three metals were still in use; and private businessmen still played a major role in currency issue. Similarly with the balance of payments: Iran went from settling its trade accounts with bullion – with a surplus in trade to the north more than offsetting a deficit to the south and east, thereby producing the net bullion imports needed to sustain and expand the money supply – to largely relying on bank transactions to settle trade imbalances. But bullion flows continued to play a role, both in settling trade imbalances and as a means of expanding the money supply, and in 1925 Iran remained one of the few countries in the world still wedded to a silver standard rather than gold one.

Several issues about Iran's monetary system from the sixteenth through the nineteenth centuries would benefit from additional research. One is that the role, extent and character of credit extended by bazaar merchants are not entirely clear. Bills of exchange were widely used, especially in long-distance trade. So too were letter of credits which could be endorsed and transferred to another party. It is not clear to what extent these functioned as effective quasi-monetary instruments – that is, to what extent they were readily exchangeable. Nor is it clear what proportion of trade, either long-distance or local, was conducted with such instruments as distinct from payment in coin.

Another issue meriting further investigation is the role of provincial governments in relation to that of the central government. Two particular issues in need of additional research are regional coins and copper money. On the first, various regional silver coin systems flourished at different times. It is not clear what role the provincial governments played in these regional coins. Perhaps some of the these regional variations reflected weak central government control over the region in question; in other cases, they may have been the vestiges of earlier times; in still other cases, the regional coins may have been fully sanctioned and controlled by the central government, perhaps to fit with local preferences. The second and closely linked issue is copper money, which seems to have been done almost exclusively by provincial governments until late in the nineteenth century. The practices adopted by governors seem to have differed considerably, and it is not clear which approaches were most common and which were unusual.

On a different front, the cycle of fiscal problems and coin debasement deserves further exploration. It is not clear how effective at addressing the state's fiscal problem was debasement compared to such other techniques as raising exactions from provincial governors. Nor is there good evidence on what role the debasement/fiscal shortfall cycle played in the weakening of the Safavid state. From what little we know, a plausible argument could be made that bad monetary policy was an important part of the Safavid's downfall, which if true would be an interesting example of how monetary policy affected pre-modern states

Indeed, there are many other issues we wish we had the time and opportunity to explore in more detail. But such is the curse of the historian, always wishing to know more.

Bibliography

Archival Sources

The Netherlands

National Archief (*NA*), The Hague. Eerste afdeling (first section).

Records of the Verenigde Oostindische Compagnie (VOC) (Dutch East Indies Company).

Overgekomen brieven en papieren (Letters and papers received). Vols. 1139, 1146, 1150, 1162, 1174, 1177, 1178bis, 1185, 1201, 1203, 1210, 1224, 1226, 1233, 1234, 1226, 1242, 1243, 1252, 1265, 1284, 1285, 1291, 1292, 1297, 1304, 1307, 1315, 1332, 1343, 1352, 1360, 1364, 1372, 1398, 1406, 1425, 1434, 1448, 1459, 1476, 1493, 1501, 1507, 1549, 1559, 1642, 1644, 1667, 1694, 1714, 1732, 1737, 1763 1776, 1798, 1812, 1848, 1856, 1857, 1870, 1877, 1879, 1886, 1897, 1913, 1947, 2186, 2232, 2252, 2253, 2254, 2255, 2269, 2322, 2323, 2357, 2426, 2416, 2417, 2448, 2476, 2477, 2510, 2511, 2537, 2546, 2584, 2593, 2680, 2705, 2724, 2748, 2864, 2885, 3003.

Bataviasch uitgaande brievenboek (Batavia's outgoing letterbook). Vols. 783, 873, 882, 866, 968, 1009, 1015.

Collectie Geleynssen de Jong Vol. 141, 147.

Great Britain

India Office Records (IOR), London.

Records of the English East India Company (EIC).

Letters from Persia. Original Correspondence. Vols. E/3/11–E/3/52.

Factory Records Persia and Persian Gulf G/36/92, G/40/2–G/40/5.

National Archives, Kew Gardens, Great Britain.

FO (Foreign Office) Files. Public Record Office, London (transcripts of Crown copy-right records in the PRO appear by permission of Her Majesty's Stationary Office). FO 60/125, 157, 248, 314, 456, 542 and 581. FO 881/5728 and 5808.

State Papers Vol. 110/20.

Archives of the British Bank of the Middle East (BBME) (held by the HSBC), London.

France

Bibliothèque Nationale, Paris.

[Vachet], 'Journal d'un voyage en Perse commencé au mois de décembre de l'année 1689'. Mss. Fr. 24516.

Archives des Affaires Etrangères, Paris.

MD, Perse 5 and 8.

Documents and Collections

Accounts and Papers (*AP*) Government of Great Britain, Parliamentary Papers.
Baladouni, Vahe and Margaret Makepeace (eds). *Armenian Merchants of the Seventeenth and Early Eighteenth Centuries: English East India Company Sources.* Philadelphia: American Philosophical Society, 1998.
Berchet, Gugliemo (ed.). *La Repubblica di Venezia e la Persia.* Turin: G.B. Paravia e Comp., 1865; repr. Tehran: Imp. Org. f. Soc. Services, 1976.
Brosset, M.-F. (ed.) and trans. *Collection d'historiens arméniens.* 2 vols. St. Petersburg: Imprimerie de l'Académie impériale des sciences, 1874.
—— (ed.) and trans. *Histoire de la Géorgie depuis l'antiquité jusqu'au XIXe siècle.* 2 vols. St. Petersburg: Imprimerie de l'Académie impériale des sciences, 1849–58.
Chick, H. (ed.) and trans. *A Chronicle of the Carmelites in Persia and the Papal Mission of the XVIIth and XVIIIth Centuries.* 2 vols. London, 1939; repr. London: I.B.Tauris, 2012.
Coolhaas, W.Ph. (ed.). *Generale Missieven van Gouverneurs-Generaal en Raden aan Heren XVII der Verenigde Oostindische Compagnie*, 8 vols. The Hague, 1960–1985.
Diplomatic and Consular Deports (*DCR*), Government of Great Britain, Parliamentary Papers:
(a) Miscellaneous Series no. 590, 'Report on the Trade and General Condition of the City and Province of Kermanshah', by Mr. H.L. Rabino (cited as DCR 590).
(b) Annual Series: DCR no. 241, 318, 445, 1671, 2260, 2896, 3729, 3953, 4179, 4794, 4811, 4994, 5048, 5083.
Dunlop, H. (ed.). *Bronnen tot de geschiedenis der Oostindische Compagnie in Perzië.* The Hague: Martinus Nijhoff, 1930.
Foster, William (ed.). *The English Factories in India 1618–1669.* 13 vols. Oxford: Clarendon Press, 1906–27.
Hakluyt, Richard. *The Principal Navigations, Voyages, Traffiques and Discoveries of the English Nation.* 8 vols. London, J. M. Dent & Sons, ltd.; New York, E.P. Dutton & Co., 1907.
Lorimer, John Gordon (ed.). *Gazetteer of the Persian Gulf, Oman and Central Arabia.* Calcutta. 2 vols in 6 tomes. Calcutta: Superintendent Government Printing, India, 1915.
MacLean, H. W. *Report on the Conditions and Prospects of British Trade in Persia.* London: HMSO, 1904.
Military Report on Persia. 4 vols. Simla: General Staff, 1924.
Morgan, E. Delmar and C.H. Coote (eds). *Early Voyages and Travels to Russia and Persia.* 2 vols. London: Printed for the Hakluyt Society, 1886; repr. New York: B. Franklin, 1967.
Purchas, Samuel. *Hakluytus Posthumus or Purchas His Pilgrimes.* 8 vols. Glasgow: J. Maclehose and Sons, 1905.
Sainsbury, *Calendar of State Papers, Colonial Series, East Indies, China and Persia, 1625–1629.* London: HMSO, 1884.
Saldanha, J.A. *The Persian Gulf Précis* 8 vols. Calcutta: Superintendant of Govt. Printing, 1906; Repr. Gerrards Cross, 1986.

Published Primary Sources

Abraham of Crete. *The Chronicle of Abraham of Crete.* Trans. and edited by George A. Bournoutian. Costa Mesa, 1999.
Amin al-Dowleh, Mirza `Ali Khan. *Khaterat-e siyasi.* Edited by Hafez Farmanfarma'iyan. Tehran: Ketabha-ye Iran, 1339/1960.
Arnold, A. *Through Persia by Caravan.* New York: Harper and Bros., 1877.
Asaf, Mohammad Hashem. *Rostam al-Tavarikh.* Edited by Mohammad Moshiri. Tehran: Amir Kabir, 1348/1969.

Astarabadi, Mirza Mehdi Khan. *Tarikh-e Jahangosha-ye Naderi*. Tehran: Donya-ye Ketab, 1368/1989.

Baker, Valentine. *Clouds in the East: Travels and Adventures on the Turkoman Frontier*. London: Chatto and Windus, 1876.

Bakikhanov, `Abbas Qoli Aqa. *The Heavenly Rose-Garden. A History of Shirvan & Daghestan*. Trans. by Willem Floor and Hasan Javadi. Washington DC: Mage, 2009.

Ballantine, Henry. *Midnight Marches through Persia*. Boston: Lee and Shephard, 1879.

Barbosa, Duarte. *The Book of Duarte Barbosa*. Trans. by Mansel Longworth. London: Printed for the Hakluyt Society, 1908.

Basir al-Molk Seystani. *Ruznameh-ye khaterat-e Basirat al-Molk Seystani*. Tehran: Ashna, 1374/1995.

Basseer. 'The Role of Financial Intermediaries in Economic Development: The Case of Iran, 1888–1978', DBA 1983 George Washington University, 81–112.

Basset, J. *Persia, the Land of the Imams*. London: Blackie, 1887.

Benn, Edith Fraser. *An Overland Trek from India*. London: Longmans, 1901.

Berichte über Handel und Industrie. Band 14, Heft 7, Juni 1910.

Beygdeli, Mohammad Reza (ed.). *Tarikh-e Beygdeli. Madarek va Asnad*. Tehran: Bu `Ali, 1367/1988.

Bidlisi, Sharaf Khan. *Cherefnameh ou Histoire des Kourdes*. Edited by V. Vel'iaminof-Zernof, 2 vols. St. Petersburg: L'Académie impériale des sciences, 1860–62.

Binning, R.B.M. *A Journal of Two Years' Travel in Persia, Ceylon, etc.* 2 vols. London: Wm. H. Allen & Co, 1857.

Blau, Otto. *Die commerzielle Zustände Persiens*. Vienna: Decker, 1858.

Bourges, M. de. *Relation du voyage de monsigneur l'évêque de Beryte, vicaire apostolique du royaume de la Cochinchine par la Turquie, la Perse, les Indes, etc. jusqu'au royaume de Siam & autres lieux*. Paris: D. Bechet, 1668.

Bradley-Birt, F.B. *Persia - through Persia from the Gulf to the Caspian*. New York: E.P. Dutton and Co., 1909.

Chardin, Jean. *Voyages du Chevalier Chardin en Perse etc.* Edited by L. Langlès, 10 vols. and atlas. Paris: Le Normant, 1811.

Chardin, John. *Travels in Persia 1663-1677*. Repr. Mineola NY: Dover Books, 1988.

Chelebi, Evliya. *Travels in Iran and the Caucasus 1652 and 1655*. Trans. and annotated by Hasan Javadi and Willem Floor. Washington DC: Mage, 2010.

Conolly, Arthur. *Journey to the North of India*. 2 vols. London: Richard Bentley, 1834.

Cook, John. *Voyages and Travels through the Russian Empire, Tartary, and Part of the Kingdom of Persia*. 2 vols. Edinburgh: Printed for the author, 1770; repr. Newtonville: Oriental Research Partners, 1997.

Curzon, G.N. *Persia and the Persian Question*. 2 vols. London-New York: Longmans, Green and Co., 1892; repr. London: Cass, 1966.

D'Allemagne, Henri-Réné. *Du Khorasan au Pays des Backhtiaris*. 4 vols. Paris: Hachette, 1911.

De Bode, C.A. *Travels in Luristan and Arabistan*. 2 vols. London: J. Madden & Co., 1845.

De Bruyn, Cornelis. *Reizen over Moskovie, door Persie en Indie*. Amsterdam: Rudolph en Gerard Wetstein, Joannes Oosterwyk, Hendrik van de Gaete, 1714.

De Sercey, Comte. *Une Ambassade extraordinaire. La Perse en 1839–1840*. Paris: L'Artisan du livre, 1928.

Della Valle, Pietro. *Viaggi di Pietro della Valle il pellegrino*, 2 vols. Edited by C. Gancia. Brighton, 1843.

——. 'Extract of the Travels of Della Valle' In John Pinkerton (ed.), *A General Collection of Voyages and Travels*. vol. 9. London: Longman, Hurst, Reese and Orme, 1811.

Dickson, William Edmund Ritchie. *East Persia. A Backwater of the Great War*. London: E. Arnold, 1924.

Don Juan. *Don Juan of Persia. A Shi`ah Catholic 1560-1604*. Trans. and edited by G. Le Strange. London: George Routledge and Sons, 1926.

Du Mans, Raphaël. *Estat de la Perse.* Edited by Charles Schefer. Paris: E. Leroux, 1890.

Dunlop, H. *Perzië, Voorheen en thans.* Haarlem: De Erven F. Bohn, 1912.

Dupré, A. *Voyage en Perse fait dans les années 1807, 1808, 1809.* 2 vols. Paris: J.G. Dentu, 1819.

Eastwick, E.B. *Journal of a Diplomat's Three Years' Residence in Persia.* 2 vols. London: Smith, Elder & Co, 1864.

Ehtesham al-Saltaneh. *Khaterat-e Ehtesham al-Saltaneh.* Tehran: Zavvar, 1366/1989.

Eichwald, Eduard. *Reise auf dem Caspischen Meere und in den Caucasus unternommen in den Jahren 1825–1826.* 2 vols. Stuttgart und Tübingen: J.G. Cotta, 1834.

al-Esfahani, Mohammad Mehdi b. Mohammad Reza. *Nesf-e jahan fi ta`rif al-Isfahan.* Edited by Manuchehr Setudeh. Tehran: Amir Kabir, 1340/1961.

E`temad al-Saltaneh, Mohammad Hasan Khan. *Montazam-e Naseri.* 3 vols. Tehran (lithograph) 1298–1300/1880–83.

——. *Ruznameh-ye khaterat.* Edited by Iraj Afshar. Tehran: Amir Kabir, 1345/1966.

E`tesam al-Molk. *Safarnameh-ye Mirza Khanlar Khan E`tesam al-Molk.* Edited by Manuchehr Mahmudi. Tehran: Manuchehr Mahmudi, 1351/1972.

Ettehadiyeh, Mansureh and Sirus Sa`dvandiyan (eds). *Siyaq-e ma`shiyat dar `ahd-e Qajar. Hokmrani va molkdari* (majmu`eh-ye asnad-e `Abdol-Hoseyn Mirza Farmanfarma). 2 vols. Tehran: Tarikh-e Iran, 1362/1983.

Evliya Efendi (Çelebi). *Narative of Travels in Europe, Asia and Africa in the Seventeenth Century.* 2 vols. London: Printed for the Oriental Translation Fund of Great Britain and Ireland, 1834; repr. New York: Johnson Reprint Corp., 1968.

`Eyn al-Saltaneh, Qahraman Mirza Salur. *Ruznameh-ye khaterat.* 10 vols. Edited by Mas`ud Salur and Iraj Afshar. Tehran: Asatir, 1376/1997.

Fasa'i, Hajj Mirza Hasan. *Farsnameh-ye Naseri.* 2 vols. Tehran, lithograph, 1314–16/1894–96; repr. Tehran: Amir Kabir, 1357/1988.

Ferrier, J.P. *Caravan Journeys and Wanderings in Persia, Afghanistan, Turkistan and Beloochistan.* London: J. Murray, 1856.

Floyer, Ernest Ayscoghe. 'Journal of a Route from Jask to Bampur,' *JRGS* 47 (1877): 188–201.

——. *Unexplored Baluchistan.* London: Griffith & Farran; repr. Quetta: Gosha-e Adab, 1977.

Forbes, Frederick. 'Route from Turbat Haideri, in Khorasan, to the River Heri Rud, on the Borders of Sistan'. *JRGS* 14 (1844): 145–92.

Francklin, William. *Observations Made on a Tour from Bengal to Persia in the Years 1786–7.* London: T. Cadell, 1790; repr. Tehran: Imp. Org. for Soc. Services, 1976.

Fraser, J.B. *Narrative of a Journey into Khorasan in the Years 1821 & 1822.* London: Longman, Hurst, Rees, Orme, and Brown, 1825; repr. Delhi: Oxford University Press, 1984.

——. *Travels and Adventures in the Persian Provinces and the Southern Banks of the Caspian Sea.* London: Longman, Rees, Orme, Browne and Greene, 1826.

——. *Travels in Koordistan, Mesopotamia.* 2 vols. London: Richard Bentley, 1840.

——. 1838. *A Winter's Journey from Constantinople to Teheran,* 2 vols. London: Richard Bentley, 1838; repr. New York: Arno, 1973.

Fryer, John. *A New Account of East India and Persia Being Nine Years' Travels, 1672-1681.* 3 vols. Edited by William Crooke. London: Printed for the Hakluyt Society, 1909–15.

Fumeni, `Abd al-Fattah. *Tarikh-e Gilan dar vaqaye`-ye salha 923–1038 hejri qamari.* Edited by Manuchehr Setudeh. Tehran: Entesharat-e Bonyad-e Farhang-e Iran, 1349/1970.

Gemelli-Careri, Gio Francesco. *Giro del Mondo.* 6 vols. Napoli: Giuseppe Roselli, 1699.

Gmelin, Samuel Gottlieb. *Travels through Northern Persia 1770-1774.* Trans. by Willem Floor. Washington DC: Mage, 2007.

Gobineau, Joseph Arthur Comte de. *Trois ans en Asie.* In idem, *Oeuvres,* 29–401. Paris: Gallimard, 1983.

Goldsmidt, Sir F.J., et al. *Eastern Persia. An Account of the Journeys of the Persian Boundary Commission, 1870–71–72.* 2 vols. London: Macmillan and Co., 1876.

Golestaneh, Abu'l-Hasan Mohammad Amin. *Mojmal al-tavarikh.* Edited by Modarres Razavi. Tehran: Daneshgah, 2536/1977.

Gordon, Thomas Edward. *Persia Revisited.* London: Arnold, 1896.

Greenfield, J. *Die Verfassung des Persischen Staates.* Berlin: Franz Vahlen, 1904.

Grey, Charles (ed.) and trans. *A Narrative of Italian Travels in Persia in the Fifteenth and Sixteenth Century.* 2 vols. London: Printed for the Hakluyt Society, 1873.

Grothe, Hugo. *Wanderungen in Persien.* Berlin: Algemeiner Verein f. Deutsche Literatur, 1910.

Häntzsche, J.C. 'Specialstatistik von Persien' *Zeitschrift d. Gesellschaft fuer Erdkunde* 4 (1869): 429–49.

Hanway, Jonas. *An Historical Account of the British Trade over the Caspian Sea.* 4 vols. in 3 tomes. London: Dodsley & others, 1753.

Hedges, William. *The Diary of William Hedges, esq. (afterwards Sir William Hedges), during his Agency in Bengal: as well as on his Voyage out and Return Overland (1681–1697).* Edited by R. Barlow and H. Yule. 3 vols. London. Printed for the Hakluyt Society, 1887–89.

Herbert, Thomas. *Travels in Persia, 1627–1629.* Edited by W. Foster. London: George Routledge and Sons, 1929.

Höltzer, Ernst. *Persien vor 113 Jahren.* Edited by Mohammad Assemi. Tehran: Vezarat-e Farhang va Honar, 2535/1976.

Jamalzadeh, Mohammad `Ali. *Ganj- e Shayegan. Owza`-e eqtesadi-ye Iran.* Berlin: Kaveh, 1335/1916; repr. Tehran: Entesharat-e Daneshgah-e Tehran, 1376/1997.

Jaubert, P.Am. *Voyage en Armenie et la Perse.* Paris: Pélicier-Nepveu, 1821.

Jones, Sir Harford. *An Account of the Transaction of His Majesty's Mission to the Court of Persia in the Years 1807–11.* London, 1834 ; repr. Tehran : Imp. Org. f. Soc. Services, 1976.

Kaempfer, Engelbert. *Am Hofe des persischen Grosskönigs (1684–85). Das erste Buch der Amoenitates exoticae in deutscher Bearbeitung.* Trans. and edited by Walther Hinz. Leipzig 1940; repr. Tübingen: Horst Erdmann Verlag, 1977.

Khatunabadi, Sayyed `Abd al-Hoseyn. Vaqaye` al-sennin va al-a`vam. Gozareshha-ye saliyaneh az ebteda-ye khelqat ta sal-e 1195 Hejri. Tehran: ketabforushi-ye Eslamiyeh, 1352/1973.

Khvandamir. *Habib al-Seyar.* 4 vols. Edited by Mohammad Dabir-Siyaqi. Tehran: Ketabforushi-ye Khayyam, 1362/1983.

Kosogovski, V.A. *Khaterat-e Kolonel Kasakufski.* Trans. by `Abbasqoli Halabi. Tehran: Ketabha-ye Simorgh, 1344/1965.

Kroell, Anne (ed.). *Nouvelles d'Ispahan 1665–1695.* Paris: Société d'histoire de l'Orient, 1979.

Krusinski, Judas Tadeuzs. *The History of the Late Revolutions of Persia.* 2 vols. London: Printed for J. Pemberton, 1733.

Küss, W. *Handelsratgeber für Persien.* Berlin: Selbstverlag, 1911.

Lacy O'Brien, H. de. *Banking in Persia.* London, 1873.

Landor, A.H.S. *Across Coveted Lands.* 2 vols. London : Charles Scribners Son, 1902.

Le Bruyn, Cornelius. *Travels into Moscovy, Persia and part of the East-Indies*, 2 vols. London: A. Bettesworth, 1737.

Leandro di S. Cecilia, F. *Persia, ovvero secondo viaggio d'Oriente.* Rome: Angelo Rotilj, 1753.

Lerch Johann Jacob. 'Nachricht von der zweiten Reise nach Persien welche der kaiserl. Russische Collegienrath Herr Dr. Johann Jacob Lerch von 1745 bis 1747 gethan hat'. *Magazin für die neue Historie und Geographie* (*Büschings Magazin* X). Halle, 1776, 376–476.

Lockyer, Charles. *An Account of Trade in India.* London: Printed for the author and sold by Samuel Crouch, 1711.

Lorini, E. *La Persia economica contemporeana e la sua questione monetaria.* Rome: Ermanno Loescher, 1900; repr. Tehran: Imp. Org. f. Soc. Services, 1976.

MacGregor, Charles Metcalfe. *Narrative of a Journey through the Province of Khorasan and the N.W. Frontier of Afghanistan in 1875.* 2 vols. London: W.H. Allen & Co, 1879.

MacKenzie, Charles F. *Safarnama-ye Shomal.* Trans. by Mansureh Ettehadiyeh. Tehran: Gostareh, 1359/1980.

Malcolm, John. *The History of Persia.* 2 vols. London: J. Murray, 1815.

Marsh, H.C. *A Ride through Islam.* London: Tinsley Brothers, 1877.

Marvi, Mohammad Kazemi. *'Alamara-ye Naderi.* Edited by Mohammad Amin Riyahi. Tehran: Nashr-e 'Elm, 1369/1990.

Mashizi (Bardsiri), Mir Mohammad Sa'id Mashizi. *Tazkereh-ye Safaviyeh-ye Kerman.* Edited by Mohammad Bastani-Parizi. Tehran: Nashr-e 'Elm, 1369/1990.

Melgunof, Gregorii Valerianovich. *Das Suedliche Ufer des Kaspischen Meeres.* Leipzig: Leopold Voss, 1868.

Membré, Michele. *Mission to the Lord Sophy of Persia (1539–1542).* Trans. and edited by A.H. Morton. London: School of Oriental and African Studies, 1993.

Milburn, William. *Oriental Commerce.* 2 vols. London: Black, Parry & Co, 1813.

Minorsky, Vladimir (ed.) and trans. *The Tadhkirat al-Mulūk, A Manual of Safavid Administration.* Cambridge: Cambridge University Press, 1943; repr. 1980.

Mirza Mohammad. *Ruznameh-ye Mirza Mohammad Kalantar-e Fars.* Edited by 'Abbas Eqbal. Tehran: Sherkat-e Chap, 1340/1961.

Mitford, Edward Ledwich. *A Land March from England to Ceylon Forty Years Ago.* 2 vols. London: Allen & Co., 1884.

Mofidi Bafqi, Mohammad Mostowfi-ye. *Jame'-ye Mofidi.* 3 vols. Edited by Iraj Afshar. Tehran: Asadi, 1340/1961.

Momtahen al-Dowleh. *Khaterat-e Momtahen al-Dowleh. Zendeginameh-ye Mirza Mehdi Khan Momtahen al-Dowleh.* Tehran: Amir Kabir, 1353/1974.

Monajjem, Molla Jalal al-Din. *Tarikh-e 'Abbasi. Ruznameh-ye 'Abbasi ya Ruznameh-ye Molla Jalal.* Edited by Seyfollah Vahidniya. Tehran: Vahid, 1366/1967.

Monshi, Eskander Beg. *Tarikh-e 'Alamara-ye 'Abbasi.* 2 vols. Edited by Iraj Afshar. Tehran: Amir Kabir, 1350/1971.

——. *History of Shah 'Abbas the Great* (translation of Monshi) 2 vols. Trans. and edited by R.M. Savory. Boulder: Westview Press, 1978.

Al-Monshi, Mahmud Ebn Ebrahim al-Hoseyni. *Tarikh-e Ahmad Shahi.* 2 vols. Moscow: Edareh-ye Entesharat-e Danesh, 1974.

Morier, James. *A Journey through Persia, Armenia and Asia Minor in the Years 1808 and 1809.* London: Longman, Hurst, Rees, Orme, and Brown, 1812.

——. *A Second Journey through Persia, Armenia, and Asia Minor ... between the Years 1810 and 1816.* London: Longman, Hurst, Rees, Orme, and Brown, 1818.

Mostowfi, 'Abdollah. *Sharh-e zendegani-ye man.* 3 vols. Tehran: Zavvar, n.d; 3rd edn 1371/1992.

Mostowfi, Hamdallah. *The Geographical Part of Nuzhat al-Qulub.* Edited by Guy le Strange. Leiden, E.J. Brill; London, Luzac & Co, 1915–19.

Mostowfi, Mohammad Mohsen. *Zobdat al-Tavarikh.* Edited by Behruz Gowdarzi. Tehran: Mowqufat-e Doktor Mahmud Afshar, 1375/1996.

Mounsey, A.H. *A Journey through the Caucasus and the interior of Persia.* London: Smith, Elder & Co., 1872.

Nasiri, Mirza Naqi. *Titles & Emoluments in Safavid Iran.* Trans. and annotated by Willem Floor. Washington DC: Mage, 2008.

Nasiri, Mohammad Ebrahim b. Zeyn al-'Abedin. *Dastur-e Shahriyaran.* Edited by Mohammad Nader Nasiri Moqaddam. Tehran: Entesahrat-e adabi va tarikhi-ye Mowqufat-e Doktor Mahmud Afshar Yazdi, 1373/1995.

Nasrabadi, Mirza Mohammad Taher. *Tazkereh-ye Nasrabadi.* Edited by Vahid Dastgerdi. Tehran: Ketabforushi-yi Furughi, 1361/1982).

Nezam al-Saltaneh Mafi. *Khaterat va asnad-e Hoseyn Qoli Khan Nezam al-Saltaneh Mafi.* 2 vols. Edited by Ma`sumeh Nezam Mafi, Mansureh Ettehadiyeh, Sirus Sa`dvandiyan, and Hamid Rampisheh. Tehran: Tarikh-e Iran, 1361/1982.

Nizam al-Mulk, *The Book of Government, or, Rules for Kings: The Siyar al-Muluk, or, Siyasatnama of Nizam al-Mulk.* Trans. by Hubert Drake. Richmond, Surrey: Curzon, 2002.

O'Donovan, Edmond. *The Merv Oasis.* 2 vols. London: Smith, Elder & Co., 1882.

Olearius, Adam. *Vermehrte newe Beschreibung der muscowitischen und persischen Reyse.* Edited by D. Lohmeier. Schleswig, 1656, facs. repr. Tubingen: Niemeyer, 1971.

Olivier, G.A. *Voyage dans l'Empire Othoman, l'Egypte et la Perse.* 6 vols. Paris: Agasse, 1802–07.

Orsolle, E. *Le Caucase et la Perse.* Paris: E. Poon, Nourrit et cie., 1885.

Ouseley, William. *Travels in Various Countries of the East, more particularly Persia.* 3 vols. London: Rodwell & Martin, 1819–23.

Polak, Jakob Eduard. *Persien, Das Land und seine Bewohner.* 2 vols. Leipzig: F.A. Brockhaus, 1856; repr. Hildesheim-New York: Georg Olms, 1976.

Porter, Robert Ker. *Travels in Georgia, Persia, Armenia ... during the years 1817, 1818, 1819, and 1820.* 2 vols. London: Longman, Hurst, Reese, Orme, and Brown, 1821–22.

Poullet, P.A. *Nouvelles relations du Levant.* 2 vols. Paris: Chez Louys Billaine, 1667.

Preece, J.R. 'Journey from Shiraz to Jashk, via Darab, Forg, and Minab,' *RGS*, Supplementary Paper I (1885): 403–37.

Qazvini, Budaq Monshi. *Javaher al-akhbar.* Edited by Mohsen Bahramnezhad. Tehran: Miras-e Ketab, 1378/2000.

Rabino, J. 'Banking in Persia', *Journal of the Institute of Bankers* 13 (1892): 1–56.

——. 'An Economist's Notes on Persia', *Journal of the Royal Statistical Society* 64 (1901): 265–82.

Rashvand, Mohammad `Ali Khan. *Mojmal-e Rashvand.* Tehran: Ayeneh-ye Miras, 1376/1997.

Richard, Francis (ed.). *Raphaël du Mans, missionnaire en Perse au XVIIè s.* 2 vols. Paris: L'Harmattan, 1995.

Rumlu, Hoseyn Beg. *Ahsan al-tavarikh.* Edited by `Abd al-Hoseyn Nava'i. Tehran: Babak 1357/1978.

Sam Mirza, *Tazkereh-ye Tohfat-e Sami.* Edited by Rokn al-Din Homayun Farrokh. Tehran: Asatir, 2nd edn, 1384/2005.

Sanson, F. *Estat présent du royaume de Perse.* Paris: Veuve de J. Langlois, 1694.

Schillinger, Franz Casper. *Persianische und Ost-Indianische Reis.* Nuremberg: Lochner, 1707.

Schlimmer, Joh. L. *Terminologie Médico-Pharmaceutique: Française - Persane.* Tehran (lithograph), 1874; repr. Tehran: Daneshgah, 1349/1970.

Schwartz, Benjamin (ed.). *Letters from Persia written by Charles and Edward Burgess 1828–1855.* New York: NY Public Library, 1942.

Sheil, Lady. *Glimpses of Life and Manners in Persia.* London: J. Murray, 1856; repr. New York: Arno, 1973.

Shirazi, `Abdi Beg. *Takmilat al-akhbar (Tarikh-e Safaviyeh az aghaz ta 978 h.q.).* Edited by `Abdol-Hoseyn Nava'i. Tehran: Nashr-e Ney, 1369/1990.

Sirjani, Sa`idi (ed.). *Vaqaye`-ye Ettefaqiyeh - gozareshha-ye khofiyeh-nevisan-e Englisi.* Tehran: Entesharat-e Novin, 1361/1982.

Sistani, Malek Shah Hoseyn b. Malek Ghayas al-Din Mohammad b. Shah Mahmud. *Ehya al-Moluk.* Edited by Manuchehr Setudeh. Tehran: Bongah-e tarjomeh va nashr-e ketab 1344/1966.

Siyaqi-Nezam, 'Fotuhat-e Homayun (Les Victoires augustes, 1007/1598)'. Edited and trans. by Chahryar Adle. Dissertation, Paris, 1976.

Southgate, Horatio. *Narrative of a Tour through Armenia, Kurdistan, Persia and Mesopotamia.* 2 vols. New York: D. Appleton and Co., 1840.

Speelman, Cornelis. *Journaal der reis van den gezant der O.I. Compagnie Joan Cunaeus naar Perzië in 1651–1652*. Edited by A. Hotz. Amsterdam: Johannes Müller, 1908.
Stewart, Col. C.E. *Through Persia in Disguise*. London: George Routledge & Sons, 1911.
Stirling, Edward. *The Journals of Edward Stirling in Persia and Afghanistan 1828–1829*. Edited by Jonathan L. Lee Naples: Istituto universitario orientale, Dipartimento di studi asiatici, Istituto italiano per il Medio ed Estremo Oriente, 1991.
Stocqueler, J.H. *Fifteen Months' Pilgrimage through untrodden Tracts of Khuzistan and Persia*. London: Saunders and Otley, 1832.
Stolze, F. and F.C. Andreas. 'Die Handelsverhältnisse Persiens', *Petermanns Mitteilungen*. Ergänzungsheft nr. 77/1885. Gotha: Justus Perthes.
Stotherd, E.A.W. Lt. *South-West Persia. A Reconnaissance from Bushire to Arsinjan via Lake Niriz*. Simla, Govt. Central Printing Office.
Strabo. *The Geography of Strabo*. Edited by Leonard Jones and J R Sitlington Sterrett. Cambridge, Mass.: Harvard University Press, 1960–69.
Struys, Jan Janszoon. *Drie aanmerkelijke en seer rampspoedige Reysen Door Italien, Griekenlandt, Lijflandt, Moscovien, Tartarijen, Meden, Persien, Oost-Indien, Japan, en verscheyden andere Gewesten*. Amsterdam, by Jacob van Meurs, op de Keysers-Graft, en Johannes van Someren, in de Kalverstraat, 1676.
Tahvildar, Mirza Hoseyn Khan. *Joghrafiya-ye Esfahan*. Edited by Manuchehr Setudeh. Tehran: Entesharat-e Daneshgah-e Tehran, 1342/1963.
Tate, G. *The Frontiers of Baluchistan: Travels on the Borders of Persia and Afghanistan*. London: Witherby and Co., 1909.
Tavernier, Jean-Baptiste. *Les Six voyages de Turquie et de Perse*. 2 vols. Paris: G. Clouzier, 1676.
Texeira, P. *The Travels of Pedro Teixeira*. Edited and trans. by W.F. Sinclair. London: Printed for the Hakluyt Society, 1902.
Thévenot, Jean de. *Livre troisième de la suite du voyage de Mr. de Thévenot au Levant*. Paris: C. Angot, 1689.
——. *Suite du voyage de Levant*. Paris: C. Angot, 1674.
——. *The Travels of M. de Thevenot into the Levant*. Trans. by Archibald Lovell. London: Printed by H. Clark, for H. Faithorne, J. Admason, and C. Skegnes and T. Newborough, 1687; repr. Westmead, 1971.
Torkaman, Eskandar Beyg and Mohammad Yusof Mo'arrekh. *Zeyl-e tarikh-e `alam-ara-ye `Abbasi*. Edited by Soheyli Khvansari. Tehran: Ketabforushi-ye Eslamiyeh, 1317/1938.
Tournefort, Jean Pitton de. *Relation du voyage du Levant*. 2 vols. Paris: Imprimerie royale, 1717.
Vahid Qazvini, Mohammad Taher. *Tarikh-e jahan-ara-ye `Abbasi*. Edited by Sayyed Sa`id Mir Mohammad Sadeq. Tehran: Pazhuheshgah-e `olum-e ensani, 1383/2004.
[Villotte, Jacques]. *Voyages d'un missionaire de la Compagnie de Jésus en Turquie, en Perse, en Armenie*. Paris: J. Vincent, 1730.
Von Riederer, G.S. Ritter. *Aus Persien*. Vienna: R. von Waldheim, 1882.
Waring, Edward Scott. *A Tour to Sheeraz*. London; T. Cadell and W. Davies, 1807; repr. New York: Arno Press, 1973.
Wills, C.J. *In the Land of the Lion and the Sun*. London: Macmillan and Co., 1893.
Wilson, S.G. *Persian Life and Customs*. New York and Chicago: F.H. Revell Co., 1895.
Yate, C.E. *Khurasan and Sistan*. London and Edinburgh: W. Blackwood, 1900.
Zak`aria of Agulis. *The Journal of Zak`aria of Agulis*. Translated by George A. Bournoutian. Costa Mesa, Cal.: Mazda, 2003.
Zarrabi, `Abdol-Rahim. *Tarikh-e Kashan*. Edited by Iraj Afshar. Tehran: Ebn Sina, 1342/1963.

Modern Studies

Abduallaev, Z.Z. *Promyshlennost i zarozhdenie rabochego klassa Irana v kontse XIX-nacale XX vv.* Baku, 1963. As translated and printed in Issawi, *Economic History*, 299.

Adamiyat, Fereydun. *Andisheh-ye taraqqi va hokumat-e qanun-e `asr-e Sepahsalar.* Tehran: Amir Kabir, 1351/1972.

Afshar, Iraj. 'Enqelab-e deram dar zaman-e shah`Abbas-e dovvom', *Tarikh. Zamimeh-ye majalleh-ye daneshkadeh-ye adabiyat va `olum-e ensani* 1 (2535/1976): 267–74.

`Ala' al-Dini, Bahram. *Sekkehha-ye mesi-ye Iran.* Tehran: Yasavoli, 1391/2013.

Album, Stephen. *Checklist of Islamic Coins.* Santa Rosa: Steven Album Rare Coins, 3rd edn, 2011.

——. 'Iranian Silver Denominational Names, 907–1295/1501–1878, part one'. *Pricelist* 52 (1987): 20.

——. 'The Coinage of Nur Award, Atabeg of Lur Buzurg, 751–57 H./A.D. 1350–56', *The American Numismatic Society Museum Notes* 22 (1977): 213–39.

Album, Stephen, Michael L. Bates and Willem Floor. 'Coins and Coinage,' *EIr.* 6 (1993): 14–41.

Allen, James W. and Willem Floor. 'Copper'. *EIr.* 6 (1993): 258–60.

Amanat, Abbas (ed.). *Cities & Trade: Consul Abbott on the Economy and Society of Iran 1847-1866.* London: Ithaca, 1983.

Amin, A.A. *British Interests in the Persian Gulf.* Leiden: E.J. Brill, 1967.

Arasaratnam, Sinnappah. *Merchants, Companies and Commerce on the Coromandel Coast.* New Delhi: Oxford University Press, 1986.

Ardakani, Hoseyn Mahbubi. *Tarikh-e mo'assasat-e tamaddoni-ye jadid dar Iran.* 2 vols. Tehran: Entesharat-e Daneshgah-e Tehran, 1353/1974.

Arunova, M.R. and K.Z. Ashrafiyan. *Gosudarstvo Nadir-Shakha Afshara. Ocherki obshchestvernnykh otnoshenii v Irane 30-40-x godov XVIII veke.* Moscow: Izd-vo vostochnoi lit-ry, 1958.

Astarabadi, Mirza Mehdi Khan. *Tarikh-e Jahangosha-ye Naderi.* Tehran: Donya-ye Ketab, 1368/1989.

Attman, Artur. *The Bullion Flow between Europe and the East 1000–1750.* Gothenburg: Kungl. vetenskaps- och vitterhets-samhället, 1981.

——. *The Russian and Polish Markets in International Trade 1500–1650.* Gothenburg: Institute of Economic History of Gothenburg University, 1973.

Aubin, Jean. 'L'avènement des Safavides reconsidéré'. *Le Moyen Orient et l'Océan Indien* 5 (1988): 1–130.

——. 'Deux sayyids de Bam au XVe siècle. Contribution à l'histoire de l'Iran Timouride'. *Akademie der Wissenschaften und der Literatur. Abhandlung der geistes- und sozialwissenschaftlichen Klasse* 7 (1956): 375–501.

Avery, P.W, B.G. Fragner and J.B. Simmons. '`Abbasi'. *EIr.* 1 (1985): 86.

Avery, P.W. and J.B. Simmons. 'Persia on a Cross of Silver 1880–1890.' In Elie Kedourie and Sylvia G. Haim (eds), *Towards a Modern Iran: Studies in Thought, Politics and Society*, 1–37. London: Frank Cass, 1980.

Axworthy, Michael. *The Sword of Persia. Nader Shah from Tribal Warrior to Conquering Tyrant.* London: I.B.Tauris, 2006.

Bacqué-Grammont, Jean-Louis. *Les Ottomans, les Safavides et leurs voisins.* Istanbul: Nederlands Historisch-Archeologisch Instituut te Istanbul, 1987.

Baiburtian, Vagan Arakelovich. *Armianskaia koloniia novoi Dzhul'fy v XVII veke.* Erevan: Izd-vo AN Armianskoi SSR, 1969.

Bakhash. 'The Failure of Reform: The Prime Ministership of Amîn al-Dawla, 1897–8'. In Edmund Bosworth and Carole Hillenbrand (eds), *Qajar Iran: Political, Social, and Cultural Change 1800–1925*, 14–33. Edinburgh: University of Edinburgh Press, 1983.

Barrett, Ward. 'World Bullion Flows, 1450–1800'. In James Tracy (ed.), *The Rise of Merchant Empires: Long-distance Trade in the Early Modern World 1350–1750*, 224–54. Cambridge: Cambridge University Press, 1990.

Bastani Parizi, Mohamamad Ebrahim. *Ganj `Ali Khan*, Tehran: Asatir, 3rd edn 1368/1987.

Benn, Edith Fraser. *An Overland Trek from India*. London: Longmans, Green & Co., 1909.

Berichte über Handel und Industrie. Band 14, Heft 7, Juni 1910.

Beygdeli, Mohammad Reza (ed.). *Tarikh-e Beygdeli. Madarek va Asnad*. Tehran: Bu `Ali, 1367/1988.

Biddulph, C.H. 'Countermarked Mughal and Suri Coins'. *Journal of the Numismatic Society of India* 25 (1963): 39–46.

Bosworth, Edmund C.E. *The Ghaznavids, their Empire in Afghanistan and Eastern Iran 994:1040*. Edinburgh: Edinburgh University Press, 1963.

Bournoutian, George A. *Eastern Armenia in the Last Decades of Persian Rule 1807–1828*. Malibu: Undena, 1982.

Braudel, Fernand. *The Mediterranean and the Mediterranean World in the Age of Philip II*, 2 vols. Transl. by Siyân Reynolds. New York: Harper & Row, 1972; repr. Berkeley: University of California Press, 1995.

Braudel, F. and F.C. Spooner. 'Prices in Europe from 1450 to 1750'. In *The Cambridge Economic History of Europe*, vol. 4, 378–486. Cambridge, 1967.

Broome, Michael. *A Handbook of Islamic Coins*. London: Seaby, 1985.

Browne, Horatio F. 'A Report on the Condition of Persia in the Year 1586: Lettera, Sacra Cattolica Real Maestà', *The English Historical Review* 7 (1892): 314–21.

Bushev, P.P. *Posol'stvo Artemii Volynskogo v Iran v 1715–1718 gg*. Moscow: Nauka, 1978.

Chaudhuri, K.N. *The Trading World of Asia and the English East India Company 1660–1760*. Cambridge: Cambridge University Press, 1978.

Dale, Stephen. *Indian Merchants and Eurasian Trade, 1600–1750*. Cambridge: Cambridge University Press, 1994.

Davidovich, Elena A. 'The Monetary Reform of Muhammad Shibani Khan in 913–914/1507–08'. In Devin DeWeese (ed.), *Studies on Central Asian History in Honor of Yuri Bregel*, 129–85. Bloomington Indiana University Press, 2001.

——. *Istoriia denezhnogo obrashcheniia srednevekovoi Srednei Azii. Mednye monety XV-pervoi chetverti XVI v. v Maverrnnakhre*. Moscow: Moskva: Izd-vo 'Nauka', Glav. red. vostochnoi lit-ry, 1983.

Davis, Ralph. *Aleppo and Devonshire Square: English Traders in the Levant in the Eighteenth Century*, London: Macmillan, 1969.

Deyel, John S. 'The Development of Akbar's Currency System and Monetary Integration of the Conquered Kingdoms'. In John F. Richards (ed.), *The Imperial Monetary System of Mughal India*, 13–67. Oxford: Oxford University Press, 1987; repr. New Delhi, 2000.

Ederer, R.J. *The Evolution of Money*, Washington, DC, 1964.

Emerson, John and Willem Floor. 'Rahdars and their Tolls in Safavid and Afsharid Iran'. *JESHO* 30 (1987): 318–27.

Entner, Marvin L. *Russo-Persian Commercial Relations, 1828–1914*. Gainsville, Fl: Florida University Press, 1965.

Ettinghausen, Richard. 'Stylistic Tendencies at the Time of Shah `Abbas'. *IS* 7 (1974): 593–628.

Farahani, Daryush Shahbazi. *Tarikh-e sekkeh (dowreh-ye Qajar)*. Tehran: Pelikan, 1380/2001.

Faroqhi, Suraiya. *Pilgrims and Sultans: The Hajj under the Ottomans 1517–1683*. London and New York: I.B.Tauris, 1994.

Ferrier, R.W. 'British-Persian Relations in the 17th Century'. Dissertation, Cambridge University, 1970.

——. 'An English View of Persian Trade in 1618'. *JESHO* 19 (1976): 182–214.

Floor, Willem. '`Abbasi'. *EI*^{3}.

——. *Commercial Conflict between Persia and the Netherlands 1712-1718.* Durham, UK: University of Durham Occasional Paper Series no. 37, 1988.
——. 'The Decline of the Dutch East Indies Company in Bandar `Abbas (1747–1759)'. *Moyen-Orient et Ocean Indien* 6 (1989): 45–80
——. 'Coal'. *EIr.* 5 (1992): 871–73.
——. 'The Dutch on Khark Island: A Commercial Mishap'. *IJMES* 24 (1992): 441–60.
——. *The Afghan Occupation of Persia, 1722-1730.* Paris: Cahiers Studia Iranica, 1998.
——. *A Fiscal History of Iran in the Safavid and Qajar Period.* New York: Bibliotheca Persica, 1999.
——. *The Persian Textile Industry in Historical Perspective 1500-1925.* Paris: L'Harmattan, 1999.
——. *The Economy of Safavid Persia.* Wiesbaden: Reichert, 2000.
——. *Safavid Government Institutions.* Costa Mesa, Cal.: Mazda, 2001.
——. 'Dutch Trade in Afsharid Iran (1730–1753)'. *St.Ir.* 34 (2005): 43–93.
——. *The Persian Gulf. The Rise of the Gulf Arabs. The Politics of Trade on the Persian Littoral 1747-1792.* Washington DC: Mage, 2007.
——. 'Weights and Measures in Qajar Iran'. *St.Ir.* 37 (2008): 57–115.
——. *Guilds, Merchants and Ulama in Nineteenth Century Iran.* Washington DC: Mage, 2009.
——. *The Rise and Fall Nader Shah.* Washington DC: Mage, 2009.
——. *Textile Imports into Qajar Iran. Russia versus Great Britain. The Battle for Market Domination.* Costa Mesa, Cal.: Mazda, 2009.
——. 'Who were the Shamkhal and the Usmi?' *ZDMG* 160 (2010): 341–81.
Floor, Willem and Patrick Clawson. 'Safavid Persia's Search for Gold and Silver'. *IJMES* 32 (2000): 345–68.
Floor, Willem and Mohammad Fagfoory. *Dastur al-Moluk, a Safavid State Manual.* Costa Mesa, CA: Mazda, 2007.
Fragner, Bert. 'Social and Internal Economic Affairs'. *The Cambridge History of Iran* 6, 491–567. Cambridge: Cambridge University Press, 1986.
Gaastra, F.S. 'The Exports of Precious Metals from Europe to Asia by the Dutch East India Company, 1602–1795'. In J.F. Richards (ed.), *Precious Metals in the Later Medieval and Early Modern Worlds,* 447–76. Durham: Carolina Academic Press, 1983.
Gaube, H. and E. Wirth. *Der Bazar von Isfahan.* Wiesbaden: Reichert, 1978.
Geidarov, M.Kh. *Remeslennoe proizvodstvo v gorodakh Azerbaidzhana v XVII v.* Baku: Izd-vo Akademii nauk Azerbaidzhanskoi SSR, 1967.
Gharavi, M. 'Un medecin des Lumières. Simon de Vierville et son voyage en Perse'. *Moyen-Orient & Ocean Indien, Europeéens en Occident au XVIIe siècle* (1994): 35–155.
Gilbar, Gad. 'Demographic Developments in Late Qajar Persia, 1870–1906'. *Asian and African Studies* 11 (1976): 125–56.
Glamann, Kristof. *Dutch-Asiatic Trade, 1620-1740.* Copenhagen: Danish Science Press; The Hague: Martinus Nijhoff, 1958.
Gmelin, Samuel Gottlieb. *Travels through Northern Persia 1770-1774.* Translated by Willem Floor. Washington DC: Mage, 2007.
Golestaneh, Abu'l-Hasan Mohammad Amin. *Mojmal al-tavarikh.* Edited by Modarres Razavi. Tehran: Entedahrat-e Daneshgah-e Tehran, 2536/1977.
Gopal, Surendra. *Indians in Russia in the 17th and 18th Centuries.* New Delhi: Naya Prokash, 1988.
Gorgijanize, Parsadan. *Istoriia Gruzii.* Tbilisi: Izd-vo Metsniereba, 1990.
Habib, Irfan. 'A System of Trimetallism in the Age of the 'Price Revolution': Effects of the Silver Influx on the Mughal Monetary System'. In John Richards (ed.), *The Imperial Monetary System,* 137–70.
Haider, Najaf. 'Precious Metal Flows and Currency Circulation in the Mughal Empire'. *JESHO* 39 (1996): 298–364.

Hennequin, G.P. 'Nouveaux apercus sur l'histoire monetaire de l'Egypte à la fin du Moyen-Age'. *Annales islamologiques* 13 (1977): 179–215.

——— . 'Problèmes theoriques et pratiques de la monnaie antique et médievale'. *Annales islamologiques* 10 (1972): 1–51.

Herzig, Edmund. 'The Armenian Merchants of New Julfa, Isfahan. A Study in Pre-modern Asina Trade'. Dissertation, University of Oxford, 1991.

Hinz, W. 'The Value of the Toman in the Middle Ages'. In M. Minovi and I. Afshar (eds), *Yadnameh-ye Irani-ye Minorsky*, 90–95. Tehran, 1969.

Honarfar, Lotfollah. *Ganjineh-ye asar-e tarikhi-ye Esfahan*. Isfahan: Saqafi, 1344/1967.

İnalcık, Halil. 'Harir'. *EI²* 3 (1971): 211–18.

———. 'The Ottoman Economic Mind and Aspects of the Ottoman Economy'. In M. A. Cook, *Studies in the Economic History of the Middle East*, 207–18. *Oxford:* Oxford University Press, 1970.

Issawi, Charles. *The Economic History of Iran 1800–1914*. Chicago: Chicago University Press, 1971.

Jackson, Peter. 'Čāv'. *EIr.* 5 (1992): 96–97.

Ja`fariyan, Rasul. *`Elal-e bar oftadan-e Safaviyan*. Tehran: Sazman-e tablighat-e Eslami, 1371/1992.

Jones, Geoffrey. *Banking and Empire in Iran*. 2 vols. Cambridge: Cambridge University Press, 1986.

Kasravi, Ahmad, *Pansad saleh-ye Khuzestan*. Tehran: Khaju, 1362/1983.

Ketzer, Peter. 'Copper from a Statistical Viewpoint'. In *Copper in Nature, Technics, Art and Economy*. Hamburg: Norddeutsche Affinerie, 1966.

Khachikian, Levon. 'The Ledger of the Merchant Hovhannes Joughayetsi'. *Journal of the Asiatic Society*, 4th ser., 8 (1966): 153–86.

Kukanova, N.G. 'K voprosu o torgovle Rossii s Iranom v 50–80e gody XVIII v'. In N.A. Kuznetsova (ed.), *Iran (Sbornik statei)*, 181–94. Moscow: Nauka, 1971.

———. *Ocherk po istorii russko-iranskikh torgovykh otnoshenii v XVII-pervoi polovine XIX veka*. Sarank: Mordovskoe knizhnoe izdatel'nostvo, 1977.

Kurts, Boris Grigor'evich. *Sochinenie Kil'burgera o russkoi torgovle v tsarstvovanie Alekseia Mikhailovicha*. Kiev: Tip. I.I. Chokolova, 1915.

Kuteliia, Tinatin. *Catalogue of the Iranian Copper Coins in the State Museum of Georgia*. Tiflis: Metzniereba, 1990.

———. *Gruziia i sefevidskii Iran. Po dannim numizmatiki*. Tbilisi: Metsniereba, 1979.

Laere, R. van. 'The Larin: Trade Money of the Arabian Gulf'. *Oriental Numismatic Society Occasional Paper* no.15 (1980).

Lambton, A.K.S. *Qajar Persia*. Austin: University of Texas Press, 1988.

Li, Ming Hsun. *The Great Recoinage of 1696 to 1699*. London: Weidenfeld and Nicholson, 1963.

Lockhart, L. *Nadir Shah*. London: Luzac and Co., 1938; repr. New York: AMS, 1973.

Lombard, Maurice. 'Les bases monétaires d'une suprématie économique. L'or musulman du VIIe au XIe siècle'. *Annales E.S.C.* 2 (1947): 143–60.

McCabe, Ina Baghdaniatz. *The Shah's Silk for Europe's Silver*. Atlanta: Scholars Press, 1999.

Mahdavi, Shireen. *For God, Mammon, and Country. A Nineteenth Century Persian Merchant Haj Muhammad Hassan Amin al Zarb (1834–1898)*. Boulder: Westview Press, 1999.

Markov, A. *Inventarniy katalog' musulmanskikh' monet'*. St. Petersburg, 1896.

Markova, O.P. 'Russko-iranskaia torgovlia v poslednie desiatiletiia XVIII veka', in *Uchennye Zapiski Institut Vostokvedeniia. A.N. Azerbaidzhan SSR*, 1 (1959): 103–22.

Martinez, A. P. 'Regional Mint Output and the Dynamics of Bullion Flows through the Il-Xanate'. *Journal of Turkish Studies* 7 (1983): 121–73.

Masson Smith, Jr., John and Frances Plunkett. 'Gold Money in Mongol Iran'. *JESHO* 11 (1968): 275–98.

Matthee, Rudolph (Rudi). 'The Career of Mohammad Beg, Grand Vizier of Shah `Abbas II (r.1642–1666)'. *IS* 24 (1991): 17–36.

——. 'Politics and Trade in Late-Safavid Iran: Commercial Crisis and Government Reaction Under Shah Solayman (1666–1694)'. PhD Dissertation, UCLA, 1991.

——. 'Changing the Mintmaster: The Mechanization of the Mint in Qajar Iran'. *Itinerario* 19 (1995): 109–29.

——. 'Between Venice and Surat: The Trade in Gold in Late Safavid Iran'. *Modern Asian Studies* 33 (1999): 231–65.

——. *The Politics of Trade in Safavid Iran: Silk for Silver, 1600–1730.* Cambridge: Cambridge University Press, 1999.

——. 'Mint Consolidation and the Worsening of the Late Safavid Coinage: The Mint of Huwayza'. *JESHO* 44 (2001): 505–39.

——. 'The Safavid Mint of Huwayzah: The Numismatic Evidence'. In *Society and Culture in the Early Modern Middle East: Studies on Iran in the Safavid Period.* Edited by Andrew J. Newman, 265–91. Leiden: E.J. Brill, 2003.

——. *Persia in Crisis: Safavid Decline and the Fall of Isfahan.* London: I.B.Tauris, 2012.

——. 'The Safavid Economy as Part of the World Economy'. In Willem Floor and Edmund Herzig (eds), *Iran and the World in the Safavid Age*, 31–50. London: I.B.Tauris, 2012.

Meilink-Roelofz, M.A.P. 'The Earliest Relations between Persia and the Netherlands'. *Persica* 6 (1974): 1–50.

Migeod, Heinz-Georg. *Die persische Gesellschaft unter Nasiru'd-Din Shah (1848–1896).* Berlin: Klaus Schwarz Verlag, 1990.

Miles, G.C. *The Numismatic History of Rayy.* New York: American Numismatic Society, 1938.

Moosvi, Shireen. *The Economy of the Mughal Empire – A Statistical Study.* Delhi: Oxford University Press, 1987.

——. *People, Taxation and Trade in Mughal India.* Delhi: Oxford University Press, 2008.

Morgan, Jacques Jean-Marie de. *Feudalism in Persia: Its Origin, Development and Present Condition.* Washington DC: Government Printing Office, 1914.

Morineau, Michel. *Les retours des trésors américaines d'après les gazettes hollandaises (XVIe-XVIIIe siècles.* London-New York: Cambridge University Press; Paris: Maison des sciences de l'homme, 1985.

Mostafavi, Mohammad Taqi. 'Yek farman-e jaleb-e tavajjoh az Shah Tahmasp-e avval', *Yaghma* 3 (1329/1950): 133–35.

Mo`tazed, Khosrow. *Hajj Amin al-zarb. Tarikh-e tejarat va sarmayegozari-ye san`ati dar Iran.* Tehran: Entesharat-e Janzadeh, 1366/1987.

Pakhomov, E.A. *Monety Azerbaidzhana.* 2 vols. Baku: Izd. Akademii Nauk Azerbaidzhanskoi SSR, 1959–63.

Pakhomov, E.A. and D.A. Kapanadze. *Monety Gruzii.* Tiflis: Metsnireba 1970.

Pamuk, Şevket. *A Monetary History of the Ottoman Empire.* Cambridge: Cambridge University Press, 2000.

——. 'Money in the Ottoman Empire'. In Halil İnalcık and Donald Quataert (eds), *The Ottoman Empire: Its Economy and Society, 1300–1914*, 947–80. Cambridge: Cambridge University Press, 1994.

Pearson, Michael N. *Pilgrimage to Mecca: The Indian Experience 1500–1800.* Princeton: Darwin Press, 1996.

Perlin, Frank. 'Money-use in Late Pre-colonial India and the International Trade in Currency Media'. In Richards (ed.), *The Imperial Monetary System of Mughal India*, 231–73.

Perry, John R. *Karim Khan Zand.* Chicago: Chicago University Press, 1979.

Prakash, Om. *The Dutch East India Company and the Economy of Bengal 1630–1720.* Princeton: Princeton University Press, 1985.

——. 'Foreign Merchants and Indian Mints in the Seventeenth and Early Eighteenth Century'. In D.S. Richards (ed.), *The Imperial Monetary System of Mughal India*, 171–92.

——. 'Precious Metal Flows, Coinage and the Prices in India in the 17th and the Early 18th Century', in H. G. van Cauwenberghe (ed.), *Money, Coins and Commerce: Essays in the Monetary History of Asia and Europe*, 55–75. Leuven, 1991.

Rabino di Borgomale, H.L. *Coins, Medals, and Seals of the Shâhs of Īrân, 1500-1941.* Hertford: Stephan Austin and Sons Ltd, 1945; repr. Dallas: Numismatics International: 1973.

——. *Mazandaran and Astarabad.* London: Luzac and Co., 1928.

Radzhabli, A.M. 'Iz istorii monetnogo dela v sefevidskom gosudarstve'. *Trudy Muzeia istorii Azerbaidzhana* 4 (1961): 44–67.

Rakhmani, A.A. 'Iz istorii monetnogo obrashcheniia v sefevidskom gosudarstve (XVII v.)'. *Gruzinskoe Istochnikovedenie* 3 (1971): 44–67.

Ricardo, David. 'High Price of Bullion'. In E.C.K. Gonner (ed.), *Economic Essays by David Ricardo*, 3–39. New York: A.M. Kelley, 1923; repr. 1966.

Richards, D.S. (ed.), *The Imperial Monetary System of Mughal India.* Delhi: Oxford University Press, 1987.

Ronall, Joachim O. 'The Beginnings of Modern Banking in Iran'. In K-.H. Manegold (ed.), *Wissenschaft, Wirtschaft und Technik, Studien zur Geschichte. Wilhelm Treue zum 60. Geburtstag*, 255–63. Munich: Bruckmann, 1969.

Sandrock, John. *Copper Cash and Silver Taels: The Money of Manchu China.* Baltimore: Gateway Press, 1995.

Santen, Hans van. *De Verenigde Oost-Indische Compagnie in Gujarat en Hindustan, 1620-1660.* Meppel, 1982.

Schwartz, Benjamin (ed.). *Letters from Persia Written by Charles and Edward Burgess 1828-1855.* New York: NY Public Library, 1942.

Seifeddin, M.A. 'Monetnaia sistema v Azerbaidzhane v XIV I pervoi polvinie XV v'. *Numizmatika i Epigrafika* 11 (1974): 196–208.

Sha`bani, Reza. *Hadis-e Nader Shahi.* Tehran: Daneshgah-e Melli, 2536/1977.

Shubbar, Jasim Hasan. *Tarikh al-Musha`sha`yin wa tarajim `alayhim.* Najaf: Matba`at al-Adab, 1385/1965.

Simmons, Jeremiah Benn. 'The Evolution of Persia's Monetary System between Safavid Power's Consolidation in 1502 and the Employing of Belgian Mint Management Experts in 1901'. Dissertation, University of Cambridge, King's College, 1977.

Sircar, D.C (ed.). *Studies in Indian Coins.* Delhi: Motilal Banarsidass, 1968.

Slaby, Helmuth. *Bindenschild und Sonnenlöwe.* Graz: Akademische Druck, 1982.

Smith, John Masson Jr. and Frances Plunkett, 'Gold Money in Mongol Iran'. *JESHO* 11 (1968): 275–98.

Soucek, Priscilla. 'Coinage of the Qajars: A System in Continual Transition'. *IS* 34:1–4 (2001): 52–88.

Spufford, Peter. *Money and its Use in Medieval Europe.* Cambridge: Cambridge University Press, 1988.

Spuler, Berthold. *Die Mongolen in Iran.* Leiden: E.J. Brill, 4th edn, 1985.

Steensgaard, Niels. *The Asian Trade Revolution of the Seventeenth Century: The East India Companies and the Decline of the Caravan Trade.* Chicago: University of Chicago Press, 1973.

——. 'The Route through Qandahar: The Significance of the Overland Trade from India to the West in the Seventeenth Century'. In Sushil Chaudhury and Michel Morineau (eds), *Merchants, Companies and Trade: Europe and Asia in the Early Modern Era*, 55–73. Cambridge: Cambridge University Press, 1999.

Stern, S.M. 'The Coins of Amul'. *Numismatic Chronicle* 7th series, 7 (1967): 205–78.

Subrahmanyam, Sanjay. 'Precious Metal flows and Prices in Western and southern Asia, 1500-1750: Some Comparative and Conjunctioral Aspects'. In Sanjay Subrahmanyam (ed.), *Money and the Market in India 1100-1700*, 186–218. Delhi: Oxford University Press, 1994.

Supple, B.E. *Commercial Crisis and Change in England 1600-1642: A Study in the Instability of a Mercantile Economy.* Cambridge: Cambridge University Press, 1959.

Şahillioğlu, Halil. 'The Introduction of Machinery in the Ottoman Mint'. In Ekmeleddin Ihsanoğlu (ed.), *Transfer of Modern Science & Technology to the Muslim World*, 261–81. Istanbul: ISIS, 1992.

——. 'The Role of International Monetary and Metal Movements in Ottoman Monetary History 1300–1750'. in Richards (ed.), *Precious Metals in the later medieval and Early Modern Worlds*, 263–304.

Treue, Wilhelm. 'Copper Trade from Prehistoric Times to the Present Day'. In *Copper in Nature, Technics, Art and Economy*, 93–104. Hamburg: Norddeutsche Affinerie, 1966.

Tucci, Ugo. 'Le emissioni monetarie di Venezia e i movimenti internazionali dell'oro'. In Idem, Mercanti, navi, monete nel Cinquecento veneziano, 275–316. Bologna: Il mulino, 1981.

Vilar, Pierre. *Or et monnaie dans l'histoire.* Paris : Flammarion, 1974.

Von Glahn, Richard. *Fountain of Fortune: Money and Monetary Policy in China 1000-1700.* Berkeley and Los Angeles: University of California Press, 1996.

Warminton, E.H. *The Commerce between the Roman Empire and India.* Cambridge: Cambridge University Press, 1928.

Welin, W.S.L. 'Wasit, the Mint-Town', *Bulletin de la Société Royale des lettres de Lund.* 4 (1955–56): 127–69.

Wood, H. 'The Gampola Larin Hoard', *Numismatic Notes and Monographs*, no. 61. New York, American Numismatic Society, 1934.

Yaganegi, Esfandiar Bahram. 'Recent Financial and Monetary History of Persia'. PhD Dissertation, New York University, 1934.

Yakta'i, Majid. *Tarikh-e dara'i-ye Iran.* Tehran, 1340/1961.

Zarinebaf-Shahr, Fariba. 'Tabriz under Ottoman Rule (1725–1730)'. PhD Dissertation, University of Chicago, 1991.

Index

www.ingramcontent.com/pod-product-compliance
Ingram Content Group UK Ltd.
Pitfield, Milton Keynes, MK11 3LW, UK
UKHW020905190926
475560UK00010B/283

9 781780 760797